Heaven and Hell to Play With

The Filming of
The Night of the Hunter

Heaven and Hell to Play With

The Filming of *The Night of the Hunter*

Preston Neal Jones

LIMELIGHT EDITIONS
New York

First Limelight Edition   August 2002

Copyright © 2002 by Preston Neal Jones.

All rights reserved including the right of reproduction in whole or in part in any form.
Published by Proscenium Publishers Inc., 118 East 30th Street, New York, NY 10016.

Manufactured in the United States of America.

Library of Congress Cataloging-in-Publication Data is available from the publisher.

ISBN: 0-87910-974-2

Designed by Mulberry Tree Press, Inc. (www.mulberrytreepress.com)

A deep bow and Thank-You

To the late Louis Grubb,

a man with no "Right-Hand Left-Hand,"

just two right hands.

Miss you, babe.

To the Night-Blooming Cereus

ACKNOWLEDGMENTS

One of the dangers in seeing a long-time labor of love finally brought to fruition is that there may be people who helped along the way whose contributions elude my memory now that I'm finally ready to acknowledge them. For any such omissions, I offer my apology, beg forgiveness, and throw myself on the mercy of the court.

Because an oral historian depends, like Miss Dubois, on the kindness of strangers, first and foremost among those who must be thanked are the people who consented to be interviewed and gave so generously of their present to delve into their past. Some of these gifted people shared not only their memories but also their precious artifacts, while still others helped to arrange interviews with their former colleagues. Hilyard Brown, to my delight, illustrated one of his recollections by dashing off a few sketches like the ones he did for Laughton and company over dinner every night during the shooting of *The Night of the Hunter*. To all these interviewees, I bow deeply and hope humbly that they will feel their memories have been treated with respect and affection on these pages. Interviews were conducted circa 1974–1977, with the exceptions of the conversation with Lou Grubb, which took place in New York City in 1995, and the talks with Terry Sanders and William Phipps, which took place in Los Angeles in 2001. Lillian Gish was interviewed by telephone in Manhattan; Davis Grubb at a friend's Manhattan apartment; Robert Mitchum at his office in Los Angeles; Paul Gregory at his home in Palm Springs; Stanley Cortez at the A.S.C. Clubhouse in Hollywood; and Sonya Goodman, Robert Golden, Hilyard Brown and Don Beddoe at their respective homes.

Bill Chapin gave this project his blessing, although for personal reasons he was unable to participate, and I extend to him my appreciation and best wishes for the future. The late Lou Grubb was a fervent supporter of this project, for which he supplied many indispensable elements, from family photos to copies of his brother Davis's unpublished writings and his sketches for Laughton. To the Grubb family goes my heartfelt condolences at the loss of Lou, and my lifelong gratitude for the love and beauty he and his beloved brother brought to this world.

For permission to quote from the unpublished correspondence of James Agee, (as well as offering general encouragement), I am indebted to Mr. Paul Sprecher, administrator of the James Agee Trust.

Heaven and Hell to Play With, in embryonic form, was published as an article in the Library of Congress anthology entitled *Performing Arts/Motion Pictures* (1998). Members of the staff at the Library were very helpful in providing access to invaluable archival material donated by the late Elsa Lanchester. In addition to correspondence and documents relating to the production of *Hunter*—including the Walter Schumann score sheets—the Library shared transcriptions of many interviews with friends and colleagues of Laughton which Miss Lanchester had commissioned at a time when she was planning to write a biography of her late husband. (That project eventually became a book by Charles Higham.) Ms. Iris Newsom, editor of the Library's *Performing Arts* series, was a most gracious and helpful supervisor, and was instrumental in obtaining frame blow-ups of *Hunter* from a skilled technician named Patrick Loughney. Biographers, film critics and historians had written about *The Night of the Hunter* in many books and periodicals, but my Library article was, I believe, the first study to be blessed by such illustrations. For the first time in publication, certain key elements of Grubb and Laughton's imagery, as realized by Brown's art direction and Cortez's cinematography, could be presented visually for the reader, and that holds true for this expanded book version of my essay. Thanks for the use of these and other copyrighted visual materials goes to Paul Gregory Productions, MGM/UA, Universal Pictures, Time-Warner, and Columbia Pictures. I have tried to contact holders of copyrights before publication. If informed of any omissions, I will strive to rectify them as soon as possible.

Special thanks are due to Robert Gitt, preservation officer at the UCLA Film and Television Archive. He and his staff have not only produced a brand new, visually pristine print of *Hunter,* they have also catalogued and preserved many hours of raw footage and out-takes from Laughton's masterpiece. I spent three days viewing this material in the expert company of Mr. Gitt and his associate Nancy Mysel, and the experience, with all due respect to H.G. Wells and Norman Mailer, was an incredible Time Machine journey. For all three of us, I daresay, it was a thrill when someone pointed out that we were the first people to be looking at this footage since Laughton sat down with Robert Golden in the late autumn of 1954.

Ms. Pat H. Broeske, Mr. Tom Weaver and Ms. Lucy Chase Williams formed an honor guard, a triumvirate of distinguished authors of books on film who guided me through many pitfalls and helped me up after many a pratfall. Their innumerable services ranged from reviewing manuscript to introducing me to a key interviewee. Tom Weaver also gave me permission to quote from an interview with William Phipps in one of his own books on film history. (Check out Tom's interview with Yvette Vickers to learn of the strange fate which awaited Shelley Winters' mannequin after its "performance" in *The Night of the Hunter* . . .) Jon Burlingame, another fine writer of film books, was generous with his experience and expertise.

An excellent article about the *Hunter* restoration/preservation appeared in the January, 2002 issue of *American Cinematographer*. The author of that article, Jeffrey Couchman, is writing a thesis about *The Night of the Hunter*, and has been most generous in sharing some of his research with me. Joseph A. Marcello, an excellent—and award-winning—composer in his own right, walked me through the Walter Schumann score on more than one occasion, offering unique insights into its mastery and its mysteries. Mr. Marcello also afforded me the opportunity to screen *Hunter* and discuss it with his film students at Northfield Mt. Hermon school.

Over the years of this book's long gestation, I have received practical and moral support from a host of wonderful people, whose contributions defy categorization (and alphabetization): Harvey Sid Fisher, David Light, Elaine Capogeannis, Jon Orovitz, Alexander Payne, Warren Sherk, Michael Chapin, Cindy Kunishige, Linda Danly, John Morgan, William Stromberg, Sam Rosen, Jan Contreras, William Eustace, Richard Heft, Coro Chase, Richard Creviston, Bet MacArthur, Richard Orton, Lorin Hart, James A. Contner, Helen Hicks, Ross Care, Miss Wendy Keagy, Cooper Graham, Lynne Walker, Nancy Quad Kirk, Deidre Crumbley, Beth Gottlieb, Jason Rabinowitz, Lauren Eve Rabinowitz, George Gerdes,

Deborah Feldmann, Sam Park, Rose Sasanoff, Stephen J. Strauss, James A. Strauss, Sperry DeCew (who I'm sure would want me to mention that he hates this movie), Brian Chic, Dorothea Petrie, Dennis Brown, Jane Barnett, Sara Prejean, the late Raymond Massey, the late Frederick S. Clark, and the late Allan Sloane.

Thanks are due to a most conscientious copy-editor, Nina Maynard and a most diligent designer, Joe Gannon. Finally, and above all, I must thank most deeply Mr. Mel Zerman of Limelight Editions for saying yes. (My favorite word, in case you were wondering, Professor Lipton).

Heaven and Hell to Play With

The Filming of *The Night of the Hunter*

INTRODUCTION

"One night when I was very, very small, I saw a shooting star and my mother explained it was a world burning up. Can you imagine my horror a few weeks later when the air was full of fireflies?"

— Davis Grubb, author of *The Night of the Hunter*

It was **Mother Goose** with goose bumps. It scared the living Levis off a young kid in Maine named Stephen King, and it has had the same impact on many another child and grown-up. It drew inspiration from D.W. Griffith and the German expressionists, but there has never been another movie, before or since, like *The Night of the Hunter* (United Artists, 1955).

A tale of terror told from a child's point of view, *Hunter* was the only film directed by the late actor Charles Laughton. Underrated by many critics, ignored by most of the public, this 1955 film nevertheless had a vision and a vitality which today mark it as a major achievement, while other, more successful pictures of its period have been largely forgotten. *Hunter*'s haunting visuals seem to leave a particularly indelible imprint on the memories of those who see it when they are very young. But even adults can have a hard time shaking loose some of the film's imagery—and the ideas behind it.

In 1992, *The Night of the Hunter* joined the select rank of pictures chosen for inclusion in the National Film Registry at the Library of Congress. More recently, *Hunter* made the cut of the American Film Institute's "100 Greatest Thrillers." And Laughton's lone opus continues to appear on many critics' and scholars' all-time best lists because, as the late Pauline Kael has pointed out with regard to *Hunter*, "truly frightening movies become classics of a kind."

The original advertising come-ons—"The Scenes, The Stars, The Story—but above all, the Suspense!"—offered no indication of the unusual nature of the film. And if, today, *Hunter* is a classic of a kind, it is not entirely because of its power to frighten. At the time, Laughton's producer and partner, Paul Gregory, told a reporter, "I was determined to film (the Davis Grubb book), because I want as many people as possible to share the warm feeling of hope I received from this haunting novel." Laughton, like Grubb, was striving for more than the jolts and shudders to which most suspense stories limit themselves. Because he was aiming for the heart as well as the gut, Laughton brought to his film a tenderness and compassion almost unheard-of in the horror film genre and all too rare in films of any category. *Hunter* is at once nightmare and nocturne, and one leaves the theater haunted not only by the hand of HATE, the scream of rage, the threat of the knife, but also by the faces of the children, the moonlight on the river, the music of the lullaby.

Although Laughton collaborated with many distinguished talents to realize this project, any discussion of the creative force behind *Hunter* must begin with the man who wrote the story, Davis Grubb. When *Hunter*, his first book, was published in 1953, *The New York Times* called Grubb's work "a brilliant novel," and went on to say, "Make no mistake about it, *The Night of the Hunter* is a thriller which commands one's frozen attention. It is also a work of beauty and power and astonishing verbal magic." To the *New York Herald-Tribune*, *Hunter* was "part idyll, part nightmare, a terrifying and impassioned narrative" which told "with subtle lyricism and a compelling sense of evil how the consequences of a crime of violence enmesh and all but destroy the innocent."

Grubb's innocents are two Ohio River Valley children of the Depression era, Pearl and John Harper. While robbing a bank of ten thousand dollars, their father, Ben, kills two men, for which he is condemned to hang. Ben Harper dies without revealing the money's hiding place. Enter the force of evil, personified in "Preacher" Harry Powell, a self-ordained, itinerant gospel-spouter with LOVE and HATE tattooed on his fingers, a man whose outward piety cloaks the madness within. He is a Bluebeard who has married and murdered a dozen widows, using their money to spread his version of the Lord's word. Preacher ingratiates himself into widow Willa Harper's household, but soon realizes it is not the mother but her two children who alone know the secret of the blood money. Little John's child instinct senses the menace to which the rest of the community is blind, and the war of wits between Preacher and the boy becomes a life-and-death struggle. Ultimately, there is only one savior to whom the children can turn: the river.

In the Hollywood of the fifties, this would have been strikingly original material to be tackled by anyone, let alone an actor embarking on his first film-directing venture. But British-born Laughton was always an unusual actor—*A Difficult Actor*, as Simon Callow has called him in his much-praised biography of that title. Charles Laughton, a corpulent man, often joked that he had "a face like the backside of an elephant," a self-deprecation only hinting at the inner demons which tormented him all his life. "Laughton was a stadium of nerves," Paul Gregory recalls in the pages which follow, "Unhappy, an unhappy man . . . I had a nervous stomach from the time I was in business with him until the time it was over." Nonetheless, Laughton's titanic war with himself struck sparks which fueled a dynamic creative spirit. He possessed one of the most expressive voices in the English-speaking theatre, and the sensitivity and imagination to create a character from the (often painful) inside out. Belying his poetic nature, he excelled at bringing to life tyrants and despots, from his drumstick-tossing Henry VIII to his keelhauling Captain Bligh. For all his lack of glamour in the commonly accepted sense, Laughton nevertheless became one of the stars of Hollywood's golden age.

By the early fifties, he was still a major character actor, though chiefly in supporting parts. Then, at the instigation of Paul Gregory, a young MCA agent full of ambition and ideas, Laughton began a whole new career. Gregory's idea, which would eventually launch his own career, first came to him while watching Laughton's enthralling reading of a passage from the Bible on television. Gregory sensed the contemporary studio audience's delight in the age-old art of the storyteller, and he intuited that other audiences around the country would welcome the chance to see the famous film star working his magic in-person. Here was an opportunity for Gregory to mount his first production, starring a famous performer, with a budget that would be minuscule compared to the cost of producing a full-scale play. On fire with his idea, Gregory persuaded the actor to let him book a cross-country reading tour. The surprising popularity of that first tour, as well as subsequent ones, led Laughton to direct a series of successful stage productions: George Bernard Shaw's *Don Juan in Hell*, Stephen Vincent Benet's *John Brown's Body*, and Herman Wouk's *The Caine Mutiny Court Martial*. In open defiance of the theatrical taboo immortalized by H.L. Mencken, Gregory and Laughton were growing rich by overestimating the taste of the American public. Eventually, Gregory started looking for the right property with which to bring Laughton's directorial skills to the silver screen.

Laughton biographer Callow, himself a highly esteemed actor (*A Room with a View, Shakespeare in Love*), expressed to this writer the opinion that, "artistically, it all came together for Laughton in *The Night of the Hunter*. Frankly, I think if I had my book to start over again, I'd devote it entirely to that one film." The elements which all came together in Laughton's film, not surprisingly, shed light on the conflicting forces within the artist himself. As Gregory remembers, "I think Charlie could see himself in the rendition of it. Yes, he could put you through miseries, but there was much that was saintly in Charles Laughton, too. And with the young children aspect of it, and the devil in Preacher Powell and all that, you see, that gave Laughton both heaven and hell to play with, and he was the master of both of those at that time."

Heaven and hell for Charlie to play with—and play with them he did. A lesser artist than Laughton might have to busy himself through an entire career to break half the Hollywood shibboleths that Laughton shattered in this single work. As the mad, murderous zealot, Laughton cast heroic he-man Robert Mitchum. Against Tinseltown tradition, the script stayed remarkably faithful to the original novel, even though this meant killing protagonist Shelley Winters before the film was half over, and several years before Hitchcock was to do away with Janet Leigh in the first half of *Psycho*. Laughton ensured that his music composer and his editor, rather than start their work after the footage was shot, participated during the entire making of the movie. With his art director and his cinematographer, Laughton created a visual style which forsook objective realism for the images of a child's dream world. He used devices such as the iris-in which, outside of cartoons (and Welles' *The Magnificent Ambersons*), had not been seen since silent picture days. He employed highly effective but rarely utilized gambits, such as helicopter shots (nowadays an action movie staple), and devised images that had never been seen in the movies before, from the boy photographed through the leaf shadows on his wall, to the murdered woman sitting in her car beneath the river.

The end result was a film which earned wildly mixed notices from the press and a resounding veto at the box office. To some, it was artistic, to others, arty. To Hollis Alpert of the *Saturday Review*, who made *Hunter* the subject of one of that magazine's rare movie-oriented cover stories, it was one of the Ten Best of the Year, exploring the expressive qualities of the medium more than any other film of 1955. (In that regard, perhaps only Kazan's film of Steinbeck's *East of Eden* comes close.) *Time* gave the picture a glib pan, and didn't include it on its list of movies currently worth seeing. William K. Zinnsser, critic of the *New York Herald-Tribune,* placed the film among his Ten Best, yet the redoubtable Bosley Crowther of the *New York Times* thought Laughton's first effort a nice try that had misfired. Crowther did allow that *Hunter* had a few dramatic moments equal to von Stroheim's *Greed*, and added that he would look forward to Laughton's next effort. Dorothy Manners' review in the *Los Angeles Examiner* began by stating, "If it was Charles Laughton's intention to scare the scalps off the watchers of *The Night of the Hunter, . . .* he succeeded where this non-paying customer is concerned. Seldom has an entire production sustained the nightmarish feeling of helpless terror as does this picturization of Davis Grubb's symbolic novel." Not many people paid for the chance to have their scalps raised in 1955, however, and Gregory and Laughton's chain of hits was broken.

The film's box-office failure denotes more than one irony. A bestselling novel had not guaranteed a ready-made audience for the movie version. (This was one old Hollywood custom Laughton and Gregory had not wanted to break.) And star Robert Mitchum, then at the height of his popularity, which was to endure for over four decades, was seen by relatively few movie-goers in what is probably his finest performance.

> "You never know what they tell you. You never find out if it's real or a story."
>
> —Davis Grubb, *The Night of the Hunter*

Why wasn't the film a hit? In the following pages, some of the people closely associated with the film speculate on this question. More to the point, they describe the many acts of creation which Laughton inspired, guided and fused to produce this rare film. (In the process, they also shed light on the pictures of such other film-makers as David O. Selznick, John Ford and Orson Welles.) In presenting this montage of memories, supplemented by archival material, the interviewer has, wherever possible, stepped back to let the subjects speak for themselves. The author hopes that their distinctive personalities will be heard through the silent medium of print. (Perhaps the most lamentable limitation of these transcriptions is their inability to duplicate on the page Mr. Mitchum's gift for mimicry; in listening to the tape of his interview, the author can almost swear he was listening to Laughton himself in Mitchum's recreated conversations.) The opinions expressed by these men and women may not in all cases jibe with the opinions of the author; they certainly do not always jibe with each other's; perhaps this is inevitable in a creative enterprise in which so many talented people have participated. Laughton himself, of course, was a remarkable person, and the memories and insights of his associates—often at wide variance with each other—combine to evoke a portrait of the artist and the man.

The qualities which Laughton and company brought to the screen in 1955 may have seemed too innovative to acquire a wide audience then, but the film lives on, gaining new admirers with each revival at arthouses, museums, schools, festivals and, of course, television. Like the children described in "Rachel Cooper"/Lillian Gish's curtain speech, it abides, and it endures. Today, in its forty-seventh anniversary year, *The Night of the Hunter* remains a film ahead of its time.

—*P. N. J.*
Hollywood, April 2002

INTERVIEWEES

DAVIS GRUBB
author

LOUIS GRUBB
author's brother

PAUL GREGORY
producer

ROBERT MITCHUM
"'Preacher' Harry Powell"

LILLIAN GISH
"Rachel Cooper"

DON BEDDOE
"Walt Spoon"

HILYARD BROWN
art director

STANLEY CORTEZ
cinematographer

ROBERT GOLDEN
editor

MRS. SONYA GOODMAN
widow of composer Walter Schumann

TERRY SANDERS
second unit director

WILLIAM PHIPPS
actor/friend

PREPRODUCTION

"You're absolutely crazy.
Audiences won't sit still for that sort of thing."

—Charles Laughton to Paul Gregory

In a sense, the man who made *Frankenstein* was also responsible for *The Night of the Hunter*. It was, after all, James Whale who introduced Charles Laughton to Paul Gregory. Whale had been the director of such thirties chillers as *Frankenstein, The Invisible Man* and *Bride of Frankenstein* (which had featured Mrs. Laughton, Elsa Lanchester, in the title role). In getting the distinguished actor together with the budding entrepreneur, the long-retired film-maker could not have known that he was setting the wheels in motion for yet another classic terror-film, but that is where eventually the Laughton/Gregory acquaintanceship would lead. In time, Gregory, the impoverished impresario, suggested to silver-screen luminary Laughton that the actor should read the Bible to audiences across the United States. Laughton's response was immediate and—as Gregory would come to learn—characteristically vehement.

Paul Gregory (producer)
"You're absolutely crazy," he told me. "Audiences won't sit still for that sort of thing." But I said I thought they would stand still, and would he give me a chance and see if I couldn't book him for ten weeks? At that time, I was an agent at MCA, and I said, "If I can't book you, I won't quit MCA. But if I can book you, and it's successful, then we'll do something." So, in my after hours at MCA, I booked him the ten weeks. It wasn't easy. He was right on that one score. It wasn't easy. But there was an audience there that I went out and got. And it was enormously successful, and that started our business relationship together.

I think we worked so well together because, primarily, Laughton was an enormously sophisticated man, and I'm not. At that time I wasn't, anyway, and I still don't think I'm any way near as sophisticated as Charles Laughton. He was a very good editor for me. I was a real retriever; I would go out and get things and bring them back, and I loved books and literature and all that sort of thing, but Charles could cut through it. Charles had a great sense of show, which I'm not sure I always have, and we worked well together.

Later on, when we were on our way to Montreal on a reading tour, I said to him that I would like to do a drama quartet. He said, "It's absolutely a wild idea, what do you mean, a drama quartet?" I said, "Well, in chamber music, they have four instrumentalists on the stage; I'd like to see four actors on the stage, doing material worthy of performance that would not be done otherwise." He said, "Like what?" I said, "Well, I don't know, but Shaw's preface to *Back to Methuselah* is one of the most fantastic things I ever read." And with that, he shot around and said, "It's crazy people like you that there should be more of in this goddamned business. I've *got* the material. Did you ever read the Hell scene from *Man and Superman?*" So, that's how we came to do Shaw's *Don Juan in Hell.*

Of course, Laughton had been in the film business with Erich Pommer, and I was told by Erich Pommer when I met him, "You watch and see, he'll screw you," he said. "He'll kill you." And I said, "Well, that's all right," you know, "It's nice to be warned." But Laughton, he was a stadium of nerves. He was just an enormous collection of nerve-ends all the time, unhappy, an unhappy man, which contributed to many, many problems. I had a nervous stomach from the time I was in business with him until the time it was over, because I never knew when he would go on, when he wouldn't go on—"Jesus Christ, there are three thousand people out there, why the hell wasn't it *three* thousand dollars?" There was never, ever, ever, ever a time when the man could look at you and say, "Boy, it was terrific."

Here's a man *grateful.* There was no one more grateful than Charles for his reading success. But we would be going into Omaha, say, and the people in the press wanted to see him, he'd say, "Goddamn press, I won't see the sons of bitches! What do they want to see me for?" The woman that was giving the thing would say, "There's going to be a party afterwards." He'd say, "No! Goddamn it, why does she want to have me come to a party? Why do you let these things happen?" Everything was just afoul, you see. And someone would come to him and say, "I want to take your picture." "No, no!" And he'd cover his face with his hands and run. You see, he had no grace to handle his easing in and easing out of the situation. And he wouldn't let someone else handle it.

You see, he loved to torment you. He loved to torment me. He'd call me up at one o'clock and he'd say, "I have a fever of a hundred and two, I don't know if I can make it tomorrow, I don't know, old boy." He wouldn't have a fever at all. He just thought that I didn't have enough to worry about.

One quarter of the Drama Quartet is *Time*'s cover boy, March 31, 1952. The devil in the corner holding a microphone pays homage to Laughton's stage role in *Don Juan in Hell* and, implicitly, his new-found fame as a storyteller.

Because of his ugliness, he felt people hated him, thought he looked ugly: his unattractiveness, his hunchback and what–have–you. You know, he was deformed, and he covered it all up with pads and coats. He was a *tragic* man, and I'm here to tell you. He was a tragic man. I saw him one time in Cincinnati make a fuss that was unnecessary over a blind man. You see, it was grotesque, he made such a fuss, he talked to the blind man and told him how beautiful he was, and all of this, and the blind man really wasn't beautiful at all. He just stood there, going, "Uh-huh . . . Uh-huh . . ." It was grotesque. Laughton wanted to take him and read to him. Oh, it was unbelievable, some of the instances.

Charles was the kind of man that could only make a rose bloom in a heap of garbage. He couldn't make it bloom in a beautiful, cultivated field, he had to have trash, and turmoil, and hideousness, and people at each other's throats, and then he'd sit there and, "Aahhh, look at it grow," you see, and have a rose. It kills people, you know, it kills people. This is the way his readings were, this is the way *Don Juan in Hell* was, this is the way *John Brown's Body* was . . . And then we did *Hobson*. We didn't produce *Hobson's Choice*, but I had set it up for Charles to do it for Alexander Korda in England. We went to England, and right there he started a thing. He liked David Lean, the director, but Robert Donat was to have done the young man's part, and Robert had this awful asthma attack, so John Mills was called in, and right away Laughton wanted out. He said, "I don't want to do it with John Mills, blah-blah-blah-blah-blah." He had a reason to make a big fuss, you see, and he couldn't stand until he could see everybody going at it, and then, (*beatific smile,*) he would come in and, "Well, I'll do it, old boy."

Mrs. Sonya Goodman (widow of composer Walter Schumann)
Almost from the very beginning, Mr. Laughton and my late husband had a very compatible, creative relationship. Mr. Laughton did not have to go into details to get his ideas across to my husband. When they worked on the *a cappella* chorus for the stage production of *John Brown's Body,* Mr. Laughton would just say, for example, "I want them to sing fire sounds here." My husband would sit down at the piano and play some music, or hum the vocal texture, and Mr. Laughton would say, "Yes, exactly like that."

When I first met Mr. Laughton, I was in such awe of him and his acting ability that I was overwhelmed and too shy to speak. But then, he had an amazing ability to put people at their ease. My husband convinced me that Mr. Laughton was a very nice man and wouldn't bite my head off, but I was still shy. And then we went to have dinner with him and Elsa one

Following his *Don Juan* success with another staged reading, Laughton directed (L to R) Tyrone Power, Dame Judith Anderson and Raymond Massey in *John Brown's Body*.

evening. As you walked into the Laughtons' house, you were silhouetted against the sky. Mr. Laughton was sitting at a desk at the far end of the room, speaking to someone on the telephone, and he said, "A beautiful vision in green has just entered my doorway." Now, of course, I just lapped it up, and lost all my fears from that moment on.

He had gotten all dressed in a beautiful suit, which was so amazing because we were the only guests. (Elsa was working on a picture at that time, and she couldn't join us until later in the evening.) We had a delightful dinner, he was the most attentive and considerate host, serving us himself, commenting on the food and the wine, hopping up and asking us if there was anything we wanted. And then we spent the rest of the evening looking at his art collection. He was a bulky man, but so agile as he would quickly hop on a bed and pull down a piece of porcelain from a high shelf just to show it to us. And he pronounced it the original, correct way, "pors*lane*." Some employer had once asked him what salary he wanted for a job, and Mr. Laughton had said, "I want that painting." So,

Under Laughton's tutelage, matinee idol Power surprised critics and audiences with his dramatic intensity. (Here he single-handedly recreates the battle of Gettysburg.) Laughton would offer up a similar revelation when casting the leading male role in his first film-directing project.

he had in his bedroom a magnificent Rubens, called *The Assignation of Paris,* which I believe is presently hanging in a museum in Washington. "I want you to really look at this," he said, and we all sat down in front of it. The main characters in the painting were four nudes, and Mr. Laughton said, "Look at that luscious skin tone. Don't you feel that you could just bite her ass?" He was a very voluptuous man, in that respect.

Mr. Laughton often came to our house to work with my husband. He got very involved in our two young children, very playful, asking them questions about their lives, reading them bedtime stories. Then, another evening, he called us at eleven o'clock at night to invite us to visit. It seemed that the Laughtons had a whole annual ceremony, calling friends in to watch the night-blooming cereus burst into bloom. It's a beautiful flower on an ugly cactus plant, and once a year it blooms for twenty-four hours.

Mr. Laughton liked to swim in the nude, but because there were ladies present that evening, he put some swimming trunks on. We were in the pool, and as the hours progressed, the blossoms opened up bit by bit. Pretty soon it was open to its fullest extent, and when it started to close, the Laughtons picked the blossoms and gave them to us all, and pictures were taken of us wearing our new flowers. Mr. Laughton was just a magnificent, delightful, fun-loving man who could completely lose himself in the moment.

Another lady with fond memories of the night-blooming cereus was legendary actress Lillian Gish, who told Elsa Lanchester's biographical researchers that she always loved going to the Laughton home. Like Schumann's wife, Miss Gish recalled Laughton phoning her one afternoon and inviting her to come see the night-blooming cereus, several of which blossoms he picked for her. Such sensitive qualities and such appreciation, Miss Gish felt, were remarkable in such a giant. (She thought she would fool everyone somehow by taking her cereus blossoms home and secreting them in a cupboard so dark that they wouldn't die. But the next morning,

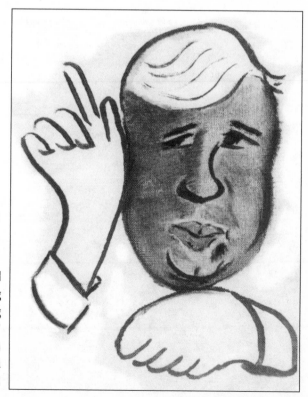

"He got very involved in our two young children . . . reading them bedtime stories." Caricature of Laughton by Mrs. Sonya Goodman.

un-fooled, the blossoms were gone.) Laughton, according to Miss Gish, always spoke so proudly of his wife, Miss Lanchester, whenever they were apart: "You'd think he had given birth to Elsa." The reverse, apparently, was not true, according to an old family friend of the Laughtons. Actor William Phipps (*Crossfire*, *War of the Worlds*, and the voice of Prince Charming in Disney's *Cinderella*), had known Charles and Elsa since the early forties.

William Phipps (actor/friend)

Elsa was not very supportive of Charles, in anything. She found all of the negative things about whatever he did, she never really supported him. She was really the devil's advocate, is another way of putting it. You know, looking at all the things that could go wrong, and all the bleakness, instead of saying, "Hey, it sounds good, do it." She didn't like Paul Gregory. And he didn't like her. I think she resented everything Charles did, because, he was *it*. Like, when they would go out in public together, Laughton would say, "They never ever even noticed her," they'd just looked at him, they didn't say hello to her. People's eyes went right to

William Phipps, circa the late nineteen-forties, early nineteen-fifties.

him. What a show-stopper that man was, you know, what a presence. He'd walk into a room, and everything would stop. It might have been that way even if he weren't a famous star.

Miss Gish is right, Charles was a fan of Elsa's work. And, he even loved her. And vice versa. How would I describe their relationship? Symbiotic, for one. Enabling, for another. Appearances—you know, we're talking about the twenties, thirties and forties. Elsa, though she acted the hurt maiden about her husband being homosexual, didn't have a man friend at all. All of her male friends were pansies—by which I mean, her coterie, her entourage, the people around her . . . There's a difference between "pansy" and "homosexual," you know, pansies are people, they can't help themselves lisping and being effeminate. She had a couple of girl friends, who worked with her at the Turnabout theater, but they weren't around her very often, she really only saw them at the theater. The rest of her friends were all pansies.

All the time that I knew Charles and Elsa, there were many times that they had really bad spats, bad quarrels. And Laughton's friends would say what a horrible bitch she was, and her friends would talk to her about him on the other side. So, he would talk about leaving her, and I never used to get into it. All I would say to him, and I said to him many times, I said, "Laughton, the love between you and Elsa, you will never leave her." And he wouldn't listen to that, but, when it blew over and things would cool down, he used to say to me, "You son of a bitch, you're right! You're the only one who says that, and you're probably right, I'll never leave her." And of course, he never did.

Paul Gregory

And it wasn't just *Hobson*, it was always that way. With *Caine Mutiny*, we started with Herman Wouk doing the draft of the script, and Laughton didn't want to have anything to do with *The Caine Mutiny*. He said, "It's a man's play and I don't know anything about it, it's too male for me," and so forth, and I insisted that he could direct it. If he could direct our other shows, he could direct *Caine Mutiny*. But, he had other little interests at the time, which made it difficult to pin him down. And so we got involved with Dick Powell, who was wrong, but we had Henry Fonda, Lloyd Nolan and John Hodiak signed, and we were going into

PAUL GREGORY

Millions of theatergoers throughout the country who would win the jackpot if the question happened to be, "Who is the dynamic producer who is giving people beyond the shadow of Broadway the very best in living theater" will not protest, perhaps, if no note is made herein that (1) Paul Gregory was born Jason Burton Lenhart (MGM saw him as another Gregory Peck when he first arrived in Hollywood and changed his name to Paul Gregory); (2) His first production effort was staging comic strips in a hen house in his birthplace, Waukee, Iowa; (3) He starred at the age of 14 in a radio program of his own on Station KSO in Des Moines (he read from the classics and one of his favorite acts of precocity over the airwaves was to read Stephen Vincent Benet's "John Brown's Body," an epic poem which he eventually produced for the theater in 1952); (4) The idea for a concert series was born while he was attending Drake University and his successful bookings of Artists on the Campus paid for his tuition in his second year; and (5) he appeared on the screen in "Brief Interlude" and "Sing a Jingle" in the days before he realized that he really wanted to be a producer.

Paul Gregory at thirty-two, energetic to a point of exhausting his co-workers and with ideas for the theater that could keep a whole regiment of producers busy, takes his place, as producer of "The Caine Mutiny Court Martial, in a list of the most active theater producers in the country.

Working in Hollywood, a continent away from Broadway earth that is believed to contain the only nutrients for living drama, Gregory is the first producer to create productions primarily for the vast audiences removed from the trail which road shows generally follow. His offerings have all been embraced by New York critics and have packed theaters on Broadway, but they go forth designed to stir the minds and hearts of Americans who are rarely privileged to see plays. He has turned the entire country into a gigantic arena composed of the smallest hamlets and the largest cities, and his players move against a stage that retains its vigor because of his belief that drama and the communication of living, passionate, ennobling words are the legacy of all men.

Prior to the presentation of "The Caine Mutiny Court Martial," Gregory produced Bernard Shaw's "Don Juan in Hell" starring Laughton, Charles Boyer, Agnes Moorehead and Sir Cedric Hardwicke; a theater adaptation of Stephen Vincent Benet's "John Brown's Body" with Tyrone Power, Anne Baxter and Raymond Massey, and the national reading tours by Laughton. He is shortly to launch "That Fabulous Redhead" starring Agnes Moorehead and Robert Gist, and a show being especially conceived for Tyrone Power; and his maiden musical "Something to Rave About," with Marge and Gower Champion.

The producer is profiled on a page from the program of his stage presentation, *The Caine Mutiny Courtmartial.*

rehearsal in three weeks, and didn't have a director. I'd gone to Harold Clurman, Danny Mann, Josh Logan, they'd all turned down my script. It was this old crap-o that you got and still get in the theatre today, this "What is the motivation?" It wasn't enough that the drama of the moment was sufficient motivation, they had to know who was the grandfather of the court judge, and who were the wives of the others, if they had children—it was just such nonsense, I'd never heard such crap.

It was all an outgrowth of the Method, you see. So, when Charles Boyer told me that Dick Powell, who was being considered for one of the parts, really wanted to direct, I said, "Well, God, has he ever directed in the theatre?" Because, directing in the theatre is another cup of tea than directing in the movies or television. After I met with Powell and was leaving his house, Dick said he didn't want to play in anything where he'd have to run a year or two, "But," he said, "I'd sure like to direct it." Well, the way he said it made me think, "What the hell, I've taken chances on many, many people, and maybe Dick Powell could direct something in the theatre if I stood by him." I did not bargain on this ego the size of Mount Vesuvius. Up to the moment we went into rehearsal, I could talk to him and tell him anything. The minute that we went into rehearsal, he had on his Cecil B. DeMille boots and gloves and you couldn't get near him, so after a week I had to fire him.

I called Laughton, who was languishing around in England, and I said, "Get on a plane, you're directing this, we're in rehearsal, and if you don't, it'll ruin us, get over here." And so that's how Laughton loved to be brought in. He came in like the white god on the stallion; you know, the white savior. He worked on the script, and he directed it, and was brilliant, brilliant. And *Caine Mutiny* went on and became the great hit and so forth and so on. And, I'll tell you a story of Laughton, this was typical of the man. We were sitting at a Boston press conference, and one of the members of the press at the luncheon turned to Laughton and said, "How did you ever decide to do *Caine Mutiny*, Mr. Laughton?" Charles looked at me, and he looked down at the table, and he hemmed and said, "Well, I read the book, and I—I just thought this had to be done. I just thought it had to be put on stage." So, later, we're walking down the hall, he puts his arm on my shoulder, he says, "Oh,

Paul, I can't help it. I *couldn't* say it was your idea." Well, I don't give a damn, really, but that's a very keen insight to dear old Charles.

In reminiscing about his old business partner, Gregory sometimes sounds as if he has an ax to grind, not unlike a divorced spouse discussing his once-beloved ex. William Phipps recalls that while it lasted the Gregory/Laughton team was a happy as well as a productive union.

William Phipps

My first meeting with Laughton was in 1941. One night I was in the Maxwell Coffee Shop on Hollywood Boulevard, and the person sitting next to me, who I guess was also a night owl like me, turned out to be an English professor at UCLA. His name was Tom Sherabeck, and we started talking. He mentioned being a friend of Laughton, and invited me over to meet Laughton some day, and I met him then, briefly. And then along came Pearl Harbor. I was out here in California, alone, I was twenty years old, I had no relatives, no family, nothing—except my brother. So, when I got the news that my brother was killed in the war, it happened to be about the time I met Laughton. And he let me pour out my grief, he just listened, he was a sounding board. The fact that he had two brothers of his own, Tom and Frank, that had a lot to do with his empathy. (This leads me to remember that, in Laughton and Elsa's house, there was not a photograph in the place of anybody—of her, or him, or anything else—except by his bed, he had a little picture, maybe three inches by five inches, of his mother. That was all. Of course, the walls were all covered with his fabulous art collection, but there were no other photographs. Most people in Hollywood, they have all kinds of photos and posters and memorabilia on their wall—but not Laughton.) He had been in World War One; he had been gassed. But he only mentioned it once or twice in passing, like an aside, because he was concerned that it might affect his bronchial tube, but he would never go into it.

I went into the navy for three years, and I got one letter from Laughton while I was in the navy. Then, when I got out of the navy, I went into what was called The Actor's Lab. It was the most famous school then, and more prominent since. And I was cast in the lead of Sidney Kingsley's play *Men in White*. There were only two performances, a matinee and an evening. Russ Johnson, who later played the Professor on *Gilligan's Island*, and I were cast in the leads, and so there were two casts from the class that we were in. We drew straws to see who would do the matinee and who would do the evening performance, and I drew the evening. Laughton, at the time, was casting Brecht's *Galileo*, which has about fifty speaking parts, so it's tough to cast, as you can imagine. So, he was going all around town. (There was a lot more little theatre then, I think, than now.) And, he came to this one performance of *Men in White*, and he brought with him Helena Viegel, Bertolt Brecht's wife. (She'd been the number one stage actress in Germany before Hitler.) They went right to me, and Laughton said, "Young man, you're very impressive, the audience liked you," etc., etc.—I won't go through it all. And Helena Viegel kept saying, "Ja! Ja! Ja!" She was probably more instrumental than anybody in getting me to do *Galileo*. She was living in Santa Monica, and she had me come out to the house, and gave me breathing exercises. She took me on as a protege.

I remember one time when we were rehearsing *Galileo*, Laughton was down below in the atrium in the foyer, talking to this little man in a suit, and Laughton said, "Billy, come here, I want you to meet somebody." And I went over, and I thought, "I wonder who this little man is?" And Laughton said, "Billy, this is Charlie Chaplin, Charlie Chaplin, Bill Phipps." Can you imagine? Charlie Chaplin! I think it was that night, after rehearsal, we ended up at the place across the street on La Cienega, a restaurant called The Ready Room. It was like two restaurants, one in front and one in back. We went to the back, Charlie Chaplin, a couple of people from *Galileo*, Laughton and I. We were sitting at the table, and Laughton kept gently prodding Chaplin to do *schticks*. And, Chaplin got to doing things . . . Well, I'll tell you. This whole dining room, maybe seventy, eighty people, little by little, people stopped eating . . . the waitresses stopped waiting . . . the bartender stopped serving drinks . . . they all became quiet, everything stopped to watch Charlie Chaplin. Magical, magical moment. Little by little, they got to realize they were in the presence of greatness—"Let's not miss this!" And everybody was just enthralled. And it went on for like two or three hours! And, one of the things I remember Laughton had Chaplin doing was playing himself— when he was a little boy—playing a little girl! Now, here he is, the adult, playing himself as a little boy, imitating this little girl. But of course, Charlie Chaplin was brilliant, he could do anything. And Laughton used to say, "The greatest living actor is Charlie Chaplin." Which was true.

Laughton and I got to know each other better during *Galileo*, and then I became one of the students in Laughton's Shakespeare class. Shelley Winters was one of the other students, but I already knew her. I used to see Shelley Winters a lot socially, in pubs and restaurants. As a matter of fact, she and I went to Slate Brothers restaurant once, and we appeared in the columns the next day as an "item," but we were just friends. She was John Ireland's girlfriend. In addition to Shelley, some of the other students were Kate Lawson, Arthur O'Connell and Denver Pyle, among others. There was one room at Laughton's house that he called the "classroom," and it was sealed off from the house. To get in, you had to go outside and go in a separate door, both back and front. And we had classes in luxury. There was a bar, there was coffee, there was a fireplace, there was a library, and recording stuff. In Laughton's class, Shelley could never really, for want of a better description, "crack" me, as in crack open the safe, to get in. I would usually get there early, to talk to Charles about the class and what was coming up, etc., and so I always sat in the same chair. And every time I would get up to get some coffee, or go to the men's room, Shelley, no matter where she sat, would go over and sit in my chair. That could be maddening, but I didn't let it, I just ignored it. But invariably, and even if I sat in a different chair . . . She wouldn't say anything, she'd just get up and go sit where I was sitting. And I never "bit." I never said anything, I didn't start a thing. Could have been the start of something big, it could have been an affair, but I was not attracted to her, you know. Now, this'll kill you: I went to the airport some time later to get on an airplane to go to Paris to shoot a picture Charles was starring in, *The Man on the Eiffel Tower*. Lockheed Constellation—sleeper all the way, LAX to Paris, and I got a window seat. I'm ready to go to Europe, but the plane sits there for a while, and they said, "Well, we're waiting for somebody." The flight was delayed because of Shelley Winters—and she happened to have the seat next to me! Can you believe the coincidence? She was going back to New York for the premiere of *A Double Life* with Ronald Colman, which made her a star. And sure enough, I got up to go to the bathroom—she took my window seat.

But, when we got to New York, you know what? She took me, on Universal's expense account, to every Broadway show. I had a week or two before I had to go on to Paris, and she treated me, courtesy of Universal, to all the shows.

I always liked Shelley. But I don't think she was getting very close with Charles Laughton. I remember one time, I had dinner with her and her sister, Blanche, who was married to George Boroff, who had the Circle Theater. Shrift was their maiden name, Shelley Shrift and Blanche Shrift. We were having dinner, just the three of us one night, and Shelley was being critical of Laughton, and I just laid her out. Because I thought her criticism was very unfair, and she was criticizing him from a selfish point of view, like maybe things in the class weren't going *her* way, or what *she* wanted. So I told her off, and she just clammed up, she had nothing to say. If she says in her book she spent a lot of time with Laughton, I don't think so. Knowing Charles as well as I did, I think he would have given Shelley Shrift short shrift. I don't think Laughton was ever that close to Shelley.

I first met Paul Gregory about the time that he took Laughton out on his reading tours. And, I always liked him. You met him—charming man. And later on, he hired me for a couple of small parts in his productions, *The Day Lincoln Was Shot* on television, and the film *Harlow*, with Carol Baker. Laughton had a funny description of Gregory (*laughs*): he said he looked like an Argentinian pimp. What's an Argentinian pimp? I don't know. But this was humorous, it was spoken with affection, it wasn't a put-down, no. Because, he was quite the dude, then, Paul Gregory. He was always dressed-up, and he was charming, he was witty, and very cheerful, always very cheerful. And very handsome.

Paul Gregory

Anyway, going from theatre to the movies was a natural progression for us because, first of all, every time we would do a reading tour, Charlie would become so exhausted . . . He really wasn't well; he would go out on tour for five or six weeks and then he would just *fade*. Oftentimes, we would have to cancel a week's dates. We had to have the understudy take over for him in *Don Juan in Hell* for six weeks, at one time. He would fade. And, his genius was such—and he was a genius, no two ways about it, the man was a genius—that I looked to *any* medium that would permit us the facility of working together and not wear him down. So, we did television, and I tried to get things going like *Three for Tonight* that he didn't really *have* to do. And I still called them "Paul Gregory and Charles Laughton" productions, or "Charles Laughton/Paul Gregory," I forget how it was billed. It wasn't necessary how it was billed, anyway, I never gave a damn about billing. I tried to do things that he didn't have to get so involved in, and even *then*, he was saying, "You're trying to do things so that you don't have to be bothered with me anymore." He was the most insecure human being I've ever known in my life, and that's why he was so unhappy.

So, anyway, we thought of movies. I told my old friend Harold Matson, the literary agent, I was looking for something that Charles and I might do as a picture. Then, one day, he sent me the galleys of *The Night of the Hunter*.

"I never understood Hollywood," said Davis Grubb in a 1974 interview with this author. "I had been there for the first time in 1949, right at the tag end of the Raymond Chandler Hollywood. I lived in a place that was just starting to get seedy on Kenmore Avenue, right below the Ambassador Hotel and the Brown Derby, and it was just full of character. I was drinking in the local taverns—not bars, Hollywood taverns—on streets like Rampart in L.A. and little streets off Wilshire. I got into the habits of the night crawlers and people who went around at night looking for what-

Davis Grubb in the early ninteen-fifties, around the time of *The Night of the Hunter's* first publication.

Louis Grubb, Davis' younger brother.

ever: loneliness, or drugs, or sex. A lot of that later went into *The Night of the Hunter,* in a funny way. It's very strange, where inspirations, such as they are, or, as they're so called, come from."

By the time Davis Grubb was seven, he knew he wanted to write. With his younger brother, Louis, he grew up in the Ohio Valley. It was a world of rural beauty and pervasive poverty he would describe vividly in *Hunter* and such subsequent novels as *The Voices of Glory* and *Fools' Parade* (also filmed, starring James Stewart, in 1971). Louis Grubb, who became an artist in Manhattan, recalled with fondness and pride his brother and the childhood they shared.

Louis Grubb (author's brother)
My father was an architect from Wheeling. My mother was the daughter of a steamboat captain whom my grandmother tamed and convinced him that that was not a very ethical profession. His brother was also a captain, and was in fact the character "Uncle Birdie" in *The Night of the Hunter.* He finally retired and after ran a boat across from Ohio to Moundsville. I was born in 1930, which was not a great year to be born, and Dave had been born in 1919. We were basically ten years apart. Dave and I were bitter enemies, because he was terribly jealous of me. Because, he had been king of his world, cock of the walk. (*Smiles,*) Of course, I was a wonderful child, a perfect child.

When I was still very young my father took sick, and my mother started reading library books in the bathtub at night. She didn't want father to know she'd decided she might need to pursue a career. Mother had never worked up until that point, but my father was ill for a year, and died of a lung problem. We never knew if it was lung cancer or tuberculosis. Mother with her two boys left Moundsville and finally got a job in Clarksburg as a children's social worker for the state. Dave had written his first short story, obviously influenced by Poe, called "The Horrors of the Rue Morgue," on paper which was pieced together by yarn, about the age of six or seven. I just found it again the other day. And Dave began to write short stories in Clarksburg. He also wrote quite a few radio plays for WBLK in Clarksburg.

Eventually, Dave and I became friends. There was a point that I had to gather some wildflowers for a botany class in high school, and Dave volunteered to take a long, long walk with me outside of town. So, we walked through some fields, and we collected these wildflowers, and something happened. I don't even think that Dave knew. But, there was some sort of magic that happened between the two of us, and after that point, then, we were friends. We would often go to the recreational poolroom. I guess I must have been fifteen or sixteen and Dave was about twenty-five or twenty-six, and we would shoot pool together. I wasn't very good. I would have an Orange Crush, and Dave would have a beer. And then I would have another Orange Crush, and Dave would have another beer. Dave would win the first game, and then, when he would have the second beer, I would win the second game. So that, by the third game, I was the Minnesota Fats of Clarksburg.

This pool hall was a wonderful place. On Saturday, farm people would come in to do their shopping. Families would drive in on their trucks, usually, and the women and the children would go off to do the shopping, and they would drop the husbands off at the recreational poolroom. Some of the husbands would play pool and the others would sit on the two sets of bleachers looking down on the poolroom. And then, towards the end of the day, when the women were ready to go back to the farm, they'd bring their children and their bags of whatever they'd bought, and then they'd stand outside as long as they could, and then they'd come in, outraged, and grab the husbands. And the husbands, for the most part, were embarrassed, while Dave and I would be standing there with our Orange Crush and beer.

Lou Grubb remembered one of many incidents which made its impress on his brother's consciousness, later to emerge as a crucial component of his most famous story:

Louis Grubb

That pool hall is where Dave, several months later, went back to have a beer by himself and sat down next to a man who was having a beer. Dave looked over, and saw that the man had LOVE tattooed on one hand, and HATE on the other. Dave was so horrified that he got up and left. And obviously he never forgot that.

As a young man, Davis Grubb began writing short stories and selling them to the pulp market and better magazines, such as *Collier's*. Most of his short stories—and all of his subsequent books—were set in the West Virginia of his childhood and long family history. As the author told a local public television station late in his life: "I just can't think of taking off on any book without a West Virginia base, because I can't quite visualize things happening in the world without their happening here." But this was a realization reached upon reflection, and something of which the author was not aware when he came to write his first novel. At the time of *Hunter's* publication, however, Grubb did tell the *Reader's Digest*, "Being born and raised within sight, smell and taste of the river had an influence on my mind and soul that seems to have survived all others. Although I have not been to the bottom lands in more years than I can remember, the music and grandeur of the Ohio River have never left me and I think they never will."

Davis Grubb (author)

Being asked where he gets his idea isn't the worst question to a writer, but it may be the unanswerable one. Because, where a book comes from is like the roots of a tree, there are so many of them.

By the early fifties, I was back in Philadelphia, working as an ad copywriter. My agent was Don Congdon, who was Harold Matson's as-

sistant and who has been a priceless friend through the years. I broke
with him recently because the whole agent–writer relationship has
changed very fast in our time, and our break was a very sad one. But, it
was Donald who encouraged me to try my first novel. I'd been in California for a winter, knocking out a few short stories, and reaching the
end of that period in which the short story would satisfy me as a form.
I wanted to try something longer. It was like I had been making short
trial runs in my backyard, and now I wanted to fly the Atlantic.

So, I couldn't think of a theme for my first novel, until I came up with
two things, one of which was based on a horrifying derivation of a nursery rhyme outlined in a book called *The Oxford Dictionary of Nursery
Rhymes*, by a very charming writer named Opie. (*Actually, Peter and Iona
Opie. P.N.J.*) According to him, the origin of the song "London Bridge
Is Falling Down" is based on a custom immemorial the human has created of burying alive, in the foundation of a bridge, a child to appease
the river gods, who were offended by the bridge being built over their
water. I was going to update this, I think, into the seventeenth century,
because I thought England in 1630 was one of the extremely interesting
times: a time when a lot of the alchemy, magic rites and actual participation in the world of fairies, elves, Oberon and all the great mystic figures of English mythology were just being suppressed, primarily by the
Puritans. Shakespeare's time was full of that. I'm still going to do the
book; it may be my next one, because I want to do a fairy story.

Instead of exploring the nursery rhyme mythology, the young writer
decided to pull an unfinished story out of his horsehair trunk.

Davis Grubb

I might have written a book with more international interest if I'd written a novel set in England in 1630. But, for better or worse, I picked
my second idea, which was to go back to a story I had once started
called "Gentleman Friend." This one was about a little boy and his sister whose mother gets involved with a traveling salesman at a time when
they're looking for a lonely-hearts killer in the town. I've forgotten
what kind of salesman this guy was, but he wasn't a preacher.

Louis Grubb

"The Gentleman Caller" was Dave's version of something that had really happened, not with a preacher, but with a man who had advertised in the pulp magazines of the time, love/romance magazines, looking for a widow with children. And, in fact, I think his name was Harry Powell, and he did live in Clarksburg, and he was arrested, and tried, and convicted. He may have been executed, I'm not sure. But, they found bodies of widows and children under the floor in the garage of his house. The motivation was money, same as Preacher. He advertised for widows with children specifically because he felt that they were vulnerable, because this was the early thirties, and they were very hard times. So, any woman who had children would be looking for a husband. He was even worse than Preacher.

It's a hard world for little things.

Davis Grubb

There was a murder in "Gentleman Friend." I hadn't finished the story, because I'd known it wasn't right. I didn't know at that time that it was going to be a novel, just as I later didn't know when I wrote a certain chapter of *Voices of Glory* that it was eventually going to become *Fools' Parade*. It never became a chapter, because it got to be too long; it was like a yeast culture. The others had turned out to be nice fifteen-to-twenty page chapters with a successful ending—as successful as any ending ever can be to a cartoon of human life—but nothing would stop *Fools' Parade* until I put it aside and later came back to it. I worked six months on the novel, which later became the Jimmy Stewart movie. But it wouldn't have worked as a short story, any more than "Gentleman Friend" would have. It was like a certain wire that will not carry that much electric current, it'll burn out. I'm not using the metaphor "current" in a sense of implying any great power in my work, I'm just saying that some ideas have too much load for a short form to carry.

I don't remember the exact moment when I decided to change the salesman into a preacher. But I knew that I had to say something about the gap between promise and gift, which I'd seen all my life in the Christian Church. I had to make some social comment as a human being who had gone through the experience of hearing wolves in sheep's clothing in the pulpit. I had been through the astonishment of a child in reading about a lady whom I'd heard was a great Christian, Aimee Semple McPherson; suddenly she's caught in her love nest, in probably the most human situation of her life, out in the western deserts, and this was a big scandal.

At that time, there was afoot in America a great attempt to make Christ into an account executive for the whole system. In the twenties, a man named Bruce Barton wrote a book called *The Man Nobody Knows*, and he made Christ into kind of a super-salesman. He sort of changed the gesture of crossing yourself into an extension of a lodge handshake. It was really an interesting experiment, and for better or for worse I think it still survives, because you hear in the voices of men like Norman Vincent Peale a kind of Rotary expansiveness, a hail-fellow-well-met. I can't mimic it, but the minute I hear it, I recognize it. I'd heard it all my life, and it seemed to come to life about the time of Barton's book.

I had a chip on my shoulder about preachers, I think, from childhood. You see, I saw how preachers talked in the pulpit and then, because our family was friendly with our preachers, I saw them in their homes. And there was some terrible dichotomy . . . Well, it was left hand in the pulpit and right hand in the home, or vice versa. They were either hell and brimstone in the pulpit and then very kind and rather passive at home; or else, they would speak about human kindness, and come home to dinner that Sunday and taste the coffee, look at their wife and say, "You call this coffee?" and throw it out the window. I saw that happen.

A very little boy in our neighborhood named Pal was the son of the Episcopal minister. He was always coming to our house for dinner on Sunday, which is an immemorial custom in W.A.S.P. America, to have the preacher over. And he would say, "Can I have a piece of your chicken, Davis?" I'd say, "No," and he would say, "Aw, have a heart." That phrase kept haunting me through the years, and I put it in Preacher's mouth when I wrote *Night of the Hunter*. As for Pal, he had a tree-house in his backyard down on Lafayette Avenue. Lord, I envied that tree-house. Then I found out that one of the main reasons why Pal had the tree-house was to hide from his father, the minister, who used to beat him unmercifully. His father couldn't climb the tree.

So, I had a very graphic picture of the church at that time. And, there's another guy who went into that image of Preacher. My mother was always digging up little children in whorehouses or abandoned car chassis or someplace and bringing them in and trying to repair them and help them repair themselves. Well, she found these two children, a little boy and a little girl, brother and sister, who were in some kind of sexual bondage to this strange man. He was in his forties or fifties, and very solicitous, kind of unctuous, in fact. Mother could never find out what went on, what ritual was taking place. It may have been an utterly harmless thing, but it had a definite sexual overtone, and my mother was pretty sensitive to that kind of thing. She got the children away from him. But I sensed, in these children's faces, a kind of delighted terror that such a thing could be.

All of these things went into *The Night of the Hunter.* Do you remember a little child actress named Sybil Jason? She was in a kidnap movie that came out in 1934, just after the Lindbergh kidnapping. You see, the image of the abused child was very strong in the thirties. We had the Lindbergh case. We had a man in California named Hickman. We used to read about all that in the rotogravure section of the papers.

Louis Grubb

One very funny thing when I was a kid. Mother decided we needed a vacation, and we went to Rehoboth Beach, Delaware. She had a brown Pontiac coupe, and there was a drop seat in the back. Dave and I were both very tall, but Dave was older so Dave sat in the front seat and I had to sit in the drop seat in the back. We would be going through small towns, and Dave and I had become really good friends, and as we would be driving through these towns, Dave and I would yell out the window, "Help! Help! Help! We're being kidnapped!" And Mother would say, "Oh, dear God, you both need keepers." Then she would speed up.

Davis Grubb

There were all kinds of monsters roaming the land. I can't think of people like Pretty Boy Floyd, Alvin Karpis, and these guys, I don't know what they were like. I suppose they were probably guys with very primitive ideas about acquisition in a very acquisitive society. But I don't think of them in the same light that I would a man like Harry Powell, the name I gave to my preacher character.

Of course, there were other characters in *Hunter* beside the children, their mother, and Preacher—chiefly Rachel Cooper, the old farm ' woman who rescues the youngsters.

Davis Grubb

There again, so many things went into her. My mother was a liberal, I suppose the word is. A thinking person. Our house was full of quarrelsome books. Karl Menninger's *The Human Mind,* books by Dorothy Thompson, books by Sinclair Lewis, and later, books by Rebecca West who, in my opinion, is the best living writer in English. It was a critical house.

Louis Grubb

We were a very political family. My father had all the classics around the house. I wasn't around to hear this talk, but there was a lot of talk about Roosevelt and what was going on. There was talk about communism, and psychiatry, and we were brought up basically with really intelligent friends.

Davis Grubb

My father was a conservative. Then, when he died, my mother became a social worker, and I saw this little world of frightened children under her hand and care. She was a magnificent social worker, working hand in hand with this wonderful farm woman outside Clarksburg. My mother was half of the model for Rachel Cooper and, later, for Marcy Cresap in *The Voices of Glory.* My mother was a more sophisticated woman than the original of Rachel, but I just knew a lot of Rachels.

And I knew that women held this country together during the pioneer days, and I think they held it together during the Depression. I don't think the country ever would have made it without women. I don't think women's lib has struck on this point yet. If they have, I don't think they've emphasized it as much as they should: the times when women have linked hands and saved the country. I don't think there's any question about it. I saw the pride of men broken who had been strong, self-sustaining people, taking care of their families. I saw that broken. And the reaction to that, in most men, is a terrible social anger. And I've seen the women appease that, and probably save us from great violence.

There was another woman I based the character of Rachel Cooper on, physically and so many ways. She went to church in Glad Bell, West Virginia, once and they asked her for a contribution, and she didn't go back to church for twenty-five years. She was that kind of woman, and I think I mentioned that in the book.

And what of the characters in the first half of the story? What of the townspeople who are all part of little John's world at Cresap's Landing?

Davis Grubb

There's Walt and Icey Spoon, with their ice cream parlor. Well, there was a Spoon family who ran a confectionery in Moundsville. We were always afraid they might be offended. Actually, my agent was very upset; I wasn't, because I knew they were lovely people and wouldn't mind a bit.

Old Uncle Birdie with his wharf boat is John's pal. I've changed Uncle Birdie into Uncle Gene in the play I've written from the book, because he was based on my Uncle Gene Cresap. He was my grandmother's brother, born about 1815, who started out with a skiff, operating a ferry service at Moundsville—drunk most of the time, I am told. I loved him, because he always smelled like a fruitcake. And he was like a fruitcake. You could slice him and there was always something jolly and merry inside, like a piece of cherry. He would always boom out when he'd see me, "That's my boy down there!" He kind of cussed, but cursing is a river art that goes back to Mike Fink and the keel-boat men. Mark Twain wrote about it, but I knew about it long before I read *Tom Sawyer* or *Huck Finn*.

Anyway, these were some of the roots and origins of the characters with which I tried to populate a scary story. But, as I said, it would be impossible to trace all the elements that worked on me from childhood to adulthood, which went into my first novel. For example, I learned a lot of the devices of producing fright in people through a story from old silent movies, because they, too, were a big part of my growing up. My brother just missed that; he was born in 1930, so he wasn't around when talking pictures started. I remember it was a big deal when they put up an enormous sign in Wheeling: "Vitaphone."

The Hunchback of Notre Dame had a big impact on me. I admire Chaney enormously. I just remember the Griffith pictures vaguely. I know I used to feel great grief at the sorrows of Lillian Gish when I'd see her in the movies. And I always felt great grief for Chaplin. I never could laugh at Charlie Chaplin when I was little. His pictures always seemed to me nothing to laugh about: somebody who had to eat his shoe, who was so hungry he saw this guy turn into a chicken and start pacing around the cabin. Chaplin always made me sad.

But if I'm going to talk about the actors I learned from when I was growing up, I can't leave out the name of Charles Laughton. I can't put into words what he contributed to my life, because he started to contribute to my whole, apperceptive mass as a writer when I was nine or ten years old. So, we kind of worked together till the time when he started to direct movies.

Once all the elements were in place, the actual writing of *Hunter* was completed in only six weeks. Agent Matson had no trouble selling the book to the prestigious Harper & Brothers, which set about preparing a place for Grubb's first novel on its 1953 roster. In the meantime, Matson had not forgotten Paul Gregory's clarion call in search of movie material.

Paul Gregory
When Harold Matson sent me the galleys of *The Night of the Hunter,* I read it and—you see, I've never been short of an opinion. When I think something's good, I say, "Go." So I didn't send the book to Laughton and say, "What do you think of this?" I sent the book to Charlie and said, "I think this is what we ought to do."

Charlie read it and called me up at four in the morning and said, "You're absolutely right. We should do it."

Davis Grubb
Laughton never told me why he chose my book for his first directing job, but apparently it hit him right between the eyes. Because, Paul Gregory later told me that Laughton was staying at the St. Moritz then, on the same floor with Gregory. Gregory said, "Here came Laughton wallowing down the hallway in his nightshirt, waving this book, saying, 'We've found it, we've found it!'"

"In reading the story by Davis Grubb," Laughton later wrote in a magazine article, "we couldn't put it down. And, we bought the story as we figured if we liked it that much, the chances were that Normal, Illinois, and Grand Forks, North Dakota, and Wilmington, North Carolina, would like it too."

Paul Gregory

So I got on the horn and got ahold of Harold Matson to get an option. I told him we wanted it, and I said, "I authorize you to up my bid by 15 percent over any bid that comes in." So, I assume that's why we got it.

Davis Grubb

A friend at the ad agency in Philadelphia where I was a copywriter called me at about 1 A.M. and said, "You're in Louella Parsons' column this morning!"

I said, "Drink a cup of coffee, and get back to sleep."

"No," he said, "seriously." He kept insisting, so he finally got me awake, and I got dressed and went out and bought a paper at Spruce and Broad Street. I came home, and sure enough, it said Paul Gregory and Charles Laughton had just bought *The Night of the Hunter* for $75,000, or $80,000, something like that. I didn't know a thing about it. I was just stunned.

Then I called my agent, I think the next morning, and he told me all about it. So, then it all started. It's quite an impact, you know. Laughton called me that afternoon, and was very expansive and charming. He kept saying, "Man, who are your masters? Who are your masters?" It put me in a rather awkward position. I tried to tell him that they were people as different as Howard Pyle, and Hans Christian Andersen—who was one of Laughton's favorites—and Sax Rohmer, who wrote the Fu Manchu stories, I loved him. I still do. And I read mystery stories avidly when I was a kid. My father did, too; we always shared our mystery stories. I'd finish one and pass it on to him.

Night of the Hunter in the new edition is in the "Mystery/Detection" section at Doubleday's bookstore downtown. I have no idea why. That's like putting Rebecca West's *Black Lamb and Gray Falcon* in the Animal Husbandry department. I don't mean to make any comparison, I hasten to add. *Black Lamb* has been kind of my Bible through the years. I've recently finished her life of St. Augustine, which is just breathtaking. I'm realizing now that Preacher wouldn't have been possible in a Christian mural, which *Night of the Hunter* is, in a way—in a parable—without the influence of St. Paul and St. Augustine. Because, I don't believe that the great credos or creeds become twisted or distorted in history. I think that history has a way of making greatness out of even twisted minds. But I do think that St. Paul and St. Augustine had an influence on the teachings of Jesus of Nazareth which caused it to come out not exactly like He had envisioned it. Paul had his own problems, which we can only surmise at through history. Apparently he was a man who was, to say the least, very ambivalent toward women. In fact, I mention St. Paul in one of the passages in the book. I think I almost thought of St. Paul as resembling, in some way, Preacher.

The Book-of-the-Month Club used to give out a little pamphlet with short book reviews. There was a lovely review of *Night of the Hunter* by a man I admire very much, the late Christopher Morley, and Lord, he just blew his top. He said the flight down the river was worthy of Mark Twain, the book was full of Barrie, and Stevenson, he likened it to Dickens. And these, of course, are my gods. It embarrassed me, because I know how great Dickens is. Dickens, to me, is almost as great as Shakespeare, much as I dislike the phrase, "as great as." Dickens is great because of, like Balzac, the enormous population of his work. The point of a good book is to crowd as much into it as possible without making it cluttered.

It's funny, I feel enormous affinity for Charles Dickens, and I don't remember reading that many of Charles Dickens' books. I know I spent hours and hours in the parlor poring over those books before I learned to read. It's like, people have tried to turn me on to Tolkien for years, and I can't read him, for some reason. Lots of times, I've found that when I can't read a writer, it's not because there's something in him that goes against my grain, it's that he is doing so exactly in his time what I want to do in mine, it's a waste of time for us to examine each other's working procedure.

Davis Grubb's literary processes aside, all Paul Gregory cared about was that the author's story was precisely what he had hoped to find for his first feature film. Decades after the fact, Gregory has a ready answer when queried about his decision to purchase the film rights to Grubb's first novel.

Paul Gregory

Because it paralleled emotionally, I guess, aspects of my life. The little children that are deserted . . . My father had left our family when I was very young. I have a deep feeling for little children. I love them, and I have a deep feeling about what life hands young people, the bag of tricks it puts in your hands before you begin to know what it's all about. And that touched me deeply, the trip down the river, and the old woman, and I thought it would touch other people. In fact, I have never done anything that I didn't like personally. (*Laughs*) And that's why I haven't done too much.

Davis Grubb

Now, what things corresponded in my book with Laughton's methods, thoughts or feelings, I couldn't tell you. But my watching Laughton in villainous roles through the thirties helped to create the book which Laughton later saw himself in. That's how it works, in a funny way.

Paul Gregory

I'll tell you an interesting thing, I think Charlie could see himself in the rendition of it. I've spoken of some of the miseries he could put you through, but there was much that was saintly in Charles Laughton, too. And with the young children aspect of it, and the devil in Preacher Powell and all that, you see, that gave Laughton both heaven and hell to play with, and that doesn't happen often, you know. He was the master of both of those at that time. The man was a saint/sinner. Now, I don't think the saint/sinner aspect had anything to do with his unhappiness. I think that was his nature, that's like an alligator is an alligator. He *was* a saint/sinner, period.

Here again, and I can say this because this is absolute truth, I don't know what Charles would call himself, but he was anti-religious, absolutely anti-religious in the denominational sense. And he felt that ministers and people like that were all bogeymen. And I think that he felt that it was a marvelous opportunity to show that God's glory was really in the little old farm woman, and not in the Bible-totin' son of a bitch.

Although elsewhere in these pages producer Gregory will assert that his partner was "not the man on fire," Laughton revealed to fellow artist Grubb a more passionate side to his nature. "He told me," Grubb remembered, "of the decades he had obediently submitted to the biddings of a director"—well, not all *that* obediently, if Laughton had been completely honest—"and now he had had his fill of that and wanted to direct a movie himself. And he was searching, searching for just that property which he would make into the film which had, he often told me, been his lifelong dream."

Davis Grubb
Laughton said—and I hope I don't misquote him, because he said a very heavy thing—"Hollywood has been looking for forty years, Davis, to find a story about the church, what it is and what it does, and you've found a way of doing it that we can put over." And I guess he was thinking of books like *Elmer Gantry,* which still had a few more years to go before it would be made into a brilliant film.

"Like all actors," Grubb once wrote, "—like all writers worth their salt—Laughton was more than a little mad." Grubb also perceived Laughton as being somewhat "left of center," a very dangerous position to be in at that time, although the two men very rarely discussed politics. Grubb's own political philosophy was such that, as he admitted, "I brooded for two months over the defeat of Adlai Stevenson and the execution of the Rosenbergs (whose children—orphaned by their parents' electrocution—I had, in part, patterned the orphans in my story after.)" Laughton, blessedly, managed to get through the McCarthy era without being blacklisted, although his affiliation with Brecht and *Galileo* had raised a few pairs of bushy eyebrows at the House Un-American Activities Committee.

Davis Grubb
Laughton was not against the church in a leftist sense, which would have been common to that period, say, in the sense that "religion is the opiate of the people." Because Laughton was not a fool, and only fools would say a social structure like the church, with all its psychological implications, is merely a tool of capitalism. Laughton didn't seem to have a political mind in the small sense, but a very political mind in a large one. He would be far more interested in the politics of Richard II

than he would in that of Stalin, because he would see similarities, and I'd say he felt, "Why look to a smaller model like Stalin, when you can look to an original like Richard II?"

Whatever the implicit criticism of the church which may have resided between the lines of Grubb's novel, the author had attempted to emphasize more positive elements, and these, too, had struck a chord with the about-to-be first-time director.

Davis Grubb

There were other things that Laughton also wanted to get across: love, and mercy. And the fact that, in proportion to the existence of an evil, there's always in nature a corresponding and somewhat resultant good. No question about that.

A couple of years later, when the finished film was about to open and Laughton was speaking with journalists to drum up publicity, he ventured a few words on the subject of *Hunter* and his perception of it. "It's really a nightmarish sort of Mother Goose story," Laughton told *Saturday Review*'s Hollis Alpert. "But our theme," as the director told *Collier's* Evelyn Harvey, "like that of the book, is really the plight of little children who must learn that evil has many disguises, and kindness is often where you least expect to find it." Laughton told Grubb that he had first used that expression, "nightmarish Mother Goose story," the night he initially read the novel, woke up Paul Gregory, and spent the next two hours enthusing over their discovery. Amongst his other descriptions that first night: "A beautiful ballad; a folk tale; and real Americana."

Paul Gregory

But to have Charles come right out and say, "This is what I want to say," no, he never did. That was what I wanted to say. I wanted to say all those things that were hateful about being an orphan, and about the massive movement of life in its indifference to the little soul that has to struggle and scratch away to make it.

In a strange way, Preacher himself is an isolated, perhaps even orphaned figure . . .

Paul Gregory

I thought of Preacher as motherless and fatherless. In fact, I'm not certain he was even born out of a woman. Sometimes I think people like
that aren't born at all, they're just suddenly materialized, they have no
youth or anything.

Davis Grubb

I never worked up a biography for Preacher: where did he come from,
what kind of parents did he have, that sort of thing. I often thought of
that, but it didn't interest me. I guess, subconsciously, I was interested
in him as a symbol. Which is always a mistake for a writer. I think if I'd
had more texture and depth and dimension to Preacher as a man I
would have lost something of the symbolism, but . . .

Understand, I don't sit down and say, "I'm going to take this guy as
a symbol of that . . ." It all works inside you, like the little wheels are
turning right now in that tape recorder. I don't know what any of the
symbolism is about in *Night of the Hunter.* I mean, if there is any. I assure you, I hope I'm not sounding pretentiously modest, but I had no
knowledge of what I was setting up. I really think it would take a very
strong artist to set out deliberately to write a symbolic novel. Because,
I think it would get so out of hand if he knew what he allegedly was
doing. For example, if I'd known ahead of time that I was going to put
into a book the things people have since told me that I put in, I would
have been a pain in the ass beyond belief.

I suppose if I'd wanted to I would have sketched in a detailed face to
tell you more about Preacher, whereas with a few lines I said something
about a whole group generically. Harry Powell was a phony preacher, but
he was a real preacher as a phony. I think that the position of a preacher
in our time, with what's happening in the world, must be, to say the very
least, equivocal to his own conscience. You see, most people think that the
enemy of Christianity in our time is communism. The enemy of Christianity in our time is the equivocation of Christianity itself on certain issues. The support of Government policies, the almost unfeeling drift to

the right in human affairs in the past . . . Well, I'd have to check my Rebecca West and find how long that's been going on, but I suspect since the early days of the second or third century: an attempt to appropriate the marvelously convenient idea of having people believe that if they don't have anything in this life they'll have infinite riches in the next. This adapted itself so ingeniously to the purposes of a state run by people who were making a lot of money. I think that gap is obvious to anybody who's involved in the church, and I think that has made it so that people are concerned more about their individual salvation than about the salvation of humanity. The latter is, for the time being, kind of not in prominence.

I've had a very close look at the Christian Church in Louisiana for a year or so, and it confirmed every inference I'd drawn when I was five years old: of hypocrisy, of cant, of bigotry, of separation from other human beings spiritually, of making out God to be kind of a weakling who is cowering in the presence of the devil. I don't think that's true. I am a Manichaean, I guess. I'm told, I don't know. I didn't start out reading the Manichaean philosophy and deciding that "This is my thing," I just put things together, and somebody said, "Gee," when I told them about it, "you're a Manichaean." I believe that God is evil and good, both. So, I believe that the symbol of Preacher is partly authentic.

I've known some preachers who were angels, incidentally. I wrote about one in my little Christmas book, *A Tree Full of Stars.* And Rachel has seen both kinds of preachers, too, which is why, when she is confronted with Harry Powell, she knows him for what he is. I believe I put that act of recognition into an interior monologue in the book.

Getting back to the way I handled Preacher, there are certain things a writer does. He puts up signals on a character, without sketching them in any detail, which are directed at the reader to let him start improvising himself. It doesn't always succeed, because sometimes you just produce a few lines that don't suggest any human dimension or emotion or action or anything else. But I think if you put in too much, you rob the reader of that fecundity of his own imagination. I think that there *should* be holes in a story. A friend of mine, a very fine writer, looked at *Voices of Glory* the other day, and he was very effusive in his appreciation of it. But, he said, "You throw away so many characters. You mention little stories in passing that make me wonder who they are, and I start to think about them." To me, that's the *point* of good writing, you see. Hardly anybody does that now. There should be little vignettes all through a story that could possibly go off on a trip. That's the only way a work of art becomes organically a living thing.

I could have written this story as a more "realistic" novel. But then I'd have to go into depth to Preacher's make-up, some way flash back to his origins. I like to write a book where the reader does that himself. Where he says to himself after the book is over, "I wonder what happened to so-and-so . . . and to somebody else," among other things. That is the historian quality which a work of art should have. I hear themes of beauty and fascination in Bartok that he throws away. So does Gershwin. Maddening. And you think, "Jesus, why didn't he . . ." Well, I can see why he didn't. Because it's building up to this other theme, or that other climax.

You know what an historiated initial is? In the old books, the Howard Pyle books and others, they always had the first initial of the first word of a chapter drawn with a lot of little things happening in it. I like that to happen in every letter of a book I write, if I can. If I can do it with the sound of a word, or the juxtaposition of two words that clash together like brass cymbals, or one that gives you a slight tinkle . . . I felt the other day of the way the rain comes down a meadow suddenly on a windy day: It limps. I suddenly realized that the words, "limping rain," might be combined. Those words are just as important as a trumpet blast or a sound of a violin. And it's hard for someone who isn't mechanically a writer to know what I'm talking about. They'd think this is all pretentious, arty bullshit on my part.

Although not a writer, Laughton clearly found the workings of Grubb's technique neither pretentious nor phony. In fact, he was about to invite Grubb to stretch the definitions of his craft in an unexpected way.

Davis Grubb

Anyway, there was Charles Laughton on the phone, and oh, he started to work right away. Laughton was all work, you know. Mind you, he couldn't call me at home, because I didn't have a phone then. Now, I had studied art at Carnegie Tech. Long before I learned to eat or hold a fork, my father, who was an architect in Wheeling, a great person, was teaching me how to sketch in the little breakfast nook in our house at

318 Seventh Street in Moundsville. I talked to Laughton about this, and he said, "Is there any way you can give me drawings of what you saw in your mind while you were writing the story—?" He would send me telegrams and letters from Hollywood, saying, "I need sketches of—" and then he would list five different scenes, say, or five different expressions on the faces. I gather he sometimes wanted to see how I saw an expression on a character's face in a certain situation.

Somewhere along the line, I think there was some discussion of the possibility of my doing the script. Laughton never mentioned it to me, but my agent said that I could probably pick up an extra $20,000 if I'd go out there and work on it. And I've kicked my ass around the whole East Coast ever since that I didn't, because it would have given me a screen credit, which might have led to some work. But these things, you never know, they rearrange your life, and the next thing you know, you don't turn out the last ten books that you turned out under other circumstances.

Paul Gregory

I never met Grubb until well into the project. It seemed he had some kind of phobia, I never quite understood what it was: he wouldn't go on trains, or he hid, or he did something strange; he had to bicycle from Philadelphia to New York, and I had to fly in and out so quickly that by the time he got there I was always gone. I think we were in the second week of shooting when I finally met him. I had to go back to New York, and I met him in Harold Matson's office.

Like often with writers, he wasn't impressive at all. He seemed like some kind of a little figure that had been hidden in a library sorting books or something. And yet, you read his words, and they're gigantic. His phrasing and his descriptions, the imagery that comes out of the man's words is compelling and wonderful. You feel like maybe you're going to meet a god figure, and it's always rather disappointing when you meet someone that looks like a mild-mannered mortal. It has nothing to do with what their talent is, what they can write. (Same thing with Shaw. When I met Shaw, I wasn't prepared for this tiny little man, wasn't prepared for him at all. And he wasn't prepared for me, I'll tell you that. But he was such a giant that, maybe it's my fantasizing, but I just expected somebody, you know, larger than life.)

Davis Grubb

I was going to a shrink, then, a psychiatrist, and I didn't want to break
with that, and I couldn't leave Philadelphia. I had friends there, and very
soon my mother came up from Baltimore, and my brother, and a whole
family unit was sort of set up there. I had a girl in Philadelphia . . . And
if any girls in Philadelphia hear this interview, they'll wonder which one
I'm thinking of. Also, I loved Philadelphia. I knew a young cop around
those days named Frank Rizzo, who's now mayor. But all of that is why
I didn't want to go out to L.A. to work on the film.

I didn't get a phone for a long time, I wouldn't go to New York, and I
was very nervous, and I was frightened by the sudden attention. Because,
you know, I was just making sixty dollars a week in the ad agency, and suddenly this thing happened. I'd thought I was all washed up, right before I
sold the book. I figured, "Well, I've only sold a few short stories to *Collier's*," You know, "I'm a washout." So all of a sudden came this enormous
fireworks of success, which was a wonderful thing. People say success is
dangerous, and all that. Of course it's dangerous, but so is failure. Success is
like a heart attack, and failure is like cancer. A writer's life is just constant
repetition. In my case, chicken on Sunday and feathers all week. I hit it very
big, and then went on to demonstrate that I'm not very astute at managing
money, because money is not interesting to me, it's only a tool. I don't have
a great passion to accumulate it, or I would have accumulated some.

Signifying Grubb's improved station in life would be a visit from his
new employer, a man who had been a legend to movie-goers since 1933,
when he'd tossed a drumstick over his shoulder in his Oscar-winning portrayal of Henry VIII. Although it is not known exactly what specific issue
Davis Grubb was feeling nervous about at the time (perhaps refinements
in the movie-sale contract), a telegram from Laughton, then in Manhattan, to the author dated April 2 clearly evinces his enthusiasm and the fact
that he was, as Gregory will later describe him, "on the track":

DEAR DAVIS GRUBB PLEASE DON'T WORRY ALL THAT IS JUST BIG
BUSINESS FIDDLE FADDLE ANXIOUSLY AWAITING YOUR CALL CAN I
COME DOWN TO SEE YOU ON SUNDAY= CHARLES LAUGHTON

Davis Grubb

Laughton came to Philadelphia to meet with me. I'll never forget his first words to me: "I welcome you to the Aristocracy of the Arts." I lived in a tiny, second-story apartment on Sixteenth and Pine Street, and he ran up the steps, almost two at a time. When I asked him why, he said, "Because I'm so big, that's the only way I can get up."

Then we went out to Gray's Delicatessen to get some take-out food. Of course, it was a thrill to meet him, just to walk up Spruce Street and have a traffic cop say, immediately, "Hi, Mr. Laughton." He had a kind of stolid, stalking walk. He was just out of another world. I've known people back home that are different from the mainstream of sidewalk society, as he was, but I never knew anybody quite like him.

We brought the food back to the apartment. He sat there very elaborately eating a turkey drumstick, and when he finished he threw it over his shoulder. Broke me up. He did it just for effect, of course. It was like giving me his signature or something.

"Underneath the heavy layer of actor," Grubb once wrote, "there lived in Charles Laughton a first-rate writer . . . Laughton was a born writer: I have enough intuition to know one when he's within whistling distance." How much writer Laughton would turn out to be in the service of *The Night of the Hunter* Grubb could never have dreamt at this first meeting. Apparently the novelist gathered his impression simply from the way Laughton could express himself when chatting with the young writer about Hollywood and its denizens. As Grubb recalled, "I once remarked that Marlene Dietrich had always struck me as a strange and bewitched kind of genius. 'Yes,' Laughton sighed. 'There is a quality about Marlene that rather suggests jeweled whips.'"

One of the aspects of his encounter with Laughton which the author never forgot was that, for all the hours director and author shared together, they spent very little of that time talking about the novel. In retrospect, Grubb came to intuit Laughton's feelings: "Laughton already knew the book. Now, he felt, he had to know *me*, to do the kind of fanatically accurate adaptation he had in mind." Although Grubb had no way of knowing it then, this approach mirrored the way Laughton would later deal with actors during the casting process for *Hunter.* In the pages that follow, we will hear from more than one actor who would meet with Laughton and be astonished to discover that Laughton didn't want him to read any lines, he only wanted to talk with him so he could get to know him as a person—only then could Laughton determine if the actor was right for the role. During the course of his time spent getting to know Grubb, Laughton also saw to it that Grubb got to know Laughton. Grubb later recalled Laughton fondly for his "rather wistful Dickensian quality. He was a man of both the nineteenth and twentieth centuries." Laughton shared with Grubb his childhood as a "fat, ugly, pimpled bellboy" in his parents' seaside resort hotel at Scarborough. (The youth had executed his duties so perfectly that three visiting Sitwells assumed that, of course, the boy must be *acting* the role of bellboy. And, they helped him go off to study theatre.)

That child, of course, grew up to be a genuine actor, and Laughton shared with Grubb many of his theatrical experiences—including the gala night in Paris which he recalled as "the most terrifying experience of his whole career." The event was a benefit, and Laughton had been honored by the invitation to portray Moliere's *Le Médecin Malgré Lui* (*The Doctor in Spite of Himself*) in French, before an illustrious and expensive-ticket-buying audience. As Grubb recreated the actor's nightmare, "The play ends with Moliere's eloquent and famous *tirade*. Laughton—always the great improvisor—thought up a bit of stage business with which to conclude the *tirade*. This consisting of something, he assured me, which never fails in theatre. He roundly slapped the nearby chambermaid on the ass. A deathly silence fell over the audience. Laughton, feeling he had profaned this sacrosanct moment in the play, looked up at Elsa in her golden plush box seat beside the President of France. Her face was covered with trembling hands; weeping in sympathy and humiliation for him. Laughton managed to make it till the curtain descended. At which moment the crowd went mad. And it was then—and only then—that he learned that it was sacred tradition in *La Comédie-Française* never to applaud that hallowed tirade. One would as soon applaud a great prayer! And he was born triumphantly out of the theater that night on the shoulders of the adoring crowd."

Of course, *some* of Laughton's visit with Grubb *was* spent discussing the book. "Grubb hates to travel," Laughton subsequently explained to *Collier's* magazine, "so I went to Philadelphia and sat in his study for five straight days asking him what he'd seen in his mind while he was writing the book." Grubb elaborated, "It was easier to draw the answer than tell it." The result was over a hundred roughly-sketched line-drawings. In subsequent years, the sketches were gathered into a portfolio to be sold as a collector's item. Eventually, they were acquired by famed director Martin Scorsese, who after a few years donated them to the Margaret Herrick Library of the Academy of Motion Pictures Arts and Sciences. The frontispiece to this unique treasury is a note, "To Whom It May Concern," written by Grubb and dated August 10, 1973:

The 119 drawings enclosed in this case represent a collaboration which I believe to be unique in the history of film-making. Long before the script by James Agee and Laughton was even begun, Laughton assured me with considerable passion that he intended the film to resemble as nearly my mental pictures in writing the book as was possible to achieve. He quoted Irving Thalberg, his first and best friend in Hollywood, as saying to him once, "Charles, you can't make a good film unless the writer is in the chair." This statement contains a certain ambiguity inasmuch as Thalberg shortly afterwards fired Erich von Stroheim for this very ideal. Indeed, Laughton resembled von Stroheim in his obsessive quest after the most precise possible resemblance between the film and the novel. He told me once of the months he spent in the British Admiralty Archives poring over maps, charts, log-books, records, diaries and the like in preparation for his role as Captain Bligh in *Mutiny on the Bounty*. He was—like von Stroheim—compulsive in this passion for verisimilitude.

Long after I had sold the screen rights to Laughton and Gregory for *The Night of the Hunter* and was well into my second novel I began to be subjected to a daily barrage of wires, phone calls from Hollywood and letters asking me for sketches, more sketches, and yet more sketches of what this or the other scene looked like in my mind. So incessant was this interrogation that it kept me busy dividing my time between the new book—*A Dream of Kings*—and making drawings and sending them off airmail special to Laughton in Hollywood. He would even ask me to draw the expression on a character's face during certain scenes.

Cresap's Landing, as sketched for Laughton by Davis Grubb.

I have seen *The Night of the Hunter* perhaps a dozen times in the past 18 years since it was made and can only declare—perhaps immodestly—that I was not only the author of the novel from which the screenplay was adapted but was the scene designer as well. Any film student comparing these drawings with the actual picture frames of the movie can see what I mean. If such a practice of collaboration between director and the original writer of the adapted novel ever occurred prior to this, in the whole history of the film industry, I do not know of it.

In the introduction to this book, I mentioned that on several occasions an interviewee would remember Laughton or his working methods in a way that was at variance with the memories of another interviewee. The truth, I think, must lie somewhere between the two. Occasionally in my research, I have felt that the same must be said of the truth when an interviewee contradicts not another interviewee but *himself. . .*

Davis Grubb

He stayed five days, and I drew him some pictures. We were always just talking about the book, that's all we talked about. I had been filming *Night of the Hunter* in my head as I wrote it. My ideal cast was mostly made up of people who were already dead. I kept thinking of Marie Dressler as Rachel. And I kept thinking of Walter Huston as Preacher. Mother had taken me to see him and Jeanne Eagels in *Rain* on the stage in Wheeling, it might have been 1924. He would have been magnificent as Preacher.

But of course, Laughton needed a star who was still breathing—and bankable. Laughton also insisted that a different image was required: "People who sell God, Davis, must be sexy." According to Laughton's actor friend William Phipps, Laughton had just such an actor in mind.

William Phipps

Charles called me up and said, "Come over to the house, I've got a book for you to read." I drove over, he took *Night of the Hunter* and handed it to me, and took me personally, almost by the hand, to the library, and he says, "Read this book, and don't come out till you've finished." Honest to God, he made me read it at one sitting. I could get coffee, I could have one of the servants bring me something to eat, but I had to finish the book. He really wanted my gut reaction to it. (He wanted my gut reaction on a lot of things.) And when I read it, I said, "Wow—this is a *movie!*" I said, "My God, this'll make a great movie!"

He was all hot to approach Gary Cooper to play the preacher. Laughton had done a movie with Cooper and Tallulah Bankhead and Cary Grant called *Devil and the Deep* (1932) years before. He wanted Cooper, but I kept saying, 'No, I think Gary Cooper is wrong for this." And, I think he *would* have been wrong, because he was too much the All-American hero to be this sadistic preacher. It just wouldn't work, *I* don't think.

Laughton's friend Phipps was not the sort to discourage one idea without offering another idea in its place. Dubious as he was about Laughton's friend Cooper, Phipps happened to have a friend among his own thespic acquaintances who he felt just might be ideal for Preacher.

William Phipps

I'd first met Bob Mitchum when he was in the army. Not many people know that he was in the army very briefly. There was a place on Sunset Boulevard called Victor's. Everybody used to go there, and I mean *everybody* in Hollywood, stars, directors, etc. I had just gotten out of the navy, and it was my hang-out at the time, and I remember going into the bar. This soldier in uniform was sitting there, and we started talking, and I thought, "My God, what a fascinating man." It was the Mitchum persona, it was evident, it was obvious. At least, it was to me, it probably wasn't to other people. Because, I remember working on several westerns later on with a director by the name of Frank McDonald. I was on the set one day, and Frank McDonald was a nice man, he was very gentle, he was very funny, but for some reason or another he hated the fact that Mitchum had become a movie star. And I remember his saying to me, "Look at that man. Can you imagine, he's a movie star? My God!" He just couldn't believe it.

Mitchum, he was so aware . . . Most people don't know how aware he was of his greatness . . . I remember, so early on in his career, like when he was doing the movie with Bill Holden and Loretta Young, *Rachel and the Stranger.* I remember his saying to me, one day, "I like doing this, but I want to get my own movies." You know, he realized that he should be *the* star. And he knew that he was going to be. He never talked about it in those terms, but you could just tell by his actions, you know, and by his saying things like that.

But, after that night at Victor's, I didn't see Mitchum again until my first picture, *Crossfire* (1947), which of course was one of the first movies to tackle anti-Semitism. My first scene was with Mitchum and Robert Young, which is the tag of the movie, but was shot the first day, at night. I'm on the set for the first time, and it's the last scene in the movie! It's where Mitchum and I walk up to Robert Young, as he is holstering his gun after he has shot Robert Ryan, and I'm a Southern boy, I walk up to him and I say, "Did you have to kill him?" And Robert Young says, "He's been dead for a long time and didn't even know it." So. It was my first time in front of the camera, I was twenty-five years old, just out of World War II, I'd just fallen off the turnip truck. And this business is cruel. Nobody on the set, but *nobody*, came up and introduced themselves, not even the director, Eddy Dmytryk—nobody. And of course, I was scared to death, really, literally scared to death. So, Mitchum and I walked up and hit a mark in front of the camera, and I said the line. Well, I would miss the mark three or four times, I didn't want to look down, and I'm shaking and I'm scared. And also, on stage, you walk up to somebody and maybe look at him and pause—beat, beat—and talk. Dmytryk came over to me; he said, "I know you're doing this like you're on stage, but, as soon as you hit the mark, start talking." "Oh, okay." So, while we're shooting this, Mitchum and I had to walk out of frame and walk back in on the take. One time, when we're way back there, I said to Mitchum, "This is my first picture, y'know." He says, "You're kiddin'." Because, it was so obvious. But, he didn't say it unkindly. You know, he didn't say it snidely and sarcastically, he said it with humor, and said it in a way that amused *me*. And so then I was all right.

That final scene of *Crossfire* ends with soldier Mitchum suggesting to soldier Phipps that they go have a cup of coffee. His arm paternally on the younger man's shoulder, Mitchum walks with Phipps into the final fade-out. Moments after this shot was in the can, art imitated life . . . after a fashion.

William Phipps

And then, after we'd made this take—and that was all we shot that night—Mitchum took me over to his car. And I remember he had an old Buick. We got in the car, he picked up a full bottle of Vodka and a full bottle of Scotch and he says, "Take your pick." So, we sat there and had a few drinks. I didn't realize what a wonderful thing he did, *then*. You know, it was just like, guy to guy. But this was typical of Mitchum, he was very kind to me in ways that I sometimes didn't even recognize until years later, because he never drew attention to them himself. Most people, if they do something nice for you, you know, if you don't acknowledge it in some way they'll manage to point it out to you or mention it so that you'll say, "Thank you," but Mitchum never did that. He was subtle. If he wanted to do something kind to you, he just did it, he never mentioned it. And he was, I realized, very fond of me, he was very kind.

Gentlemen's Agreement that year won the Oscar for Best Picture, and *Crossfire* was far superior to *Gentlemen's Agreement* on the same subject. But they couldn't nominate or vote for *Crossfire* because of the blacklisted people who had made it—the "Red Scare," then—Adrian Scott, Dmytryk,

John Paxton. I remember Shelley Winters saw that picture and loved it, and then some time later she told me, "I didn't think you were an actor, I thought you were a kid from Tennessee."

From that time on, Mitchum and I did a lot of things together. After his famous pot bust, he used to ask me to join him whenever it was time for him to go see his parole officer. So, Mitchum would light a joint, we'd both get high, and then drive down to the police station to see the parole officer. There was no waiting room or anything, there were people waiting to see the officer running along from one story to the next on the steps. There were pimps, and maybe a few murderers, I don't know. It was really awful, but they were so wonderful, they'd see Mitchum and say, "Hey, man, we're here with Mitchum." And they were all stoned, too, either half drunk or smoking pot. Mitchum would go in for his appointment, then he'd come out and say, "Hey, the parole officer loves hearing about kissing Jane Russell." I remember he once said, "If I don't get back into movies, I can tour the country. All those people back there will love hearing about Jane Greer and Jane Russell. I can go on for hours, and they'd pay to see it." And he was right. The parole officer never knew Mitchum was smoking pot, he couldn't tell. People don't know, unless they're an expert, especially if they don't know somebody well. I remember one time, I had seen one of Mitchum's pictures and I'd never seen it before—I forget the movie—and I said to him, "Hey, I saw *Such-and-such!*" He said, "Could you tell which scenes I was high?"

And I said, "No, I couldn't," and you couldn't, 'cause Mitchum was always the same. And he would be stoned out of his *mind* some times. I remember one time, Mitchum and I were going into Victor's. And, you know, cops, they'll do anything to hassle a celebrity or get their name in the paper. And we had been smoking pot, and we started in—they stopped him, and searched him. He didn't have anything on him. And he says, "Better luck next time."

But, you want to know something? The first time I ever smoked pot, it wasn't with Bob Mitchum. It was with Charles Laughton. In 1941, when I first met him, he was going through the motions of trying to get into shape and stay healthy, which of course he never did. So, he got a trainer, named Tom, you know, somebody to throw the medicine ball around with, and do steambaths, and all of that. So, one day I went some place with them. I don't remember any of the details, all I remember is, Tom and Laughton were in the front seat and I was in the back seat, and they started smoking pot. And I didn't know what to make of it, I'd never been around it before. Tom urged me to try it, and I was reluctant to do it, and Laughton said, "Go ahead, Bill, it won't hurt you, I wouldn't say so if I thought it would hurt you. Try it." I tried it, and *loved* it. So, Laughton and I smoked pot together many, many times after that. It would be at his house, Elsa would be working at the Turnabout, we'd smoke pot, and I'd always turn on jazz. You know how jazz is when you're stoned. He didn't know too much about jazz until I started smoking with him, but he got to love jazz like you wouldn't believe.

(**Apparently he also** came to know jazz musicians. Billie Holiday once told Davis Grubb that Laughton "had eaten and loved her mother's chittlins and black-eyed peas and rice." Piano-great Oscar Peterson tells a hilarious story in his memoirs about introducing himself to Laughton at an airport and praising his artistry. When Laughton inquired about Peterson's own profession and was told that he was a jazz musician, Laughton immediately asked, "Got any pot?")

William Phipps
Anyway, by the early fifties I was good friends with both Mitchum and Laughton. I was a very busy actor, but my mission in life was to get Mitchum and Laughton together. Both of them were very big in my life at that time, and they didn't know each other. Then, when Laughton had me read *Night of the Hunter,* I thought, "My God! This is it!" "Robert Mitchum would be great," I said. But he didn't know Mitchum. It went on for weeks. Laughton kept saying, "Gary Cooper," and I kept saying, "No, Mitchum," and he kept saying "No," he didn't want to hear about it. He'd worked with Cooper, he knew Cooper well, and he didn't know Mitchum or his work.

Now, the first time that Mitchum and Laughton met was in the parking lot at Lucy's, the popular hang-out across the street from Paramount. One day, Laughton's car was pulling in . . . Laughton didn't drive, that's part of the reason I spent so much time with him. He loved having me drive him places so we could talk about theatre, and Brecht, and whatever.

Laughton got out of the car at Lucy's, the driver got ready to go, and some guy came up to Laughton and said, "Hi, Charles, how are you?" He said, "I'm fine, but who are you?" He says, "I'm Bob Mitchum." And Laughton says, "For Christ's sake, don't tell Phipps, he'll kill me!" Which meant that I'd talked so much to Laughton about Mitchum, and Laughton didn't know who he was.

If Grubb fancifully marks the beginning of his collaboration with Laughton at the moment he first viewed the actor's villainy on screen, then perhaps it could be said that, for Laughton, the collaboration began the moment he started reading the galleys of *The Night of the Hunter*. The association intensified during Laughton's Philadelphia visit and remained a dynamic interchange between the two men as the days progressed towards production. As Grubb happily recalled, they became close friends—"it was almost like a sexual union." And why not, with their common goal of reproduction (from one medium to another)? (Interestingly, cinematographer Stanley Cortez, as will be seen, fondly remembers his collaboration with Laughton as "mental intercourse.") The first-time author said that he grew so comfortable with Laughton that he felt free to phone the actor at 4 o'clock in the morning if he was troubled and needed reassurance about his own current project—his next novel, the Civil War coming-of-age story, *A Dream of Kings*. "Charles was always in good humor, and didn't seem to mind such an intrusion."

Davis Grubb

It's been written that I wrote these single-space letters to Laughton. I don't know. We were writing at length, and I used to write him so fast that I'd be full of ideas. And I think I did contribute something to the film, other than the novel.

Whether or not there were numerous letters from Grubb to Laughton, only one seems to have survived, but it's a six-page, single-spaced corker. Dated April 19, 1954, it is in response to a hand-written letter from Laughton (again, the only one extant) and a note from Walter Schumann asking questions relevant to the music. Also, it probably harks back to conversations they had shared in Philadelphia. Although in retrospect, many

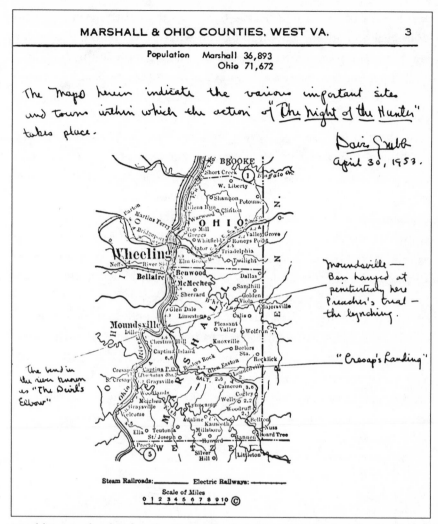

MARSHALL & OHIO COUNTIES, WEST VA.   3

Population   Marshall 36,893
                   Ohio 71,672

The maps herein indicate the various important sites and towns within which the action of "The Night of the Hunter" takes place.

Davis Grubb
April 30, 1953.

Moundsville —
Ben hanged at penitentiary here
Preacher's trial —
the lynching.

"Cresap's Landing"

The bend in the river known as "The Devil's Elbow"

Steam Railroads:_____ Electric Railways: --------
Scale of Miles
0 1 2 3 4 5 6 7 8 9 10 ©

In addition to the sketches the director had requested, Grubb inscribed and mailed to Laughton a book of West Virginia maps, citing therein all the spots which had figured prominently in *The Night of the Hunter.*

years later, Grubb would pay Laughton the posthumous compliment of claiming that he knew more about *The Night of the Hunter* than its author did, at this early stage Grubb found it necessary to question and revise some of Laughton's perceptions about the characters and relationships he had created. "First of all I want to discuss the problem of Willa and Ben. It is my feeling now (and it was my feeling when I wrote *The Night of the Hunter*) that the relationship of Willa and Ben contained, at its outset, most of the seeds of doom which later bore fruit in (a) Ben's crime and (b) Willa's liaison with Preacher. I think you will discover hints of this in the novel in many places. After all, Ben's job was a good one for those hard times; his greed was based on a kind of hysterical feeling that he was not giving his wife and children the best. Willa's concern over finding out where Ben hid the money shows how deeply the same kind of economic neurosis of those times had eaten into her. (An idyllically loving wife would have been concerned with getting her man out—NOT just with finding the money.) It was also established that Willa and Ben's pre-marital relationship had been pretty furtive and guilt-ridden at the outset. It was established that they were drinking on the night of their honeymoon (not in itself a sign of unhappy thinking but, I think, in their case—in their milieu—it would be). Ben, I would imagine, resented living on land and in a house that had come from Willa's parents—or, at least, her uncle. What I am trying to say is simply this: I do not believe that Willa and Ben's relationship was quite as physically and emotionally perfect as you seemed to feel. It was violent sexually because it had begun on such forbidden terms. It is not easy to go into this problem without making an analysis of sexuality which perhaps belongs in a wider religious and psychological consideration than I have the time or wit to make here. Let me say simply that I

Two of Davis Grubb's character portraits for Laughton: Ben Harper; and his wife, Willa (resembling a young Bette Davis).

do not believe any such purely innocent and guilt-free sexual relationship has existed between man and woman since that theoretic Eden from which all such judgements seem to date. And yet it would be well to remember that it was not Sin which the snake brought into the garden—it was Guilt. Otherwise it would not be so simple a matter to flip the coin from the face of Love to the wings of the eagle. In short, I think we must understand how easily Willa slipped from the physical sensuality with Ben to the spiritual sensuality with Preacher. And the bud of guilt was there from the beginning for Preacher to bring so quickly into flower. 'I've been punished,' Willa might well think. 'Yes, he has come to punish me for the Joy me and Ben had together. It is revealed how He punished the both of us! He drove Ben to steal and murder because of his lust for me! And he drove me to shameful greed, too, wanting to know where the money was hid. It is God's judgement and his punishment for them bad things we done.' And ecstacy slips so quickly from the loins to the praying hands and if you let yourself feel what people are thinking and feeling at one of these tent revivals (or in any church, I think) you will know what similar things these two scarlet ecstacies are. The whole Christian ethic is woven thusly—the gold thread of the spirit and the scarlet thread of the flesh and I think perhaps you sensed, wisely, that this was so when you said you thought Shelley Winters would not understand this, being of a more mellowed and temperate faith—a faith, certainly, through centuries piled upon centuries, of a more charitable disposition toward sexual matters. So much for that. I simply do not think we can show Willa and Ben as Darby and Joan or as pre-snake Adam and Eve without leaving unanswered the question: 'How could she endure such a man as Preacher if she had been so happy with Ben?' Preacher, you see, brought Willa the punishment she had felt (perhaps since childhood) that she deserved. And there was a little of the same thing in Willa and Ben that there was so much of (horribly) in Preacher."

Davis Grubb

Laughton kept in touch with me about the studios and stars they were sending the project to. Sam Goldwyn, I heard from Laughton, was interested at one point. Laughton came in very excited one day and told me, "Gary Cooper is reading *Night of the Hunter,* and we're going to hear from him soon." So finally we got Cooper's reaction. His agent, or Mrs.

Cooper, or somebody said that he was afraid of it. I gathered that he'd read it and thought it was a good book, but he was afraid for his image.

William Phipps

I think, in looking back—I didn't think of this until I started talking to you—I'd pitched Mitchum so often that I think Laughton probably talked to Gregory and other people, telling them, "Phipps is talking about Mitchum." And, probably, Gregory—I'm just surmising, now—Gregory said, "My God, yes, Mitchum, if we could *get* him . . .!" But, Laughton never said that to me.

Paul Gregory

When Laughton first called me after he'd read the galleys, he said, "Who do you see as the Preacher?" And I said, "I see Bob Mitchum." He just capitulated, he thought it was such a great idea for Mitchum.

I really loved Bob Mitchum, you see, I loved his qualities. He's got all these side things to him that are wonderful, you know. He's kind, he's good, he's mean, he's a son of a bitch, he can cut you up, and he can write a beautiful piece of poetry—he's got all of these things, and that's what I felt Preacher Powell was. I felt that Preacher had an awful lot of that in him, in order to be fascinating. He couldn't have been just a man with a Bible and a switchblade. He had to have been able to say to a woman, at some time or another, something to charm her. And he had to be able to charm a child. And there had to be some fantasy in him, as mad as it was, there was fantasy in him. So, it had to be Mitchum. If it had been John Carradine, it would have been ridiculous, but that's what one of the geniuses somewhere along the line suggested.

Davis Grubb

I never really offered any casting suggestions for Preacher, I just wistfully said I wished Walter Huston were alive. And I wished Marie Dressler were alive . . .

I did mention John Carradine, who later told me at P.J. Clarke's one night, very honestly, "My agent tried for weeks to get me that part. But," he said very kindly, "I would have considered it the greatest role of my career." I will never sell Mitchum short as an actor, he's a brilliant actor. But don't ever sell John Carradine short. John Carradine would have brought a whole toy box full of surprises to that part. He would have done it with imagination, and panache. He would have brought something to it that Mitchum couldn't have brought to it because he wasn't that old, he wasn't that much of a veteran.

And yet, Mitchum brought to it a kind of a robust corruption that was just invaluable.

Robert Mitchum ('Preacher' Harry Powell)
For a while there, I made the same movie about twenty times; it was called *Pounded to Death by Gorillas*. But no, I wasn't surprised when Charles asked me to do *Night of the Hunter*. I'd known Charles for a long time. We'd never discussed the possibility of working together, but then, he'd never directed a picture before.

Always, whenever he'd call up, he'd say (*softly*), "Hello, Bob?" I'd say "Yes," and he'd say, "Charles here." So this time, I said "Yes?" and he said, "I've found a book to make into a film, and the main character is the most dreadful shit." And I said, "Present."

Then he said, "I shudder that it should even be implied that I know what a dreadful shit is, because I'm making my living reading the Bible about the country, you know. But this character is the most *dreadful* shit." I said, "Okay," and that was it.

The actor has been quoted many times giving this account of his being brought on board the *Hunter* project, and it serves, perhaps, as a typically terse—and fanciful—Mitchum abridgement of history, but there is another version of the story, less short and sweet, which differs to varying degrees from not only Mitchum's recollection but also producer Gregory's.

William Phipps
When Laughton said he was going to get Gary Cooper, I kept saying, "No, I don't think so, I think Bob Mitchum would be better." Well, he didn't know anything about Mitchum, really. I don't think, at this point, he had met him at the parking lot at Lucy's or not, but, either way, he still didn't know his *work*.

So, one day we're in his home, and he says, "All right, have you got Mitchum's phone number?"

I had his phone number, and I called him, I got him on the phone, he was home in Mandeville Canyon, and I said, "How are you?" He said, "Fine," and I handed the phone to Laughton. Laughton told him, "This character's a shit—a real meanie. So, if you play it, you've got to play it in a way that you don't give your little kids nightmares!" Mitchum's children were very young then. "I don't want you to scare the hell out of your kids," Laughton told him. He said, "I'll send you the book," Bob said, "Okay." It was a very short conversation.

So, he handed me the book, and he said, "Take this out to Mitchum," you know, and I said, "No, I won't." He said, "What do you mean, you won't?" I said, "I will not take it to him unless you go with me." And he said, "No, I won't go." He insisted he wouldn't go with me. And I said, "Well, then give it to somebody else. I'm not gonna go take a book to Mitchum unless you go with me." "No, no, no, no!" he cried out. This went on for an hour or two, but I was adamant. Finally in frustration he said, "Okay!"

I had a Mercedes Benz roadster then, with the bucket seats, white, black leather, and Laughton loved that car. Of all the cars *he* ever had, he liked my Mercedes Benz roadster, because we had the top down all the time. So, he got in the car, we drove out to Mandeville Canyon, and, this day, we had the top up. I remember that because, otherwise, Mitchum would have seen him immediately. We parked in the interior of the grounds where Mitchum lived, and I went up and knocked on the door and I said, "Here's the book, Mitch," and he said, "Okay, Willy. Come in." He looks, and he says, "Who's that in the car?" I said, "Oh, a friend of mine came along," so he looked, and he went out to the car. And he of course saw who it was and he said, "Come on in for a drink." So we went in and had a drink. Mitchum had some relatives there that day. Mitchum told me a couple of days later that the relatives had wanted to come over to the house, and he'd said, "What do you want to come over here for? It's dull here on Sunday, and nothing ever happens." Then, when the relatives were there, all of a sudden, this bigger-than-life Charles Laughton walked into the room! It made a liar out of him, made him feel like a fool (*laughs*). Because for Charles Laughton to walk into a room, believe me, it was like leading an elephant into a living room. Wherever he went, he would stop traffic—people would just stop and stare. He had that kind of presence, as you can very well imagine.

Paul Gregory

And so I got the galleys to Mitchum, and he just went wild over it.

In fact, Mitchum went wild in almost the precise way Laughton and Gregory themselves had gone wild. As the actor's sister Julie explained to Mitchum biographer Lee Server in his book, *Baby, I Don't Care,* "Bob told me he was going to do that one to show people not to follow some character because he's got a Bible in his hands, or because he's got his collar on backwards, to alert people to these kinds of characters. And he was always very sympathetic to the exploitation of children, always very sympathetic to the innocence of children. He thought this would get that out there." These thoughts echo, respectively, one of Laughton's prime motivators (as recalled by Gregory) and the chord struck in Gregory's own heart when he'd read the novel. Is it any wonder that director and prospective star would soon find themselves simpatico? "I suppose," mused Elsa Lanchester in her autobiography *Elsa Lanchester Herself,* "it was inevitable that Charles and Mitchum would work together. They were kindred spirits, both what you call rebels, with no respect for formal religion or Hollywood society."

Paul Gregory

Mitchum and Laughton and I got together, and now, here is where Laughton was unbelievable. When Laughton was on the track, there was no one like him in the world. Laughton was actor enough, and sufficiently oversized, even, as an actor, that he could convey to the most extraordinary talent what he saw and what he felt. And so, the minute I saw that they were both on the track, I disappeared out of the house and left them, because I knew that Laughton had Mitchum wrapped up. I just knew that there was no question that Mitchum would say, "That's that," and indeed he did.

As Gregory elaborated to Lee Server, Laughton reported back to his producer partner. "He was on the ceiling with excitement about

Producer Gregory, (R to L), director Laughton and their star, Robert Mitchum, pose for pre-production publicity pictures with a script and the novel.

Mitchum. He said that Mitchum had been wonderfully enthused, had so many ideas to offer." Server records that, "Mitchum quoted from the book by memory and at one point got up before his adoring host and began crashing about the living room acting out the love/hate sermon, the story of 'right hand/left hand,' knuckles upraised. 'Of course,' said Gregory, 'they had had quite a few drinks.'"

William Phipps
After the first occasion of spending any time with Mitchum, Laughton said to me—he was very *moved*—he said, "My God! What a great Macbeth this man would make!"

Davis Grubb
When I learned that Robert Mitchum was going to play Preacher, I was pleased and dazzled. I was just like a little kid with somebody saying to him, "Hey, Tom Mix is going to play Patrick Henry in your story!" Wow, I thought, this is great. I wasn't as critical as maybe I should have

been, though if I had been critical I probably would have been a pain in the ass to Laughton.

Davis Grubb wasn't the only one who was thrilled. With Mitchum, the box office heavyweight, on board, Gregory was able to seek financial backing from United Artists. Initially the corporation founded by "the lunatics (who) have taken over the asylum" in the twenties (Chaplin, Fairbanks, Pickford and Griffith), UA was by the early fifties under the direction of New York lawyers Arthur Krim and Robert Benjamin. There was no studio overhead for UA, because UA had no studio. Their modus operandi was to provide fiscal backing and shared ownership to producers of independent features.

Paul Gregory

So with that, then, we went ahead and set up production. Harry Cohn, the head of Columbia, was staying in New York at the time. He called me up and said (*harshly*) "I hear you got this book, *The Night of the Hunter!*" And he said, "Well, come on up here, I want to talk to you about it!" That's how he talked, he was a rough old guy. I liked him. I've always liked rough people, because I've always felt that I knew more quickly where I stood with them than I did with someone smooth and slick and so on.

So I went up there and had a meeting with him, and he said, "Well, I want to read the book before I make any deal!" I said, "Well, haven't you read the book?" He said, "*No*, I haven't read the book! My office just sent me a wire that you've got Mitchum and that you're in New York. I'd like to do a picture with Mitchum," and so on. So, he read the book. The next day he called me. He said, "Well, if they're not fuckin' on every ten pages, you haven't got a movie!" And I said, "Well, Mr. Cohn, they're not fucking on every ten pages, and I probably won't have a movie." So, that was his point of view.

One of the reasons I was in New York at that time was that we had started on negotiations with United Artists. I'd met with Cohn because you're always looking, even when you're negotiating. Because, United Artists screw you right up against the wall and have you so cross-collateralized that you have to make ten pictures to make a dime on one.

With a United Artists deal finally signed and sealed, Gregory and
Laughton were free to begin hiring a production team. As Grubb has mentioned, there was some discussion of his adapting his own novel for the
screen, but nothing came of this. On the one hand, Grubb told Laughton
that he thought he ought to stick to his own field, and on the other, it was
decided that the financial backers would wish to see a more experienced
craftsperson in the writer's chair. Although Laughton subsequently com-
plained to Elsa Lanchester that James Agee was foisted on him by United
Artists, Agee's biographer Laurence Bergreen reports that Laughton had
met Agee at Salka Viertel's famous Hollywood salon, and had in fact requested the author/poet/screenwriter's services from his agent, Ilse Lahn.
Agee's most successful screen credit up until then, although he had not
written its improbable climax, had been *The African Queen*. Agee's earlier
book, *Let Us Now Praise Famous Men,* about his journeys with photographer Walker Evans among sharecroppers, indicated an empathy for the time
and milieu of Grubb's Depression-era backwoods novel, and his other writings revealed a poetic nature which, it was felt, might prove appropriate for
adapting Grubb's tenderhearted tale of terrorized children.

Paul Gregory
We made a deal with United Artists, and then of course we had to write it.
Actually, Laughton was perfectly capable of writing the script. After all, he
had done the *John Brown's Body* script, he had cut the *Caine Mutiny Court
Martial* script . . . But we hired James Agee to do the script. From what I
had read of his, such as *Let Us Now Praise Famous Men,* I felt he had a basic
feel for this, and would have sympathy and understanding and capacity.

Agee at this time was living in Manhattan with his wife, Mia. Paul Gregory's offer of $15,000 for ten weeks' work—the agreement thereto was
signed in May, 1954—was sufficient to lure the writer back to Los Angeles, where he promptly booked himself into the legendary Chateau Mar-
mont on Sunset Boulevard. Had they been in a position to know their
scribe more intimately, Gregory and Laughton might have had second
thoughts about the assignment. "He was a man of excesses and extremes,"
according to Mia's posthumous assessment in Ross Spears' and Jude Cas-

A portrait of James Agee, painted by his grandson David Sprecher (from a photograph by Florence Homolka).

sidy's *Agee: His Life Remembered,* "and that is inevitably to some extent self-destructive. He was a slightly larger-than-life person, so he tended to overdo whatever he was interested in doing at all. Anything." As it turned out, that "anything" included everything from drinking—to screenwriting.

Agee hadn't been back in L.A. long before he had begun an adulterous affair with a woman named Tamara Comstock, a relationship designed by both parties to self-destruct after Agee's *Hunter* assignment was completed, whereupon, it was planned, he would return to Mia and their two children back east. Agee reported for duty at Laughton's Curson poolside to begin their discussions of the script. To Curson, and anywhere else he wandered, Agee invariably carried a bottle of Jack Daniel's.

Davis Grubb

I don't want to be sitting here pretentiously saying I think it should have been this or that in my movie, because it wasn't my movie. I was a very small collaborator, and many people brought more gifts than I to whatever kind of a Spanish inn this was. I feel it's a very modest contribution to have provided a good story. I think that whatever Agee, or whoever the writer was, did was just as original as my book.

Laughton and Gregory began populating their "Spanish inn" with an experienced production team, which would prove indispensable in helping the first-time director realize his vision: production manager Ruby Rosenberg, assistant director Milton Carter, art director Hilyard Brown, editor Robert Golden, and cinematographer Stanley Cortez, whose chief claim to fame had been shooting Orson Welles' follow-up to *Citizen Kane, The Magnificent Ambersons.* Laughton had worked with Rosenberg, Carter and Cortez on another film a few years previously.

Stanley Cortez (cinematographer)
You'll undoubtedly want to know how I first met Charles Laughton. A picture called *The Man on the Eiffel Tower* (1949) was just about to start, and they were having trouble over there with film emulsions and things like that. I was asked to leave here on ten hours' notice to go to Paris. Well, I didn't know Charles Laughton from Adam. When I arrived, a cocktail party was being given for Franchot Tone, who was also in the cast. When I was introduced to Charles, the first words out of his mouth were, "So you're taking the picture over. Well, I'm very happy to meet you, you big bastard." So I said, "I'm very happy to meet you, you fat son of a bitch." And from that moment on, we became the dearest of friends.

He liked me immediately, because of, call it what you may, forthrightness, an independent spirit, or a courage to express yourself no matter who the man might be. My respect for him was always there, of course. He used to call me "the Brooklyn Spaniard."

People don't know this, but Charles Laughton directed many sequences in *Man on the Eiffel Tower.* There were situations on that picture where the director had a problem, the problem could have been resolved, but, to skip the details, he was relieved of the directorship and Burgess Meredith, who was in the cast, took the picture over. Well, when Burgess was in a scene with Franchot, we'll say, or somebody else, Laughton would take the directorship over. But when they were *all* in the scene, who was left but Cortez? So I functioned in two positions, and I was very happy to do that.

If Mr. Cortez was in the mood to "skip the details" about *Eiffel Tower's* original director, cast-member William Phipps is happy to supply them.

William Phipps

I don't think I've ever told this story. His name was Irving Allan, he was co-producer, with Franchot Tone. He had never directed before. Being insecure about never having directed before, he was going around shooting exteriors. He kept Laughton and Franchot and Burgess all waiting to go to work. This went on for about two or three weeks, and I'd come back every day and tell Laughton and Burgess exactly what the man had done. In the stuff he was shooting, I'm all over Paris, tailing Franchot, and I climb the Eiffel Tower, and I'm going in and out of places, entering and exiting buildings. So he was "safe," shooting that. And, the way he was setting the camera up, he might as well have been on the back lot at MGM—which I told Laughton—because, all he'd shoot was a doorway. You don't shoot a doorway in Paris, you shoot the doorway, but you get the street, and the people, and the *Sacre Coeur*, or something! I told Laughton about that, and about the crude and coarse way Allan would talk at his actors.

So, it came time for Laughton to work his first day. I'm getting ready to go to the set with him from the *Georges Cinq* Hotel. There's a limousine, a French driver. Twice that morning, Laughton and I waited in the limousine for Allan—this is summer, it's hot—and twice, he never showed up. We go back up the second time, we go to Mr. Allan's room, Laughton knocks on the door. When Allan opens it, Laughton says, "Mr. Allan, I don't think this is very funny. Acting is an old and honorable profession. You will never, ever keep me waiting again. And I am not going to work with you." So, Laughton called in Franchot for a meeting and he told him, "I will not do this movie, I will not work with this man," he says, "And Phipps has told me everything that's happened on the shoot so far. This can not continue." Laughton realized, "Well, we'll never make a fucking movie with a clod like this," you know, so Laughton says, "I will not do the movie unless Burgess directs it." ` So, by the end of the meeting, Allan was off the picture, and Buzz Meredith was in. There were some contractual obligations, and they had to let Allan keep his title as co-producer, but it was a small price to pay not to let him direct the picture.

The Laughton-directed footage in *Eiffel Tower* opens the film with a feeling of mystery and intrigue, and closes it with an exciting chase that, unlike his predecessor's version with its doorway-fetish, captures the fabled

city in all its full-color glory. For the first-time (albeit uncredited) director, preserving Paris on celluloid was a labor of love.

Stanley Cortez
But when they all went back to the States, Charles and I were left, and
we did many sequences around *Sacré-Coeur.* Charles knew Paris perhaps
better than most actors do, and he found many of the locations for us
in the film, things that were there that even the French crew didn't
know existed. I have a photo somewhere of myself standing in front of
one of the buildings near *Sacré-Coeur* beside a bronze plaque. On the
plaque is the name of Wolfgang Mozart and the date of the night he
spent at that building. The building is a brothel.

Charles Laughton was the only British actor ever to appear in an all-
French Molière play, in which the dialogue was in French. And so when
he and I went to the *Comédie-Française,* where his play had been held
many years prior, the audience remembered it. When Charles and I
walked in, they all rose in unison in deep respect for Charles Laughton.
We spent many, many weeks in Paris, and Charles really showed me the
city. This developed a very warm relationship between Laughton and
myself which was the prelude to *The Night of the Hunter.*

I think that much of our communication was instinctive, unspoken.
You're with a man eight hours a day . . . And on Sundays, we would take
long walks, and I really learned a great deal from him. As a matter of fact,
it was Charles who got me interested in Japanese art. I would often see
Charles in the Pickwick Book Store down here on Hollywood Boulevard, rummaging through all kinds of books. Charles was very much involved in the Kabuki players of Japan that he would tell me about, and
about artists like Otramara, and Hosaki, and Hiroshihi. Actually, he and
I would sit in his house by the hour, at his pool, and he would tell me
all these wonderful stories, and that in itself was a rarity, to have this great
artist express himself to you. Anyway, from then, I would see Charles and
his dear wife Elsa very often at their house.

Oddly enough, I found myself photographing, of all things, *Abbott and
Costello Meet Captain Kidd* (1952), kind of a satire, really, and of all people,
my dear friend Charles Laughton playing Captain Kidd. And, as time went
on, he was getting involved in *The Night of the Hunter* with his wonderful

friend and partner, Paul Gregory. I was on the same lot, doing *Black Tuesday*. This was the RKO Pathe Studios, where I had done *Magnificent Ambersons, Since You Went Away, Diamond Queen,* many films. I would see a lot of Charles, he and Paul would visit me sometimes on the set, and we would sit and have our little talks about what was going on. Paul Gregory made it official when he called me into his office one day and said, "Stan, we're starting *Night of the Hunter* on a certain date. Charles would love to have you do it." I could never say "No" to Charles Laughton, and I said, "Nothing would please me more, Paul, than to do it with both you and Charles." But instinctively, I had known all the time that this was going to happen, because of the repartee and the rapport over the last few months. I knew that Charles and James Agee had been working on the script.

William Phipps
Stanley Cortez shot *Man on the Eiffel Tower,* and he was kind of a strange man, difficult, stubborn, bull-headed. Once, in the early days of TV, I worked with a very talented cinematographer who, because this was TV, had to do a whole thirty-day show in two days. He used to set up, (*rapid delivery*) "Put this light here, put that light there," (*snaps fingers*) "Ready!" You know? And I remember his saying at the time, "I could take two hours to set it up, or ten minutes, still it'll all look the same." That was not Stanley Cortez. Stanley Cortez was slower than molasses in December. In fact, because he was so slow, I was very surprised when they hired him to shoot *Night of the Hunter.* Very surprised. Maybe it was because Laughton liked to work with people he'd worked with before, it was more comfortable for him. But once they started shooting, no, there weren't any problems with Stanley, not that I know of. Somebody probably lit a fire under him. And, he had Ruby Rosenberg, who was production manager on *Man on the Eiffel Tower.*

Robert Golden (editor)
It was while I was on *Black Tuesday* (1954) for Hugo Fregonese that I got the assignment on *Night of the Hunter.* Fregonese was leaving for Europe or someplace, and he was leaving the picture in my hands. He wanted to be sure that the dubbing and everything would be done right, and he wished I wouldn't do this other assignment. He said, "Bob, I

plead with you. Laughton will just charm you to death, and you won't have time to give to my picture." I said, "Trust me, trust me." But— Laughton was pretty charming . . .

The production unit for *Night of the Hunter* was the same unit under which I had been working at RKO Pathe, which were the Selznick Studios. Paul Gregory had gone to this already-existing production unit for his crew. That included Stanley Cortez, Hilyard Brown, the art director, and myself. Milt Carter, the assistant director, was not part of the unit, they brought him in from the outside.

Hilyard Brown (art director)
It may not have been a great hit at the box office, but I've gotten more jobs just from mentioning that I did this one picture, *The Night of the Hunter.*

I did a show called *Black Tuesday* for producer Leonard Goldstein. He was going to be executive producer for *The Night of the Hunter,* but he died before we started shooting. My first meeting was with Laughton and Paul Gregory. Laughton asked me to read the book, and he said he would like to do the whole film from the little boy's point of view and how everything affected him. Mitchum was the heavy in the whole thing, but essentially it was a story about a little boy and his sister. We didn't want to make it "fairy tale," though. Fairy tales are told *to* little boys, little boys don't tell fairy tales.

Stanley Cortez
I met Agee at Charles' home, and in fact I would bring certain camera equipment to Charles' home so that he could be familiar with some of the lenses and apparatus. It was only a way of refreshing Charles' mind, or memory, as to what the different lenses would do in terms of angle and depth of field, just give him sort of an outline, a working knowledge. Actually, Charles was not too involved with these mechanics, he would depend upon me for that. You know, Charles was a very sensitive guy, and very deep. Once I had delivered to him what I felt about the potentials of the script in terms of camera technique, then he would enlarge on that in terms of the dramaturgy, the whole structure of the script and the dramatic values, and I would become the pupil. It is one

thing to have an idea, something else to have somebody enlarge on the idea, which is what Charles was doing.

While Laughton and Cortez, in concert with Agee, were conducting their cinematic tutorials, Gregory undertook the process of assuring that there would be actors and actresses to place before the cameraman's learned lenses.

Paul Gregory

Charles turned the whole casting of it over to me, because we trusted each other tremendously. Just as, later, I knew what he would do with scenes, I wasn't on the set watching everything, I didn't have to.

Shelley Winters had been one of the students in Laughton's group at his little school there in his house. And we wanted for the children's mother a voluptuous kind of actress, and someone that didn't have to be in front of the mirror and up at the hairdresser every five minutes. We wanted someone that would be willing to let her hair blow, and be a little frowzy, but still have that pathetic quality.

In light of Gregory's apt description of the requirements for portraying Willa, it is ironic that not only was Miss Winters not his first choice but he was in fact hoping for a casting coup which would have been every bit as offbeat as Mitchum for Preacher: Betty Grable. Voluptuous she certainly was, but, even though her best days as box-office queen were behind her, she was known for glamorous Technicolor musicals, notwithstanding her one forties foray into *film noir, I Wake Up Screaming.* Miss Grable strung Gregory along for weeks, according to Mitchum biographer Lee Server, hesitating, hemming and hawing, before finally declaring herself out of the running.

The Night of the Hunter was expected to start shooting in mid-August, but by June, with Agee and Laughton still hard at work on the script, Paul Gregory Productions had only a Preacher, not a Willa. As Davis Grubb remembered things, both Anne Baxter (whom Laughton had directed onstage in *John Brown's Body*) and Grace Kelly were very anxious to play Willa, but Laughton wanted Shelley Winters from the beginning. (Grubb personally felt Baxter would have done well as Willa but Kelly would have been too patrician.) Elsa Lanchester claimed that Shelley Winters as Willa was her suggestion, to which her husband quickly concurred: "Many people saw in Shelley the temperament of an uncontrolled, bitchy, selfish, catty woman," she wrote in *Elsa Lanchester Herself.* "I must say that I have always seen her as a good actress, and Charles not only saw her as a good actress but he penetrated that brash exterior of hers. In those days she was really a vulnerable, fragile woman, a frightened girl. It was all bravado, this other thing. She knew that Charles understood that. Of course, Shelley had been one of Charles's students in the Shakespeare class and he was naturally flattered by her adulation, but he also saw her in the part. And Shelley was magnificent and fragile and touching in *The Night of the Hunter.*"

According to Miss Winters' second volume of autobiography, *Shelley II,* she returned one morning from a walk with her baby daughter to find a copy of the Davis Grubb novel on her doorstep. "In it was a letter from my lovely and brilliant teacher, Charles Laughton . . . I parked the carriage under a tree in my garden and made sure the baby was fast asleep and sat down and read that whole powerful novel. I had done nothing important for two years, and I was trembling with joy at the thought of being directed by Charles Laughton and working with Robert Mitchum . . . After reading the book, I ordered my agent" (*the estimable Paul Kohner*) "to make the best deal he could with United Artists, but, in any case, *I would do this film.*"

For Miss Winters the attraction was not only the role and the story but her loving mentor/pupil relationship with Laughton dating back to the late forties. In those pre-*A Place in the Sun* days, she had made one good film, playing a sexy, ill-fated waitress opposite Ronald Colman in his Oscar-winning role as a schizophrenic actor in *A Double Life.* Feeling that she still had much to learn, Miss Winters had joined the actors taking Shakespearean instruction from Laughton in his home. She believes that he was instrumental not only in improving her acting technique but in facilitating her growth as a person, especially in helping her find the self-confidence to do what she needed to do professionally and personally. (One sticking point, apparently, was the actress's accent, an ungainly mixture of St. Louis and Brooklyn, which Laughton encouraged her to lose.) She came to regard Laughton not as an Englishman but as a "universal citizen," one whose shared knowledge of acting, art, travel and life broadened her horizons and opened up her spirit to new possibilities. One of Elsa Lanchester's re-searchers paraphrased Miss Winters, "She came to understand by studying the Bard with Laughton that all men were *alone* and lonely, and this helped her to feel less lonely and alone herself. She got the idea from the classes that verse, Shakespeare's or anyone's, is merely a means for holding ideas together." Her devotion to Laughton's classes became so all-enveloping that cameramen at Universal were starting to complain about the circles under her eyes. Studio chief Bill Goetz thought she was losing rest because of some love affair, when actually she had once missed a romantic tryst with a big movie star because of her absorption in the class. When she explained to Goetz that it was Laughton's classes which were occupying her ex-tracurricular time, the executive said, "You tell Charles Laughton, we don't do much Shakespeare at Universal, and you need sleep."

The arrival of Grubb's novel on Miss Winters' doorstep came at a time of deep personal crisis in her marriage to prominent Italian actor Vittorio Gassman. Miss Winters recalled visiting Laughton in hopes of discussing her personal problems but found him at poolside hard at work with James Agee on the *Hunter* script. To her surprise, Winters was told by Laughton that in order to play Willa she would have to work at regaining her old accent. When she protested that it had been at his insistence she had lost the accent in the first place, Laughton told her, "In this life we never forget our bad habits, Shelley. They stay around somewhere and are easily recalled when we need them."

After Agee left for the day, Laughton and his protégé sat by the pool, sipping Camparis, and discussing her future with Gassman. Laughton had met her husband, and had argued with him over the relative virtues of Shakespeare in the original English versus in Italian translation. But now, with a heavy heart, Laughton suggested to Miss Winters that Gassman, being a true actor, would inevitably have to return to his homeland to play all the great parts in his native tongue. "That is the language he thinks in," Laughton explained, as quoted by Miss Winters in her first book, *Shelley, Also Known as Shirley,* "both consciously and unconsciously. It is the one nearest to his soul. You cannot translate the great ideas of men of literature into a second language when you act. You must learn and feel and com-municate in your first language. Maybe some genius who had learned a second language when very young has been able to do it, but I doubt it.

Words are our first impressions of how the world and its occupants are."
From his experience having acted Moliere in French that long-ago night
in Paris, Laughton was in a unique position to hold forth on the matter,
and Miss Winters reluctantly had to acknowledge the wisdom in what he
said. Soon, she hoped to be enacting the part of widow Willa, but she
knew she would no longer be playing the role of Mrs. Vittorio Gassman.

Meanwhile, casting proceeded for the supporting parts. Veteran character actor Don Beddoe won the part of befuddled but warmhearted ice
cream purveyor Walt Spoon in a matter-of-fact way.

Don Beddoe (Walt Spoon)
I think that was just an ordinary booking thing—I mean, the casting agent
called up and said, "Go out and see Paul Gregory and Charles Laughton,"
and they said, "Yes, you'll do fine for this part." I don't remember reading for the role. I think Laughton just took a look at me, or had seen me
work in something, and decided, yes, I was right. I was doing a soap opera
at the time called *General Hospital*—the same one that's still on—and I
played the head of obstetrics in this hospital. And when this offer came up
to do *The Night of the Hunter,* I went to them and said, "I'd like to do this,
if it isn't going to screw you up too much." I had no contract with them,
but there are certain obligations to people that you've worked with, and I
did want the transition to be a pleasant one. The director of *General Hospital* said, "Oh, well, go ahead, that's too good a shot to miss," with
Laughton, Mitchum, Paul Gregory and all the rest of it. So he said, "Go
on, I'll use you again some time." They wrote me out of the show. He said
that I was away on a convention. I never did go back.

Paul Gregory
I'd seen the young actor, Peter Graves, and thought of him for the father.
He was certainly good in this. There's an enormous under-the-surface
talent in him—I still think Peter has not had his moment.

Years later, when fondly recalling his brief experience on *Hunter* for
Miss Lanchester's researchers, Peter Graves stated that he was under
contract at the time to United Artists, hence he was recommended to
Laughton and Gregory for the role of Ben Harper. After a brief chat

with the director and producer, Graves was told by Laughton that he would be exactly right for the part.

Paul Gregory

As to the casting of the boy, I just saw a lot of children, and Billy Chapin looked to me like he could be out of Peter Graves and Shelley Winters.

Davis Grubb

I never had an image in mind for Willa, nor the kids. Of course, I asked Laughton who were the greatest child actors he'd ever known, and he said, "There are no child actors. There are child performers. Acting is an art you have to learn over years and years." I don't know whether I agree with that or not. I've seen children alone, acting out things, sometimes brilliantly.

Grubb once recalled that Laughton had fond memories of working with little Margaret O'Brien on *The Canterville Ghost* in the forties. "She used to come sit on his knee, and he would tell her stories about the famous ladies of the English theatre." At the conclusion of filming, when the rest of the cast were giving their elaborate farewells, O'Brien was nowhere to be seen. Then, as Laughton was walking off the set, she jumped from behind a telephone booth, grabbed him around the neck and hugged him, saying nothing. "It was such an eloquent goodbye that for a moment Charles almost lost control." Now, Grubb's novel was about to offer Laughton the chance to bond with another child as once he had with Margaret O'Brien.

Ten-year-old Billy Chapin was not the only professional acting child in his family. He had an older actor brother, Michael, and his sister, Lauren, would achieve television immortality as Kitten, the youngest daughter in Robert Young's long-running *Father Knows Best* series. Young Bill had won an award for his stage work in *Three Wishes for Jamie;* his filmography by this time included the title role in *The Kid From Left Field* and soon he would portray a clergyman's son in *A Man Called Peter.* To find out whether Billy might play the stepson of a phony clergyman, a meeting was arranged with Laughton at the director's home in Hollywood. Mrs. Chapin and her son rendezvoused with Paul Gregory at his office, then she followed in her car while Gregory drove her son toward Curson. When

Mrs. Chapin noticed that Gregory's Cadillac seemed to be swerving a bit, she discovered that Billy was sitting in the producer's lap and steering. Despite this adventure, the trio arrived safely *chez* Laughton, where the famous host, instead of offering one of his gourmet meals or potent martinis, inquired of his young guest, "Billy, do you like to swim?"

"Yes, but I don't have any trunks."

"Oh, that's alright, I have some that you can use."

While Billy splashed around the pool in a voluminous pair of Laughton's trunks—held on by a carefully tied belt—Laughton and Gregory conferred briefly by themselves. Later, as Chapin and his mother recollected for Elsa Lanchester's researchers, "Laughton came to the edge of the pool to chat in a personal way about impersonal matters. He really wanted to see if the two of them could establish the right kind of rapport. Laughton was not so interested in the child's ability to read the part, but more in his personality and sensitivity." After the boy's dip, Laughton offered him a meal, and the conversation continued casually and naturally. It was "love at first sight" for Charlie and Billy, and the part of John Harper was his.

According to *New York Times* correspondent Helen Gould, "'Never,' Mrs. Chapin marveled, 'never once did Mr. Laughton or Mr. Gregory ask Billy what he thought of the part, or what he had done. They just wanted to get to know him as a natural boy. I've been in this business for seventeen years, and I've never come up against anything like that before!'"

"What I want is a flexible child," Laughton told Davis Grubb, "and Billy is exactly that." As Grubb recalls, Laughton would be very pleased with Chapin's sensitive portrayal in the film—but little sister Pearl was another matter. For this role, Laughton cast Sally Jane Bruce, five years old but already a veteran of TV, radio, and such films as *Mischief Makers* and *My Wild Irish Rose*. Little Sally was the sister of Jewell K. Edwards, who worked with the Spade Cooley Band. According to a United Artists press release, the talented tyke got her big break by singing with a full orchestra for a contest sponsored by a Los Angeles newspaper. Winning that competition led to her first role, in a Joan Davis comedy, and ultimately to the attention of Paul Gregory. (I have found no record of any films she may have made after *The Night of the Hunter*.) Laughton told Grubb that he found little Sally Jane to be "a repulsive little insensitive pie-faced teacher's pet"—and yet, as will be seen, this was precisely why he cast her as Pearl.

But there was still one more vital role to fill—the children's savior, old Rachel Cooper.

Davis Grubb

Then I heard Laughton was talking to Ethel Barrymore about playing Rachel. But, he said, he was afraid she was just too frail.

"The trouble with Barrymore," wrote Laughton in a springtime letter to Grubb, "is that she is rather Hudson than Ohio River Valley. I am coming round to the idea of Jane Darwell for Rachel. We talked about her. You remember her in *Grapes of Wrath*."

Davis Grubb

And he was talking about Helen Hayes. He was also talking about Agnes Moorehead, a formidable actress I used to watch doing the radio show, *Dupont Cavalcade of America,* when I was a page boy at NBC in 1940. Laughton came in one time with the corners of his mouth just twitching in amusement and announced that Miss Moorehead had had an astonishing vision. She told Laughton on a plane flying to California that God had told her she was to play Rachel.

I don't know whether Laughton had to tell her that he and God might not see eye to eye on the casting, but Laughton could handle that situation very well. Laughton knew a great deal about God. I remember one afternoon we were drinking up at the St. Moritz, and he began to chant a soliloquy which was unfamilar to me, because I'm a miserable Shakespeare scholar. It was the line about, "No, no, no, no! Come, let's away to prison: and there we two will sing like birds," and everything. I said I felt it was Dylan Thomas, whose work was a great influence on me then, but he said, "No, that's from *Lear.*"

I said, "Will you write it down?" He wrote it down on a piece of stationery. We were both kind of high, and he missed a couple of words, but I saved it. Of course, *Lear* is like Mozart's 40th Symphony, or *Don Giovanni,* it's perfect, you see. But Laughton said he hadn't realized what *Lear* was about until he was at Stonehenge once. He said he was standing there looking at the huge stones and suddenly it dawned on him what *Lear* was. "It's primitive man," he told me, "prehistoric man, with his knuckles brushing the earth, and his other hand stretched toward God."

Paul Gregory

When Laughton and I had our little meetings, he talked about the possibility of Louise Fazenda, the woman who married Hal Wallis, to play Rachel Cooper, the old farm woman. And we had Louise over, and she was very dear, and very sweet, and she wasn't right. She was too buxom, she didn't have enough sinews to her to let you believe that she would milk the cow, or get out there and plant the potatoes, and pick the beans, you see—she looked too much like Jane Darwell. They were too big for the Depression, you know what I mean? There wasn't enough muscle to them. Jane Darwell had come across all right as the Depression character Ma Joad in *The Grapes of Wrath,* but that was a different character altogether, she was fighting life. This woman wasn't fighting life, and this woman wasn't bitter. She was an angel. She had muscle, she had guts, and she believed in what was right. We needed somebody who would embody all that for us.

Ultimately, Laughton and Gregory decided to offer the part of the old woman to a legend of the screen, a lady whom Laughton would come to call, with respect and affection, "The Iron Butterfly."

Paul Gregory

Charlie said to me that we ought to have somebody that was birdlike in this role, and immediately Lillian Gish hit me. I knew Lillian, and Laughton knew Lillian. I said, "Well, what about Lillian Gish?" He said, "Oh my God, old man, you'll never get her." It was a relatively small part, and she'd said she would never make any more pictures. I think she was unhappy with *Duel in the Sun* (1946), and I think she felt it was a waste. And, Lillian's a purist, you know, she's absolutely wonderful.

Well, I just got on the phone and called her, and then I had Laughton call her.

Lillian Gish (Rachel Cooper)

The Museum of Modern Art called and told me that Charles Laughton was over there with a group of people, rerunning all my old movies, and did I know why? I knew him, but I hadn't heard from him and I didn't know why he was in New York.

After a week or two, Charles telephoned and told me he was about to direct his first film, *The Night of the Hunter.* He'd been to the museum with his cameraman and writer, and would I come over and have tea with him and his group at the museum?

Describing that meeting for Elsa Lanchester's researchers, Miss Gish recalled meeting Laughton at his hotel for tea with Gregory and Agee. She confessed that she hadn't really noticed Agee very much because he hadn't said much, "But then, when Charles was around, no one said much, we just listened. And of course, he always had so much to say that was interesting."

Lillian Gish

When I went over, he said that they had run and rerun the Griffith films because he felt the one person he could learn from was Griffith. Griffith's were his favorite films, he said. They were so exciting, you sat up straight in your chair because you didn't know what was coming. "And now," he said, "I go to the pictures and they're all leaning back, relaxed, kind of not interested. I want to sit them up straight again and have them leaning forward!" Then he said, "The museum has agreed to send these films to the coast so that all my staff can see what I'm after with *The Night of the Hunter.*"

Davis Grubb

Charles Dickens was, to the confusion of a lot of critics today, not only a great writer but an extremely popular one. It's like we had a man with the versatility and the agility of, say, a Carson McCullers or a Faulkner, who was as popular as James Bond in our time. People actually waited on the wharfs of New York when the serialized episodes of *The Old Curiosity Shop* were coming over on the Great Westerner ship. They waited on the wharfs to yell to the crew before the ship docked, "Is Little Nell dead? Did she die?" Because they'd been hung up since the last episode. I don't think we have that excitement. It's probably because of the diversity and diffusion of the media.

Soap operas are considered bad art, and in many cases they are, but some of the soap operas of the thirties and forties offered a lot. One of them in particular I'm thinking of, *Vic and Sade,* was first-class American humor, right up there with Ring Lardner and some of the others. You see, there's a question of popular literature, which was discussed at length by G.K. Chesterton in his marvelous book, *Charles Dickens,* published about 1910, I guess. (*It was 1906.*) And he said it isn't that people prefer bad art, it's that people demand a certain kind of story, and if they can only get it in bad art, that's where they'll take it. Most of the themes of soap opera—boy meets girl, and so forth—are as malleable in concept, though not, certainly, in expression, as in Shakespeare and Homer.

Paul Gregory

Charles was wild, he played the Griffith movies all the time. And he was interested in some of Orson Welles' things. He thought *Citizen Kane* was marvelous.

Lillian Gish

After we left the museum, Charles and I walked ahead. "There's a part I'd like you for," he said. "I'll send you the Grubb book and the script, and you let me know if you're interested." I read it, and it was a very fine story of the basic human equation, a story of the battle of good and evil. I thought I could help him, so I told Charles I certainly was interested in the part.

When Miss Gish agreed to play Rachel, Laughton's film was assured a link to Griffith which was not only aesthetic but also flesh and blood. United Artists, the company co-founded by Griffith was, alas, under different management by now, and they wanted their pound of flesh.

Paul Gregory

I said to United Artists, "You're not united artists, you're united against the artists." Because, what happened is, they wanted our picture, and then they put up every obstacle under the sun to keep it from happening. They said, "Here's the money, here's the distribution, now, here are your conditions, here are the deadlines, here are the this-and-that . . ."—which makes you frigid. It's an awful simile, perhaps, but if you're going to have sex with someone and you're told you have to get your rocks off in the first minute, it sort of limits you, doesn't it? And that's what they do. That's why we went into production so quickly.

Doubtless the fiscal strictures imposed by UA were an important factor in determining (much to Mitchum's displeasure, as it turns out) that, instead of shooting *Hunter* on location, Laughton would lens his film in Hollywood, as quickly and as efficiently as possible. This decision, in turn, necessitated the hiring of a second unit which *would* travel to Grubb's home turf in West Virginia, to shoot background projection plates for certain scenes, as well as shots of the Ohio River and surrounding countryside which could be intercut at various points with the L.A. footage. Paul Gregory Productions assembled for this purpose a film crew of old pros, but—as if harking back to the Biblical quote so key to *Hunter*'s story, "A little child shall lead them"—Laughton turned to a young man fresh out of film school to lead these seasoned Hollywood men. A short film crafted by two brothers in the enclosed academia of UCLA, *A Time Out of War,* had actually found an audience outside in the real world. This Civil War vignette told of a temporary truce between two Union soldiers and a Rebel who meet on opposite banks of a river. Not only had the brothers' little movie been broadcast on television but it had also found theatrical distribution and, even more remarkably, gone on to win the Academy Award for Best Short Subject. *A Time Out of War* was the work of Denis Sanders and his three-years-younger brother Terry. In the late sixties, Denis shared his memories of the Laughton collaboration with Elsa Lanchester's biographical researchers. Although Denis had been the writer/producer/director on *A Time Out of War*—it was his master's thesis—and brother Terry merely the cinematographer, apparently it was the look of the film which most captivated Laughton. So taken was Laughton with the film's documentary-like mood and atmosphere that he decided to contact Terry.

Terry Sanders (second unit director)

This was my first job out of UCLA. Barry Atwater, the actor who played the Southerner in *A Time Out of War,* was a friend of an actress friend of Elsa Lanchester—her name escapes me right now. But she saw the film, told Elsa, Elsa told Charles, Charles called me. I was living in Beverly Hills, Charles was in Hollywood. And I hear this voice, "Hello, this is Charles Laughton." And of course, you think it's a joke, because you've never had a call from Charles Laughton. But, it wasn't a joke, he said, "Could you come over? I'd like to talk to you." I got in the car and went over to Curson. I ring the doorbell, and the door opens and there, filling the whole door frame, is Charles Laughton, and he says, "Brother Sanders!" And I said, "Brother Laughton!" And that sort of broke the ice, and then we proceeded to talk about his project, which of course was his first directorial job, *The Night of the Hunter.* He was impressed with the scenes of the river in *A Time Out of War,* and since *Night of the Hunter* takes place along the Ohio River, he thought I would be the perfect person to go and direct the second unit while he stayed with the first unit at the Lee ranch. I had photographed *A Time Out of War,* and Charles would have had me film the second unit for *Hunter,* but of course the union wouldn't allow that. Charles was interested in the gestalt of our film, he wanted the river feeling . . . He loved *A Time Out of War,* he loved the flow of the river, he loved the images, the figures, the three soldiers . . .

As the August start of production loomed, another crisis arose which applied pressure to Gregory and Laughton, but for this one they could not blame United Artists. Unless, that is, there had been any truth to the notion that UA had been responsible for the team's hiring of scriptwriter James Agee. For all his nocturnal carousing, Agee assured Laughton that he was hard at work turning their poolside discussions into concrete pages for the *Night of the Hunter* screenplay. And in truth, he was working prodigiously, and in apparent high spirits. In a typed note of apology to Laughton before taking a week off to complete a long-standing previous assignment, Agee stated, "Clearly, during this week, I should not receive payment from you and Gregory . . . I can only hope to assure you that it need in no way seriously worry you; that at the rate I've been going, the past couple of days, we will have a first draft ready for further anvilling, much sooner than I had estimated—even taking into account a week's necessary interruption. Nevertheless, I'm exceedingly sorry to have to report this—and fully as sorry to have to interrupt work which is going so fast and well, and which so excites me. If it will help assure you, I'll of course be glad to send along all copy so far written, just as soon as I can get it typed. (A problem: Since most people find my handwriting difficult, I am my own quickest typist.)"

Ah, if only his typing had been Agee's biggest liability. And, if only Laughton *had* been able to get a sneak peek at what Agee was typing. Or, had he? As so often in this account of the creation of *Hunter*, we are presented with several versions of history at some variance with each other, and we must look for the elusive, quicksilver truth in the space between.

Paul Gregory

James Agee was a poet, he was a very big talent, there's no two ways about it. But he had a drink problem.

Robert Mitchum

I didn't meet Davis Grubb until a long time later. But Jim Agee used to stay at my house for a while. Not voluntarily, I think, he just fell over on the couch a couple of times. I don't think we discussed the novel, but he must have been happy with it, he wrote six pounds' worth on it. It was like a WPA work, it was a six-pound treatment.

Which, according to Gregory, was about five pounds too many . . .

Paul Gregory

Agee produced something, but it was nothing we could use, absolutely nothing. It was bigger than the book. Mr. Mitchum never saw that script. He may have heard about it later, but we never gave it to him. Well, it looked like a dictionary. I looked at it and thought, "My God! Where do you start here?"

Davis Grubb

Laughton ran into all kinds of trouble. He came to me very dejected one day and said, "I just got Agee's finished script, and it's about six hours long. I don't know how *Griffith* would have screened it. It's got everything Agee ever felt about the Depression . . ." It pulled the plug, apparently, on things Agee wanted to say about America in the twenties and thirties, and Laughton said, "We can't do it."

Paul Gregory
After about six weeks, Agee became so incapacitated that we had to skip it, and Laughton wrote the script. I would say Laughton was the real one who wrote that script.

Once again, it would seem, Laughton had to become the knight on the white steed. With mere weeks to go before cameras had to roll—else lose Mitchum—Laughton set about writing the screenplay for *The Night of the Hunter,* "occasionally incorporating some of Agee's simpler ideas," as the latter's biographer Bergreen put it. Agee was heartbroken that his magnum opus had so deeply disappointed Charles. For the better part of two weeks, the drunken and weeping writer resided at Paul Gregory's Santa Monica home, complaining that Laughton was killing him by rewriting his script. "He was a wonderful writer," admitted Gregory to Mitchum biographer Lee Server, "but the poor man was tormented by something. I don't know what. At times he would cry for hours. I went and sat with him . . . one night, and he just sobbed and sobbed. I thought he might commit suicide. I had never seen such behavior." Eventually, Tamara Comstock came and retrieved Agee, returning him to the Chateau.

Davis Grubb
Laughton was very upset about the script, but finally one day he said, "We've got it back together, with the assistance of a $2,500-a-week stenographer." Now, who that was, I have no idea.

The implication, of course, was that Laughton had pulled in an anonymous but highly-priced writer to get the job finished. On the other hand, Grubb related the same tale in slightly altered form to Elsa Lanchester's researchers, giving a different spin to Laughton's lament. This version, according to Grubb, had Laughton phoning him in distress and saying, "We can't possibly use the script by Agee. It would run six hours. It's as if we had been paying $2,500 a week for a mere secretary. The man's a hack writer!" Although this last may seem an unfair description of a man with Agee's gifts, under the circumstances Laughton could be excused his anger. By incorporating breadlines and other such aspects of the Depression, along with stream-of-consciousness montages of dubious filmability, Agee had completely shifted emphasis away from the novel's basic concept. With that peculiar set of blinders which is a part of every General Issue alcoholic's kit, Agee had apparently focused on what most interested him personally in the material, filtering out the parts of Grubb's story—and Laughton's instructions—which did not directly apply. "Charles had tremendous compassion toward children," Grubb recalled, "and he was fascinated with their 'innocence and endurance.' He lacked an understanding of the Depression, and was never interested in causes; therefore, it's understandable that he didn't like the additions Agee had made to the original novel in his telephone-book-sized script. It's true that I felt strongly myself about the Depression, having lost my own home in it, but it merely served as a context within which to deal with the age-old struggle between good and evil."

It has been said that the on-screen credits for virtually every film of that era should be taken with a grain of salt due to all the "fronting" for blacklisted writers. Papers in the Laughton/*Hunter* file at the Library of Congress indicate that Blake Edwards—later of *Pink Panther* fame—may have made some contributions to the screenplay for *Hunter*. What is more likely, however, is that Laughton had consulted with Edwards when Paul Gregory Productions was preparing *Hunter* for the screen and *Three for Tonight* for the stage, with a blanket payment covering any and all assistance Edwards may have been able to offer. In the sixties, two volumes of *Agee on Film* were published. The first volume contains the writer's distinguished magazine criticism; the second contains five scripts, including *The African Queen* and *The Night of the Hunter*. (More will be said later by second unit director Terry Sanders, about both the script for *Hunter* and its publication in *Agee on Film* . . .)

Davis Grubb

I don't think that script in *Agee on Film* had any resemblance to the script that I heard Laughton describe. Now, where that script is, I don't know.

Maybe Miss Lanchester has it. Some people at the University of South Carolina said in their thesis on my novel that Agee's book, *A Death in the Family,* had been influenced by *Night of the Hunter.* I can't imagine how, though it may have worked out that he said in *Death in the Family* the things that Laughton had not allowed him to say in that six-hour script.

Paul Gregory
Oh, there were all kinds of arbitration with the Writers Guild over the screen credits, and in the end they insisted that Agee receive the credit and the only credit, which was absolutely ridiculous. I must say, I didn't follow any of that, but I can tell you that Agee's script was not what was shot.

As you know, we were absolutely faithful to the book. How many studios do you know that buy things and then the picture comes out and you wouldn't even recognize it, you wonder why they paid the price for it? But I *wanted* what I bought.

The consensus seems to be that Agee refused to let Laughton and Gregory look at his script until that fateful first draft was finished, whereupon Laughton had no choice but to take over. Perhaps that is true. Perhaps not. There is precious little documentation of the *Hunter* screenplay process; but what there is includes a cordial memo from Laughton to Agee discussing script matters and dated July 16—barely a month before the camera was due to roll. Just two weeks prior to that memo, on July 2, Gregory sent Mitchum as much script as he had to send, referred to as "Revised First Draft," accompanied by this note (addressed to personal assistant Reva Frederick):

Dear Reva:

Here is a copy (up to page #103, the entrance of Rachel) of *Night of the Hunter.*

Charles wanted me to be sure and tell you and Mitch that there are another twenty-five pages coming, approximately, which we expect to have in just a few days; and that en toto, another five to seven pages will come out of the over-all script. There are places where a little "tightening up" will be necessary, etc.

Please call me when you have read it, as I am anxious to know if you are as thrilled as we are.

Sincerely,
Paul Gregory

On the one hand, there is no reason to doubt the original existence of that notorious, six-pound Agee first draft, although it is presently nowhere to be found. On the other hand, it seems that, after receiving it, Laughton, at least for a time, kept Agee on the payroll and at the typewriter. To what degree he served as Laughton's writer and to what degree as his stenographer, we can never know completely. But clearly, a point had come where Laughton felt compelled to take charge.

Terry Sanders

I wound up spending a lot of time with Laughton. I don't remember the exact sequence, but very soon I was sitting down with him, going over the script—which, incidentally, he had written. You know, I saw James Agee's script, which was about three hundred pages in a black binder, I remember, and was a fascinating document but was not a shooting script. It was not even a screenplay. It was much more of a compendium, almost, of all the research and ideas and so forth. It was incredible. I mean, someone should publish it, but it was not something that you ordinarily go and try to shoot. It was three or four inches thick, it was like two or three times the size of a normal script.

I know that Charles wrote the screenplay for his film. *Night of the Hunter* was one of those books where you could almost tear the pages out and start directing, like John Huston did with *Maltese Falcon*. It was the kind of book one really looks for, you know, because it short-circuits the need to create the screenplay out of a few little ideas or so. I mean, the characters are there, the story is there, the plot and the whole thing. Charles was very, very clear that there was a completion of the contact with Agee. The work was finished. I guess he felt it was not satisfactory, probably Paul did, too. I think Charles just—he may have had help from one of his several assistants, but I doubt it—I think he just took the book and wrote it. I never heard Blake Edwards' name connected with this, ever.

I contacted Blake Edwards and asked if he had any light to shed on *Hunter*'s authorship, but he never responded.

Terry Sanders

First, Charles and I spent a lot of time just going over the script and what he needed in the way of the second unit shots. I don't know the time-frame, exactly, but I had ample meetings. There was no rush to it, as I recall. It was, like, sitting down in what he called "the school room," which was a room that had a big table, and a piano; it was their workroom, with books all over. It had wooden captain's chairs. I don't think he was teaching acting at this time; I think "school room" probably related more to maybe his background in England. I guess his family were hotel people. And he liked the house on Curson, because it was a little like the English inn, you know? A little sort of lobby area, and a stairway upstairs . . . I think it had a feeling of England, somehow.

I probably sat down with him no more than two or three days, going over the script and making drawings and discussing things. Here's my production book, and this is a list of the second unit locations, and these are location breakdown sheets which I got from UCLA and used on feature films. It's just a way of making notes, like this one, "Helicopter shot." And the sketch shows that it starts wide on the river and moves in. And these are for the shots of Mitchum's driving along, with a double, and also shooting the plates behind him when they shot him in the car in Los Angeles. A lot of the shots had been drawn by the art director, Hilyard Brown. He was a great sketcher. Charles drew some sketches, too. He used this thin pencil—I should have given him a heavier pencil. He was pretty minimalist. In this sketch here, for example, these two lines are the river. He was just trying to give a sense of flow, and screen direction, that kind of thing. These numbers in the corner are scene numbers. These sketches are basically just little reminders that I could use. A lot of these shots, of course, are helicopter shots, and they were already planned and written into the shooting script. Laughton clearly had in mind what he wanted. He was not floundering around at all, he knew exactly what he wanted. It may have been a little unusual to use helicopter shots, but . . . *Everything* hadn't been done that much, at that

BREAKDOWN SHEET | Hel. ˅

PRODUCTION NO_____ TITLE "NIGHT"   PAGE 2

NAME OF SET DESERTED HOUSE-DAY (EXT) INT   NO. OF SCENES 2

CAST: (7 or 8?) ⌐ children	CAST AND WARD-ROBE CHANGE Bring back costumes ?	SCENE NUMBERS AND SHORT RESUME OF ACTION
		Sc. 4 M.L.S. DESERTED HOUSE (HELICOPTER) CAMERA moves straight down. Children are in yard, playing hide-and-go-seek. As we move down, they scatter—all except "IT". ONE CHILD RUNS TO THE OPEN OUTSIDE CELLAR DOOR AND STOPS. CAMERA PAUSES— ✓
EFFECTS:		
		✓
MUSIC AND MISCELLANEOUS HELICOPTER		
		Sc. 7 M.L.S DESERTED HOUSE (HELICOPTER) (Sc. 4, cont'd) CAMERA STATIC. Children are gathered around en-trance to cellar. CAMERA holds for a moment, then PULLS UP + AWAY (toward the right — DOWN RIVER).
CONSTRUCTION ESSENTIALS:		
		DISSOLVE OUT.
ESSENTIAL PROPS: a) HOUSE (DESERTED) b) OPEN, OUT DOOR CELLAR ENTRANCE.		Ⓟ (can be shot past production)

A sample page from Terry Sanders' second unit breakdown book reveals a Hilyard Brown sketch and instructions for capturing—via helicopter shot—the early scene of children discovering the body of one of Preacher's victims.

point, you know, but certainly other films had used helicopters, it was not like breaking new ground. And, the Bell helicopter was around. The helicopter shots were very important. Charles had probably seen it in some other film, possibly the Nicholas Ray film, *They Drive by Night*.

So, it was probably a couple of days of going over the script. And then, I guess, Paul Gregory said, "How much do you want, to do this?" I could have said a lot of money, I was too dumb. I think I said, about, "Three hundred a week," or something like that.

Laughton, ostensibly "to keep peace in the family," hired brother Denis as a "dialogue director." For both brothers, the collaboration with Laughton would prove to be a tremendous learning experience and an invaluable introduction to professional Hollywood filmmaking. The same could not always be said, however, of their association with some of Laughton's colleagues.

Terry Sanders

Stanley Cortez was very remote. He did nothing to help us in the second unit, or guide us, or give us any advice at all. Which led me to feel that . . . I don't know if he resented that there was a second unit, or whatever; he was just not helpful. And I always felt he was not happy about something. He seemed to be an unhappy man, generally, and maybe bitter . . . I don't know, it just gave me a strange feeling. He was not helpful.

Whether it contributed to the director of photography's dour mood or not, while young Sanders was about to go off and point a camera at Davis Grubb country, Cortez and the rest of Laughton's loyal crew were to stay behind in Hollywood and recreate that unique territory, river and all, on a soundstage and at the Rowland V. Lee ranch in Chatsworth. Gregory's and Laughton's mood, already darkened by the necessity for the latter to re-write Agee's script, could not have been brightened by the fact that their production was still minus the actress they wanted to play Willa. Hoping to pin her down, Gregory exchanged a series of cables with Shelley Winters, then overseas filming Christopher Isherwood/John van Druten's *I Am a Camera*, and her agent in Hollywood.

JULY 12, 1954

MISS SHELLEY WINTERS

LONDON (ENGLAND)

DEAR SHELL,

I HOPE THIS REACHES YOU AND THAT YOU HAVEN'T GOTTEN LOST IN THE STEAM BATH. WE EXPECT TO HAVE SCREENPLAY COMPLETED BY END OF THIS WEEK. AT THAT TIME WILL HAVE BUDGET APPROVED AND CAN ADVISE STARTING DATE OUR PICTURE. WE DO WANT YOU. WE ARE NOT HEDGING. IT IS JUST THESE LITTLE ELEMENTS WHICH MUST BE FIRM BEFORE WE COMMIT OURSELVES. BLESS YOU

PAUL GREGORY

JULY 13, 1954

DEAR SHELLEY:

AM WORKING CLOSELY WITH PAUL KOHNER AND WILL ADVISE.

PAUL GREGORY

JULY 26, 1954

MR. PAUL GREGORY

HOLLYWOOD, CALIF

I JUST KNOW THERE MUST BE SOME VALID REASON FOR YOUR FAILURE TO CABLE ME YOUR DECISION ON SHELLEY WHICH YOU PROMISED FOR LAST TUESDAY AFTERNOON=PAUL KOHNER

JULY 26, 1954

PAUL GREGORY GREGORY ASSOCIATES

AM DOING FILM I AM A CAMERA STOP DIRECTOR WAITING STARTING DATE PLEASE CABLE A YES OR NO ON YOUR FILM

IMMEDIATE REGARDS=SHELLEY WINTERS

JULY 26, 1954

MISS SHELLEY WINTERS

DESPERATELY WANT YOU OUR FILM. HAVING PROBLEM RE YOUR SALARY. AM TRYING TO WORK OUT. WILL ADVISE YOU IMMEDIATELY I HAVE WORD.

BEST REGARDS,

PAUL

JULY 27, 1954

PAUL GREGORY GREGORY ASSOCIATES

DO NOT KNOW WHAT AGENTS HAVE DISCUSSED WITH YOU I AM ALREADY
IN 90:0/0 TAX BRACKET FOR 54 AND DOING PLAY IN 55 PLEASE CABLE
FINANCIAL OFFER AND DATES INVOLVED DIRECT TO ME HENRY COR-
NELIUS WAITING MY DECISION URGENT REGARDS=SHELLEY WINTERS

Gregory cabled a reply on July 28, offering $25,000, an amount which
happened to be a third of Mitchum's up-front fee. (Unlike the deal ten-
dered Miss Winters, Mitchum's agreement with Gregory also included potential profit participation.) Apparently, Miss Winters' reply to Gregory was
favorable, because:

JULY 29, 1954

MISS SHELLEY WINTERS

DEAR SHELLEY:

PLEASE LET'S HAVE NO PUBLICITY WHATEVER AS WE HAVE AN ENOR-
MOUS BREAK THAT WILL BE MADE FROM THIS END. BEST

PAUL

That same day, a copy of the script was mailed with this cover letter:

Miss Shelley Winters
Dear Shelley:

By the time you have received this, you will have had further
cables from me. Needless to tell you that Charles and I are both
thrilled to death that you are going to be with us, as we wanted
you more than anything.

We think you will like the script. You will see that the part of
Willa is a wonderful one; and with you in it, Charles is certain he
can get all the excitement that the part of Willa has in the story.

Looking forward to seeing you soon, and God love you,

Cordially,
Paul Gregory
Gregory Associates, Inc.

So at last, they had their cast, and with no time to spare. In a mere fort-
night, Charles Laughton would be faced for the first time with the challenge that confronts every movie director—to paraphrase his producer
partner: to get all the excitement in the story. Miss Winters, as she recalled
for the Lanchester researchers, was now welcomed into the Laughton film
society. She sat in when the director screened Griffith's *Broken Blossoms* for
his team, and remembered Laughton remarking, during the famous
frozen-river chase, on "how clearly one could hear the cracking of the ice
floes because of the pictures." By contrast, with Shakespeare, said
Laughton, "one sees through the ears." She also recalled that, throughout
the making of *The Night of the Hunter,* she got the impression from everything Laughton said to her that the Grubb story was "some kind of classic folk tale"—and he wanted his film to be the same.

II

PRODUCTION

"Visit the set? Well, if that fat son of a bitch doesn't know what he's doing, I'm dead anyway."

—Paul Gregory to a United Artists executive

Under the insistence of UA, *Hunter* commenced principal photography on August 15, 1954, with a bare-bones shooting schedule of only thirty-five days.

Robert Golden

The picture went into production very fast. There wasn't as much time as is usually given for preparation of a big production. Because it was Laughton's first screen directorial effort, he needed a great deal of help with the mechanics, the technical end. (For instance, during the making of the picture, he could never get straight on "complete reverses," the rule that, if you're shooting two people talking and you reverse the angle, you're careful not to have the people jump across the screen, which is very disconcerting.) And, because he didn't have time for this preparation, we met every evening after the day's shooting—Laughton, Brown, Cortez, Carter, Walter Schumann, the composer, and myself—to plan the next day's work. This was done through the entire making of the picture. We ate a lot of food, and we drank a lot of booze doing this, but—the job got done.

Hilyard Brown

I read the book—it was some book, wasn't it?—and I read the script, and I came up with ideas of where I thought we should do the various pieces, how I thought they should be done, and what we were physically capable of reproducing out in the open or on a stage, in order to get across what Laughton wanted to get across. That's what an art director does, essentially, that's my principal contribution to motion pictures: How To Do It.

Because Laughton said he was approaching the film from the boy's point of view, I'd often design and build sets but only put in the things the boy paid attention to. You know, little boys don't attend to everything that comes along. They run up and down the street and they see certain buildings and certain things, and everything else in-between is a blank. The boy paid attention to the fences along the street that he could hit with a stick. I decided I'd put a picket fence along there, and there wouldn't be any house behind it at all, just a vacant place with a fence. The boy remembered this shop because Miz Cunningham used to yell at him, and he re-

113

". . . a picket fence with no house behind it at all." Pre-production water color by Hilyard Brown.

membered this place because that's where the ice cream parlor was, and he remembered the little floating shack down at the end where the old man, Uncle Birdie, lived. So, those were the places we put in. Remember the street in the second half of the picture where Lillian Gish and the kids went

Cresap's Landing. Pre-production water color commissioned by Hilyard Brown from Allan Abbott.

to town? Quite often there would be whole vacant places with no building at all, but just a sign that flashed "Hot Dogs," or "Coca-Cola," because this was what the little boy would remember.

Davis Grubb

It's funny, there happens to be a town in West Virginia that is kind of down and out economically, and on their main street they have about five frame office-building fronts, like in a western movie set. There's nothing behind them, they just want to look prosperous. Really, it's true.

Looking at the sketch today, I can see that Birdie's wharf boat is correct, but the damn waterfront is not right. You see, with those pylons it looks like it belongs on the coast of a sea, or along the Chesapeake Bay. There were never any pylons where I grew up.

Uncle Birdie's Wharf Boat. Pre-production water color by Hilyard Brown.

Hilyard Brown

Laughton got out a whole lot of stuff to show the rest of us how he hoped to approach the picture. He used every facility at hand to portray to us what he was trying to do. And he ran a lot of silent pictures for us. They weren't entirely Griffith pictures, he also ran *Greed,* and *The Four Horsemen of the Apocalypse,* and some others. Laughton really believed that motion pictures were motion pictures, not talking pictures. He felt that in many ways talking pictures were not as well-done as the old-time silent pictures because, in the silents, the visual images had to carry the whole thing, with just those few little lines in between. Laughton was a very visual storyteller. That's probably one reason that Stanley and I were so greatly involved with him, because that's our end of the business, the visual end.

Terry Sanders

I remember that D.W. Griffith's presence kind of hung over everything. I particularly remember in *Birth of a Nation,* Laughton loved the shot in the homecoming scene of somebody's back with the mother's arm reaching through the doorway to embrace his back, but you never see her face . . . He was struck by certain kind of images and subtle approaches that Griffith had. Laughton was very infatuated with Griffith, with Lillian Gish, of course. And he got from the Museum of Modern Art, because he had great contacts there, an original print of *Intolerance.* A tinted print. I had gone through UCLA seeing the films of great masters and so forth, including Griffith, and I saw probably a dupe of a dupe of a dupe, in 16mm, and it just looked like it was developed in mud. It was still pretty interesting. But, I got the impression at UCLA that, well, in those days, they didn't really have very good photography, or good lenses, or they didn't know how to develop film, or whatever. I saw the original tinted print of *Intolerance,* and it was sharper and clearer than anything, than anything of that time, or *any* time. It was so incredibly sharp. Of course, it would be, because the nitrate base is actually a better base than the acetate. It's clearer and sharper. And then, the lenses . . . Everything looked amazing.

But, another time, Laughton ran *A Time Out of War* for Stanley and some other people, and he didn't know that Denis and I were in the back of the auditorium. And at the end, he said that it was even better than Griffith. That was . . . Wow. He didn't know that we were there.

Hilyard Brown

One reason *The Night of the Hunter* had a lot of light and shadow is because Stanley was experimenting with Tri-X film. Of course, with Tri-X you get some tremendous contrasts, blacks and whites. I think Stanley's contribution to the whole thing was that extreme black and extreme white with very few intermediate tones. It was a little bit shocking.

Stanley Cortez

Unfortunately, that picture was made in black and white. I don't know why we didn't use color, even though that picture was done in 1954. I think it was Charles' feeling that it should be black and white because of the story content, and I believe we all concurred with that thinking. But in hindsight, I feel that, well, maybe we should have gone color. I say that because, as films are being shown today on television, if our picture were made in color perhaps it would have more of a presentation. But then, who the hell knows? Had I used color, I would have used it with pastel shades, or desaturated shades, which we didn't know about in those days but which I thought about then. And I was a little bit skeptical about taking that step, because, when you talk about desaturation and those things, the laboratories were not as prepared then as they are today. In addition to the laboratories, we had certain other problems on the picture, the design, the slowness of the film, and working with children, all these things.

As soon as I agreed to do the picture, I read the novel; I always read the novel if there is a novel to be read. This one was great. When you read a book you're going to be filming, either you're for it or against it. If it's not right, then you're fighting it, you're on the defensive. If you think it's right, you're with it, you want to help it, you start thinking about images. The sharp contrasts in this picture, that was strictly my invention, and fortunately Charles agreed with that interpretation. How did I decide on this approach? You don't decide, you feel. After you read the script, you feel those things.

Tri-X had first come out around then, and I had used it on *Black Tuesday,* where I experimented with a scene shot entirely by the light of one candle. I understand Mr. Kubrick is saying that *Barry Lyndon* is the first feature to shoot scenes with nothing but the light from some candles, but actually our scene with just one candle was the first. Anyway, the sensitivity on the Tri-X was faster than on the film we were used to using. I used it on *The Night of the Hunter* not because of the technical phase but strictly for its dramatic properties. I *wanted* those deep blacks, because I felt that it would give me an added dramatic punch in there

"It was a little bit shocking," as Hilyard Brown described the look of *Hunter*. Here, Mitchum and Sally Jane Bruce in a scene lit by Stanley Cortez to take advantage of high-contrast Tri-X film.

when a sequence called for it. I'm a firm believer in black. I don't want to use the word "startle," but it holds you, like a diamond and its reflections, it magnetizes you. You don't know why, but it's there. The contrast is there, but the average person in the audience doesn't know why he's magnetized or why he gets a certain impetus from the imagery that he sees, and it's the contrast that does it.

Hilyard Brown

We'd all meet every night, but very seldom on the set. I would usually get them to walk through and look over a set long before it was ready to be shot, when the first physical portions of it were done. From my sketches, they already knew roughly what the set was going to be like and how the thing was going to work.

Quite often, we'd meet at a restaurant, where Laughton would order and pay for everything. Naturally, he was a big gourmet, and knew all the good restaurants, and all the good chefs; he knew exactly what to order, how to order it, and which wines to have. Saturdays and Sundays, we met around the pool at his house. Their cook would serve lunch and coffee, and we'd go right on working until it was done, then meet on Monday and go back to work.

At each nightly meeting, Milt Carter would tell Charles what sequence we were going to shoot the next day, what stage we were going to be on, and how he was prepared for all the various mechanical operations on the set. Then Laughton would tell us what he hoped to get out of the scene, what the scene meant to the picture as a whole and how he hoped to portray that. Sometimes he would get a book and read passages of Dickens to illustrate what he was attempting to put into the scene and why he was doing it this way. Or, he'd ask Walter Schumann to play some music on the piano, a certain piece to create a certain mental attitude and mood between the six of us who were meeting.

I would illustrate on a big pad of paper how the set worked, where the various major elements were, what the mood was. And then I'd make up lots of continuities—storyboard sketches—of each camera setup in each scene and how they were going to be done. Everybody would be talking, it was a completely cooperative thing. Stanley would say, "Well, if you shoot it from over here, Hilyard, and you give me a piece here, I can slide in past that, and we hide this while we're going by . . ." Sometimes I'd have to do a little alteration to the set, sometimes he would have to alter his setup or movement to accommodate the set, which was actually already built and dressed long before we got to this. But everything I could do to help Stanley, I did, and everything he could do to help me, he did. That went for all of us.

And then, when we got through the evening, we'd have twenty or thirty rough sketches of camera moves, the position of the set, the physical aspects of the thing. We'd turn them over to Milt Carter, and the next morning he would turn them over to the grips. We'd say, "All right, we're going to shoot this one first, this one second, and that one third. And while we're changing the makeup, we'll shoot this and this and this . . ." So, there was a complete continuity, not only of what was going to be in the picture but a continuity of how it was going to be shot for the day. The grips and the electricians and everybody knew exactly what we were attempting to do, and they could get two jumps ahead of us. They knew what equipment was needed or if they were prepared to do all these things. If they weren't, they would get prepared for the afternoon shooting. They just went as smooth as clockworks. It's the only show I've ever done that way, and it really paid off.

"The Blue Men." In Davis Grubb's novel, Ben Harper dreams in his prison cell—which he shares with Preacher Harry Powell—of the day he was arrested for the bank robbery which claimed two lives:

> Now, from the corner of his eye, Ben sees the blue men with the guns in the big touring car coming down the road beyond the corner of the orchard. John's mouth is a white little line as his dark eyes follow the blue men. They circle and walk slowly in through the dead grass that rims the yard.
> Now I'm goin' away, boy.
> John's mouth breaks and trembles but then it tightens back into thinness again. He makes no sound.
> Just mind everything I told you, John.
> Yes, Dad.
> And take good care of Pearl. Guard her with your life, boy.
> Yes, Dad.
> Who's them men? Whispers Pearl at last.
> Never mind them. They come and I'm goin' off with them, children . . .

There were other sketches involved in the production process, of course, those provided to Laughton by author Grubb. His drawings are cartoon-like in their simplicity, a quality which enhances the child's point of view that Laughton recognized would have to be the key to telling Grubb's story on film. The drawings cover virtually every important character and scene in the novel. An enterprising publisher, should he secure the rights to print these drawings, could produce an edition of *The Night of the Hunter* thoroughly illustrated by its author.

Stanley Cortez

Charles showed me some sketches of Grubb's. Charles was very much involved with Grubb, and that contributed a great deal. But these sketches didn't contribute too much to my own thinking, they were strictly an academic outline, so to speak.

Academic or not—and there's no denying that Grubb's illustrations were in complexity barely a step or two above James Thurber's—the sketches must have been deemed valuable by Laughton, because on his next film project, (sadly never realized,) *The Naked and the Dead*, he would ask Norman Mailer to repeat the process and create drawings of scenes from his novel. In fairness to Cortez, however, it is likely that Grubb's line drawings would be more instrumental to a director in his staging than to a cinematographer in his lighting. Grubb himself had nothing but praise for Cortez, and tended to downplay his own visual contributions.

Davis Grubb

I liked the photography. I think I may have suggested to them the use of helicopter shots, because so many of my drawings were made from an aerial elevation. But the interplay of light and shadow, of course, that was all Cortez' genius.

Stanley Cortez

But the sketches that Hilly Brown made were definitely part of the whole structure. Yet that's merely a guide, you know. I've had many films where they've gotten too involved with the sketches. I did a picture for Selznick many years ago called *Since You Went Away* (1944), and they had all kinds of sketches, and they would really go by these damn things. I finally said, "Well, for Christ's sake, put 'em on a wall and photograph *them!* Why do you do the scene?" Actors have to have a certain amount of leeway. Sketches are strictly a guide, and anybody who goes with these things to the nth amount of detail, I think, is out of their minds.

One of the most wonderful things about working with Charles was that he had the faculty of getting out of people behind the camera as much as he got out of those in front of the camera. I found myself, as I am on all my films, to be totally absorbed in what I'm doing, from an artistic and a professional point of view. But with Charles it superseded all that. It became a highly personalized thing. We would spend hours every Sunday, he and I, just talking. It wasn't only Cortez involved, we had a team of marvelous people on this thing. It wasn't a question of one knowing more than the other, it was a question of how can we best combine all of our talents to help a great man like Charles Laughton. It's very rare that you can get guys like Hilly Brown and Bob Golden and Milton Carter and Ruby Rosenberg, the production manager, and myself, all together to do as much as we possibly could for Charles Laughton. We were his dedicated cabinet, you might say. We had a thousand meetings, we wanted to know what Charles was thinking so that we could do for Charles what he wanted, in our own way, of course. He would read out of the Grubb book, or some piece of poetry, or something like that. It was his way of getting us in a frame of mind. On weekends, Walter would play some of the music that he would compose for the film, and since I love music I would sit there fascinated by Walter playing not only the music for the film but other things as well.

Don't misunderstand me, when Charles was wrong, we as a group would say to him, "Charles, don't you think . . ." We would try to help him, you know; we didn't always agree with him, and he realized that what we had to say were very valid statements.

But we were the ones, we were the nucleus, we were with Charles all the time. Most of the picture was shot from sketches that were made on the tablecloth in a restaurant down here on La Cienega Boulevard. Hilly Brown would draw sketches on the white tablecloth, and that's how many ideas in the picture were formulated. And the nice thing about meeting with Charles at the Somerset Restaurant after each day's shooting, it wasn't only that we could have a couple of drinks and have dinner while we were meeting, but good old Charles would sit with his back to the audience, to the people there—he didn't want them to know he was there, he didn't want to be bothered with signing autographs. But how could you miss that marvelous figure: the baggy pants, the rear end, the broad shoulders, the tousled hair?

Paul Gregory

Whenever we did the reading tours, all of Charles' problems with local people and the press could have been handled if he had *allowed* someone else to handle it. But he wouldn't allow it. Then he would say "No" to all these things, and then he'd say, "Let's go get something to eat," and he would sit in the most conspicuous place in the restaurant, so that he *would* be noticed. Or, he would start reading something and do it so loudly that people would realize Charles Laughton was in the restaurant. So you see, there was no rhyme or reason to any of it. The dear man had no sense of himself in proportion to anything else.

"I wasn't anywhere near the set during the production," Davis Grubb remembered. "Yet I know Laughton was at top form. And a little mad. Obsessed. In the trance I get into myself when the writing really flows."

Robert Golden

I'm certain that Paul Gregory had a very active interest in the picture, but the personal relationship between Gregory and Laughton was a very close one, and they had a wonderful understanding: each was to do his part and be left alone by the other. The only time Gregory showed up at one of our nightly meetings was when we had a severe problem with the production outfit, which was finding fault with the way we were doing things from a financial standpoint. He was there as a troubleshooter, to protect Laughton.

Hilyard Brown

Paul Gregory very seldom came around to the set. In fact, a lot of times, we wouldn't see him from day to day. Somebody at the office of United Artists, which was financing this thing, said to Gregory, "Don't you think you should go out there and keep your finger on what's going on?" Gregory said, and these were his exact words, "Well, if that fat son of a bitch doesn't know what he's doing, I'm dead anyway."

Robert Mitchum

Paul Gregory didn't come around much, only to smile a lot, bring some of his mother's grape pie.

Paul Gregory

Old Mitch, God, the things he could put you through. The police would call me at home every morning at five-thirty and tell me that the light was on at Mitchum's house, because I had an arrangement with the police to let me know when he drove out on his way over to location. And then I'd leave and follow him to make sure he didn't stop someplace. It's the truth, absolutely the truth. Well, you know, in those days, Mitch was on booze, he'd been arrested for marijuana, he was all of this and all of that. It's neither here nor there, I love him, I *love* him, but when you hire Mitchum you hire a character, you know. He may be different now, but he was a rebel, you know, he was against everybody and everything, but, with it all, he turned in, I think, the best acting job in his career. I don't think he's ever done anything equal to it.

And I must say, he always showed up at the set on time.

William Phipps

He had to have his pot. He could work so well behind it. I couldn't. Of course, he didn't care about what it did to his timing or anything else, he just didn't care about that. As long as he could talk, and stand up in front of the camera . . . Was he smoking pot during *Hunter*? You know, I kind of doubt it. I don't think he was doing it during shooting. The reason I doubt it is that I think this was one picture where he really wanted to do it. He wanted to make a good movie, and he and Charles got along great, and had great respect for each other.

Robert Mitchum

No, I didn't study any dialects for the picture, or any criminal psychopaths. I *knew* that character. I just did it. That's supposed to be my profession. You know, if I can't do that, then . . . Charles and I didn't have a lot of conferences before shooting, he didn't have *time* for that. He was locked into a date, and it was really a mighty labor for Charles. You've got to remember, it's the first time that Charles had ever directed, much less written, a motion picture. And he edited it, too. Now, that, for a first time, was really an achievement.

Robert Golden

Of course, it's very unusual for the editor—or, for that matter, the composer—to be on the set throughout the shooting. When Billy Wilder started directing at Paramount, the famous editor Doane Harrison was assigned to Wilder and never left his side. There are other cases, but this was the only time it's ever happened in my own experience. As a matter of fact, Laughton wouldn't allow me to leave the set to do any cutting during the whole making of the picture. Laughton wanted me to be with him the whole time. There were two reasons: First, the help that he needed, which I would say was secondary to the other reason, which was that he wanted to supervise the editing himself. Laughton was the primary instrument in every phase of this picture.

He knew the theatre like no one I've ever met, every phase of it. He was demanding, he consumed you, but it was really a lot of fun. It was wonderful to be associated with him, but what *he* did was extraordinary. His effort was absolutely immense. We were all very respectful of him for having this whole thing in his head. I think the reason the picture was so good with so little pre-production time was that it was so implanted in Laughton's mind and he was a brilliant artist. Yet at the same time, one of the reasons that the picture was not the commercial success it should have been was that there really wasn't enough time. It wasn't something he wanted to keep to himself, because he realized how important we were to him. But there wasn't enough time to explain, really, everything he wanted to do. When he was telling us, it was an intense, I'm-trying-to-do-something/I-want-to-do-it-so-badly/please-help-me kind of a feeling. He had it so within him, he was not going to let it get lost. When I speak of Laughton not having the time to convey his whole vision to these people around him—how could he have done it? I mean, when you think of all that he had in his mind. Whatever is on the film, it was in him.

One of the reasons he was very cautious in trying to have us understand what he wanted was because time becomes of the essence when you're making a picture. That's why he was so intent upon being there with all the cutting. I think I understood him the least of any of the other people around him. Like, Hilyard Brown, he said, "This man is a genius." Whatever Laughton wanted to do, Hilyard Brown would break his back to do. Stanley Cortez was the same way, and so was Milt Carter. And I didn't feel that way. I couldn't tell you why I didn't appreciate Laughton as much as these others did. You might say I respected him but didn't venerate him.

Hilyard Brown

Laughton was never unsure at any time. There was never a man more sure of what he was doing. He didn't always do exactly what he said he was going to do, because we all threw in our two cents' worth and sometimes somebody came up with another idea which superseded, or helped, or improved. We all got mixed up in everybody else's business, it was a really cooperative project. Stanley Cortez was telling me how to do this, and I was suggesting to him how to do that, and we were all whispering ideas here and there in Laughton's ear. But in the end, Laughton had the final judgment of how it was going to be done.

I think he impressed me more than any director I've ever worked with. He had a great facility to get the best out of everybody, to get people to do what he wanted, the way he wanted it done, and to be appreciative of how it was done when it was finished. He was very kind to everyone. Now, I don't mean "kind" in the sense that he'd pat you on the back and tell you nice things. He had a kindly attitude toward your ideas. If you had an idea, he would help it along and get the most out of it. Most people are not kind to ideas, you know, they either accept them or they reject them. But he was not of that nature.

The script commences with a disembodied voice quoting the Biblical passage warning against false prophets in sheep's clothing. But during shooting, Laughton came up with something much more effective than a mere, disembodied voice. The main title credits in the film itself are presented against a starry sky. Following the last credit, we see superimposed against those stars the benign face of Lillian Gish as Rachel Cooper, who will not appear in the actual story until its third act. Clad in a simple farm dress and dark shawl, it is she who reads from the Bible, and we see the faces of her orphans, also imposed against the night sky, almost as if in a Sunday School choir, listening intently. (Although later in the film, when Rachel "adopts" Pearl and John, all her other orphans are female, here, there is one boy—presumably to balance out the imagery—and another girl, whom we will never see again. Laughton fills out the screen by including the face of Sally Jane Bruce, who of course plays Pearl, not one of Rachel's original orphans.) "Now, you remember, children," Miss Gish ~~improvising on thoughts provided by Laughton), "how I told you last Sun~~ the good Lord going up into the mountain and talking to the people? And how he said, 'Blessed are the pure in heart, for they shall see God.' And how he said that King Solomon in all his glory was not as beautiful as the lilies of the field? And I know you won't forget, 'Judge not, lest ye be judged,' because I explained that to you. And—then the good Lord went on to say, 'Beware of false prophets . . .'" (While shooting this monologue, Laughton the experienced Bible-reader suggested to Miss Gish that she smooth down the pages of the Good Book, and encouraged her to be nonchalant and not give a damn about any slip-ups, assuring her there was plenty of film in the camera.)

Right away, the audience is presented with imagery which is at once abstract but heartfelt. Coupled with Schumann's beatific underscoring, the image of Miss Gish and the innocent wonder of the children set the scene magically for all that is to follow—both the nightmare and the nocturne. This opening gambit also reveals Laughton's kinship with the silent cinema, resurrecting a syntax of expression in which film-makers were unafraid to intercut the progression of story with unabashedly symbolic images to help project the mood. We can think of the title characters in *The Four Horsemen of the Apocalypse* (1921), the clowns ringing 'round the globe in *He Who Gets Slapped* (1924), or the storm in *The Wind* (1928) (which had also starred Miss Gish).

While younger brother Terry was off filming the second unit, Denis Sanders found that his duties as nominal "dialogue director" included running lines with actors, performing errands and, best of all, when he wasn't observing the day-to-day activities on the set, engaging in discussions with Laughton about his script and his plans for filming it. The director shared

with the young beginner his fondness and admiration for the talent and the
strength of "the Iron Butterfly," Miss Gish. Laughton also explained to
Sanders that one of his goals was to structure *Hunter* like a picture from
Griffith's silent era, "for instance . . . with the bridging techniques, the
train, the birds, and so forth, he wanted to create an abstract quality."

Robert Golden

Anything that's in the picture that's not in the Agee script was probably
Laughton's. He didn't ad-lib a script on the set, but he rewrote the Agee
script before shooting started. I remember La'' ;
didn't always know what Laughton want،
Laughton's. But I can't remember for certain if those first shots in the
picture were his idea or not, the face of Lillian Gish in the stars, reading the Bible to those children.

Paul Gregory

That was dear Charles Laughton. That was the angel, the saint, absolutely the saint in Laughton. Those were the ideas that he would have
that were absolutely lovely. Lovely. Whether it was right or wrong, it
was a lovely idea, a lovely, pure idea.

Davis Grubb

And don't forget that lovely theme comes in there, that lullaby.

The opening imagery may have been Laughton's idea—but it was not
his only idea. At one point, he considered appearing on-camera and
reading the Bible passage himself, and even shot this alternate opening to
the film which still exists, along with approximately nine hours of raw
out-take footage housed at the UCLA Film and Television Archive. Although the Lillian Gish version of the introduction had been shot late in
production, on October 2, Laughton experimented with his own rendition—as an afterthought?—on October 21, two weeks after the official
last day of production. In these particular out-takes Laughton is in a business suit and tie, kerchief in breast pocket, and eyeglasses, shot against a
black background, just as Miss Gish had been. Presumably, Laughton,
like Miss Gish, would have been superimposed optically against the

starry sky. If so, his dark clothes might very well have made him appear more eerily disembodied than Rachel. This is the avuncular, informal Laughton of his reading tours and televised Bible readings, using the book and his eyeglasses for props as much as tools. This is the man whose riveting persona first inspired Paul Gregory to create their theatrical partnership—but it is the wrong man to open *The Night of the Hunter.*

As with his storytelling performances, when Laughton is not "reading" the text he is improvising his own introductory remarks, without a set script but expressing a clearly pre-determined sequence of thoughts. Here, (for example) is how Laughton begins one take: "Hello. Um, before we start this epic, (*pause for a self-deprecating smile*), I wanted to remind you of some words from the Sermon on the Mount. You all know the Sermon on the Mount, I suppose our lives are largely ruled by the things that are written in the Sermon on the Mount." (Apparently, he is presuming that his hoped-for cinema audience will be predominantly Christian, as have been the folks in middle America who flocked to his concert appearances.) "The Lord's Prayer is in the Sermon on the Mount. There are some other very beautiful things. There's a lovely one, here, that you remember, 'Blessed are the merciful, for they shall obtain mercy.' You remember that thing, maybe, that 'Solomon in all his glory was not as beautiful as the lilies of the field.' Oh, and, 'Judge not, that ye be not judged.' Wonderful thing—that we all try to live by and find it very hard to. However—the part of the Sermon on the Mount that has to do with our story is this part here: 'Beware of false prophets—which come to you in sheep's clothing—but inwardly they are ravening wolves. Ye shall know them by their fruits.'" Laughton continues with the Biblical text, and the reference to the good tree which cannot bear evil fruit and vice versa, but he is less sure of the wording and stumbles at a couple of spots. When someone off-screen offers to cut, Laughton snaps, "No, don't cut. Don't cut. This is all voice." And indeed, by that point in the monologue in the actual film, Miss Gish is no longer on camera but merely narrating footage of West Virginia shot from a helicopter by Terry Sanders. Clearly, as Robert Golden has stated, Laughton kept the whole film in his head at all times.

And just as clearly, director Laughton knew enough to fire actor Laughton from this on-camera appearance as host/master of ceremonies. The objectification effect from Laughton personally introducing his "epic" might have been appropriate for a story written by one-time Laughton collaborator Bertolt Brecht, but not for one by Davis Grubb. Far better to open with Rachel Cooper, a character organic to the story, and Lillian Gish's warm portrayal drawing us immediately into a world of fairy tales told to children, to the child in us. It is not known whether Laughton had to be persuaded not to use his own footage to introduce the film, but the man praised by Gregory for his showmanship and sharp editing skills probably looked at both versions and quickly came to the correct decision on which to keep and which to scrap.

Robert Golden

Laughton had sought help from Billy Wilder beforehand, and I think there were others. And of course, he ran all those D.W. Griffith pictures and pointed out his favorite moments to us. That iris shot later on in the picture, which came directly from Griffith, that's what Laughton wanted to do, even though it may have seemed old-fashioned. How brilliant he was to do things like that.

"Ye shall know them by their fruits," the Bible warns. The fruits of Preacher Powell's false prophecy are presented immediately in the film as a counterpoint to Rachel Cooper's narration, when children playing hide-and-seek discover the body of a murdered widow in an outdoor cellar stairway. This high-angled view was one of many shot on location in Grubb's beloved West Virginia by Terry Sanders' second unit. The house was real, but the cellar doorway was movie-making artifice placed against a wall. The next shot, showing the woman's feet on the cellar steps as the camera pulls back up to include the youngsters, was created in the studio. (In editing, Laughton decided the camera held just a tad too long on the feet, and he had Robert Golden shorten it by a few seconds, noticeable in a tell-tale jump in the children's shadows.) But the following image, in which the high pull-back continues, is another one of Sanders' helicopter shots. Gish's narration, "A good tree cannot bring forth evil fruit, neither can a corrupt tree bring forth good fruit—wherefore by their fruits ye shall know them," resumes over another helicopter shot of Preacher driving his car through the countryside. When the camera cuts from this long-shot of a double to Mitchum in medium close shot in his car, the rear projection

"Ye shall know them by their fruits." Hilyard Brown's pre-production sketch *(see page 105)* translated into a helicopter shot photographed in West Virginia by Terry Sanders' second unit.

footage behind him, and the subjective shot moving through a small town, was photographed by Sanders and his second unit crew.

Terry Sanders

How the crew got together, I don't know. But it was like an I.A. crew and at that time, how old was I? Probably twenty-two, twenty-three, and it seemed like the average age of Hollywood craftspeople, cameramen and so forth, was about sixty-seven. This was the feeling I had. Film schools almost didn't exist except for UCLA, USC and NYU. No one was even aware of them, really, they were tiny. Hollywood was not only highly unionized, but they were closed-shop unions, so nobody could get in, particularly the cameraman's union, unless your uncle or father happened to be in the union, you know; it was that kind of thing. And the director's, the same thing. So, even though I was the second unit director, I didn't get credit at all. I probably could have insisted on getting something, but again, I was naive. But, I'm credited by Elsa and everybody else, so . . . Good. But, I don't know how the crew got together, why they picked the cameraman they did, and the assistant cameraman. And then, Frank Parmenter was the production coordinator. He was an old-timer, a big, beefy guy, totally uninterested in the film, really, in the story, it was just a job of work for him.

I have the shooting script, and my production book from that time. This front page has to do with *Time Out of War,* in that Floyd Crosby—who's the cameraman who did a lot of Pare Lorentz's documentaries, and also did *High Noon* and a lot of Fred Zinneman's other films, and *Old Man and the Sea,* most of Roger Corman's early films—he taught at UCLA. So, these are just notes on photography that I got from Floyd that I guess I brought along for the *Night of the Hunter* job, so I could remind myself of things. And here's the map I had, it's just a road map.

We went off three weeks shooting the second unit, (looks like, from my production booklet, August 16, I flew to Pittsburgh), but first we were location scouting in the small plane and all that. We actually flew first to Minneapolis and then up and down the upper Mississippi to try to find the location, then we wound up along the Ohio. Mississippi had just been suggested as a good portion of river. I don't recall exactly why. Those were the two possibilities, the upper Mississippi River and the Ohio. I don't know why we went to Mississippi, because the Ohio is where it takes place, although, it was so industrialized in the fifties, I guess, compared to the thirties, that it was probably felt, "maybe it's too dirty and too industrialized." I never met Davis Grubb, unfortunately. He probably had suggestions to Charles . . .

I can't remember if it was two trips or one trip, but I do remember that, on the first day of shooting, the batteries for the camera were totally dead. Completely dead. And we had this helicopter sitting there, at great cost, like five hundred an hour or something, and the batteries were dead. So, that was an embarrassment for the assistant cameraman, because it took two days to send these batteries back and get new batteries. And of course, in those days the batteries were big, too, they were like suitcases.

But the camera operator was great. It was interesting. He didn't do a thing until it came to a panning shot, and then his arm was like a marvel of robotics. He would just grab on to the tripod and he would move the camera, it was like perfect all in one take. So I realized, "Perhaps people do have great skills"; and he certainly did. I think there was a grip along, too, who could rig things. I think that's about it.

So, we shot a little every day. Riding in the helicopter, that was fun. I wasn't in the helicopter when the actual shot was being taken because there wasn't enough room in these little helicopters. But, going to the location, that was amazing. I was sitting in the Bell helicopter, you see, just in a bubble, on a chair, that's like you're sitting in a field, and you don't see the aircraft. It's just like levitation: rising . . . It was pretty extraordinary, just rising above the ground in a chair. So, that was fun.

Laughton and I were in daily contact on the telephone, because, for various reasons, I found myself saying "I'm quitting" every afternoon, because I had a conflict with this guy who was the production manager and who had total control of all the money, so you couldn't do a thing without asking him. I always had the total power of knowing what was needed to be shot, because, I had the relationship with Charles in which he'd told me exactly what he needed. I had the script, I had the drawings, I had everything. Frank had the money. And also, he pretended that he had a lot of powers; it was a power struggle. His big thing was, we'd come into town, and he would interview for all the doubles. He would pick them. And, he'd do it in a hotel room. Mothers with their children would come. I don't know what happened with the mothers (*smiles*), but it's possible that he used his power to cast as a "casting couch" kind of thing. Anyway, that seemed to be his job. But, we would discuss where we were going to shoot, and then he would always cause some problems, "You can't do this, can't do that," and I would like, two or three o'clock every afternoon, wind up calling Laughton and saying, "I'm going to quit." And then Gregory, or one of the production people back there, would get on the phone and talk to Frank and say, "Listen, do what he says," and Frank would totally change his tune and say, "Okay, well, we can do that." But it seemed to me like every day there was some kind of power struggle, and it was getting to be not worth it.

For the local citizenry, however, the presence of Sanders and company was like a holiday. The West Virginia towns of Martinsville, Sistersville and Moundsville (home of the state penitentiary) threw out the red carpet, and some communities staged contests and community picnics when word went out that there would be some casting for doubles and extras. "Hollywood Makes West Virginia Famous," declared one local paper, whereas it might have been more accurate to state, "Holly-wood is famous in West Virginia," as the second unit often drew big crowds of locals to observe it's doings.

Denis Sanders, Terry's brother, accompanied Laughton, Cortez and assistant director Milt Carter on one expedition to the Rowland V. Lee ranch in Chatsworth, California, in search of location shots which could be mixed with the footage from the second unit. Denis was impressed with how Laughton, despite having little photographic experience, "had an eye and knew exactly what he wanted. He knew the kinds of scenes that he needed to match with the photography which he asked Terry to secure for him."

As Davis Grubb heard the story from Laughton, production had ac-tually started when a local delegation of Los Angeles clergy came call-ing on Laughton and Gregory, hoping to persuade them to abandon *Hunter* as an insult to the church, because of its treatment of ministers. They thought it was a great indignity to show a preacher as a malignant, schizophrenic murderer and opportunist. Laughton, in his most master-ful deadpan, with great calmness but power, addressed their leader thus: "Do you mean, Reverend Sir, to say that the character of the Preacher reminds you of yourself?" Which, apparently, ended the witch-hunt then and there. The delegation left without another word.

Robert Golden

That first scene of Mitchum, talking to God while he's driving along that graveyard—how new could that be? It's just a process shot, an old device, but it's brand new, the fact that he was talking to God the way he was about the widows he's killed. You don't do those things. That's why I say it's new.

In a pre-production memo to James Agee regarding certain lines and actions in the script, Laughton had written, "I understand that Mitchum is a little doubtful about talking to himself in the old Essex at the begin-ning. It's too bad, but I'm damned if I know how else to do it. If you see him it isn't necessary to mention this." If Mitchum had any qualms about his soliloquy to God, he had quelled them by the time the sequence was shot against a back-projection screen on Sept. 25. "Say when," said

Mitchum, and on cue he launched into his chat with the Almighty. On most takes, he gave the emphasis to, "Well, *now* what's it to be, Lord? Another widow?" but in the take that Laughton picked Mitchum begins more conversationally, "Well, now, what's it to *be*, Lord? Another widow?" (One take had to be interrupted when the projector ran out of Terry Sanders' footage and the background suddenly went black.)

At the time of *Hunter*'s release, at least one newspaper repeated a story found in the film's official press kit: "A pocket dagger which Robert Mitchum uses . . . in the unusual suspense drama, 'The Night of the Hunter,' has an interesting history. It actually belongs to the author of 'The Night of the Hunter,' Davis Grubb. He found it one day while walking along the banks of the Ohio River on the West Virginia side. It was engraved—Harry Powell—and author Grubb used the name as the central character in the book." Press kit or not, that isn't quite the way the author himself remembered it.

Davis Grubb

I bought a switchblade knife in a shop in L.A. in 1949. I didn't know why I bought it. It was rather a frightening thing to find myself owning, but I figured that it was interesting. I'd heard about it, because this was during the Zoot Suit period in America and there were quite a lot of them around. They used to sell them openly in the L.A. stores.

I carved Preacher's initials "H.P." in it after I'd written the book, because it suddenly became a prop for a play I was setting up. But then I gave it to Laughton. Laughton always said it wasn't the knife they used in the movie, but it always looked to me like the one.

Following Preacher's heart-to-heart with the Lord, the very next scene finds him in a burlesque house watching a hootch dancer "hard at work," as the script puts it. While Schumann's blaring brass and percussion add oomph to the young lady's choreography, we view her voyeuristically through the sly suggestion of a keyhole created by the interplay of the big solo spotlight against two parted curtains. In the outtakes, the dancer—an uncredited Gloria Pall—can be seen making her entrance, but very effectively the film cuts to her in mid-routine. On-set the hootchy-kootchy choreography was performed to a playback of

Walter Schumann's piano rendition of the brazen, brassy tune he later realistically arranged for horn and drum on the soundtrack.

Stanley Cortez

With the shadows in the burlesque house, we introduce the evilness, not only of the man but of the whole scene. The lighting, contrast, the whole thing has a powerful influence to set the audience, without their knowing it, into the mood of the character of Bob Mitchum.

But it is not only the lighting. Laughton has Preacher reach his HATE hand into his coat pocket: his hatred of the woman on stage is written all over his "sour and aggressive" (*script*) face. In the out-takes of Mitchum in the audience, the playback music is still being heard, suggesting that Laughton had the dancer continue her performance off-camera for Mitchum to focus on and react to—or, at the very least, kept the raunchy tune playing to sustain the mood. Out shoots the switchblade tearing the pocket cloth (perfectly in time with the burlesque house's bump-and-grind band). Back to the close-up of Preacher—and this is *not* specified in the script—his face, granite-hard a moment before, has now gone

One good hand adjusts another: Laughton positions Preacher's hand of HATE in the burlesque house, then steps out of the shot so that Cortez can photograph the character's disgust and revulsion at the off-screen dancer.

slack. The burlesque sequence was shot early in the schedule, on August 18, but the insert shot of the knife cutting through the jacket was done without Mitchum's participation weeks later during post-production, on October 21. If you look carefully at the shot you can make out the pull-wire trailing from under the jacket at the bottom of the screen to the special trap used to spring the blade through Preacher's coat pocket. Not only does this sequence introduce Preacher in brilliantly cinematic shorthand, it slips past the Breen Office a highly sexual allusion with profoundly disturbing implications about the sickness of a man who cannot distinguish his sexual impulses from his violent ones. "There are too many of them," Preacher tells the Lord, "you can't kill a world."

Laughton derived this sequence from two passages in the book which delve into Preacher's history prior to becoming Ben Harper's cellmate. "He would pay his money and go into a burlesque show," Grubb writes, "and sit in the front row watching it all and rub the knife in his pocket with sweating fingers; seething in a quiet convulsion of outrage and nausea at all that ocean of undulating womanhood beyond the lights . . ." Another scene finds Preacher about to strike at a prostitute: "He had his fingers around the bone hasp and he was already fumbling for the button that held back the swift blade but God spoke to him then and said there wasn't any sense in bothering. There was too many of *them*. He couldn't kill a world." There soon follows a third scene, also involving Preacher and a prostitute. This scene was not used at all in the movie, but it was well remembered by the film's star.

Robert Mitchum

Charles and I wanted to go to West Virginia to shoot the picture. The other place, which would have been ideal, was Oxford, Maryland. Would have been a mother deal. I really don't know why we couldn't go. So, we shot that burlesque house scene on a set. That was really instead of the scene from the book, in the hotel room, where he carves a cross on the whore's belly, (*pantomimes, nice and easy*), like that. They didn't want to shoot that, or couldn't, so these other two scenes at the beginning were used, sort of false introductions, because the hotel scene is the real introduction, isn't it?

Anyway, the burlesque scene, that's what I wanted to accomplish on lo-

cation. Because, on location, it'd be for real. But there, in the studio, all
the light was . . . They paid no attention to it, really, probably because they
had a lot of extras. It wasn't realistic, really. Okay, the picture was stylized,
but I think they failed in that scene.

Here Mitchum begins presenting a theme to which he will return continually in these recollections, and in which he reveals that he was very
much in sync with Grubb's story, (recalling that un-used scene from the
novel he'd read over two decades earlier), but perhaps less so with
Laughton's vision of how it should be presented on film. And yet, as Gregory pointed out, Mitchum put his complete faith in the director and let
Laughton lead him light-years away from any of his previous performances. Actor-director Don Taylor reported to Elsa Lanchester a story
Laughton had told him about watching the *Hunter* rushes with his star at
the Hal Roach Studio: "Mitchum got up and went outside. Charles followed him. Mitchum had thrown up. Charles said, 'What's wrong?'
Mitchum answered, 'I didn't know I could be so good.'"

Winters' recollections of the *Hunter* experience also include a similar
sense of revelation. To Miss Lanchester's researchers she explained,
"Charles was a marvelous director. Somehow (Mitchum and I) never
felt we were being directed. Only when (we) saw the rushes did (we)
realize how everything worked together." In *Shelley II* she wrote,
"Every day of shooting was a joy. I played a character unlike any I'd ever
played before or since. Charles Laughton directed the film slowly and
carefully. And we knew when we saw the first rushes that we were part
of something classic and timeless. *Night of the Hunter* is probably the
most thoughtful and reserved performance I ever gave."

Don Taylor and Laughton had become friendly when both had
acted—though not together—in *The Blue Veil* (1951). As it happens, what
reunited them was the 1955 press junket to Des Moines for the premiere
of *The Night of the Hunter*. On the flight to the American heartland,
Laughton shared with the rising actor (and future director) his adventures
as a first-time movie-maker. As Taylor's reminiscences were recorded by
Lanchester's researchers, "Charles told him that the main job of directing
was in learning how to communicate with actors. He said Mitchum, who
had the reputation then of being 'somewhat of a naughty boy' had given

Charles no trouble at all because, as Charles explained, 'Being an actor I knew what to expect and I anticipated almost each action, and therefore I had no trouble with him at all. As an actor, I understood him, and as an actor he worked.'" Taylor's own assessment was that this performance "was one of the most important acting steps that Mitchum ever took, that he reached out and took a chance, and that it shows in the picture." In his own subsequent directing, said Taylor, he "has tried to remember, or certainly has learned, what Laughton meant, that the main job is communication, communication between the director and the actor."

But, back to the burlesque show: A state trooper claps a hand on Preacher's shoulder and arrests him, not for one of his many murders, but for the theft of the car. A brief, one-shot scene shows Powell being sentenced by a stern judge to Moundsville Penitentiary, after which one of Terry Sanders' helicopter shots of the prison gives way to his aerial survey of riverbank residences. The film then cuts to a high-angle shot, booming down to a lower angle, of young John and Pearl, playing with her rag doll, "Miss Jenny," in an idyllic, flower-strewn meadow. (On the soundtrack, the somber bell of the penitentiary has given way to a brief orchestral statement of Schumann's river/"Pretty Fly" theme.) "Go and dress Miss Jenny, kids," Laughton can be heard cuing the youngsters in the raw footage. This idyll is interrupted when the children's father Ben speeds up in his car and leaps out, wounded in the shoulder, holding a gun and a wad of money. Knowing the police will soon be there, Ben speaks rapidly to his children about hiding the money for their future benefit. For this pivotal moment, Laughton cues Peter Graves with a sense of urgency: "Pressure, pressure, pressure all the time! All right—*go!*"

Ben hurriedly settles on a hiding place for the stolen money—not shown to the audience or visible to the troopers who drive upon the scene, sirens blaring. Ben swears his son to secrecy, to never reveal the money's hiding place, not even to his mother, and to guard Pearl with his life.

Robert Golden

With all the wonderful people he had working, Laughton was the best performer. Watching him work behind the camera was really watching the best performance in the picture.

Hilyard Brown

Laughton himself would often play the little boy at our conferences,
saying, "This is what the little boy thinks about what he does . . ." He
was a tremendous actor. He could have played the ten-year-old boy, and
he would have been believable.

As a matter of fact, Laughton did play the little boy—off-camera. Actually, he played virtually every part in the picture. In Pearl's close-ups,
Laughton played John off-camera, simultaneously feeding her John's
lines and directing her performance. During John's close-ups, Laughton
reversed the process and played Pearl for Billy Chapin. During Shelley
Winters' close-ups, Laughton was Preacher; and during Mitchum's
close-ups, Laughton was Willa.

Laughton brought imagination to even the most routine of a film director's functions. For example the obligation to say "Cut" after a
take—Laughton often ignored it. Having gone to the trouble of utilizing all that poetry and music to establish for his actors a certain mood
on the set, Laughton sought to sustain that feeling by engaging in a
highly unorthodox technique. Rather than calling "Cut" between takes,
Laughton instructed Cortez to keep the camera rolling while he con-
versed with the actors and gave them further direction. He was, in effect, directing his film the way the silent movie directors used to be able
to direct all the time: while the camera was filming the actors and their
responses to his direction. This enabled the players, both child and
adult, to maintain a high level of concentration. Even when the actors
had presented Laughton with the final, satisfactory take, the director
wouldn't call "Cut," but would frequently say something to express his
satisfaction. According to the *Hunter* press book, (frankly not an unim-
peachable source,) Laughton would sometimes say, "Fine. I think that
will be enough of that." If that is what he said, the evidence is not preserved in the surviving out-takes; we do hear in them an enthusiastic
Laughton saying things like, "Wonderful," "Swell," "Beautiful," and, "A
hundred percent!" Together with his substitute variations for "Cut," he
had ones for "Action," including, "Okay, come along," to Bart and the
Guard, and, "Go on with your noise," to Miz Cunningham.

William Phipps elaborated on all of this for historian Tom Weaver: "I was on the set several times. Charles would never say *cut*, unless the camera ran out of film. 'Everybody be quiet; get settled; if you're standing up and you're uncomfortable, sit down; if you're sitting down and you're uncomfortable, stand up (*laughs*); if you've got a cough or a cold, leave; but I want it quiet until this camera runs out of film.' Then he would start a scene. I remember being there one day for a scene with Mitchum and Shelley Winters. They started it, but Charles interrupted. 'No, no, that's not right. Do it again and *this* time . . .' blah, blah, blah. Most people would have said *cut*. But in order to start up again, they have to call 'Quiet!' again, they have to slate it again, lots of things. That all takes up a lot of time, and it also breaks the mood, breaks the rhythm. Laughton did all that preparatory stuff *once*, and then never stopped until the camera was out of film. That way, he got a lot better work out of people. Still today, very few people do it that way."

In all of the surviving out-take footage, there is not a single instance of Laughton being angry or impatient with an actor, but more than once he snaps angrily at the crew when they forget to be quiet while the camera is still rolling. Whatever benefits accrued to Laughton by applying this unique method in 1954, he was also, unintentionally, bequeathing to posterity a fascinating film documentation of the process of directing *The Night of the Hunter.* (Thanks to Robert Gitt and his expert preservation team at UCLA, one can view this footage, and hear Laughton talking to his actors and, occasionally, even stepping before the camera for a fleeting moment.)

Hilyard Brown
He was fantastic with children. He and the two children got along like three little kids. Really, he had absolutely no trouble at all, and he didn't have any trouble with their parents, either, like a lot of directors have.

"The Laughton method did not call for long hours of rehearsal," as Helen Gould reported in the *New York Times*, "His modus operandi was no rehearsal at all. Instead, he caught his small fry on film when they were under his spell. If rehearsal was necessary, it was effected when they were fresh—on the set, under the lights, just before each scene was to be shot. Mr. Laughton sat under a sound boom on the edge of the set, leaning over with round-shouldered intensity as though attempting to imbue each youngster with what he wished through a sort of thought transference. 'We had to do it this way,' Mr. Laughton explained, 'because children don't retain.' Reminded that some psychologists agreed with this theory, Mr. Laughton stated, somewhat wryly, 'Perhaps, but I had to learn it through experience.'"

Hilyard Brown

Laughton and I would often go off into a corner and discuss how he was going to direct the little boy in a scene, because I had a boy of my own at home who was exactly that age. Once, we were shooting the part where the little boy's father comes home and, just before he's arrested, he gives the boy instructions about hiding the money, and makes him promise to keep the secret. I was watching Laughton and Peter Graves and Billy Chapin, a marvelous little kid, and I said to Charles, "You know, little boys, you tell them something, and before you even get through telling them, they're thinking about that butterfly over there or something. If Peter really wants to impress this kid and make sure that the kid knows exactly what he's talking about, have him make Billy look him right in the eye, and say something like, 'No, son, don't look over there, look me right in the eye. I'm telling you what to do.'" So, he did. If you'll remember, Graves made Billy look him right in the eye.

A holdover of this emphasis might be detected in the out-takes of Lillian Gish's Bible-reading prelude, shot roughly a month later. In a couple of takes, just before the "Beware of false prophets" admonition, Miss Gish cautions, "Now, pay attention." But this gambit was not used in the take put into the film.

In one angle, John swears the oath for Ben while Pearl squats in the background. Laughton off-camera delivers Ben's lines while directing Billy Chapin: "Eyes steady." At one point, property man Joe La Bella unexpectedly enters the frame and bends down over Sally Jane Bruce. Because the camera is still running, Stanley Cortez can be heard calling to him, "Get back, Joe. Joe, get back!" "What's his name?" asks Laughton, and when he gets the answer the director joins the chorus of voices calling the prop man back out of camera range. La Bella has a very good reason, however, for invading the shot: Sally Jane had been

"Make Billy look him right in the eye." Peter Graves (L) and Billy Chapin enact a crucial early scene directed by Laughton—with some helpful advice from art director Hilyard Brown.

holding her doll in such a way that it could not be clearly seen—for all one could tell, it was just a rag—and so La Bella adjusts Miss Jenny's position in Sally's arms before retreating off-camera. "Look up here, dear," Cortez calls to the little girl. "Sally. Look there, dear."

Everything back in place, Billy Chapin picks up the scene, with Laughton cuing him: "Where's your mom?"

"Out shopping. You're bleedin'." Then he realizes he forgot one word, and corrects himself: "Oh. You're bleedin', Dad."

"Yes," breathes Laughton, and cues him again, "Where's your mom?"

"Out shopping. You're bleedin', Dad."

"No," says Laughton, and gives him a line-reading: "'Out shopping. (*Softer, wondering*) You're bleedin', Dad.' Billy—where's your mom . . .?"

And so they continue. When it comes time for young John to take his dread oath, a stern-voiced Laughton off-camera is at once a blend of both father Ben and director Charles, the one indistinguishable from the other: "You don't understand it. Now, stand up *straight!* Look me straight in the eye! Hold up your right hand. Now, say this after me: 'I will guard Pearl with my life.'"

"I will guard Pearl with my life."

"And, 'I will never tell about the money.'"

"And I won't never tell about the money."

"Say again—with your right hand *up!* Looking at me. You don't know what the *heck* I'm talking about. Put up your right hand. Look straight at me. And say, 'I will guard Pearl with my life.'"

"And I will guard Pearl with my life."

"Without the 'And.' 'I will guard Pearl with my life . . .'"

Later, when the angle is close on Pearl so that she can nod her agreement to the oath, Laughton's direction is much more economical. He simply says, "Spit it out, dear." Dutifully, little Sally Jane spits out her chewing gum into the hand of a helpful crew member.

Intercut with the Ben/John dialogue are shots of the approaching police—"the blue men," as they are called by the children in the novel. (Pearl speaks lines about "the blue men" in this scene and the later bedroom-storytelling scene, but both references were cut from the final film. Much later in the script, Rachel's oldest orphan Ruby also has a line about the "blue men"—and hers, too, fell to the cutting-room floor.) "The Blue Men" were the subject of one of author Grubb's pre-production sketches (see page 120) and its childlike simplicity, or perhaps the film's modest budget, is reflected in the lone, large "P.D." stickers stuck to the doors of their autos (and already seen in out-takes to be buckling from the heat). Laughton directs Graves to keep in mind "the imminence of those guns coming at you."

Robert Golden

Laughton worked very closely with the boy. The boy had a very trying part and Laughton would go through quite a bit to have the boy reach an emotional peak. I remember particularly when the father is being picked up by the police and they're beating him up. Laughton went through every emotion he could to get the boy's reaction, when he grabs his stomach as if he's been kicked himself.

In the out-takes of Billy Chapin's reaction shot, Laughton crouches just off-camera, then reaches over and snaps his hand briskly into the boy's belly, thus cuing the boy's flinch and his stomach-grabbing gesture. "Step back and do it again," Laughton admonishes, "Don't anticipate this." And so the business is repeated until Laughton is satisfied and they move on to another beat of the boy's reaction, for which Laughton directs Billy to have "a sickly smile."

Robert Golden

Laughton thought of that whole arrest as a ballet, and he tried to stage it that way. Again, this was unusual, stepping into this hard-bitten group and expressing that. Hilyard Brown ate it up, but my reaction was, "What kind of jazz is this?"

Whatever kind of jazz it was, in point of fact, it was foreshadowing. By staging the struggle and arrest—and John's reactions to them—with very specifically choreographed movements, Laughton was implanting in the mind's eye of his audience imagery which he hoped would bear fruit through recapitulation at the film's climax. But by experimenting with this technique, Laughton was running the risk that the action would appear oddly stilted, and to some viewers it does.

Stanley Cortez

Whether the ballet idea succeeded, that's something else again. I don't think it did, actually—why, it's hard to say. It could have been too stylized. However, this was Charles' concept. Argue with Charles? Oh, God, no! One never argued with Charles, one discussed with Charles.

Terry Sanders

Denis, my brother, had been the dialogue coach on the set while I was off doing the second unit. I was on the set later on, just observing.

According to Denis's recollection, Stanley Cortez was annoyed when the Sanders brothers wanted to look through the camera, prompting the siblings to dub the distinguished d.p. "Sour Old Cortez." To Cortez's complaints, Laughton's response was a quiet, "Hush, hush, Stanley. They're just children and they're supposed to learn, aren't they? So you must let them look through the camera."

Robert Mitchum could be caustic in later years describing Cortez's working methods. "Very often, Cortez would stand out on location and look at something for a long time. And while his back was turned, the grips would put a mark, an 'x,' by the spot where he'd be standing. Then he would walk around some more, and walk around, and eventually he'd end up right back at the place where the grips had put the 'x' all along and he'd say, 'Okay, put the camera here.' But what do you expect? The guy got his name off a cigar box . . ."

"Don't!" cries John as the cops pummel his father. Then, as they drag him away, the dismayed boy can only say to himself, "Dad . . ." For the first beat—"Don't!"—Laughton encourages Billy, "Shout real. Shout at me!" The direction to say or do a thing "real" or "ordinary" is a recurring motif in Laughton's dealings with the two children, particularly Sally Jane. The director even used it with some of his adult actors. But for the next beat—"Dad . . ."—Laughton calls for a quieter expression of disbelief: "This is a guy you've known all this time. And something terrible has happened. And you just say . . ."

Instinctively picking up the idea, Billy whispers, "Dad . . ."

Paul Gregory

When they came up and arrested the father, I wanted it to be the little boy looking up, and, "Dad! Dad!" You know, with the father big, bigger than life. But for me, they lost that later on in the picture.

Stylized repetition was but one device Laughton used to draw parallels between Ben, the boy's father, and Preacher, the boy's father-figure-to-be. When Ben Harper is condemned to hang for the killing of two men in his bank-robbery, he has been brought before the same judge, and is viewed through the same camera angle (albeit with a different lens), as when Preacher was sentenced for stealing a car. These single-shot scenes occur early in the film, and they were executed early in the shoot, on August 18. Already Brown and Cortez are staking out the film's territory in the expressionist land of minimal sets. The foreground silhouette of the prisoner fills a major portion of the frame, and the judge's dock and a flag in the background are sufficient to suggest an entire courtroom.

"By a strange and unholy chance," as Grubb would later put it in his narrative script for the movie's soundtrack LP, Ben Harper and Preacher Harry Powell are confined in the same cell at the Moundsville Penitentiary. Here the literally striking imagery begins to reveal Laughton's audacious presentation of Preacher, daring to see him as not only diabolical but frequently comical. Ben Harper, asleep on the lower bunk, mumbles in his dream, "And a little child shall lead them . . ." and we hear Preacher Powell's off-screen voice trying to insinuate itself into his fellow prisoner's consciousness and persuade him to divulge, in his sleep, the secret of his blood-money's hiding place. We don't know where in the cell Preacher lurks until his face appears upside down from the upper bunk. This sight often elicits a chuckle from the audience that invariably turns to a bigger laugh when Harper wakes and immediately slugs Preacher right out of the bunk. Elsewhere, Mitchum has claimed to have contributed the idea for his incongruous entrance, yet the script clearly calls for "the face of PREACHER (to stretch) down into the SHOT, upside-down, snake-like." Possibly this was one of the many ideas the actor had brought to his first discussion of the novel with Laughton. In any case, Mitchum can take full credit for being a trouper: he executes his own fall when Peter Graves "hits" him. In the out-take, after Mitchum's fall out of the frame, we hear someone, possibly Cortez, asking, "Are you all right Bob?" "Yes." Cut.

The film had only been shooting for a few days, and this was Peter Graves' first day of work as Ben Harper. When the young actor asked Laughton a question about the character, (as he subsequently related to Miss Lanchester's researchers), "Charles . . . took him to a corner of the set, and they sat on a wooden bench and talked quietly about his part. He was gentle and soft-spoken, but he immediately got to the roots of the problem. He had a fabulous sense of communication with actors. A real desire and an ability at talking solidly about what he wanted." And, what impressed Graves the most, he asked the young actor for his point of view. By way of contrast, a few months previously, Graves had been acting in *The Long Gray Line,* a film directed by the legendary John Ford. When, at one point, Graves had started to say, "About this character, I think . . ." Ford said, "Shut up. Don't think in my picture." Now, when Laughton called, "Cut and print" on the *Hunter* bunk scene, Graves went over to the director and asked, "Was that alright?" Charles replied, "You don't have to ask that question. Do you think it was alright?" "Yes," said Graves, "I think it was." And, at that moment, he found himself thinking of phoning John Ford . . . Going from working for Ford to working for Laughton, the actor decided, was like "walking into heaven."

In the Grubb novel, Ben tells Preacher about his decision to rob the bank: "Because I was just plumb tired of being poor. That's the large and small of it, Preacher. Just sick to death of drawing that little pay envelope at the hardware store in Moundsville every Friday and then when I'd go over to Mister Smiley's bank on payday he'd open that little drawer with all the green tens and fifties and hundreds in it and every time I'd look at it there I'd just fairly choke to think of the things it would buy Willa and them kids of mine." Contrast that with Ben Harper's explanation in the film: "I robbed that bank because I got tired of seein' . . . children roamin' the woodlands without food, children roamin' the highways in this year of Depression; children sleepin' in old abandoned car bodies on junk-heaps; and I promised myself I'd never see the day when *my* young'ns 'd want." If anything has survived from James Agee's excessive, Depression-haunted first draft script, it is probably this lone soliloquy of Ben Harper. Whatever it may owe to Agee, Laughton the sharp-eyed editor recognized it as something well worth retaining, because it amplifies his theme of children abiding through the hardest of times. This emphasis will recur even in the film's most poetic section, the river journey, when the gaunt farm woman who hands out potatoes muses sadly about "Such times, when young'ns run the roads . . ."

Just as Preacher quizzes Ben in vain about the blood money, Ben queries Preacher about the religion he professes. Preacher's answer (in one of Mitchum's most diabolical close-ups): "The religion the Almighty and me worked out betwixt us." At one point in the out-takes, when Mitchum says "between" instead of "betwixt," Laughton says, "Start the scene again, only say 'betwixt' instead of 'between.'" God (or in this case Satan) is in the details, and, as Laughton's beloved Mark Twain once pointed out, the difference between the almost-right word and the right word is like the difference between the lightning bug and the lightning. Brandishing his switchblade, Preacher blasphemously quotes the Redeemer, "I come not with Peace, but with a Sword." In an early take, Mitchum releases the blade in the middle of this statement, but in the take used in the film, Mitchum—presumably at Laughton's direction—gives the moment proper emphasis by taking a beat after the word "peace,"

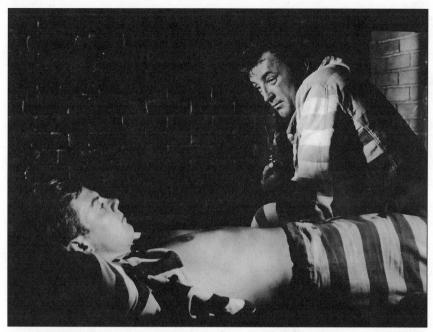

"The religion the Almighty and me worked out betwixt us."

springing the knife, and then finishing his sentence. (Knowing just when to open the switchblade was one of Laughton's key storytelling devices, as will be seen later in the film's most suspenseful scene . . .) Rather than risk divulging his secret in his sleep, Ben Harper stuffs a sock into his mouth. In a punctuation to the scene not retained in the final cut, we see the shadow of Preacher's hand tighten into a fist and pump its frustration.

Later that night, Preacher prayerfully thanks his God for bringing him to the same cell with "a man with ten thousand dollars hid somewhere, and a widder in the makin'." For the first time, we see the letters tattooed on Powell's right hand: "L-O-V-E." Underneath the fingers, however, is his switchblade knife.

Establishing shots of the prison before and after the Ben/Preacher scenes are courtesy of Terry Sanders' second unit work.

Terry Sanders

Moundsville Penitentiary in West Virginia was a wonderful set, this really nineteenth century structure. The prison yard was really picturesque. The only thing I remember about the shoot was that, when we got there, there were about three guards standing out behind it, near the wall. One of them had a hook instead of a left hand, and his shotgun was resting in the hook. They had gotten word that there was a prisoner going to try to make a jail break, and they were obviously standing right there waiting to shoot him when he came over the wall. It was a pretty horrible place.

The next few minutes of screen time, filmed by Laughton in L.A., demonstrate the director's great sensitivity to author Grubb's story, not merely by the care with which it is shot, but also by the fact that Laughton filmed it at all. So in tune with Grubb's intentions was Laughton that he saw the necessity of including certain characters whom most screen writers would have considered dispensable. But Laughton saw that these characters, the GUARD, the WIFE, and particularly BART, THE HANGMAN and his CHILDREN—however peripheral they may be to Grubb's plot—were absolutely central to the heart of his themes.

Preacher's prayer dissolves into the first of two brief scenes. The chatty guard walks Bart home, quizzing him about the man, Ben

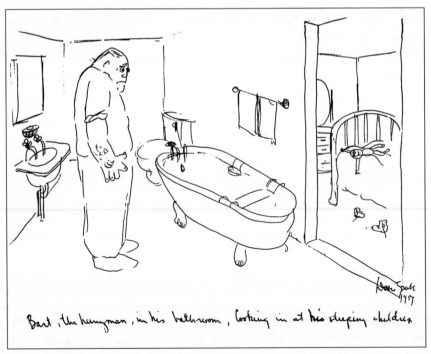

Bart, the hangman, in his bathroom, looking in at his sleeping children

The haunted hangman. Sketch of Bart by Davis Grubb.

Harper, he's just executed. (Alert viewers might spot that the hangman in Terry Sanders' long shot wears a fedora, whereas the hangman directed by Laughton sports a derby.) Concerning the hiding place of Harper's blood money, the taciturn Bart has only this to say: "He took the secret with him when I dropped him." Thus we learn that this man in the derby is the Hangman. Once inside his home's kitchen, the dialogue between Bart and his wife subtly reveals that he has never told her that his duties occasionally include execution:

> BART: (*low*) Mother: sometimes I think it might be better if I was
> to quit my job as guard.
> HIS WIFE's eyes go sharp and quiet.
> WIFE: (*low*) You're always this way when there's a hangin'. You
> never have to be there.
> BART *rinses his hands. A sigh; he takes up the towel.*
> BART: Sometimes I wish I was back in the mine.
> WIFE: And leave me a widow after another blast like the one in
> '24? Not on your life, old mister!

Terry Sanders
"Old mister," she calls him. I love that line.

They are speaking low because their two children are sleeping in the next room. Bart goes to tuck them in and regards them lovingly. The youngsters are both girls, but we can't help being reminded of the hanged man's two children, John and Pearl. One of the most poignant moments in the film now occurs as Bart adjusts his sleeping children's blanket and then is seen in close-up. Even though the children in the scene have nothing to do in their close-up but "sleep," Laughton gives them the benefit of his direction: "Don't move your body, sleepy, sleepy, quiet, all right . . . Cut." Then, to Bart during his close-up: he is to think about the hanged Ben's children and "your own children. You're particularly tender tonight because of what you've been doing. Bend down a little bit. Come up with your head . . . Come up. Stand up earlier, eyes cast down . . . Now, look up . . ." Clearly, Bart is haunted by the work he does to keep food on the table for these two precious ones. The look on his face is unforgettable,

The hangman's children—sketch
by Grubb.

and Laughton *holds on it* while bringing in the voices of children singing their cruel taunt: "Hing, hang, hung. See what the Hangman done!"

The film now dissolves to the children at Cresap's Landing, continuing to torment John and Pearl with their chant (sung to a prerecorded playback). It is a quietly powerful, eloquent transition. Schumann clearly took to heart Grubb's description of this bit of doggerel in his pre-production letter to Laughton: "I must confess that I had in mind no song at all but rather the kind of monotonous, sing-song that children make up. I think it's all the more sinister for that—something off-key—minor—dreadfully flat and heartless." As the sing-song continues, one boy pours salt into the wound by chalking on a brick wall the crude sketch of a hanged man. Not insignificantly, this picture is the image from the very first sentence in Grubb's novel: "A child's hand and a piece of chalk had made it: a careful, child's scrawl of white lines on the red bricks of the wall beside Jander's Livery Stable: a crude pair of sticks for the gallows tree, a thick broken line for the rope and then the scarecrow of the hanging man. Some passing by along that road did not see it at all; others saw it and remembered what it meant and thought solemn thoughts and turned their eyes to the house down the river road. The little children – the poor little children. Theirs were the eyes for which the crude picture was intended and they had seen it and heard along Peacock Alley the mocking child rhyme that went with it . . ."

(The uncredited actor who plays the tiny but important role of Bart was Paul Bryar. As with most character actors in Hollywood, his familiar but anonymous face enriched bit parts and small roles in TV, B-movies and the occasional first-class feature. He can be glimpsed as a racetrack bartender serving a significant drink to James Mason's Norman Maine in *A Star is Born,* filmed around the same time as *Hunter.* Towards the end of his life, Bryar contributed a bit of business as poignant, in its way, as his turn as Bart in *Hunter.* In that trenchant satire of the erotic/neurotic duality of young love, *Modern Romance* (1981), the protagonist, played by Albert Brooks, calls from a pay phone late at night to see if his former girl-friend, with whom he's desperately trying to rekindle the affair, is home yet. Meanwhile, in the adjacent booth, an old man played by Bryar is just as desperately phoning his (presumably) former wife. "He's there with you right now, isn't he? . . . Don't lie to me. I wasn't born yesterday." With a look of sad resignation, he hangs up . . .)

The hanged man's children. Pearl and John peer at the watch for sale in Miz Cunningham's window.

A happier location at Cresap's Landing for John and Pearl is Miz Cunningham's used-goods shop across the street from the schoolyard. Here, at least, John can gaze dreamily into the window at the gold watch prominently displayed. Obviously, this wondrous item is high on John's wish list. "Are you going to buy it, John?" asks Pearl, blissfully ignorant of her family's poverty, but before John can even answer his sister, obstreperous old Miz Cunningham steps out of her shop and starts grilling these two "poor, poor lambs" about Ben Harper's stolen money. So, here is another spot at Cresap's Landing where John is now made to feel uncomfortable; he grabs Pearl's hand and moves on.

In this scene, as with so many of the early episodes, Laughton is planting seeds which will yield payoffs in the final reel; one of those seeds is John's fascination with the watch. "Now, Billy," he instructs, "don't look at her (Sally Jane), don't take your eyes off the watch when she speaks to you, just keep your eyes quite steady." An insert shot, moving in to a close-up on the watch from John's point-of-view, increases the emphasis.

Elsewhere, Davis Grubb muses that he wishes he had seen a little more of Miz Cunningham. As a matter of fact, there was originally more of Miz Cunningham to be seen in this, her only scene in the movie. What few lines she has were slightly reduced in the cutting room; so gone are,

"I wish I'd seen more of Miz Cunningham." Here she appears in the wistful author's sketch for Laughton.

"The Lord tends you both these days," and, "When they caught him (Ben), there wasn't so much as a penny of it to be seen! Now what do you make of that! Eh, boy?" Even so, in the out-takes, the perfectly cast but unbilled old actress initially forgets her opening, "Uh-Hawwww!" and Laughton has to remind her of it. After all, God is *still* in the details, even if the detail isn't an actual word but a vocal sound. In this, as in many of their takes together, when Sally Jane can't help but be a distracted little girl, young Master Chapin quietly and gently gets her back on track with a whisper or a touch on her arm, showing he is both a young pro and a little gentleman. In a later take, close on Sally Jane, Laughton is again playing the off-camera character (Miz Cunningham) and he admonishes the little girl to "look at me straight, darling. Look at me straight." Sally Jane makes a face. "Ordinary. Look at me *ordinary,* darling. Put your hands back where they were, sweetheart . . . That's it."

Perhaps John's sole refuge at Cresap's Landing, aside from Birdie's wharf boat, is Spoon's Ice Cream Parlor, where the children's mother Willa (previously only glimpsed in the balletic scene of her husband's arrest) now must work to make ends meet. As the children approach, Walt Spoon (Don Beddoe) in the doorway proffers a couple of lollipops, but Willa waves the children on and they continue down the street. Walt now stands benignly on the sidelines while his busybody wife Icey (Evelyn Varden) tries to persuade the grieving young widow that it's not too soon to start shopping around for another father for her two kids. This has been apparently an ongoing conversation between Willa and Icey, and it proceeds well into the next day.

In the script, "Icey jaws down her (Willa's) back, from first moment of shot." As staged, however, there is an awkward—or, at the very least, unabashedly theatrical—moment as the camera tracks into Spoon's; only then does Evelyn Varden start her first line. In the novel, townsfolk leave the Bijou movie house at night and amble over to Spoon's for a bite. Laughton shot such a scene much as Grubb had written it but ultimately decided not to put it in the film. (As Paul Gregory later points out with justifiable pride, *Hunter* had a very tight script; this brief, nocturnal shot of the local townsfolk is probably the only complete scene shot but not used. Other deletions amount to no more than a few lines or a bit of business.) Laughton also eliminated the voices of offscreen customers. The result of this paring down is that the sense of realism is once again diminished and the abstract, dream-like atmosphere is reinforced. And it would seem to be key that this occurs in the second scene of the two women's ongoing conversation which serves as the harbinger of the hunter's imminent arrival.

The montage of Willa and Icey's chat is followed, in the script, by the image of "a short, lighted, toy-like train" fatefully carrying, we must presume, Preacher Harry Powell, on his way to court his late cell mate's "widder." Yet in the actual film, the train intrudes on the conversation/montage not once but twice and—especially supported by the menacing brass of Walter Schumann's "Preacher" motif—it looms like the locomotive from Hell. The bogey man is on his way.

Terry Sanders

I had forgotten how many second unit shots there *are* in the film. There are a lot. But I didn't shoot that train, I don't think.

Robert Golden

When the train that's carrying Mitchum is heading for the town, those were a couple of stock shots that we bought from someplace. The script may have called for a "toy-like train," but that's not what we did. I loved the sound of that whistle, and man, that big train—he's getting closer, he's getting closer—you can't do that with toy trains.

The roar of the train subsides to the nocturnal hush of the children's bedroom. (Schumann's score segues from Preacher's theme to a gentle nocturne for flute and orchestra, based on the "Pretty Fly" tune.) Pearl, under the covers, requests, "Tell me a story, John," and her brother obligingly rises and moves about, musing aloud a tale of a king in Africa who had a son, a daughter, and gold, until some bad men came along and took him away . . . Laughton, at the outset, urges his young actor, "Play it like a game, Billy. Tell me the story. Dream it away—go on."

Stanley Cortez

When I talk about conferences with Hilly Brown and Bob Golden, this was either before or after a scene was shot. But when you're on the firing line, there are two people involved, whether you like it or not, and that's the director and the cinematographer. Everything else is subservient. This is where the rapport takes place, the sensitivity. Photographing *The Night of the Hunter,* and the relationship I had with Laughton, was the most rewarding experience in my entire life and career, because of my love for this man, my great respect for him as a person and as a great artist. Period. Charles and I had a rare, rare association, and a rapport that I'd never had with anybody before—and I say this without a sense of contradiction at all, even though I have great respect for Orson Welles and all those I've worked with and for—but with Charles there was something special that's pretty hard to define. I knew what he was thinking and that what I was thinking coincided with his. Call it mental intercourse, if you want.

I don't remember whether it was Charles's idea or mine, but we did something very unusual in the scene where the two children are up in their bedroom at night and the little boy is looking at the shadows of leaves on his wall. In one shot, we reversed the angle and shot the boy through a scrim so that the wall was invisible but the shadows were not, we were photographing the little boy through the shadows. That was done with a dimmer and, actually, a series of scrims, to get a kind of depth in the shadow itself. You know in this industry, you can plan for months and months, and it doesn't always work out, sometimes you have to be innovative, you have to resort to doing something on the spur of the moment with spit and baling wire. The grips had some scrim, and a little piece of that, a bit of light here, and there it was.

Suddenly, looming large on the bedroom wall is a man's shadow. No need to guess whose—Schumann's "Preacher" motif interrupts little John's story.

Stanley Cortez
You can plan a scene thoroughly, but sometimes when you're on the set and you *hear* the dialogue and *see* the action go through, you change your whole concept of that particular scene visually. Because, when you read the script, it is one thing, but when you hear it from a live mouth it becomes something else, and however it affects you, you work accordingly, and reflect that which you hear and see. Sometimes, what one reads in the script one can't duplicate, because it just doesn't make

sense. Originally, the boy was to be looking at his shadow on the wall, and when he'd move away the shadow of Mitchum standing outside on the street below would be revealed. But how could the boy's shadow cover Mitchum's shadow which, realistically, would be so much larger? So we had Mitchum's enormous shadow enter the scene, it made more sense, and it was very effective dramatically.

I remember so clearly, at the end of the scene when the boy gets back into bed, Charles wanted to start back and move in to the boy's close-up. I said, "Charles, may I suggest that we start in and pull back?" And he said, "By God, you're right, let's do that." It was so we could surprise the audience with the visual thing, as against moving in, you see. With due respect to Charles, and Hilly, this I'll take all the credit in the world for, this was strictly Cortez.

As John and Pearl bed down for the night, and while Cortez' camera pulls away, we hear off-screen Preacher softly singing, "Leaning, leaning . . . Leaning on the everlasting arms . . ." This scene of quietly ominous portent gives way to a close-up of a loud steamboat whistle, heralding the next sequence and its bright change of mood.

Terry Sanders

That's my shot of the Delta Queen whistle. We shot a lot on and around that riverboat, which was mixed in with Uncle Birdie's wharf boat at Cresap's Landing. That's a nice set, actually. Hilyard Brown is a wonderful art director. Amazing what you could do for eight-hundred-thousand in those days.

Stanley Cortez

Remember the next scene, with the riverboat in the background while the boy is visiting Jimmy Gleason's cabin on Cresap's Landing? Well, it was impossible to go back east and do the sequence there because of the expense involved. So what we did, and it was Hilly's idea, was to go into a matte shot. The actual boat passing was done back east and then tied in with a composite done on the optical printer. We were able to accomplish, for a small amount of money, what we could have done at a big ex-

"The magic of film." Hilyard Brown's sketch for Terry Sanders envisions the matte shot which combined Uncle Birdie's wharf boat at the Lee Ranch in Chatsworth with the river boat in West Virginia.

pense by going back east. Here is where imagination takes place on a film, in the design of sets, in the lighting, in angles, and so forth.

Terry Sanders

Works perfectly. "The magic of film," huh? They did a good job.

To the shot favoring only Birdie's wharf boat, Cortez subtly brings the feel of a Griffith pastorale through use of back-lighting and, especially, a hazy shadowing effect around the rim of the screen, enclosing the image in a dark, misty, soft-focus circle. Keeping in mind the change-of-pace this scene must bring to the film's overall tapestry, Laughton interrupts his own off-camera reading of Uncle Birdie's line to exhort Billy Chapin to put more pep into his waving at the riverboat: "Hey. (*snaps fingers*) Y'look all gloomy. Faster than that! C'mon, *wave!*" (Schumann's score picks up the pace with a tune like an old river chanty, announced first by the horns and

Uncle Birdie. Grubb sketch for Laughton.

then picked up by the full orchestra, a marvelous miniature of Americana.) Uncle Birdie invites John into his shack for a cup of coffee, which, in his own case, he "sweetens" with a splash of liquor: "Man o' my years needs a little snort in the morning to heat the boilers." The exterior shots for this scene were filmed very early in September. The interiors, incorporating Terry Sanders' rear-projection footage of the riverboat, were shot a full month later. In both locations, the actor portraying old Birdie shines.

Robert Mitchum

Funny. I was just thinking about Jimmy Gleason. Picturing him, that's all. What was he like? An old Irish actor, from Bridgeport, Connecticut. Interested in baseball.

Paul Gregory

Old Jimmy Gleason, he was so dear.

Gleason, a veteran performer, had begun his career on the stage, and been among the core group of players instrumental in forming the Screen Actors Guild back in the thirties. Despite having done memorable work at virtually every studio in Hollywood (including Frank Capra's *Meet John Doe* and the classic comedy, *Here Comes Mr. Jordan,* for which he earned a supporting Oscar nomination), Gleason found his experience on *Hunter* unique. He enthused to *New York Times* correspondent Helen Gould, "Charles is just terrific. He has a brand-new way of handling people." Gleason did not elaborate on the director's method, but a sample can be overheard in Laughton's hurried instructions to the actor just before he jumps into a take of the first wharf boat scene: "Jimmy, all the charm in the world, Mark Twain, go!" That's what Laughton asks for, and that's exactly what Gleason delivers. Laughton's instruction to Chapin? "Don't forget you love him, Billy." But how could he forget—and how could we not follow suit?

Davis Grubb

I was happy when they cast James Gleason as Uncle Birdie, because I knew that no matter whether he did it with a Brooklyn accent, he would do a job that would be very interesting. I'd loved Gleason for years, he was a marvelous actor. I revel in the memory of people like that. He didn't remind me of Uncle Gene in the picture, but he shouldn't have. He had, if anything, a little too much of a city accent; he didn't do it the way Walter Brennan, say, would have done it. But oh, he was marvelous, marvelous.

It is from Uncle Birdie that John learns the news that there is a stranger in town—a man who knew John's dad at the penitentiary. Instinctively, John senses dread in this information, (reinforced by a muted reference to Preacher's theme in the underscore), and the boy quickly takes his leave of Birdie to pick up his little sister at Spoon's parlor. No sooner does he arrive at his mom's workplace, than young John discovers his mother, his sister, and the Spoons all enthralled by their conversation with Preacher Harry Powell. This is the scene where Preacher launches into his famous sermon: "Ah, little lad, you're staring at my fingers. Would you like me to tell you the little story of Right-Hand-Left-Hand—the story of Good and Evil?" By the time his warring fingers have concluded their titanic struggle for the soul of man—". . .and old Left Hand Hate is down for the count!"—Preacher has successfully seduced everyone present: Willa, Pearl, and the Spoons. Everyone, that is, except the boy.

"Right Hand - Left Hand." Grubb sketched Preacher's famous sermon in a series of sketches.

Paul Gregory

Now, I thought some of our best casting was with Evelyn Varden, who was an old burlesque and Broadway actress, and Don Beddoe. Don Beddoe is a dear man; if you get in touch with him, tell him I remember him with such love.

Don Beddoe

Isn't that nice.

Venerable character actor Don Beddoe was ninety-two years old when interviewed about his participation in *The Night of the Hunter*. Laughton's film was one of many credits racked up by this hard-working thespian whose performances had supported a host of Hollywood stars from Peter Lorre in *The Face Behind the Mask* to Cary Grant in *The Bachelor and the Bobby-Soxer.* When informed that distinguished British film historian Leslie Halliwell had described him as, "A character actor with a genial, sometimes startled look," Don Beddoe immediately said, "That means when I've blown my lines." Beddoe's recollections of his association with *Hunter* are as pleasant as Gregory's memories of working with him.

Don Beddoe

You say Paul Gregory calls Laughton a "saint/sinner"? I guess that's why he was so foul-mouthed. Charles Laughton was always on his best behavior, completely friendly and warm. I couldn't understand it, because he could be an awful, mean individual, I understood. Just gossip, that's all, such a vague source of gossip, I mean, that he was temperamental and all the rest of it. But maybe, on the other side of the camera . . . I was delighted that he was able to do this picture, because it came

"A genial, sometimes startled look." Don Beddoe as Walt Spoon.

through so well. And it didn't come through like a first attempt, at all. It was really professional, directorially.

No, Laughton never gave me a line-reading, never. His principal problem, of course, was handling Mitchum, and Mitchum has a reputation of being a bad boy about his performances and everything. But evidently there was a complete rapport between the two. Because, never has Mitchum been as good, before or since. It was a brilliant performance, brilliant performance. And he never was cockeyed on the set that *I* saw, at all, never once. Always a complete working actor. I worked with Mitchum in that picture, and then in another one, and in both cases it's been a very cordial relationship. Very cordial. Strictly man to man, with my understanding why he was a bad boy: 'cause he just felt like being a bad boy, y'know. And, his not particularly caring *what* I thought anyhow, and making it perfectly obvious, but enjoying telling me at the same time. I liked him.

Terry Sanders
Mitchum was a very bright man, a really intelligent person. What presence. There's a lot of power.

Robert Mitchum
It was an enjoyable job. I liked Charles, and I liked to work with him. So did Shelley. He was sort of the head of the family on the set, which is as it should be. He was adored. As a director, he was so grateful, he went into ecstasy whenever he enjoyed the scene.

Icey's line following the "LOVE-HATE" sermon is, "I never heard it better told." After one take on Mitchum in which Laughton has been reading Icey's part, Laughton enthuses as the character *and* himself, "I never heard it better told, by Christ, I didn't."

Years later, for the benefit of Elsa Lanchester's researchers, Mitchum elaborated on his fond memories of Laughton's direction. "He was brilliant, and inspired devotion from his actors . . . As a matter of fact, it's the last time I can remember working in a picture in which all the actors read the script." Although Laughton always entertained suggestions and valid criticisms, "One was careful not to make suggestions that

While posing for a series of publicity shots, Mitchum displayed a bit of the irreverent humor that he sometimes revealed in interviews but which has never really been captured in any of his many film roles.

would be in his own interests because Charles would simply look at you." Mitchum went on to say that "Charles's great attribute as a director was that he understood the material and helped the actors to understand it. He had the impression of the whole, he had a sense of unity and a feeling for construction. He always rehearsed the scenes and tried to explain to actors what he wanted. Because of his great appreciation of art, he had a sense of composition." On the other hand, "he dismissed symbols. He did not want to make them obvious. He was mainly interested in the story line and in the way that the story would be told. As he said, 'In a still photograph it is possible, sometimes, to have the symbol be obvious, because it is permissible. But where we have live actors moving about, obvious symbolism cannot be permitted.'"

Robert Mitchum

As to the interpretation of Preacher, Charles and I never disagreed. We never *discussed* it. And he never gave me a line-reading, or acted out a bit of business, like that LOVE-HATE tug-of-war with the left hand–right hand.

Following the LOVE-HATE sermon, the scene's next important beat occurs between Preacher and John. As Davis Grubb put it in his novel:

> Preacher smiled and patted the shaggy head with firm, quick movements.
>
> Many and many's the time, he said softly, when I sat listening to Brother Harper speak about these youngins.
>
> Now John's eyes flew to Preacher's face.
>
> What did he tell you?
>
> The room was silent. Outside the pale winter sun had appeared and they could hear the drip, drip of the melting snow on the roof.
>
> Why, he told me what fine little lambs you and your sister yonder both was! cried Preacher, his washed-out blue eyes twinkling palely.
>
> Is that all? John said.
>
> Willa stirred uncomfortably and went over to gather Pearl from the stranger's lap.
>
> Why no, boy, smiled Preacher, something new in his eyes now as if a game had begun between them. He told me lots and lots of things. Nice things, boy.

Here is how that moment is captured by the screenplay:

> PREACHER: Ah, many's the time poor Brother Ben told me about these youngins.
> JOHN: What did he tell you?
> CLOSE SHOT — PREACHER
> *He does a little take. His eyes twinkle palely.*
> PREACHER: Why, he told me what fine little lambs you and your sister both was.
> GROUP SHOT
> JOHN: Is that all?
> CLOSE SHOT — PREACHER
> *Something new enters his eyes; a game has begun between them.*
> PREACHER: Why, no, boy; he told me lots and lots of things. Nice things, boy.

That's the scene—as you can see, faithfully transcribed from the book—which Laughton shot. But, that's not quite the scene we find in the film. The difference is in the choice of shots. Laughton had the coverage to

Preacher's sermon in the film fails to impress young John—but every other soul at Cresap's Landing is captivated.

present the scene exactly as it appears in the script, had he wished, but
he decided—presumably in the editing stage—to downplay the moment
by holding on the group shot. Thus, there is no cut to a closer angle on
Preacher, no clear-cut indication that a game has begun between him
and John. With that single, simple choice of shots, Laughton has tucked
away a key turning-point in the story, and is saving it for later in the narrative—where it will have even greater impact.

An out-take reveals Laughton on the sound stage thinking of a nu-
ance he hadn't considered during the script writing, and passing it on
to Shelley Winters: "Don't move your head much, please, during this,
just the expression in your eyes. Every time he (*Mitchum*) speaks, you
cast your eyes down." But to Sally Jane, he reminds, "Look at him ordinary, dear." (Once again, prop man Joe La Bella steps in to adjust Miss
Jenny into her most photogenic position.)

The scene is punctuated with a sickly-sweet close-up of Icey over her
pot of "yummy" fudge, telling Preacher he won't get a smidgen of it unless he stays in town for the Sunday picnic. The film dissolves to that
picnic, riverbank in the background, Preacher in the foreground leading the townspeople around the table in a spirited rendition of "Bringing in the Sheaves." This is shot to a playback of a performance by
Mitchum and chorus, but Mitchum and the extras don't merely mouth
the words, they sing on-camera over their own prerecorded voices.
Choir-master Laughton can be heard calling to individual church ladies
by name: "Edna, come 'round! Come on, Margaret! Betsy, get into it!"

Mitchum recalled for Elsa Lanchester's researchers that the picnic
scene concerned him: (He) "was worried that perhaps Charles was making him too dashing as the lover in the picnic scene, and he wondered
if his wardrobe ought not to have been more seedy. Charles told him
not to worry about it, because . . . he wanted the preacher to be sen-
suous, so that he would make his evil more convincing—in the sense
that people would, quite naturally, have been taken in by him."

Hilyard Brown

I don't know if it was Stanley or me who came up with the idea, but
we thought the whole picnic scene should look like a painting by Seu-

"People who sell God, Davis, must be sexy." Illustrating Laughton's dictum, Preacher courts Willa at the picnic.

rat, the French impressionist: *La Grande Jatte.* That's why Mitchum and everybody is sort of stiff and standing up straight.

Just to dot the i, as it were, in terms of pointillist Seurat, an umbrella is seen stuck into the riverbank in the background.

Stanley Cortez
This basically was Charles' thinking. I loved the idea, and I think it came across very well. Had we done it in color, the association with the color painting could have been all that much stronger.

Nearby, Icey is still working on Willa, finally convincing—nay, forcing—her to ask Preacher about Ben's hidden money, which Willa fears may be a factor in the courtship. Icey orchestrates a *tête-à-tête* for Willa and Preacher by the riverbank. "Now Shelley," says Laughton as Winters and Varden commence their dialogue, "Angelic and all that stuff . . ." After a couple of repeats, when Laughton is satisfied that Winters has reached the right emotional peak, he urgently interrupts the two actresses: "All right, now start the scene again, and don't ever get up from that high note. Come on. Unnh! To bed! Weddings! Beds! Fresh sheets! Come on, start again!" Later, to cue Willa's walk towards Preacher, Laughton says to Winters, "All right, your mind's already on the baby shower. Go!"

Preacher tells Willa that Ben told him he'd thrown the money into the river. Greatly relieved, Willa declares, "I feel clean now. My whole body's just a-quiverin' with cleanness"; an unfortunate line which never fails to get an unintended laugh in theaters. Icey, however, is triumphant.

Davis Grubb

And Don Beddoe, he was fine. God bless him. Evelyn Varden is almost my favorite person in the whole film. I didn't know then, I found out later, that she was the original Ma Gibbs in Jed Harris' stage production of *Our Town*. I thought she was perfect as Icey Spoon. She put things into that characterization which she should have gotten *extra* for. She should have been made a member of the corporation. Because, she got across the very subtle way of middle-aged women who are promoting the marriage of a younger woman to an attractive male, they are themselves very sexually excited by the whole thing. It's a sixty-year-old *yenta*'s way of getting off. The way she'd look at Preacher, practically licking her lips. She did more with a little sigh . . .

Don Beddoe

As for *Hunter,* I didn't read the novel, just the script. Because, it wasn't that big a part, you know, Mr. Spoon. Icey Spoon's was a bigger part. She was very good in it, Evelyn Varden, she was a very good character actress. Excellent, she was excellent. And I was kind of a mousy little individual in the picture, obviously henpecked, and the only time he showed any spunk was in the big riot scene at the end, you know, when he led the whole gang of 'em.

Paul Gregory

He and Evelyn were absolutely marvelous together, you'd believe they were married always. They added a lot of much-needed humor, especially to the picnic scene.

"You'd believe they were married always." Evelyn Varden and Don Beddoe as Icey and Walt Spoon.

A prime example of the Spoons' humorous contributions cited by Paul Gregory occurs when Icey addresses the other picnickers on the topic of Willa, while Walt is munching on a piece of chicken:

> ICEY: She's moonin' about Ben Harper. That wasn't love, that was just flapdoodle. (*Agreeing nods and murmurs*) Have some fudge, lambs. (*She hands some down to John and Pearl*) . . . When you've been married to a man forty years, you know all that don't amount to a hill o' beans! I been married to my Walt that long, and I swear in all that time I'd just lie there thinking about my canning.

Laughton cues Varden on that speech by saying, "Men are disgusting, except for Mitchum. Go ahead, Evelyn." The script specifies, "In BACK-GROUND WALT looks sheepish." In the film, Walt is not in the background, he's off to the side, so he gets his own separate shot. Laughton shot footage of Beddoe improvising some amusingly sheepish expressions during Icey's revealing remarks, but, judiciously, all he kept of it was Beddoe's gesture in response to Icey's last line about "canning." The film cuts to the angle on Beddoe: he registers deep embarrassment by immediately putting down his piece of chicken, a reaction which always earns an *intended* laugh in the movie theater. (Unfortunately for the film's continuity, in the very next shot Beddoe is once again seen munching away on his chicken.)

Don Beddoe

Frankly, I don't remember that business with the chicken, so I can't tell you if it was my idea or Laughton's. But he definitely made suggestions to us as we went along. He'd say, "Well, I don't know, what d'you think—maybe so-and-so would be good there?" And of course, it *would* be good! 'Cause, he knew what he was doing about acting.

"A woman's a *fool* to marry for that. That's something for a *man*," adds Icey, in a brief speech which concludes with, "It's all just a fake and a pipe-dream," and which Varden punctuates with a priceless look of wistfulness which belies her commentary. This look also earns a laugh in theaters. Preparing Varden for a second take, Laughton counsels, "Start again. Quietly, darling, calm yourself down. This is your philosophy of life." Varden laughs quietly into the camera: "I'll never get calm if you keep talking to me . . ."

Stanley Cortez

At the end of that scene, which we shot at Rowland V. Lee's ranch, Mitchum adjusts the boy's tie; the little boy is looking up at Mitchum, and half of Mitchum's face is in darkest shadow, even though he's standing there in brightest sunlight. Very few in the audience would notice that shadow on a conscious level, or recognize it as an evil something, but those blacks and shadows impress themselves onto an audience's subconscious mind. Subconsciously, they're infected as well as affected by it—the shadow is with this evil man all the time.

Adding even more to this shot's impact is the fact that it serves a double purpose. Thanks to deep focus, while the shadowed face of Preacher fills most of the foreground, Willa can be seen hugging Icey with jubilation in the background. Over this dynamic imagery we start to hear a banjo tuning up, as the scene dissolves to a nighttime exterior at Uncle Birdie's wharf boat. Young John is examining his father's skiff, which Birdie has been repairing, while the old man accompanies himself in a song about the big boats who heave a sigh: "They blow for Uncle Birdie and the times that ere gone by." The *Hunter* press book claims that Gleason wrote the pseudo river ditty himself, and also played his own accompaniment, but the official credit sheet attributes the song to Schumann (music) and Grubb (lyrics). In the scene's out-takes, however, it does appear that Gleason is playing his own banjo, and singing the song live, not lip-syncing a playback.

Also performing live are the actual crickets which can be heard as we follow John from Birdie's place, past Spoon's, where he observes Icey and Willa in a dance of celebration, and on to his own house. (The Rowland V. Lee ranch was blessed with many rich sounds of nature which we hear in the film. Unfortunately, the location was also on many airplanes' flight path, which must have made for problems in the postproduction sound-editing process.)

Robert Mitchum

I didn't have any problems with the children. But Charles did. The little girl was living with her grandparents from Oklahoma. The grandfather was a very large guy in bib overalls, and the grandmother was equally large. Charles would be sitting there with the script, his glasses down on his nose, trying to figure out where the hell he was. The grandfather would come in and say to the little girl, "Sing your French song, honey. Come on, sing your French song." She'd sing (*mimics her tiny voice, the song from* South Pacific): "Dites-moi, pourquoi . . ." Charles would clutch his gut. Then she'd come over and sit on my lap and kiss me, and Charles would go, "Unhhhhh!"

One time, I was waiting in that narrow hallway, when the boy comes in and says, "Mom?" up the stairs, you know, "is anybody home?" And then the Preacher suddenly steps out of the shadow and says, "John." So I asked Billy, I said, "Do you think that John is afraid of the Preacher?" And he said, "Not at all." So I said, "Well, you don't know much about

John, then, and you *certainly* don't know too much about the Preacher."
He said, "Really? That's possibly why I won the Critics' Award for *Three
Wishes for Jamie.*" Charles let out a scream: "Oh!!!"—then he ran off the
set. When the kid said that, it was too much for him.

No, the boy wasn't a stage brat, but I guess somebody had made him
aware of the fact that this was Charles's first picture, and, you know,
"After all, you have the laurels." Obviously, he wasn't the boy that
Charles wanted him to be. He was an actor. Charles had to accept that
deliberate delivery. The boy's performance was a little slow to come.
There were no big problems, but that one incident just outraged Charles.

Must it be said, in young Chapin's defense, that Mr. Mitchum was
never one to avoid exaggeration or invention if it would make for a
good story? In any case, even if the dialogue between Mitchum and his
young colleague was quoted verbatim, my own inclination would be to
regard Billy's response in a kindly light. I know that if I were ten years
old, and if big Bob were pulling rank on me, I'd certainly resort to anything in my meager arsenal to defend myself, and if I'd won an award
you can be sure I'd mention it. And, for all we know, Laughton's out-
size reaction, if it was as Mitchum describes it, might have been done
deliberately for humorous effect.

Ms. Gould's report for the *New York Times* missed the Mitchum/Chapin
confrontation, but it did relate the shooting of that scene in the hallway,
specifically an episode involving Mitchum and Laughton with Billy
Chapin and his mother. In certain out-takes, a woman's voice can occasionally be heard contributing to the coaching of the children; presumably,
this voice belongs to Mrs. Chapin. In this sequence, when Preacher confronts John and tells the boy about his upcoming marriage to Willa, the
boy almost blurts out the secret entrusted by his father—"You think you
can make me tell, but I won't, I won't, I won't!"—then catches himself.
Laughton directed Billy Chapin to portray this moment of defiance by
putting the back of his hand to his forehead. "Later," writes Gould, "he
(Laughton) asked the boy's mother, 'Would a child make a gesture like
that?' 'No, he wouldn't,' Mrs. Chapin answered. Viewing the rushes that
night, Mr. Laughton voluntarily agreed: 'I was so wrong! We'll reshoot it.'"
Viewing those same rushes today, we can see in the two-shot of Mitchum

The game begins. But when Laughton gave Billy Chapin the wrong gesture—hand to forehead—he re-shot the scene with the right one: hand over mouth.

and Chapin that Laughton had the boy do the hand-to-forehead gesture over his line, and then immediately regret what he's blurted out and cover his mouth with his hand. The first takes of this scene were shot on August 19, when the film had only been in production a few days and Laughton was still getting a feel for working with the children. Hence, no doubt, his solicitation of Mrs. Chapin's input. He viewed the rushes the next day, and then, the day after that, on the twenty-first, he shot the close-up of Billy Chapin which appears in the film, with the hand-to-mouth gesture but without the awkward hand-to-brow bit.

Laughton must have felt this moment was important enough to reshoot in order to make it right, because *this* is now the beat where the director makes it clear that the game has begun between Preacher and John. "Tell me what, boy?" the man asks, and the boy answers, "Nothin'." To which, Preacher asks, "We're not keeping *secrets* from each other, are we little lad?" And this time, unlike the similar-but-down-played moment in Spoon's parlor, Mitchum is in close-up. As he says that line, there appears in his eyes what can only be described as a wicked gleam. (Interestingly, this reverse-angle shot on Mitchum wasn't filmed until five days later, on August 26. While it is not unusual for scenes in

"We're not keeping secrets from each other, are we, little lad?" Preacher tries to intimidate John—and Mitchum, between takes, tries to pull rank on Billy Chapin. John stands his ground—and so does Billy.

a movie to be filmed out of sequence, many scenes in *Hunter* were filmed piece-meal with their various component shots and angles often separated by many days of working on totally unrelated scenes.)

Stanley Cortez

Another kind of lighting came into play with that night scene, where little John comes home and finds Preacher in that narrow, dark hallway. Preacher tells the boy that he's going to marry his mother, and when the little boy slips up and starts to mention the hidden money, Preacher's eyes widen, he hopes he's going to hear where the money is. When Mitchum opens his eyes a little that way, they catch a little flash of light. I was hoping to get that glint, because I felt, dramatically, it would be a plus value to have Mitchum's eyes light up with greed. To get a light to be reflected in the eyes like that, it was a question of angle. Sometimes you're lucky, and sometimes you're unlucky. In that case, I was lucky.

In *The Magnificent Ambersons,* there's a sequence where Delores Costello walks through a big, dark room, reading a letter from her son, and you hear his words on the soundtrack. In her eyes I made sure that you saw two strong highlights. The gleam in the eyes played a very important part in that one scene because it is those two penetrating beads of light that impresses the audience that they're seeing inside those eyes into the brain. This is a highly dramatic concept which unfortunately is not being used too often. In many cases, the opportunity is there, but for some reason they aren't taken advantage of. But you can do so much with so little that it's amazing we don't do it more often.

Take our sets, for example. Some of our sets were little more than a wall, but they were very effective. That was strictly Hilly Brown.

Hilyard Brown

The film was always planned from the start to be black and white. The preliminary sketches were in watercolor, but you make sketches for actors and other people to look at. As a matter of fact, we often design and build sets and put in a lot more detail than what's necessary for the camera to see, but we build them for the actors and for the director. Of course, sometimes we don't. We did a lot of things in *Citizen Kane*—Kane's castle, for example—which were only for the camera, and on the stage they'd just look terrible, there was nothing there. Remember where Kane has filled his castle with all these millions of boxes of European statuary and everything? That set consisted of a full stage at RKO with a black velvet drape hanging around it, the boxes, a front door, a fireplace, and a set of stairs, and that's all there was to the castle. Most people don't realize that's all that was there—they say, "Oh, no, you had a whole castle there,"—but that's all they saw, because that's all that was there: the front door, the fireplace and the stairway.

In *Night of the Hunter,* there was absolutely no set for the burlesque house, and no set for the revival meeting. For the honeymoon hotel room, all we had was a door, a bed, a picture of an old general, a light bulb hanging down and a window with a shade.

The honeymoon sequence begins, in a sense, with the last moments of the Preacher/John hallway scene, because as the boy runs up the stairs Schumann's underscore for the wedding and honeymoon kicks in. The score continues under a brief scene of the children and the Spoons wav-

From the Davis Grubb novel:

*Get out of bed, Willa! He
commanded, but with a dangerous edge of anger still in his
voice, while with one arm he
pulled the window blind clear to
the sill. Now he moved across the
room, his dry naked feet whispering on the boards, and snapped
the light on. It flooded the room
with its uncharitable yellow glare
and a faint singing commenced
in the golden bulb.*

Get out of bed, Willa!

ing goodbye to Ben's old car—an economical script device eliminating
the need for Mitchum or Winters' pricey presence—and settles in to its
main tempo at the beginning of the next scene, which finds Willa in the
bathroom just off the bedroom, in her nightgown, preparing herself before the cabinet mirror. This is the most extended scene Mitchum and
Winters shared together, and also the most intense. What's more, even al-
lowing for the absence of nudity contained in the novel, this was a very
strong scene to be filmed in mid-fifties Hollywood. For Willa, this is a
scene of pivotal transition, in which, literally overnight, Preacher breaks
her spirit and transforms her into his docile slave. Laughton directs the sequence with all the hands-on attention to detail it demands, interrupting
his actors more often than usual in his quest for just the right emotion,
precisely the right note. Sometimes, Laughton got two or three short
scenes in the can during one day's shooting. The honeymoon sequence,
including Willa's bathroom preparation, took two days to shoot.

Naturally, Willa is expecting a romantic evening. The scene starts quietly enough but soon leads to Preacher's harangue against the sins of the
flesh, which stabs her to her very core. Her director, in this scene only,
parallels Preacher's theatre of cruelty, beginning on a calm, peaceful plane,
then escalating to the most cutting, shaming remarks in an attempt to
evoke from her the needed response of devastation. Although Preacher

Grubb's sketch for Laughton is re-enacted by Mitchum and Winters.

was, of course, a tremendous stretch for Mitchum, Miss Winters has in a sense a more challenging role. Preacher is always Preacher, immutable from first to last, whereas Willa, in her much briefer screen time, runs through a gamut—a gauntlet—of wrenching emotional reactions and transitions, and each must be made convincing as well as heartbreaking.

Standing before the bathroom mirror, Miss Winters is told by Laughton, speaking in tones of soft, calm deliberation, "Relax your shoulders, Shelley, before you start, will you please . . . Close your eyes . . . Now start, please."

Willa primps bashfully but expectantly, subtly but suggestively touching herself as her hands drift down from her throat; then as she opens the bedroom door, on which Preacher has hung his coat, she hears a sound when the coat slaps the door. Willa discovers Harry's switchblade in a pocket, but she is in no way concerned. "Men," she smiles to herself, as she puts it back in the pocket, then smooths the coat's rucked collar before moving on toward Preacher in the bed. With the camera, as usual, still rolling, Laughton himself steps into the shot to make the collar crooked again for another take. Strictly speaking, this is a Hollywood union no-no, the director handling a costume or prop instead of the designated crew member. But in the family atmosphere on this set, no one raises a peep against father figure Laughton.

"Men," says Shelley once more.

"Do it again, please," says Laughton, "Too fussy."

"Men."

Preacher is lying with his back to Willa, who tiptoes toward him with a look of anticipation. Laughton, making clear her desire and intention, instructs Shelley to show us "children in your eyes, darling." The first hint of cross-purposes comes when Preacher seemingly offers his hand, she reaches for it, but he merely points: "Fix that window shade." The line comes from the novel, but the business with the hands is a brilliant bit cooked up for the movie. Soon enough, Preacher announces that he was praying—and that he has no intention of "pawing" Willa "in that abominable way that men are supposed to do on their wedding night." Laughton cues Shelley's shocked reaction: "It's dizzy."

"Ohhhhhhhh . . ." She collapses on her pillow.

As this master shot continues, Preacher lights the overhead bulb and commands Willa to look at herself in the full-length bedroom mirror, all the while speaking of the sins of the flesh and ranting that the business of this marriage is to take care of her two children, not to beget more. At the scene's conclusion, Laughton is heard beaming, "One hundred percent. Lovely. Cut it."

Next, Laughton shoots the closer angles on Mitchum, with the director himself portraying Willa off-camera, and interjecting between takes, "I think that first speech was a little on the slow side, Mitch . . ." Then, the camera closes in on Shelley, with Laughton throwing her direction, delivering Mitchum's lines, and sometimes improvising even more cruel variants of them. The actor emphasizes Preacher's authoritarian stance, whereas the director hits heavily on the man's disgust. Compare Mitchum's original, "You thought, Willa, that the moment you walked in that door I'd start to pawing you in that abominable way that men are supposed to do on their wedding night . . . I think it's time we made one thing perfectly clear, Willa. Marriage to me represents a blending of two spirits in the sight of Heaven," with Laughton's, "You thought, Willa, the moment you walked in that door I'd start in to *pawing* you, and *feeling* you, in the abominable way that men are supposed

to do on their wedding nights. I think it's time we got one thing perfectly clear, Willa. Marriage to me represents *not* pawing people a'tall,
it's just two *spirits* in the sight of God, I wouldn't *touch* you!" Through
all of this, the pain is palpable on Shelley's face. So—"Cut and print."

More fine-tuning as Mitchum and Winters grapple together over the
scene. "You're wide-eyed because you want to please him, no more . . .
Face up to him, sweet, easy timing." "Get up, Willa," Harry commands.
The response, "Harry, what . . .?" is only Shelley's first line, but
Laughton immediately interrupts, "Will you start again, please, and not
make that 'Harry, what?' high-pitched. Simple question. Okay."

"Get up, Willa."

"Harry, what . . .?"

Laughton: "Do it again, please, and ask him right away."

The scene is continued to Laughton's satisfaction, and then again.
And still again. Laughton announces to his crew, "Now, turn the lights
off if you can, boys, and run this right through again." Shelley visibly
stays in character while the lighting is set up again, then Laughton tells
his actors, "Okay, kids." And after this take, Laughton says quietly, "For
God's sake cut it, that was terrible."

At one point in this grueling process, Laughton sounds very frustrated with Miss Winters, though one wonders if this attitude—which
is nowhere else evident in his direction of any of her other scenes—
might be in part a deliberate strategy to make her feel as belittled as
Willa is supposed to feel. She is sniffling. "Shelley, put your head up."
(Pause). "Knock off it." (Pause). "Oh, *Christ.*" (Pause.) "Now, then.
Keep your goddamn mouth closed. There, now. All right, Mitch." And
then Mitchum launches into his lines, inevitably perhaps slipping on
one of them: "the body of a woman, which man since Adam has profaned" comes out in the crude Southern vernacular: "The body of a
woman, which man since Adam has poontanged."

Apparently Shelley wanted to do more with a moment than
Laughton felt was called for or, perhaps, she wished to execute a
Method preparation for the take. Laughton was no fan of the Method.
He once declared, "A Method actor gives you a photograph; a real actor
gives you an oil painting." But, he let her get it out of her system, telling
her with a frustrated sigh, "Oh—! Well, if you want to scream, scream!"

She lets out with a good, loud shriek, and then Laughton quickly jumps in, "Now, hang your head! Go on, Mitch!" At the end of this take, Laughton pronounces it, "Just wonderful."

Then he asks for another. His instruction to his male star: "A little more lyric, Mitch. And, uh, not quite so heavy on the outside. We want your own deep hatred of it, your own personal dislike of this . . . crap." After Mitchum does the tirade again, Laughton says, "Try it again, Bob, for your own satisfaction. Very good, though."

"*Look* at yourself!"

"No, no, Mitch, this was a little bit too hard. More on the 'yourself.'"

At last the scene's final beat is shot, with Willa's prayer in close-up: "Help me to get clean—so I can be what Harry wants me to be." Laughton's hushed cue to Shelley: "Whisper in the night to the stars."

Even though he had had no prior collaboration with his various cast-members—save for his teacher-student relationship with Shelley Winters—Laughton quickly established a warm connection with thespians of all ages and genders on the *Hunter* set. If anyone knew the value to a film-maker of a happy, relaxed cast it was, ironically, Charles Laughton, whose rampant insecurities had proven the despair and torment of many a director and producer. No matter how quick Laughton could be to put an actor at his ease, however, there was no guarantee that every actor would be at ease with each other.

Robert Mitchum

Acting with Shelley was . . . Well, you know Shelley. She needs reassurance all the time. She'd say, "Can I have just one vodka before I—" "No, you can't!" Charles would say, "Get in there, you cunt!" Did she give me enough to react off of in the scenes? Well, I could appreciate the Preacher's problem, really.

Apparently the scream with which Winters had tried her director's patience during the shooting of the wedding night was not an isolated phenomenon. As Mitchum's lifelong personal assistant, Reva Frederick, related to biographer Lee Server, "Shelley was such a good actress, but sometimes she would have little screaming jeebies over something and Robert used to not be tolerant of that kind of attitude." Neither, as it happened, was her teacher-mentor-and-now-director Laughton. Ms. Frederick recalled an incident in which Miss Winters was "making a scene" over a perceived wardrobe problem: "And Charles just walked over to her and slapped her across the face. He said, 'Stop it!' And we were all like, 'God, did I just see what I saw?' And Shelley just blinked and snapped to and went back to the work."

Never mind that on *Hunter*'s tightly budgeted schedule there was no time for off-camera histrionics. Never mind that Laughton and Miss Winters were by this point in their lives like family to each other. (After all, had they been real father and daughter, the slap would have been just as troubling.) And never mind that this was apparently a one-time-only incident of its kind. Can there ever really be justification for a lapse like that between a director and his actor? If Laughton's action here was unheard-of, it was not, apparently, unforgivable where Miss Winters was concerned. In the span of two whole autobiographies, she never mentions the moment, and in her public utterances on Laughton she has always had nothing but kind words, i.e., "When he says 'How are you,' he really wants to know." (She once chased Paul Gregory from her dressing room when he made what she felt to be a petty remark about Laughton.) It is interesting to note, in light of the screaming/slapping incident, a letter sent by Paul Gregory to Arthur Krim at United Artists early in October, while *Hunter* was still being shot but after Miss Winters had discharged her obligations to the company. Apparently written and sent as a favor to his actress, Gregory's letter extolling her professionalism arouses speculation as to the degree it may or may not stretch the truth, and whether it was penned entirely of his own volition: "Charles and I were pleased beyond all expectations with Shelley Winters. She was cooperative and helpful whenever possible. Bob Mitchum told Charles Laughton that she was just about the greatest he had ever worked with. Shelley is a seeker after perfection and so far as we are concerned she did a perfect job for us . . . Shelley is a great talent and she should not be made to suffer from some of the loose remarks that have been passed around by some rather no talent people."

Miss Winters later admitted to Miss Lanchester's researchers that "(Laughton) got angry when Shelley was lazy, and the only time he really frightened her was when he was quiet . . . He got furious once

"Bob Mitchum told Charles Laughton that she was just about the greatest he had ever worked with." Paul Gregory's co-stars appear to be rapport personified in this candid shot.

when the camera-man said to her and Mitchum, 'Speak up.' Charles demanded that he be given the authority, but he never used it with arrogance or lack of taste."

Robert Golden

The only sequence that I cut during shooting, without Laughton being there, was a sequence they were worried about from a censorship standpoint. It was the night of the honeymoon. It has a man and a woman about to get into bed, and, of course, it's a pretty cruel scene, too. They wanted to show it to the censors, so I was allowed to go out and cut that sequence by myself. It's very difficult in this day and age to go back and realize some of the various censorship problems that existed. But, they accepted the scene as it was put together.

Oddly, the scene which most evinces fear of the censor's shears is not the powerhouse honeymoon sequence but the quiet scene immediately following it, in which John and Uncle Birdie sit in the skiff, fishing. (In the script, this scene was supposed to occur two sequences later, but Laughton re-inserted it here, perhaps to better convey a passage of time since the honeymoon.) Birdie, tying his line, informs John that "A horsehair will hold a lumpin' whale," then asks the boy if he minds him cussing, now that his stepfather is a preacher. Obviously, Birdie hasn't "cussed" at all, but that was as close as rough language could be approximated on screen in those days.

Davis Grubb

I know that they couldn't have in a movie the kind of language Birdie used in the book. Still, somebody should have worked with Agee a little more on that "cussing." Because, I knew an Uncle Dick McFadden who ran the livery stable in Moundsville and he had preserved this art of swearing. We could have whipped up something that wouldn't have been so weak but still would have passed the censors.

The brag went back to Mike Fink and those rascals who, as they were delineated in Mark Twain, would get out, click their heels in the air and say, "I'm half alligator and half man!" And then they would launch on a tirade very much like those of the poor, beautiful beggar girls in the streets of Dublin that Sean O'Casey writes about in, I think, the second volume of his autobiography. That's the way the old river fighters used to fight. They'd stand for half an hour and say what they were going to do to each other, before they ever let loose a blow.

And then they would generally come with the deadliest weapon, I think, on the frontier, which was a man's forehead. I heard of a man who ran a hotel in Hunter, West Virginia, and, to the amusement of the drummers—the salesmen—who used to congregate in the lobby at night, used to send for this guy who would, for as much money as he could get out of a drummer, give him permission to hit him in the face as hard as he could with his fist. You know, a guy with a couple of shots of Green River or Mule Whiskey in him would love to take a swing at something. The trick was, this man was like a rattlesnake. You'd swing at his nose as hard as you could, but you always got him in the forehead, and he had a skull about an inch thick. And then they'd take the poor drummer to the local doctor and patch up a broken fist. The guys actually broke their fists on this man's head, and that was a pure branch right out of the frontier humor.

But the art of profanity goes back to a time when a word was a weapon. And I think there existed in human history words which would have the power to kill. I really believe that. I think the taboo we have on certain profane words is a fear of the original, great magic power of words. You see, I'm a very literal person about mythology. I think when Christ said that with faith a man could move mountains he literally meant that at one time, or perhaps in the future—or even now—enough spiritual power could move matter. I've written stories like "The Horsehair Trunk" based on that supposition.

One of the revelations provided by a review of the *Hunter* out-takes is the fact that James Gleason was Gregory and Laughton's *second* Uncle Birdie. Footage exists of Billy Chapin playing opposite another, much less-known character actor, portraying a very bewhiskered Birdie in the gar-fishing scene. Why did the production start with one Birdie and end up with another? As his friend Bill Phipps explains, apparently this was one instance when Laughton might have wished he *had* asked his actor to read for the role at the casting session.

William Phipps
That actor's name was Emmett Lynn. I used to see Emmett Lynn a lot in a restaurant near Republic Studios; I did quite a bit of work there, westerns. And he was always drinking a lot, and he was a character. He was flamboyant, he wanted everybody to see him; he felt that he was a real "old-codger" type, but he was kind of a pain in the ass. To look at him, he looked good for the part of Uncle Birdie. And I think that's probably why they gave him the part. He probably sold himself in an interview, he was probably "on." But he was just not a good Uncle Birdie. I remember Laughton, after seeing the rushes, being disappointed, saying, "This'll never do. This man is just a stereotype. He's just playing the character and not playing the scenes, he's not being the man in the situation." He was hammy, he was "indicating" all over the place—if you're familiar with that term in acting—instead of simply *being*. Basically, he was a caricature instead of the character. He just couldn't hack

it. I remember, he was *gone*, almost immediately. So they had to replace him with James Gleason, who of course gave them the true character.

What Laughton was hoping to find in the character is indicated by his direction of Lynn in the September 4 out-takes of the gar-fishing scene. Not having seen it on the first three takes, Laughton can be heard counseling Lynn, "If you can inhabit the world of the little boy, you'll come off a thousand percent. You've got to live in the world of the little boy." After the first few lines are repeated a couple of times, Laughton feels the need to reiterate, "Just a little bit more of the little boy's world from you, Emmett. Remember. Go ahead . . ." Apparently the day went by without Laughton ever seeing or hearing what he had hoped for in Uncle Birdie. Four days later, on September 8, Laughton put Emmett and Billy back in the boat and started all over again on the same dialogue. If, as Bill Phipps remembers, Lynn had been too much of a ham, Laughton apparently saw no good in printing those first, overdone takes. What we see in the takes that Laughton did print is an actor so subdued that his delivery is three times slower than it probably needs to be. Did Laughton, in trying to rein in the ham, unwittingly swing his actor's aesthetic pendulum too far in the opposite direction? Perhaps Lynn, who must have felt insecure to be refilming his scene, was simply too nervous to find the middle ground between funny and funereal. Laughton was obviously aware of the problem, because he can be heard on this second day's attempt, just before Take Eight, cautioning Lynn, "I don't want to take the fun out of you. You're doing it very quietly, and it's gone very well. But don't take the fun out of you." There's a touching sincerity, almost a feebleness, in Lynn's folksy pledge of friendship to little John: "If ever you need help you just holler out and come a-runnin.'" But the playful spark of life, the essence of Birdie, is missing.

Three weeks later, on September 29, the scene was filmed for the third time—with James Gleason playing the old riverboat man. The camera setups and artistic Cortez lighting were exactly as before. (The scene, begun at the Lee ranch, continued shooting the next day on the soundstage with rear-projection footage.) In the film, the scene ends with Birdie landing the gar and pummeling it with his oar. Additional dialogue was shot, but Laughton and Bob Golden wisely dropped it in

The better Birdie: Last-minute replacement James Gleason charms Billy Chapin while discussing the sneaky, no-account gar—and Preacher.

the cutting room, as it merely repeats and reinforces Birdie's promise to help John if his aid is ever needed.

Not long after Willa's fateful wedding night, she has attempted to make herself over in the image of piety she thinks will please her new husband. We see Preacher urging her on as she fervently testifies to the believers at a revival meeting. As mentioned above, in the original script this was the scene immediately following the honeymoon. But Laughton must have decided—presumably in the editing process—that this made Willa's transformation too abrupt; hence, he reshuffled scenes so that the fishing sequence would precede the camp meeting. Laughton, as we have seen, took to heart Davis Grubb's pre-production admonitions regarding the Ben/Willa/Preacher triad of sensuality vs. spirituality, and it is nowhere more in evidence than here. "I might as well tell you now," Grubb wrote to his director, "that the revival meeting was held in a little tent and *not* a church. No flowers please. No organ, either. An upright piano—twangy and out of tune . . . This is a country revival meeting—not like the Jagger affair you speak of. This is the difference between a plain country-town whore-house and a fancy Brentwood brothel. The difference, if you please, between Preacher and Billy Graham or Aimee Semple MacPherson. Torch lights. Lanterns on the wagons. Headlights from the cars. Sawdust. Chairs from the local funeral parlor. A big banner with crude letters—JESUS SAVES! Folks bringing produce when they can't afford to put money in the hat. But I'll make you pictures of what I mean." Laughton and art director Brown drew from these details the barest minimum required to convey the scene: the tent and the torches. Convinced by a conniving Preacher that Ben Harper had thrown the stolen $10,000 into the river, Willa regales the makeshift congregation in a torchlit tent with the tale of her husband's tragic crime, culminating in his redemption "when the Lord stepped in."

In the out-takes of the sermon sequence, Miss Winters can be seen concentrating deeply as she prepares for Take One of her close-up. "Now Shelley, before you begin," says Laughton softly to his star, "Just do a prayer, quite high, any kind of a prayer that you know." Then, he raises his voice, "Now! Loud!" Miss winters takes a breath, and then rapidly intones, "*Shmah Ysroyel ahdenoy el o hay nu ahdenoy emhot*"—the Hebrew invocation to prayer, (translated as "Hear, Oh Israel, the Lord our God, The Lord is One"). Mitchum and the congregation add a couple of "Amens"s, then Shelley launches right into Willa's spiel: "You have all sinned!" etc. Her rendition initially verges on the hysterical, so before she is halfway through, Laughton says, "I'm going to stop you here . . ." In subsequent takes, Shelley's private prelude-prayers are more in character for Willa, being from the Twenty-Third Psalm—". . .the valley of the shadow of death, I will fear no evil, for thou art with me . . ."—and her delivery is still emotional, but now more modulated.

Laughton's instructions to the extras for their reaction shots and amens are direct and to the point. "Come on, now. Wild eyes . . . Wild as hell. This is a substitution for . . ." Mitchum, simpatico as ever, helpfully supplies *le mot juste*: "Poontang." Laughton agrees: "Poontang. All right."

All of this is necessary to build up to another one of *Hunter*'s powerfully ironic scene transitions. Whipping herself and her flock into a spiritual frenzy, (with Preacher's shouted encouragements), Willa leads them in a call-and-response:

(Revival)# 4

Willa - Yes! The Devil told the poor weak man that all
that money would just drive his wife to hell headlong HEADLONG!

Willa at Preacher's revival meeting—one of several sketches of this scene Grubb executed at Laughton's request.

WILLA: He said, the Lord to that man, you take that money and
    you throw it in the River!
PREACHER: In the River!
CONGREGATION: IN THE RIV-ER!

Laughton is meticulous in orchestrating the mounting fervor of the con-
gregants: "I want to hear that word, 'River.' Wait 'til I've said it twice, and
then I want to hear that word. Let me conduct you with me." The extras
give it all they've got, so much so that one of the women ends up cough-
ing, but not before Laughton has called "Cut" on a satisfactory take.

Now, thanks to a quick dissolve to Willa's backyard, we are finally let
in on John and Pearl's secret: The money is hidden inside her doll, "Miss
Jenny." Pearl has opened up little Miss Jenny and is cutting a couple of
bills into paper dolls representing herself and her brother. By this point,
most viewers are too absorbed in *Hunter*'s compelling narrative to notice that the cut-up currency comprises not American dollars but Mex-
ican pesos. The *Hunter* press book claims that American bills would have
been less photogenic—and, more to the point, illegal to photograph or
mutilate as the scene required. For many years, a law prevented film-

Sally Jane Bruce, Billy Chapin and Robert Mitchum in the scene which always makes audiences gasp.

makers from photographing real American currency in a scene—for fear of counterfeiting—so some substitute was always used. Several yards behind Pearl is the back porch of the house. John comes upon his little sister, is shocked to discover the bills strewn all about, and hurriedly starts to stuff the money back inside the doll.

The sight of Preacher appearing in the back porch doorway at this moment never fails to make a theater audience gasp. What further twists the screw from that moment on—while the children frantically stuff the bills back into the doll and Preacher opens the door, slowly approaching the kids—is that Laughton *holds the shot*. In real time, in one continuous take, the action unfolds until, the very second before Preacher reaches them, the children manage to hide the money. The script originally called for nine separate shots. But if this scene creates for an audience tension and suspense on the screen, it also offered the same qualities to the film-makers on the set:

Robert Golden

Hilyard always made those camera sketches the night before, and Laughton and everybody there knew pretty much what he was going to do, but you can't make a picture that way without every once in a while certain things not having been prepared for. I remember one scene, on the rather large backyard set. The little girl is taking the money out of the doll and making paper dolls out of it, the little boy comes out and sees her and says, "Pearl, my gosh, what are you doing?" They start packing the money back into the doll when Mitchum arrives out on the porch and says, "What are you doing out there?"

Now, Laughton was shooting the sequence and he'd got certain parts of it done, and there comes a crucial moment for which there was no sketch. He yelled out, "Bob Golden!" like Captain Bligh yelling "Mr. Christian!" I came over and said, "Yes, sir?" and he said, "What the hell do I do now?!"

The particular problem was, as Mitchum is standing against the steps and calls the children to him, how are the children going to get past him without his seeing the two paper dolls that are still lying on the ground and blow past him? Well, I didn't know, it wasn't in the sketch, so how the hell would I know? But, for some reason or other, I thought of the following. I said, "Why not have the camera take the place of the children as they're coming to Mitchum and the paper dolls blow past his feet?" Charles said, "You can't do that." I said, "Why did you ask me?"

In point of fact, the script does call for a "MOVING SHOT — PREACHER — JOHN'S VIEWPOINT," but Laughton was possibly nervous about whether such a subjective shot would work in this part of the scene.

Robert Golden

But Laughton didn't know what else to do. He was dependent on us for the mechanical aspects of shooting a picture, and there was nobody else there to say "You can't do that." So he shot it. Now, here we are today, and it's done all the time, using the camera in place of the individual, for a subjective point of view. But evidently, it hadn't been done much up to that time. Actually, when he said, "You can't do that," I didn't know whether you could or not.

Remember, I wasn't allowed to go into the cutting room. But, before the next day's rushes, I went there and cut the slates off of two of the three scenes that would have to go together, and made one scene out of them. I put the two scenes that had to go together, using this dolly shot as a bridge between them, and made one scene out of them to find out if it worked. A fellow who, at the time, was the head of the American Cinema Editors, was working as a cutter at the same studio. He said, "What are you doing?" I explained it to him, and he said, "You can't do that." I said, "Well, I'm doing it right now."

The next day, we ran the rushes that way, and Laughton wasn't aware that the slates were taken off these scenes to make one scene. So I found out it worked. Laughton never knew that I had done it, until Milt Carter said, "You smart son of a bitch!" He noticed it, you see.

Now, as I say, that kind of shot is done all the time. Remember that great line from *Patton,* "Glory is a fleeting thing?" Nobody knew you could do that shot, and after it was done, nobody said, "Look what he did!"

Paul Gregory

The only area that I think could have been improved upon is if the camera-work hadn't been so dark. I feel that the camera-work was too dark in the picture, and I felt it from the day I saw the first rushes, but I was overruled. And so I thought, "Well, I could very well be wrong"; I hadn't made a picture before. But I just felt you had to look too hard at it, and that made it seem less real. It began when the little girl's cutout dolls made from the money were blown past Mitchum's feet. People thought it was leaves blowing the first time it was showed. It wasn't clear, you see, and there are these areas of responsibility that I just think you have to have. I would have liked to have made it a little lighter so that I wouldn't have had to look so hard at it. I mentioned it, and of course Stanley was horrified that I would say such a thing.

Stanley Cortez

I don't remember anybody suggesting that the cinematography was too dark. If it had been lighter, you wouldn't have had any mood.

Paul Gregory

That was the only area where I felt that the unit members didn't all have the same idea. Why did they go in this direction? I felt that they had gone into it and not known it. And Lord knows, we were on such a

budget we couldn't go back and redo anything. They had allowed themselves to get carried away with all of this. You see, there can be *too much*
art direction. If you've ever watched any of my shows, you'll know that
that's where I'm an absolute tyrant, is about art direction, where the guy
wants to win the award for that particular thing and doesn't give a goddamn about the overall. I don't think it ruined the picture. But I think
that a couple of departments got carried away, and Laughton, who was
so busy at moment-to-moment stuff of directing these kids and everything, wasn't quite aware of it.

In the moment-to-moment directing of the paper-doll scene,
Laughton had to handle the final beat, in which Preacher and John
square off in the "game" they're playing. "Your mother says you tattled
on me, boy," says Preacher. "She says you told her that I asked you
where the money was hid. That wasn't very nice of you, John. Have a
heart." (This is the one scene in the film script which makes use of that
catch-phrase Grubb remembered from the clergyman of his childhood
and put into Preacher's mouth more than once in the novel.) Laughton
in the out-takes tells Billy Chapin to respond to Preacher with a "horse
laugh"—but the man has the upper hand on the boy. He has held in re-
serve this zinger: "No matter. It's your word against mine. It's me your
mother believes." These lines originated in the novel but, curiously,
were omitted from the script. (Unless, that is, the *Agee on Film* publisher
left them out inadvertently.) Apparently Laughton, who kept a copy of
the Grubb book on hand throughout shooting, noticed the oversight
and restored this crucial speech on the soundstage. The script does direct the camera to be on John's "helpless reaction." (Emphasizing John's
plight is Schumann's underscore, which commences under Billy's close-
up and continues under the following several sequences, almost without
interruption—all the way, in fact, to Willa's demise.)

The next scene depicts Willa tucking in her son at night, wearily demanding to know, from the depth of her denial, why the boy is not getting along with Preacher. Just as when he directed her to pray before
her speech in the revival scene, Laughton gives Winters a bit of business
that he knows will not appear in the film but that will set the tone for
this sequence: "Now, Shelley, before you start, you heave a great big

sigh." She sighs. He says, "Action." She begins, "Were you impudent to Mr. Powell again, John . . .?" So completely is Willa in Preacher's thrall that she is convinced her son is lying whenever he tries to tell her about Preacher pumping him about the money.

And so, the game continues. Typical is the night when Willa is still working at Spoon's and Preacher has the kids to himself in their bedroom. And typical of Laughton's meticulous direction of Billy Chapin is his handling of the boy here. In trying to get what he wants out of the lad, the director is as relentless as Preacher himself in his endless grilling. "Preacher can chat to you about baseball," says Laughton to Chapin, "and that doesn't fool you at all. And he'll eventually pop the question (*ominously*), "Where's the money hid?"

"I don't know."

"Now, when I ask it, just, much more steady than that. 'I don't know.' You see? Wait a bit now. (*Pause.*) Where's the money hid?"

"I don't know."

"Yes, but a half smile. Where's the money hid? And don't move your head. Half smile."

"I don't know."

"Where's the money hid?"

"I don't know."

"Okay, cut."

In this installment of the game, Preacher tries a divide-and-conquer gambit. Little Pearl adores him, so he cradles her in his lap and, after playful misdirection, suddenly and seriously asks her where the money is. John, who has been listening and suffering with his back turned, wheels around, grabs a brush and throws it at Preacher's head. When it connects, Pearl is not on her brother's side: "You hit Daddy with a hairbrush!" (Since in take after take, the hairbrush, probably thrown by an off-camera Joe La Bella, smacks Mitchum on the noggin, it is obviously a light-weight replica of the real thing.) This is all the provocation Preacher needs to declare his intention to take Pearl down to the parlor, without John—but with Miss Jenny. To John's horror, Pearl scoops up her doll as Preacher carries her out and locks the door behind them.

Laughton reads both Preacher's and Pearl's lines off-stage while the camera is on John and his helpless fright. "Let's do it again, we'll do it again, Billy, from the beginning. You see, the tension—gets higher, and you . . . Do you understand me?"

"Mm."

"Right. We'll start from where we were again . . ."

Laughton continues playing Preacher and Pearl, interrupting the dialogue to quickly interject a direction for Chapin's benefit: "Open your mouth slightly," or, "Now, shake, Billy. Hold your hands to your side. Shiver like you're cold. Real cold. Tighter. Turn around quickly! *Throw it at me!*" And when Pearl reaches for Miss Jenny as Preacher is carrying her out: "Now, Billy—tight! And shaking. And that half-smile . . . And you see her going for the doll on the floor. Now, try and get that! (*He does.*) Now, you went too quickly, go back and do it again. Your body would stop you going that quickly . . ." Later: "Billy, turn back. I just want you to do that quick turn, with your eyes blazing. [*To Cortez*], Is he in the right position? [*To Billy*], No, the brush isn't in, you needn't throw the brush this time. Is he in the right position?"

Crew member: "He should be a little to his right."

"A little to your right, Billy, I *thought* you were a little off . . ."

On this fateful night, a mist has come in from the river to cloak Cresap's landing. While Preacher is isolating little Pearl, her mother is bidding goodnight to the Spoons. She explains her habitual anxiousness to return home: "I'm needed to keep peace and harmony between them. It's my burden and I'm proud of it, Icey!" And with that, clutching her sweater against the cold, she turns and walks away into the fog. This is yet another set without a set, another masterfully simple, almost abstract Cortez composition: the only things visible beside Willa herself are the fog and the light from the street lamps. The script calls for Willa to deliver her last lines "with sweet radiance." That is what Laughton asks for on the set: "Radiant Christian faith. Okay, children." And that is precisely what Shelley gives him. Her make-up, if indeed she's wearing any at all, is totally plain and unglamorous, but if there is a more beautiful close-up of Shelley Winters in any film of the fifties, I have not seen it. She is lit from within. And, in the context of the story—this will be Willa's last night on earth—it is all the more poignant. (This shot was handed over to the hired special effects team of Jack Rabin and Louis DeWitt—who are responsible for the excellent riverboat matting—so that they could add even more fog to enshroud Willa as she walks away from the camera.)

From outside the Harper house, we hear Preacher and Pearl in the parlor, his efforts at wheedling the secret from her leading him deeper and deeper into frustration. Willa approaches, then stops and listens in disbelief to the conversation. Finally, we hear Preacher's threat—"Tell me, you little wretch, or I'll tear your arm off!"—and Pearl's scream. Willa opens the front door to find Pearl running from Preacher and hiding in the hall closet. Her husband, startled, stops in his tracks. (A line, "I didn't expect you home so soon," was dropped in the editing.) Willa's face registers her confusion before she heads into the closet to offer comfort to her daughter.

After a take of this action in the front hallway, Cortez points out to Laughton, "The child is screaming off-stage, Charles." So, the director calls, "Uh, uh, Sh—uh, Sally."

"Yes," she answers and skips into camera range.

"Do your screaming when you're running where we can see you, sweetheart."

"Okay."

"Okay, lovey, bye-bye."

"Bye." She cheerfully heads back off-stage where she can play-act terrified.

Laughton adds, "And that very distressed face." The slates are hit. "All right. Sally, run screaming!"

Because there is no dialogue, Laughton once again shares with the old silent movie-makers the luxury of directing his actor while the camera is actually rolling. For the close-up of Willa's reaction, Laughton here requests of Winters, "A very, very sweet smile at him. Very sweet—sweet smile, darling. Sweet smile, more than that. More than that, darling. That's it, that's it. Now, shake your head slightly. Come out. No, no, that's too much shaking. Too much. That's it. No-no, no-no, no, just sweet smile, I don't want your eyes blinking. Just a sweet, sweet smile. Shake your head slightly. Come out. Perfect."

Laughton directs Mitchum, in his close-up, to be embarrassed "like a boy."

At this point in the film, a brief transitional scene features some dishwashing dialogue between the Spoons: Walt's got a nagging feeling that something isn't quite right up at the Harper home, and Icey makes him feel ashamed for thinking even slightly ill of a man of the cloth. From this, Laughton cuts to Willa and Preacher's bedroom, and Miss Winters' final performance—though not her final "appearance"—in the film.

Paul Gregory

Shelley has a wonderful quality, you know. When she said to the little boy, "You do what I tell you, please be nice to Mr. Powell," it was tragic. She has a pathetic quality. It's that quality in her, which she wouldn't admit she has, but it's that disappointment in her that she's never been the biggest star that ever happened. It's that hurt quality in her that's beautiful. There was never a lovelier scene than her last night when she was on the bed and looking up at Mitchum and she's realized that it's all been wrong. It's just marvelous. No one could act that look, she just had it.

It should take nothing away from Gregory's praise of his star's performance that his description of the scene in question errs in one crucial detail. So far from realizing that her marriage has been for naught, Willa on her bed, arms crossed beneath her naked throat, is a picture of denial. Not even when Powell slaps her across the face—and she immediately returns her gaze to its heavenward position—can she admit to herself that God is not working some mysterious higher purpose through her marriage to Preacher, that this is about nothing but money. "But that ain't the reason why you married me, Harry," she declares in her soft, prayerful voice, "I know that much. Because the Lord just wouldn't let it be." Willa's denial of Harry's true nature, which made their misbegotten marriage possible in the first place, now pins her as motionless as a sacrificial lamb to her moonlit bed.

Willa's state of mind as she lies under her blanket and undergoes Preacher's inquisition is evoked in one of Grubb's most memorably chilling passages:

> *Answer me!*
> The fingers were around the soft flesh of her thin arm, naked under the prim, old woman's night dress: his grip banding her arm bone like a ring of thin, cold steel.

And Ben never told you he throwed it in the river? Did he?
She said.

Then she thought: Why is my lip bleeding? Why can I taste
the blood running back into my teeth and tongue? And then
she remembered that he had struck her with the dry, shiny flat
of his hand and it had happened only a second before though it
seemed like a long time.

——then the children know where it's hid? She said. John
knows? Is that it?

Later in the same scene:

But he did not hear because now the night was filled with
Whispers and they were for him. And she knew suddenly that
he was not going to ever say anything more to her as long as she
lived; that whatever was going to happen next would be not
words but a doing. But still she kept on.

And then, still later:

. . . Because that night in the hotel at New Martinsville you
showed me the way—

She paused, listening to him and then thinking: But it still
ain't enough. I must suffer some more and that's what he is
making ready for me now: the last and total penance, and then
I will be clean.

Praise God! She cried as he pulled down the window blind . . .

And there you have the author's challenge to the movie-makers. How
to film that scene, with all its dreamy, doom-laden malevolence?

Davis Grubb
Laughton told me that he'd made the murder scene to look like it was
the nave of a church. I thought that was wonderful, marvelous.

Hilyard Brown

I came up with a rather chapel-looking bedroom for Winters and Mitchum's house. A lot of these old Victorian houses are built that way. As a matter of fact, some of them have stained-glass windows that look like they've come out of a church. This bedroom was just a little piece of set behind Winters and Mitchum, they weren't even in the set, they were ten feet out in front of it. When Mitchum is holding his hand up to the moonlight, he's back there in the set, but when he goes up to her to cut her throat he's out in front on a blank stage and the set is only a background. This set was all built out of muslin, or percale, or something like that. Instead of building a solid wall and then wallpapering it, I built the thinnest kind of frame and just tacked on some figured muslin.

Stanley Cortez

So many times when you're starting to prepare a scene, it's like a writer when he starts with a blank page: How does he get started? Nothing is there, just one horrible light. How do you begin, how do you formulate, what do you plan with? On many sequences in many pictures that I do, I'll sometimes think of a certain piece of music which will give me the clue.

Take the sequence with Bob Mitchum and Shelley Winters when he's about to kill her. She's lying in the bed in the left foreground, and Mitchum is back in the right side, by the window, with the strange, poetic something about him and his hand movements. Anyway, Charles and I designed the shot, and I went ahead and started lighting it. That sequence, by the way, was lit with only about six lights, or something like that. But, in the middle of my lighting, Charles said to me, "Cortez, what in hell are you thinking about?"—in a very nice way. I said, "None of your Goddamn business, Laughton,"—with deep respect. We were like a couple of kids, he and I.

But he insisted. And I said to him, "Charles, if you really must know, I'm thinking about a piece of music." And now Charles reverted to the actor, he said, "And pray, may I ask what the goddamn music is?" I said, "Valse Triste." There was a pause. His face froze. He said, "Goddamn it, how right you are. This sequence needs a waltz tempo!"

Now, you may ask why I thought of "Valse Triste." Let me just digress there for a minute. Since music is my avocation, music plays a very important part in my career as well as my life. Jean Sibelius, the Finnish composer of "Valse Triste," based this music on a Finnish legend, or saga, and the legend is as follows. The scene takes place in a cemetery and it's New Year's Eve, and it's one minute past midnight when these sunken bones come to life and do a dance in sheer mockery of life, which is precisely what Mitchum, as a phony priest, was doing to Shelley Winters. This was my key, and my clue to the given problem, which only I in my own psyche was aware of.

Now, to express this to anybody but Laughton, they'd think, well, "Cortez is out of his mind," you know, "He's a longhaired phony," or, "An arty kind of a guy." But this was genuine, and sincere, and the moment Charles heard it, he sent for Walter Schumann to come on the set. And, for the first time in my career, a man who wrote the music saw what I was doing visually in that particular sequence so that he could interpret it musically in that sequence and in the preceding sequences involving Winters and Mitchum, such as the honeymoon scene. That was the clue, and this is how the waltz tempo was written for those scenes.

This, too, was unorthodox, working with the composer during shooting instead of simply bringing in the composer to write the music after the

Composer Walter Schumann—"Next to Laughton," according to editor Robert Golden, "the most important contributor to the picture."

whole picture has been shot and edited. Walter was a wonderful part of our family on that picture, a very warm fellow, very sensitive. You know, oddly enough, those of us who worked with Charles got to love Charles, we really did. We adored this man, we had such respect for this guy, he was so warm, and human, we would all break our fannies for this guy.

"In composing the score for this picture," Schumann remembered in an article for a magazine called *Film Music Notes* (Sept./Oct., 1955), "Mr. Laughton suggested a technique which he called 'long muscles.' We divided the music sections into six segments, each of which would become an entity. Since no one scene in the picture lasted more than a minute and a half, the purpose of the music was to form a continuity for each segment. This simply meant that I would not play each scene but write an overall composition to cover the entire segment. The first segment had consisted of the main title and establishing scenes . . . The second segment involved the transformation of Willa, the children's mother, from the time of courtship by Preacher, through the marriage to the murder scene. My first thought for underscoring these highly dramatic moments was to use an emotional and tense musical treatment. But in discussion with Mr. Laughton he used an expression I will always remember. He said, 'If the actors and I have stated it properly on the screen, then you don't have to restate it with music.' Consequently, I devised a very simple waltz which, when used against the Preacher theme, formed a dramatic background against which the actors seemed to be playing."

Davis Grubb
Schumann was a man of apparently great imagination. We were all lucky to be working with him, and with each other. It was like a bunch of guys falling in together by accident and forming the Budapest String Quartet, or a real good Dizzy Gillespie Quintet. For instance, I understand that it was Cortez who suggested a waltz, "Valse Triste," by Sibelius. Well, I'm sure Laughton would never have been able to whistle "Valse Triste." He was a very visual person, but apparently he was almost tone-deaf. He told me he had no taste at all for music. He said he really wouldn't know the difference between Bach and Brahms if he heard it.

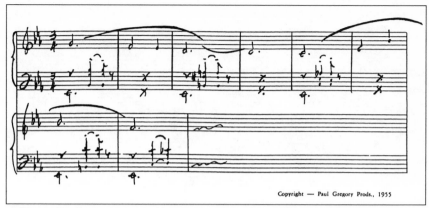

Willa's Waltz theme—inspired by cinematographer Cortez's recollection of Sibelius' *Valse Triste* while lighting the scene of Willa's sacrificial murder by Preacher.

Unfortunately, I know many people like that. It's like my being colorblind. Although, I have a theory that people who are colorblind have a compensation in which they're able to see certain other things. I haven't figured out what, but I know I see a different world than you do. And I have a feeling there are colors in the universe that we haven't discovered yet because our eyes are not capable of seeing them.

I didn't find out I was colorblind until I got to Carnegie Tech. But I should have inferred that I was colorblind, because I knew something was wrong in the third grade. We had crayons one day, and I drew a bright, leaf-green negro. I always thought it was kind of an interesting dimension in the whole concept of differences between us, but my teacher didn't think so: I got my hands beaten with a ruler till they were almost blistered.

You see, some of my schoolteachers went into that image of Preacher, too.

But Laughton was not tone-deaf in the literal sense, I'm sure, because to be tone-deaf would mean he wouldn't hear any inflections of voices, and if you listen to Laughton do a line, he sings, and chants, and whines in such a way that you know he's not tone-deaf. He may have been so absorbed in the music of the human voice that he just figured, "Why listen to sounds without words in them?"

Willa's last night on earth as scored by Walter Schumann's dance of death: Willa's
Waltz unravels as the Preacher's theme growls in the bass (*above & opposite*).

William Phipps

Laughton, "no ear for music"? Oh, but he did. Oh, God yes, he did.
Yes, he did, I remember he *loved* his Mozart. *Especially* Mozart. He lis-
tened to a lot of music. Why would he say that, I wonder? Well,
Laughton very often would say things that, if you didn't know him, you

The Music of Walter Schumann

wouldn't realize he's saying them for effect, or he didn't mean what he said, you know. Like, for instance, he used to say, "I don't know, I'm no business man," but he was a very *shrewd* man with business. Well, he used to run a *hotel.* Oh, he *did* have an ear for music. He would *have* to have, because of his feel for poetry. He was the greatest reader of poetry, I think, that ever came along.

You've heard Laughton recite the Gettysburg address. He used to compare it to a Bach fugue. Once, he was doing a thing on the radio with June Havoc, and I was there with him. He was there to read the Gettysburg Address, and the director said he was going to put music behind it. Laughton said, "No, you can't put music behind the Gettysburg address—it *is* music." The guy says, "Oh, yes I can. I'm a graduate of Juilliard, I know a lot about music, this is what I've picked, I'm putting it behind the Address." Laughton said, "No, you're not," and the guy says, "Yes, I am," Laughton says, "No, you're not," the guy says, "Yes, I am," Laughton turned to me and said, "Let's go home, Billy." He walked off the stage. Hours later, they called him back; they did not put music under it.

Hilyard Brown

There were never any disagreements among the people who were making the picture, not even between Laughton and the actors. The two principal actors were notoriously obstinate people, but they had such respect for Laughton that they never said "Boo." Mitchum, if he doesn't have real confidence in the director, I guess he can be a pretty rough guy—although I've always known him to be completely professional—but he certainly had confidence with Laughton. Most of Laughton's directions with his actors were very quiet, and very personal between the actor and the director. There was no standing back and shouting, as I've seen some directors do.

The scene begins quietly. (It is August 24, 1954.) "You were listening outside the parlor window," asks Preacher. She responds, "It's not in the river, is it, Harry?" "Answer me," commands Preacher, but Willa says, "Ben never told you he throwed it in the river. Did he?" This is when Preacher hits her; she turns her face away; then, "unruffled," as the script puts it, she returns to her upward gaze. "See God as you turn around," says Laughton to Winters, "Right." He describes for her the newfound peace in Willa's heart. God's in his heaven, and, "Satan is empty."

"The children know where it's hid," says Willa. "John knows? Is that it, Harry?"

"That's it," says Laughton, "But no pause in between 'John knows' and things. Less air in between. Right."

She absorbs the slap and says her lines again.

"Yes," says Laughton, "Cheerful, and more calm. Do it again."

She does it again.

"Right, and smile a little softer this time." He cues her slap-reaction: "Boom!"

And again: "Bang!"

And again: "Bang!"

"Do it again, please," says Laughton, who then refers to an earlier conversation he must have had with Miss Winters, "And, Shelley, when you turn your head, take it for a deeper pause after he hits you. And don't forget the *emptiness* of Satan, and the sentimentality of the religious card. Okay, now Shelley, start again, sweetheart." They start again, but Laughton quickly interrupts, "Start again, Mitch—and you've got your head down. Empty, cold statue. Iron. Iron, iron-cold, like touching metal, cold to your hand. Perfect."

Robert Golden

Mitchum wasn't easy to handle, he never has been, but Laughton did pretty good with him. Mitchum was a wild man, and he did some wild things away from the set. There were a couple of times when they were worried that he wasn't going to be there, for one reason or another. But he was always there. Mitchum had complete faith in Laughton. The scene when he's preparing to kill Shelley Winters, standing by the window with all those hand motions, that whole scene was shot very deliberately in a very stylized manner. Mitchum is quite a tough guy, and he doesn't stand for anything he doesn't want to, but he went right along with Laughton.

Robert Mitchum

Charles made a vaulted arch out of the bedroom for that scene, he wanted the effect of an inverted cross. That was his design, he explained it to me, and I said, "Okay, fine." I was against the window, he arranged the shot in the camera so that he created a vault with the light and the figure in the background.

"You gonna take it from here?" asks Miss Winters as they commence a take on this deeper view. "Go ahead," Laughton answers, "Doesn't

Hilyard Brown's "chapel-looking" bedroom—"just a little piece of set behind Winters and Mitchum."

matter about the line, just smile, Shelley, and be seraphic. Go ahead, Mitch. Start talking, Shelley. Go on." He snaps his fingers twice: "Action." While Willa prattles on in a soft, childlike voice of wonder about God's purpose in bringing them together, Preacher in the background extends his HATE hand up toward the moonlight streaming in through the window. "Uh, Mitch, would you do that gesture once more," says Laughton, "and don't speed it up at the end."

"We're still rolling," Cortez reminds everyone present.

"Smile on your face, Shelley," says Laughton.

They play the scene once more, then Laughton moves in for a closer angle on Mitchum at the window, where, twice in succession, he gestures toward his God, then pulls down the window blind, withdraws his switchblade from his coat pocket and snaps it open . . .

Laughton instructs his camera crew to print both takes, then they set up for a fuller shot on Winters in bed. Laughton addresses his one-time protege and present co-star quietly and intimately: "Shelley, sweetheart . . . Just that darling smile of yours. That darling smile, like you smile at me. That's it. Smile, smile as if you'd like . . . When you look at me

The Death of Willa
Harper—in Grubb's
sketch and in
Laughton's film.

The death of Willa Harper

when you trust me. That's it. Go ahead." Willa's monologue continues:
"You must have known about it all along, Harry."

"Keep your face still," says Laughton.

"You must have known about it all along, Harry."

"Be sorry for me," says Laughton.

"But that ain't the reason why you married me. I know that much.
It couldn't be, because the Lord just wouldn't let it."

"Now, say that again," instructs Laughton in a hushed, intimate, almost prayerful tone, "And when you say 'The Lord,' see Him. Again, sweetheart. Do it just like that. 'The way and the life and the salvation of my soul . . .' and, "The Lord just wouldn't let it . . .' You're looking at . . . You're looking at his *dear* face." Shelley repeats the speech in the same hushed rhythm of Laughton's directorial invocation, and when she says the last word, Laughton says quietly, "All right, cut, we have it."

Finally, they're shooting the full angle on the bedroom, and the moment for the sacrifice has arrived. "Smile, Shelley, please," says Laughton, "There . . . *That's* it! All right, Mitch—kill her." Preacher strides to Willa's bedside and leans over her with his free hand so that he is almost floating above her—an obscene parody of lovers, their two horizontal bodies parallel, face to face—when he extends his knife hand, the hand of LOVE, over her throat . . .

In the film, the next shot is a close-up of Willa, closing her eyes for the last time. (Her final line—"Bless us all"—was deleted in the editing.)

"Cut," says Laughton. The film, in fact, doesn't cut at this moment when we expect the blade to sweep across her throat. No, the film wickedly dissolves in a wipe that sweeps across the screen, taking us from Preacher and Willa's bedroom to the children's bedroom. John is awakened by the off-screen sound of someone trying to start up a motorcar. The lad goes to the window to investigate but, unable to pierce the fog, he returns to bed to snuggle with his little sister and her doll.

The next scene finds Preacher at the Spoons' parlor, crying crocodile tears over Willa who, he explains, has taken off during the night in their old car. Walt and Icey listen sympathetically as Preacher spins his tale of woe, and the doting couple are ready to believe any and every vile imprecation Powell has to make about their old friend Willa. (In Preacher's version, it was *Willa* who turned *him* out of the bed on their honeymoon.) In fact, Laughton advises Evelyn Varden before filming her close-up, "A woman is always delighted to know about the fall of another woman, dear. All right, go ahead, Mitch."

After doing his best to damn Willa's reputation among her oldest and dearest friends, Preacher declares to all within earshot, "Can't nobody say I didn't do *my* best to save her." And on this, the film quietly dissolves to an unforgettable image.

Davis Grubb recalled that Laughton was very concerned about making the movie "exactly like the book," and the author felt that the spirit of the whole production succeeded in evoking the atmosphere he had tried to create. Often with Laughton, however, what he had absorbed from Grubb's book would be expressed in terms of the visual artists he knew and loved so well. In addition to the already cited Seurat and *La Grande Jatte*, according to Grubb, "Charles visually had in mind . . . the flowing lines of a Manessier." To the author's mind, "many of [Laughton's] details have the precision of Bunuel," and the qualities of the revivalist meeting reminded him of Dreyer.

Davis Grubb

Well, this group that made the film was an amazing convergence of far smarter people than I am, I might say. Certainly Laughton was more experienced. I don't know, they all always just seemed to be a much sharper bunch of people than I was, maybe. Because all I had provided was the story. Things like the now-famous shot underwater was all Laughton and Cortez and Brown's idea.

Here Grubb is being extremely modest, and not just in the obvious fact of downplaying the central importance of supplying the story. The

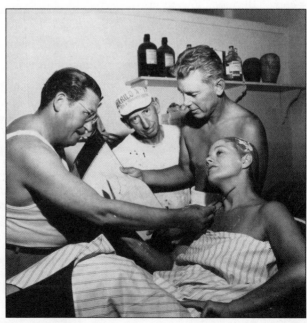

While Maurice Seiderman prepares to take a cast of Shelley Winters, from which he will replicate her mannequin, Hilyard Brown shows the actress sketches of how he intends to place her "corpse" in the front seat of a car under water.

scene of Willa's underwater corpse—perhaps the most famous in the film—is certainly an image derived directly from Grubb's novel. The author describes the terrible image not in his own words but through the drunken, horrified recollection of Uncle Birdie, trying to present his experience to the pitiless gaze of his long-dead wife, staring back at him from an old photograph:

"—'T was there I seen it, Bess. Down there in all that water. Ben Harper's old Model T and her in it!–Jesus save me!–Her in it, Bess–just a-sittin' there in a white gown and her eyes looking at me and a great long slit under her chin just as clean as a catfish gill!–O Godamighty!–and her hair wavin' lazy and soft around her like meadow grass under flood waters. Willa Harper, Bess! That's who! Down there in the deep place in that old Model T with her eyes starin' and that slit in her throat just like she had an extry mouth. You hear me, Bess? You listenin', woman? Swee' Jesus save us all!"

And yet, Grubb is right to share at least some of the credit with Laughton and company, not simply because of the artistry with which they filmed this image, but because they had the courage to film it at all. Most movies of the day would have been content to confine Willa's final resting place to Uncle Birdie's hearsay testimony. In fact, Laughton includes the scene of Birdie talking to his wife's picture, his soliloquy artfully abridged verbatim from the version in Grubb's novel. It's strong stuff, and might have evoked the power of an old radio play to bestir an audience's grisly imagination—had not the viewers of *Hunter* already been confronted, moments before, with what Mitchum might have called "the real mother deal," the actual sight of Willa's underwater corpse. Just as Willa's early demise had presaged *Psycho* by a few years, the imagery of her final fate presaged some of the shock shots in *Jaws* by a couple of decades. The script calls for the current to spare us the worst by drifting Willa's long hair across her throat, but, when shooting the scene, Laughton went for broke and let us see the wound. Fifties moviegoers, weaned on Cinemascope and Technicolor pabulum, were not prepared for this stark moment in black and white. "Frankly, it gave me quite a turn," critic Hollis Alpert would write in his admiring review of *Hunter* for *Saturday Review*. (Another writer impressed by the scene was Canadian poet and author Margaret Atwood, who would subsequently incorporate the image into one of her verses.)

Not Shelley Winters holding her breath, but Maurice Seiderman's mannequin in the tank at Republic studios.

Terry Sanders

That is an amazing shot.

Indeed it is. Author Grubb recalled that Laughton spent an extra $20,000 and three days of shooting to get the scene just right. "Special chemicals had to be used so that the water would remain clear." This shot was saved for the very end of the actual shoot, in the first week of November (officially post-production), because it involved no actors . . .

Stanley Cortez

It was a marvelous dummy of Shelley, made by a great make-up man, Maurice Siederman—we'd had him with us on *Magnificent Ambersons*. (AUTHOR'S NOTE: He had also aged Orson Welles for *Citizen Kane*.) We spent several days using a studio tank to photograph the scene of Shelley

The Music of Walter Schumann

"Water Weed"—the title given by Schumann to his scoring of the film's most famous image, Willa's corpse under water (*above & opposite*).

Winters' body sitting underwater in the car. We tried the 20th Century Fox tank, but it was too small, and paint was flaking off, and we would have had to take weeks and weeks taking all the paint off. Hilly felt that would be wrong, and that's when he found the tank at Republic.

Hilyard Brown

This was another scene that had no real set, that was just the bottom of a tank. At 20th Century Fox they couldn't make it work because they couldn't get the water clear enough to shoot through, so we finally went to Republic, where I had worked before. I put the Ford down there, and I got a fig tree and turned it upside down so that the roots of the tree looked like water willows.

Stanley Cortez

I hauled in a tremendous crane—they thought I was crazy, as they often do—and I put about ten high-powered "brutes" on a huge platform suspended above the water. These big lights poured a tremendous amount of light into the water, and we had water being pumped in, which provided that current. This was how we created underneath the water the strange, spiritual feeling of light and eerie current. We purposely played for that strange flow of the hair. I knew that the music Walter was going to write for this scene was with a waltz tempo, and that flow of the hair kind of tied in to that.

"Water Weed" is the title Schumann gave to his treatment of the submerged scene. The "Willa's Waltz" theme is played by strings in a high register. Heightening the eerie effect of the scene, the waltz seems to echo from a distant ballroom. (Significantly, though this is Willa's last appearance in the film, it is far from Schumann's last use of Willa's waltz theme. He will reprise it during several scenes involving another character who has not as yet been introduced in the story.)

Poor old uncle birdie, out fishing, sees something which will drive him to drink.

Stanley Cortez

In this scene, Jimmy Gleason as Uncle Birdie is fishing and he discovers the body when his hook gets caught on the car. That was one of the marvels of the picture: to photograph a moving shot underwater, starting on a hook that was snagged on the car, and to follow the fishing line up to the bottom of Uncle Birdie's boat. This is an achievement.

Charles was always so sympathetic, and so appreciative, when he saw what we were doing. He was really great about it.

Hilyard Brown

They'd made a cast of Shelley's face and made a rubber mask to put on a dummy. I put on a face mask and went down and fiddled around with her hair and rearranged things. I remember how it was shot, because I was down there with my face mask operating the camera. We also had a camera in a light-well with a glass window. Laughton was watching what was going on through the windows. It all had quite an effect, but it wasn't difficult to get that eerie current flowing. I think I had a water hose and just sprayed it out. It isn't very difficult to do a scene like that, (*smiles*), just get your actress to hold her breath a while . . .

Don Beddoe

I thought that one shot in the picture was just great, where Shelley Winters is in the water. I don't know how they *did* that! A dummy, you say. Did they? It was a magnificent dummy, oh, my—I thought she was just holding her breath down there. Beautiful job. Oh, that was wonderful, fantastic. I thought sure she was down there doing it.

And once again, as in the transition from the Hangman scene to the children's sing-song sequence, Laughton experiments with the technique of beginning the sound of the next scene—another song, this time Preacher's hymn, "Leaning, leaning, leaning on the everlasting arms"—before the image of the present scene has begun to dissolve. (Hitchcock pioneered this gambit in 1935's *The 39 Steps,* when he had the cleaning lady's scream replaced by the screaming whistle of the train which appears in the next shot.) Hence, the classic scene of Shelley Winters' corpse ends with the irony of her murderer's soothing hymn being sung over her wa-

"Leaning, leaning . . ."

tery grave, as if in mockery of a funeral. As Preacher continues his song,
we see him leaning against a tree outside the Harper house. The children
are hiding somewhere inside, and Preacher intends to find them.

Stanley Cortez

I think *The Night of the Hunter* was way ahead of its time. Charles had
some marvelous ideas, and he was also strongly influenced by D.W.
Griffith. Charles and I would run many Griffith films. And oddly
enough, as a punk assistant cameraman, I'd worked with Griffith, on a
picture called *Abraham Lincoln*. (And my brother Ricardo worked with
Griffith on a picture called *Sorrows of Satan*.)

   People would think I was crazy by doing some of the things I did,
because they were unorthodox, but this was between Charles and myself, we both thought alike. For instance, there was an exterior scene
with Bob Mitchum leaning against a tree outside the house, saying, "I
know you're hiding in there somewhere . . ." But until we could move
in somehow to the cellar window to see the little boy looking out, you
wouldn't know where he was hiding. This was a problem, we wanted to

move in, and we had no zoom lenses in those days. Now, I devised the following idea. We have in the camera an iris, which is not very good for the purpose that I wanted it for. So I devised a huge iris, about five feet in circumference, that I placed in front of the camera, and, instead of moving in, I irised in with this huge thing, which gave Charles the very idea that he was thinking of. I knew that way back in his mind was Griffith, and way back in my mind also was Griffith, tying in the Laughton concept. And instead of dollying in, we irised in, which was far more effective. That's one of the times when they thought I was crazy; it hadn't been done since Griffith, except when I did it once in the Orson Welles picture, *The Magnificent Ambersons*.

The iris-effect was a staple of Hollywood cartoons, but definitely not of live-action features. This was Cortez, "the Brooklyn Spaniard," at his most ingenious, and the out-take footage confirms that this effect was executed in-camera, not in postproduction optical work. (The out-takes also reveal that Cortez experimented with his iris when shooting another, unrelated scene, but Laughton decided against using it a second time.)

When the angle is reversed, we see John and Pearl atop a pile of coal, near a barrel of apples, peering out through a high window at Preacher. As John is helping his little sister down from the top of the coals, he tries to warn her of the danger afoot—and the action which must be taken:

> JOHN: Now listen to me, Pearl. You and me is runnin' off tonight.
> PEARL: Why?
> JOHN: If we stay here somethin' awful will happen to us.
> PEARL: Won't Daddy Powell take care of us?
> JOHN: No, that's just it. No.

As evidenced in the out-take footage, the children shared a bit more dialogue than made it into the final cut:

> JOHN: Someone is after us, Pearl.
> PEARL: I want to go upstairs. It's cold and spidery down here. I'm hungry.

"I know you're hiding in there somewhere . . ." One moment later, Stanley Cortez' iris reveals to us—but not Preacher—the children's whereabouts.

Compared to her generally wispy portrayal of Pearl throughout the film, Sally Jane's delivery of these complaints is uncharacteristically forthright and forceful—which is possibly why Laughton cut them. He required numerous repeats of this action and its accompanying dialogue. Part of the difficulty lay in Sally Jane Bruce's continual penchant for looking away too soon in anticipation of Preacher's off-screen sing-song "Children!" Laughton has to remind her that she shouldn't do this because both children need to react to Preacher at the same moment. Whenever it is time to begin again, a crew member scoops up little Sally Jane and places her back on top of the coals. At one point, tiring of the repetition, the little girl complains aloud, "This is a hard way to make this movie." When the final take is in the can, the precocious tyke registers her relief by saying, "That's 'Print.'"

But then, she must repeat the scene in close-up, and for this Laughton feeds her Billy's lines, all the while displaying the patience with which he often has to keep her focused on the task at hand:

LAUGHTON: Keep your dolly down, darling. Now, listen to me,
Pearl. You and me is going off tonight.
SALLY JANE: Why?
LAUGHTON: If we stay here, something awful will happen to us.
SALLY JANE: Won't Daddy Powell take care of us?
LAUGHTON: That's just it, no. I'm going to ask you that ques-
tion again. If we stay here—Keep your dolly there, dear. If we
stay here, s—look at me, dear. If we stay here, something
awful will happen to us.

And, later:

LAUGHTON: Don't go for the apples, Sally. Play with them afterwards, not now . . .

Next, coaching Billy through his close-up, Laughton has to remind
himself to clean up his customary act when with the children.

LAUGHTON (*as Pearl*): To see Dad?
BILLY: Yes, I reckon that's it.
LAUGHTON: Now, that's a lie. It's not true, what you're saying.
You know damn—(*catches himself*)—darn well your father's
dead, he's not in Moundsville at all . . .

The children crouch in hiding behind the apple barrel. ("Now, look at
me, children," says Laughton. "Large, large eyes. Very serious.")
Preacher Powell, having overheard the children, is about to descend into
the basement when the icky-sweet voice of Icey Spoon interrupts.
Keeping John's point-of-view, Laughton holds his camera on the children while we hear Icey and Preacher's off-screen dialogue. She's
brought some homemade supper for the grieving widower and his
stepchildren, and when Preacher beseeches her help in getting those
unruly kids to mind him, hide-and-seek is over.

PREACHER'S VOICE: They're down there in that cellar playin'
games and they won't mind me when I call them. I'm at my
wits' end, Mrs. Spoon.

ICEY: clucks her tongue O.S.

ICEY'S VOICE: (*yelling*) John: Pearl:

She appears at head of stairs. Her voice crackles with authority.

ICEY: John! Pearl! Shake a leg! (*She claps her hands sharply*)

. . . *A short pause; then the children, covered with coal-dust, emerge into the light and climb the stairs.* JOHN*'s head is hung in defeat.*

This brief beat, to me, is one of the best moments in the film. What viewer, remembering his own childhood, cannot identify with John's reluctance to yield to the maternal voice of interruption, and yet also identify with his powerlessness, his need to bow to her authority? The secret world of the child is his alone, and so vulnerable to being shattered by the heedless adult. Even here, where John's secret world involves no imaginary playmates but an all-too-real, life-threatening monster, the boy must submit to the well-meaning neighbor lady who could never possibly understand the boy's situation. And so, holding Pearl's hand, John trudges up the stairs to face the man from whom he's been hiding.

Robert Mitchum

When Charles would get upset with the children, I used to have to come in and direct them. Directing the kids was no big deal, directors are like auto mechanics. At least, I know some directors who *should* be auto mechanics. Charles had never directed any movies before, either, had he?

The brief moment between Preacher and Icey with the children at the kitchen doorway provides an example of Mitchum pitching in on the handling of the children: "Keep your nose low, Sally. Now, look over at me . . ." The script emphasizes the moment when Preacher's hand named LOVE moves through Pearl's locks, and in one of the outtakes Mitchum makes a chilling bit of business in the way the hand reaches, as if to crush, and then caresses. It seems a pity this chilling effect was not included in the final cut. (The still photographer, too, must have thought this was an important image, because he snapped a shot of it.) The various takes also reveal that Mitchum gave a variety of different readings to the scene's tag-line—"Now, weren't you afraid, little

(Preacher)
Weren't you afraid down there alone in the dark, children?

lambs, down there in all that dark?"—in one rendition delivering that last word, "dark," in a whisper. The version Laughton chose for the film is the quietest and simplest, perhaps in keeping with this beat of the film being the quiet before the storm. Visually, the scene ends on a close-up of John—what's he gonna do now? We hear the sound—not specified in the script—of a riverboat's foghorn calling in the night, as if to summon for John the thought of his pal, Uncle Birdie, the man who told him to come a-running if ever he was in trouble.

This cues the transition to Birdie himself—alone in his wharf-boat, drinking, in no condition to help anybody. The grizzled river man is getting drunk in his rocking chair, afraid to tell the police about Willa Harper's body because he thinks they'll accuse him of the crime. Cortez's previous iris-in to the basement window makes for a striking moment in the film, but another telling photographic effect was more the product of luck than preconception.

Stanley Cortez

Did you notice that stroboscopic effect when Jimmy Gleason rocked back and forth? Actually, it was not deliberate, that was an accidental plus. When I saw it through the lens, I knew it was going to do that, and I thought it was going to be a plus value, even though I didn't plan it that way. It was sort of a visualization of the old man's mind getting fuzzier and fuzzier, which of course is why the old man is no help later when the children come running to him for help. So, we were lucky to get that effect.

Davis Grubb

I have such an admiration for the memory of James Gleason. When he was rocking there, back and forth, he was so real. "Poor old Uncle Birdie . . ."

Laughton, the "great appreciator," as Mitchum called him, must surely have valued the contributions from an old pro like Gleason, particularly in light of some of the travails he went through in directing the children. As it turned out, Laughton's own policy of keeping his camera rolling between takes would prove providential where the children were concerned. Or, could this have been part of Laughton's conscious plan all along? Consider the crucial scene at the kitchen table, and editor Golden's recollection of putting it together:

Icey has brought to the "grieving widower" and his stepchildren a home-cooked meal. She's gone now, and Preacher is finally alone with John and Pearl. What's more, with Willa disposed of, there is no longer a need for Preacher to pretend benevolence. The greedy madman can have his showdown with the kids and get them to surrender the money's hiding place.

Robert Golden

We used to go into a room where there was a projection machine and he would run the shots back and forth, back and forth, and I'd get pretty much an idea of what he wanted. It was the hard way, it was very trying. I saw the picture again some time in the past two years, and I was amazed at how smooth the cutting was. I was amazed because I think it's impossible to dictate cutting, a personal expression, to another person. But when I say he supervised it, he *supervised* it. And I was amazed at how smooth it was.

Still, there were little contributions I could make. Laughton took a violent dislike to the little girl. He loved the little boy, but he hated the little girl. I don't know what it was, but he hated her. She must have been
something like four years old. What he was expecting, I don't know. I
guess the most wonderful picture of young children I'd ever seen was that
English picture, *The Little Kidnappers,* and I learned an awful lot from it
about children. Children's natural reactions are much better than anything
you can give them, and I think maybe that's what Laughton didn't like
about the little girl, because he couldn't give her anything. The boy was
old enough to understand what Laughton was asking from him.

There's the scene at the kitchen table, where Mitchum starts getting
angry because the girl won't tell him where the money is hid. Laughton
had a hell of a time shooting that sequence because of the little girl. She
wouldn't do what he asked her to do. Laughton was really very bad with

this little girl, he lost his temper with her. I saw things that she did react-
ing to Laughton's violence, while the camera was rolling but between
takes. I remember very vividly finding and grabbing these reactions of the
little girl that were not shot as part of the scene. I kept them and those
were the reactions we used in the picture.

There are instances where the out-takes can corroborate the memories of the film's makers; and there are others where the raw footage either disproves or at least calls into question the eye-witness testimony
taken at a couple of decades' remove from the original shoot. Although
it is possible that Laughton was hard on little Sally Jane (especially bearing in mind that we can see only a few of the takes, not the unprinted
ones), all of the surviving footage records Laughton being extremely
kind and patient with the child. What one particular out-take does reveal for certain, however, is that this production resorted to the oldest
gambit in Hollywood for finding tears: get them out of a bottle. This
particular take offers a glimpse of a glycerine tear being applied to Sally
Jane's eye by the make-up artist.

Terry Sanders
I loved all the casting. I thought the little girl was really oddly cast—and
oddly directed, too. I don't know, I just felt she was so, kind of, unnat-
ural, doll-like, and I guess he found something in her that he really
liked, but I have a feeling he never really had a real rapport with the
children. He would have liked to, but he didn't. But, Denis would have
had more opportunity to observe while the shooting was going on and
I was back east doing the second unit.

"Charles hated the little girl in the film," Denis Sanders recalled.
"On a personal and on a professional level. In fact, he had chosen her
because of her unattractive quality. He wanted the audience to particularly like the little boy and to feel little sympathy with the girl. This was
a dangerous and unconventional step to take in a movie, because audiences are supposed to like all children in film. But Charles wanted to
make this movie essentially the story of the terror of the little boy."

Davis Grubb

Charles talked to me about working with the kids on this picture. He believed the best way to direct children was to treat them with kindness, with a way of talking which was not condescending. He was particularly fond of Margaret O'Brien.

He also told me stories about the difficulties he had with the children. I think the girl was extremely talented, every bit as talented as the boy. But, he said, she kept blowing a line one morning, saying it in a strange inflection. Laughton took her aside, "Sally Jane, why did you do that?" She said, "Because Mummy told me if I did I'd steal a scene from Mitch."

Elsewhere, Grubb has testified that Laughton confessed there were times when he had to restrain himself from throttling little Sally Jane. Laughton apparently was rueful to recognize in himself such feelings, and that he tolerated in Mrs. Bruce a stage mother who controlled her daughter with an equestrian ringmaster's whip. As to Laughton's teaming with Margaret O'Brien on *The Canterville Ghost* (1942), he had indeed felt very tenderly toward the child, but he also had witnessed the treatment the girl underwent to achieve her performance, and his memories of this Grubb termed "too sad, too personal" to relate for posterity. [A hint, however, might be gleaned by reading Vincente Minnelli's memoirs, *I Remember It Well*, in which he reports on his experiences dealing with Margaret and her stage-mother while filming *Meet Me in St. Louis* (1944).] Generally speaking, however, Grubb wrote that "Laughton was—being a child himself—always at ease with children. And they with him."

Denis Sanders described the individual procedures Laughton employed for each actor. "With Mitchum, he explained the effect that he wanted. He tried to show that one doesn't necessarily have to cry, that one can manufacture tears or laughter by learning how to use the instrument that the actor possesses. He explained quietly to each of the actors what he wanted. With the little boy, he would often take him aside and whisper, because children like secrets. This worked. He did not do the lines for Billy Chapin, but told Billy Chapin what he needed to know for that particular scene. He did not necessarily explain everything that was happening in the picture because he knew that children can only concentrate on the part of the film that they themselves are directly involved in. It was as if they were sharing a secret. He would very often perform the part for the little girl—read her lines, show her how to do them—and then she would mimic Charles's performance. She would strike a pose almost identical to the pose Charles had struck for her. This was not Charles's usual way of directing, but it worked in this particular case. Charles seemed to know exactly how to approach each of the actors in this film. To make them part of a whole orchestra, to work together. They sometimes were not conscious of this fact, but the final product reveals it."

Robert Mitchum

When Charles couldn't get through to the little girl, I would talk to her. She'd listen to me. Why? For one thing, the director had a "funny accent," you know. She was from Oklahoma. I could talk Oklahoma to her, and she'd understand what I was talking about. For the kitchen scene, just before we go down into the cellar, first of all, I showed the girl how sharp the knife was. Then, when she went to grab it in the scene, I came very close to her, so she backed off fast.

"Lookee here—you want to see something cute?"

Hoping to escape Preacher's clutches, John tells the grown-up a lie: the money is hidden under a stone in the basement. But Preacher, lighting a candle, insists the children go ahead of him down into the dark cellar. Now, John is truly trapped. (The out-takes confirm that Mitchum is once more helping to direct the children, particularly little Sally Jane. After marching the kids toward the basement door, Mitchum calls for "Once more," in a very soft, un-Preacher-like voice, "And remember, not to look back at me, honey . . . Look at him.") Walter Schumann's underscore resumes at this crucial juncture, accompanying the descent into the basement with a low, lumbering rendition of Preacher's theme on horns, then introducing in the strings a rising-falling-rising motif to represent the children's plight. (Soon this theme, when sped up, will represent their flight.)

Robert Mitchum

Once we were shooting, I can't think of anything I wanted to do that Charles wouldn't let me do, not even when we came down to the cellar, and the kid tells me to dig there, and finally I'm ripping my nails off, and I say, "This is *con*crete, boy." It was spoken in the idiom, the dialect, it was almost Amos and Andy—but it fit, and Charles liked it.

Paul Gregory

Hilyard Brown is a talented man. Talented man. Now, didn't you think the basement stuff was wonderful, when Preacher went down into the cellar and the boy tipped the board and the shelf fell over and hit Preacher and so on? That was realism. There was nothing symbolic about that, nothing artsy-fartsy about that, it was a dark, old basement. And when Preacher came crouching down the steps at the beginning of the scene, we had the smaller set so that he would loom bigger against these children. You see, that was purposely done, the smaller-dimensioned set, so that he would seem, to the children, enormous. That was the point-of-view I wanted all the time.

Once again, producer Gregory refers to his regret that the film drifted away from strict realism by praising the verisimilitude of the basement set—and yet, in his very next breath, he discusses with justifiable pride the way in which the "realistic" basement was anything but real. This was another prime example in *Hunter* of Brown's gift for playing with perspective in order to lead the viewers beyond their conscious perceptions into an almost subliminal mood of the child's dream world. Which, of course, was precisely what Laughton had asked him to do.

Hilyard Brown

Charles said he wanted the cellar to look like a rat-hole. You know those glass cases filled with sand that have an ant colony inside, with all the tunnels seen in cross-section?

Well, Charles said he wanted the same kind of underground, cross-section effect. So, to emphasize that aspect, we deliberately masked out parts of the frame. As I remember, our floor plan was something like this, with steps on the right leading down into the basement:

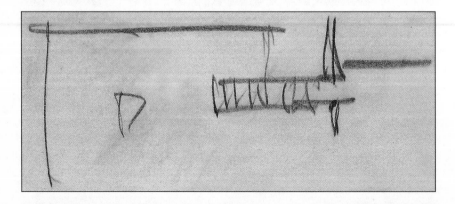

We cut some diagonal black flats
like these,

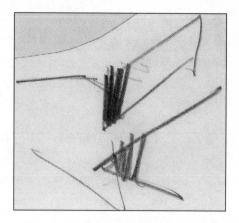

and positioned them only a few feet in front of the camera so that they
would blot out part of the set, such as in the shot of Mitchum standing in
the doorway at the top of the stairs, and again when we had the long shots
of the cellar, with Mitchum up there and the children down here.

There were whole parts of the set which you never saw, because we deliberately masked them out to achieve this subterranean effect that Laughton wanted.

And so by trapping the little boy down here in this "rat hole," the scene has been set for John to face his greatest fear and discover his deepest strength. Preacher Powell will brook no more lies. He grabs John and produces his switchblade. Even threatened by the razor edge of what Preacher believes is Jehovah's wrathful sword, John holds steadfast to the promise his father had exacted from him. He would rather die than betray that trust. Preacher senses that Pearl is weakening, so he plays on the whimpering girl's panic: "You could save him, little bird!" In the Grubb novel, the author heightens the scene's tension by having Preacher touch the blade to John's skin. Perhaps Laughton felt that this would be just a tad too intense for his fifties audience, so he omits this bit of business. Yet he maintains the same rhythmic buildup of suspense by letting Preacher brandish his closed switchblade—but having Preacher withhold the actual snapping open of the blade until the last

"You could save him, little bird!"

possible moment, on the "You could save him" line. "Pearl, you swore!" her brother reminds Pearl, but the terrified toddler can stand no more, and she tearfully blurts out the secret that the money is inside her doll.

A close angle on Pearl provides crucial cut-away moments, such as when she is responding with great agitation to Preacher's roughhousing of John. To lead her into this heightened emotional state, Laughton first disorients her: "Sally, look at me. Look here! Look here! Look here! Look here! Look here! Look there! Look there! Jump up and down a little bit! Now look here! Now look there! Now look there! That's it, cut!" For the big moment when she has to cry out, "Inside my doll! Inside my doll!" make-up applies a couple more drops of glycerine under her eyes, and Laughton adopts a highly tearful tone of voice, complete with sobs and sniffles, almost a caricature: "Cry. Cry. He's trying to kill your brother, darling, you've got to make a noise about it! Look! Look, look at what's happening over here! Now, cry out, cry out real loud like that (*Sobs*) Uhhh-huhhhhh!!—like that! (*Sobs*.) But, cry out loud, darling! Make a noise!" As she starts making audible sob sounds; he keeps increasing the pressure: "Now, hold Miss Jenny—'Inside my doll!'"

Sally Jane cries out her line, "Inside my doll, inside my doll!" but Laughton doesn't cut, he keeps her at this peak as long as he can, calling for repeat after repeat, but each with its own refinement: "Hold Miss Jenny up higher." "Can you say it louder, sweetheart?" "Yes, but look at *me* when you say it, dear." "Now *shout* it at me!" etc., until the director realizes he can't push her any further, at least in this take: "(*Crying voice*) But you looked away from me, darling. (*Instantly reverts to normal tone*) Go to your mother, dear."

Soon, the little trouper is ready to give it another go. Sally asks, "Are my tears still on?" "Yes dear, they are," answers Laughton. "They're lovely."

This tense scene, where Preacher draws his knife and issues his ultimatum, triggers John and Pearl's flight, the chase sequence which is the film's centerpiece. Yet, the cellar scene is capped with slapstick comedy. Preacher can't help laughing in astonishment at where the money has been all this time. A tight close-up on John shows him racing to size up the situation and take action. Laughton directs Billy Chapin in fast, loud, urgent tones: "Billy! Look at him! Look here! Billy! Quick! Look at him, quick! Look at me, quick! Look at him quick! Very manly! You've got

to take charge of your sister in a minute! . . . Clench your fist! Tense your
mouth! . . ." John seizes the moment, douses the candle and lets loose a
shelf of bottled preserves on Preacher's head—then grabs Pearl's hand and
runs for dear life. Mitchum—actually, a stunt-man—slides across the
fallen preserves into a pratfall while the kids are heading up the stairs.
Preacher recovers and takes after the youngsters, arms outstretched like
the ultimate bogey man. In fact, with his bare wrists yearning past his
cuffs, Mitchum somewhat resembles Boris Karloff in James Whale's original *Frankenstein*, one of the screen's all-time icons of horror.

Davis Grubb

When I see the picture now, I'm always sitting there apprehensively waiting for the laughs that used to come all the time when Preacher would slip

The bogey man
will get you . . .

on the cellar steps or something. This hurt me terribly when I first saw it;
I thought, "Jesus, I didn't plan this for comedy."

Terry Sanders

When the Preacher gets them down in the cellar, and he realizes the
money's in the doll, and he's gonna grab it and then he slips and all that,
it's sort of slapsticky the way it's staged. That's supposed to be funny. That
was probably a mistake, because I think audiences would rather be scared
than . . . There's something conflictive about that.

When something works, it works. But I'm not sure this is one of those
times. I remember one thing Laughton said about when he was in a stage
play, I think it was *Payment Deferred*. He was supposed to crawl along the
stage in a very highly dramatic scene, melodramatic, and maybe there was
a murder or something, and he has to crawl along the stage. I guess some-

body asked him, "What are you thinking when you're doing that?" And he said, "I'm just laughing to myself." So, he had that ability, I guess, to project one thing while internally feeling something quite different.

Robert Golden

That scene in the cellar when Mitchum chases the kids up to the top of the stairs and he's going to get them—Laughton played that for comedy all the way through, but it was frightening. You know, Mitchum slides across the floor when he hits those cans. But I think it was very wise of Laughton to play it the way he did, because of relief. I mean, those kids go through an awful lot, and everybody wants to see something happen to the heavy. And timing-wise, you had to do it, because there was no reason why he couldn't get them. But Laughton never had funny music in that scene. The music underneath it was terrific, it never let up, and he played the comedy against the frightening music.

Just as Preacher's hands are reaching through the door-jamb, John slams the door on his fingers, prompting a blood-curdling howl from Mitchum. John opens the door only long enough to shut it and lock it. "Wild, staring eyes, Billy," commands Laughton, "really wild!"

Robert Mitchum

We had to do that slapstick business in the chase out of the basement. We had to show, finally, when the boy slams the door on Preacher's fingers, Preacher's complete sense of frustration. I mean, a sense of, "Christ, what else?"

Charles wanted, really, to take the horror out of it. He felt if he didn't, it would be an insult to me, for some reason, because he was very fond of me. And I of him.

Seldom has a figure of evil incarnate to match Preacher Harry Powell been presented on the screen, and yet Mitchum is not the only one who recalls that Laughton felt a need to somehow soften the character's darkness a bit. Lillian Gish, as we shall see, remembered Laughton's treatment of Preacher in much the same way. Was this, perhaps, one of the reasons why Laughton exercised some restraint in the basement switchblade moment? Perhaps, but then, what of the slapstick of the cellar chase, derived directly as it is from Davis Grubb's novel? The author may have intended the scene to frighten—and he in fact succeeded—but observe how, like Laughton's staging, Grubb's prose walks the fine tightrope between horror and prat falls:

> And John thought: Because I know the cellar like I know my own room: the way among the boxes and the barrels, the way across the dank, broad stone floor to the steps, and he don't know the way and he will fall among the rakes and hoes and the apple baskets and trunks and if only I can get Pearl and me and the doll up them steps and lock him down here there will be a chance. They were halfway up the steps now and the door to the kitchen was ajar before their eyes, a bright bar of lamplight and safety in that hell of blackness, and behind them they could hear Preacher go down cursing again in another welter of crashing jars and Pearl was screaming in a high, keening wail.

This question will be examined further when it reappears in the film, but for now only one thing matters: as Grubb put it in his narration for the soundtrack LP: "The night of the hunter is at hand."

John & Pearl

Davis Grubb

From the Grubb novel: "Because a pipeline ran through the Harper yard the gas company gave them a tree lamp on a wooden post—a big box with a roof like a birdhouse with glass sides and perpetual flame within. It stood by the great oak at the road's edge and when the wind tossed the branches of the tree the light from the gas lamp made pictures on the wall of the children's bedroom." Elsewhere, Grubb wrote of the Harper house as something that "dreams and ticks" in the night. These two stills show how art director Brown and cinematographer Cortez interpreted the author's descriptions for film. In the first scene, Willa returns from Spoon's parlor to her fog-enshrouded home and hears Preacher grilling Pearl about the hidden money, so she goes around the right to investigate at a side window.

"Uncle Birdie Steptoe!" whispers John to himself, then grabs Pearl and runs from the house. Laughton, in the cutting, deleted a monologue of Preacher's in which he adopts his most honeyed voice and tries to persuade the little darlings to open the door. It was a wise cut, as the beat, however briefly, would have slowed down the momentum just as the pot is boiling at its fiercest, and also yanked Preacher out of the animal savagery so crucial to the big chase. It's much more effective to simply cut to the exterior view of the house as the kids are running away from it, then hear the

In the second scene, John and Pearl flee the house in whose basement they have just locked a furious Powell.

sounds of Preacher breaking down the cellar door. (Apparently the sound effect lasts a second or two longer than the crew had anticipated when shooting the image of the house, or perhaps this was an example of Golden's extending the footage to accommodate Schumann's score, because the camera holds on the house during most of the noise, but then the shot repeats itself for the last few seconds. Usually, by this point, the audience is much too involved in the excitement to notice the fleeting technical "glitch." As Robert Gitt, head of UCLA Film Preservation explains, "In the movie, the shot isn't long enough, and they have to make a dupe and extend it, so in the original negative—even going back to the old prints—it holds on the house, and you hear Mitchum breaking out of the door and, about three or four seconds before the end of the shot, it suddenly cuts to a less good-looking photographic dupe. They could have replaced the whole shot with a dupe, to keep it consistent, but for whatever reason the editor decided to go with the original negative . . . when the negative ran out, they extended it, to make the house-shot longer. I thought it was a replacement, something that had been done years later because of damage to the negative, but no, it's in all the old original prints, too. They hadn't let the camera linger long enough. Maybe when the music and everything was added they needed to do that extension.")

Here, with what would have been the next shot, was where Cortez again experimented with the iris effect. It's a shot of Birdie's wharfboat, with all the surrounding buildings masked out, as if to emphasize John's single-minded focus on getting to Birdie. Whereas the earlier shot had irised *in* to the detail of the children in the cellar window, here the shot irises *out* from Birdie's home, revealing the Bijou theater and other surrounding environs. Again, Laughton was wise to keep this shot out of the final cut, as it would have distracted from the suspense. (And besides, if John is focused on Birdie and his wharfboat, why would the other surroundings then impinge on his consciousness?)

Poor Birdie, not surprisingly, is passed out on the floor in a stupor by the time John races in with Pearl in tow. John pleads and shouts, but he can't wake up his old friend. (Ms. Gould's newspaper report describes how Laughton directed young Chapin: "'The knife, Billy. There's danger in the knife! It cuts! Sharp now, boy, a tight scene—like Mitch!'" (Chapin idolized Mitchum.) And when the boy turns around, his little sister is snoring, too, asleep on Birdie's cot. It is the moment of truth. Young John, in the script's eloquent shorthand, "is lost; and he becomes a man.

JOHN: (*quiet*) There's still the river."

And with that, once more he grabs Pearl, rousing her from sleep, and races out of the cabin and into the night. "Go get her!" Laughton shouted at Billy, according to Gould, and then, "He followed through with the action himself. He roughed the little girl up, then enveloped her in a bear hug (not in the script!) before dropping her back into the camera position on the rickety, dirty cot."

Hilyard Brown
We filmed the scene where Mitchum chases the kids to the river on a sound stage, all on one set. We didn't have to keep changing anything at all, just moved around and put a log here or a piece of tree there, and

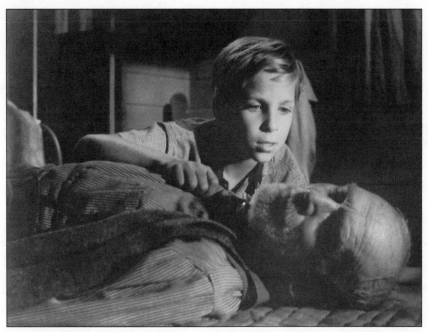

Uncle Birdie cannot keep his promise to protect John. "There's still the river."

it looked like a lot of sets instead of just one. It's very easy to fool the camera on those kinds of sets by moving to a different angle or moving a tree limb.

Here was Laughton's opportunity to restore the power of silent pictures to the screen, and he made the most of it. As if to emphasize his point, Laughton eliminated virtually all of Preacher's shouted threats, which had been found both in Grubb's novel and in the film script, that is, "Wait, you little whelps! Wait!" and *"Wait! Wait! I'll slit your guts!"* The only imprecation which remains is the single, businesslike word— off-screen—"Children!" Clearly, the director realized Preacher was more frightening as a silent, implacable, relentless bogey man. By the same token, Laughton eliminated John's panicky one-line soliloquy while clumsily trying to get the boat out into the current: "Why can't I do it when I know *how* to do it!" With these excisions, the chase can take its place beside any of the great action sequences of the silent days. The cross-cutting between hunter and prey is pure Griffith.

The shots involving Mitchum and the children together were filmed in mid-September, but some shots requiring only the children were saved for late October—officially post-production. (Out-takes reveal that, for some of the action shots here—and earlier, in the cellar—Sally Jane was doubled by a youngster named Cathy. Presumably, this was necessitated by the laws pertaining to the amount of work time allowed for a child as young as Sally.) The chase cross-cuts between Mitchum slashing viciously through the underbrush and John, dragging Pearl through muck, struggling to untie his Dad's old skiff—and struggling with his baby-sister, so bored that at one point she yawns while John is trying to get her into the boat.

"Sally, you hate it, the mud, beastly mud!" Laughton calls out (again, talking all through the action, like an old silent-movie director). "Try and make your way through it!" To Billy: "Get the rope un-done quick! Make it look tough! Make it look tough!" According to the script (as in the novel), John simply "picks her (Pearl) up and throws her into the skiff," but Laughton couldn't allow one of his child actors to do that to the other. By having Billy handle Sally more gently—and continuing to cross-cut with Preacher—Laughton actually heightens the suspense. "Help her into the boat! Help her as much as you can. Sally! Start again. Sally—don't anticipate that. Don't expect to go through the mud. Let Billy take you, you stay there. Go on, Billy, undo it. Stay there, Sally, still. Undo it, now. Un-do it. Sally, you put your hand out to him, sweetheart, it spoils it . . . Let him take you. That's it, Billy, take it off, now. Fine. Now take Sally's hand. Lift Sally into the boat, as gently as you can. Whoopsy-daisie. Whoop! Mind you don't hurt her. Now, get her into the boat, fella. Whoopee." All of this becomes excruciating on screen, when cross-cut against Preacher—and, with Schumann's powerhouse music re-placing Laughton's stage-directions. (His instruction to Mitchum, hacking and slashing ever closer toward the children? "Mitch, this is an eye for an eye. Come on." And, for a similar shot, "Look fierce. Okay, let's go.")

Then, when at last Preacher enters the same shot as the children—with John still struggling to free the boat from shore—Laughton becomes an unholy ringmaster, shouting directions of encouragement at Preacher *and* John, as if it's all a mad game—heaven and hell to play with, as Paul Gregory put it—and he'll let fate determine which will win out: "Go ahead Billy! Quick! Quick! Go on, pull the boat out! All right, *heave*, Billy! Hold it, Billy! Get *after* him, Mitch! Come and get him!"

Hilyard Brown

Where Mitchum runs out into the rushing river and can't catch the kids and starts screaming like the devil, the set had about three or four feet of water in it, and they had hoses with which they agitated the water to make it look like current. It was a fairly good-sized set, in fact it filled a whole stage. But the area we actually worked in was all foreground pieces, until they cut to that long shot of the boat drifting under the stars, which is why that's so effective after all the closer shots of the chase. In that shot, you can see how big the set was.

Here Brown is referring to what is perhaps the supreme moment of the film, when John and Pearl's skiff is caught by river currents and snatched out of Preacher's reach. This sequence remained one of the most vivid in Denis Sanders' recollection of his many conversations with Laughton. Elaborating on his intentions to make *Hunter* an abstraction and a fairy tale, Laughton told Sanders that "each of the actions had to be larger than they would have been in life. He was not trying to achieve a realistic picture, but an impressionistic one." As for Preacher's scream in particular, "Charles was consciously trying to achieve a special effect. He talked at length about how he hoped to accomplish this by mixing the visual and the auditory with the music for a final startling moment . . . Charles did this with all of the scenes. He knew that one does not simply direct a movie, one makes a movie. Charles Laughton, by instinct and his vast experience in films, understood how one must find an interrelationship of all of the elements to achieve an artistic final product. This responsibility lies with the director."

Davis Grubb

Most of the mountain communities between Pittsburgh and Nashville were built because of fear: fear of living alone, because of pirates, the Harpes and Mason, whom I mentioned in *Night of the Hunter.* They were the legendary horrors that roamed the river at the end of the Revolutionary War. They were horrible men. You hear outcries in the media today about criminals who are animals. Most of the criminals of today are gentlemen compared to those two brothers and that former soldier. Big Harpe got mad one morning because his baby was crying, and they had to maintain absolute silence in their forest hideout, so he brained it against a tree.

The boat began to spin - caught in the river's current.

One of Grubb's sketches
shows Preacher full figure,
but with bizarre, high-angled
foreshortening which gives
it more the effect of a
close-up, which was how
Laughton filmed it.

Preacher left behind by the children

I said in the novel that when the river caught the children's skiff and carried them beyond Preacher's grasp, he let out a cry which brought back memories of the Harpes and Mason, the river ghosts of all time.

Preacher's scream is the climax of the chase, in more ways than one. The transition from Powell's frustration and rage to the release—actual and emotional—of little John is an extraordinary multimedia mix of image, sound and music. The boy, through whose point of view we experience the story, is at an age when he is still innocent of sexual knowledge. Not in a sexual way, therefore, but in a purely emotional sense, this scene is a cinematic orgasm. It is unbelievable tension, followed by an explosion which quickly subsides into a strange, sweet, unimaginable peace. In terms of the film's running time as well as its dramaturgy, this moment is at the very heart of *Hunter*. And I would suggest that it taps into something deep in the human psyche, something which explains why this film is so haunting to those who first saw it when they, like John, were young and still verging on their own loss of innocence.

The Laughton-Grubb pre-production correspondence reflects this primal vision. "Now, the journey of the children down the river," the direc-

Property master Joe
La Bella hands
Mitchum Preacher's
switchblade. Now,
he's ready for his
close-up.

tor wrote the novelist, "I feel this passage must have the river behind it,
every bit of it either visually or musically. It will be a brute to shoot as it
will need so many more shots to the minute than the dialog scenes." In
reply, Grubb wrote, "I agree that the passage down the river must be lyric
and *flowing*. It seems to me that the chaos of exodus is the place where
quick fast cutting must occur. The early part of the passage down the river
must be a blessed and lyric moment of dramatic relief. I want the audience
to feel the river as the womb of safety—as the flowing breast of succor.
They must love the river as I do—as the children did. It must envelop and
embrace this sequence warmly and richly."

Robert Golden

All I can say about that moment is that a lot of care was given to it. A
lot of care. You know, to have this man Mitchum standing there screaming like a wild animal was something that, while it was being shot, could
look ludicrous. And there were no limits that Laughton wanted to put
on it. The more ludicrous it looked, the better. He encouraged
Mitchum as an actor to just let go.

Robert Mitchum

I just got in the water and did it. Charles said, "Do it once." So, "Okay." We did it in one take. Couldn't have handled too many more. We knew what we wanted. Shit. I knew what Charles was thinking, he knew what I was thinking. We had no problems, ever. I just tried to please him, you know, I was just showing off for him.

That possibility of looking ludicrous to which Golden refers was no doubt reinforced by the fact that Mitchum wasn't even really standing in the "river;" he had to *crouch* in water which otherwise would have barely come to his hips. There may have been only one take, but, as we have seen, a single take for Laughton was the equivalent of multiple takes for any other director. "All right, Mitch," says Charles, and Mitchum's very first attempt does indeed seem to be the version used in the film. "Just a minute," says the director to his crew, "don't cut. Uh, Mitch—take a deep breath, and run as long as you can. (*To Cortez:*) You haven't cut, have you?" Cortez says, "No," and then there is some maneuvering to make sure Preacher's knife isn't too close to his face. Then Laughton says, "The

"I was just showing off for Charles."

camera's still running. All right, Mitch, one deep breath." Once again, as in the film, Mitchum's scream starts deep inside him and rises rhythmically, keening and building until it bursts forth as a roar. Unlike the long sustained note we hear in the film, however, this time Mitchum screams in short staccato howls of bone-chilling pain, much like the animalistic sounds we hear later in the film after his character has been wounded. Just as Mitchum is about to run out of breath, Laughton cuts.

Paul Gregory

I don't know what they did in postproduction, but they worked on that, they just had a ball doing that particular thing. I know, because Laughton would tell me, "We've got a sound that's going to knock you right out of your seat, old boy!"

Robert Golden

The one person who understood Laughton every bit of the way was Walter Schumann, and this scream of Mitchum's was something I know they worked out between them. Pictures are a kind of an illusion, but you bring it about by very definite things. We got the scream, and we got the music, that long-held chord, and we went to the panel board and worked it out. We spent a whole week dubbing the picture, which was a pretty long session, but it was very important. Laughton was there every minute, and so was Walter Schumann.

After Mitchum screams, we cut to a couple of long shots and then an even longer shot where the kids in the boat drift down the river under the stars. I remember, in the cutting and dubbing, this was one of the things that Laughton had in his head that he was sure of. He wanted that whole shot to be extended as long as it could possibly hold on the screen. As l-o-n-g as it could possibly hold.

Laughton made sure that he had more than enough footage. In the raw shot, many seconds pass before the skiff even drifts into view. This turns out to be typical of the children-on-the-river shots, which usually begin and end with long stretches of pure river footage, and for a very specific reason: composer Schumann recalled that shots were filmed over-length in order to allow him maximum freedom for his scoring.

"As long as it could possibly hold . . ."

Davis Grubb

The sound they got for the scream wasn't right for me. It's very effective in the film, of course, but nothing could have matched what I heard
in my head when I was writing the book. Nothing could have matched
the terror that I believe every child feels at some time, of being alone,
even being hunted. Which is not just a facile metaphor. I remember too
much of my own life.

I'd *heard* that scream. Because, I used to work down at the railroad
depot on summer nights in the thirties, and I used to hear the shanty boat
people down on the water. (And I always used to envy them, because they
were obviously having a good time, drinking and fucking and fighting . . .
The girls would come up on the shore occasionally and they were beautiful girls, most of them, very scuffed and dusty-looking, muddy angels.
There were a lot of people who lived on the waterfront, and when they
became unwelcome in a river town they would unhitch their rope from
a willow and float on down to Peyton City, or Captina, or maybe down
to Parkersburg. It was kind of a nice life, I always envied it.)

Anyway, I heard sounds down there. And I used to hear trains screaming in the night, and I didn't know what trains were when I was two and three years old. They seemed like hideous monsters out there somewhere in the river fog. And then they would be followed by the enormous clash, the iron clash of a freight train or a coal train taking up slack just before it started. The sounds of it are still with me. I'm able to remember a lot of things from when I was very, very small and young. I remembered suddenly the other day, I saw a shooting star one night, and my mother explained it was a world burning up. Can you imagine my horror on the night a few weeks later when the air was full of fireflies? I thought the whole universe was going! Because, a firefly and a shooting star were, to my eyes, indistinguishable.

Stanley Cortez
Before the music was even composed for that, I had some idea as to how the music would be. And I was trying, way in advance, to think—and this may seem like a lot of baloney to you—of what Schumann would do musically so that I, in turn, could do it lighting-wise: a totality of image which embraces the tonal as well as the visual.

Hilyard Brown
It was very simple to create those stars, but very tedious. I went in front of a blank white backdrop and hung a lot of wires with some tiny bulbs of various sizes and colors. That was the easiest thing in the world, you didn't have to paint the wires or anything else. As a matter of fact, the wires could probably have been three times as large as they were. The cameras couldn't see them.

You see, the lenses aren't that good. When you go on to a set and you close one eye and you squint the other, and really squint it, that's all that the camera can see, because that's as good as the lens is. And also, the emulsion on the film is such that you can't photograph anything that small. It isn't there, it doesn't exist.

Stanley Cortez
We hung a lot of lights for the stars, and some silver leaf behind them. Sometimes we would have the silver leaf in front, and by sometimes

moving the stars themselves, diminishing the light and increasing the light gave us the impression of a glitter.

Hilyard Brown

Whenever we'd shoot the animals and the boat together, that was not process photography. There was almost no process in the picture, everything that is on the film was shot live.

Unfortunately, this is where the film-makers' memories are most sharply contradicted by the evidence preserved in the out-takes. Although there may be some general cinematic truth of a technical nature in Brown's and Cortez's recollections of the star-hanging, it does not appear that the film for which they went through this process was *The Night of the Hunter.* Or, if it was on *Hunter,* it was apparently for naught—or else it was done separately for a postproduction optical effect. The plain fact is that no stars are visible in the raw footage filmed on the river soundstage. The sky full of stars which so beautifully completes Cortez's magical shot of the skiff drifting away from Preacher was added optically by the Special Effects team of Jack Rabin and Louis DeWitt at their Studio Film Service.

From an examination of the raw footage, Rabin and DeWitt emerge as unsung heroes in attaining Laughton's goal of creating fairy-tale imagery for the river journey. Contrary to Brown's memory, every shot combining animals and the children's skiff was a Rabin-DeWitt composite. And apparently, these shots were always planned to be exactly that: composites. Although the script denotes the image of the boat, river and stars as simply a "long shot"—which may mean that the plan *was* originally to hang the stars on the stage—the shots involving animals, beginning with the bull-frog in this scene, are clearly designated as "Special Shots." (It seems, though, that Laughton kept an open mind on these shots. He included the animal images on his "wish-list" for Terry Sanders, but finally all these shots were done in-studio, all of them composites—except the turtle, who does not share the screen with the children.)

This impression of star glitter, supported by the shimmering musical chord which Schumann has miraculously transmogrified from Preacher's scream, signals a major shift in the drama's mood, and heralds the beginning of one of cinema's most remarkable passages: the montage of the chil-

dren's journey down the river in flight from their pursuer. The moment of
transition is portrayed in the Grubb novel by the following few lines:

> John? Pearl whispered.
> But he was beyond answering.
> John?
> But he was asleep. And so it was to the doll that she spoke. And
> since the game she and John and Daddy had been playing was fin-
> ished she began another one. And in the silence of the great brood-
> ing river night she whispered to the doll Jenny a little story about a
> pretty fly she had seen one day in the green, sweet leaves of the
> grape arbor. He had a wife, this pretty fly, and one day she flew
> away and he was very sad. And then one night his two pretty fly
> children flew away, too, into the sky—into the moon. But it was a
> story without an end because presently she was sleeping, too.

In the film, as John falls into his well-earned sleep, Pearl sings the "pretty
fly" story to Miss Jenny, a gentle lullaby sung in a wisp of a child's voice.
The words of her song are set to the theme which Schumann has utilized
throughout the film to portray both the innocence of the children and, to
an even greater extent, the beauty of the river on which they live:

> Once upon a time, there was a pretty fly.
> He had a pretty wife, this pretty fly.
> But one day she flew away, flew away.
> She had two pretty children.
> But one night these two pretty children
> Flew away, flew away—into the sky—into the moon . . .

Mrs. Sonya Goodman
When the little girl in the boat sings "Pretty Fly," I have a feeling that it
was not really the little girl but a young woman named Betty Benson,
who had sung Melora's song in *John Brown's Body*.

Originally, however, Laughton had a different plan for "Pretty Fly." To
begin with, there was to be no song at all. In the screenplay, as in the novel,

Once upon a time there was a pretty fly

And he had a pretty wife, this pretty fly

But one day she flew away flew away

(That very) Night his pretty fly children

(And so that)

Flew away, flew away, (flew away?) Too After their mother

Into the sky – into the moon

Grubb's hurried scrawl transforms his novel's prose into lyrics for Schumann's "river/children" melody.

Pearl merely tells her story to her doll. At some point between script and stage, although we'll never know if it was Laughton's idea or Schumann's, the child's story became a song. And whose voice was to sing it for Pearl? Remember Mitchum's story about Sally Jane Bruce's grandparents: "Sing your French song, honey, sing your French song . . ." That's right—in the original footage shot on the river sound stage, little Sally herself is singing Schumann's plaintive song, and not to a playback, but live and *a cappella*.

Even if Laughton had decided to use Sally's own rendition of "Pretty Fly" in the final film, it was a mistake to record it live on the river stage. In the out-takes, the water is making so much racket with its artificial currents that you can barely hear Laughton's directions to Sally—"You mustn't look up at me, sing to Miss Jenny"—let alone her fragile singing voice. Since this problem must have been immediately apparent the moment he saw and heard the next day's rushes, Laughton then attempted to record Sally sans the watery *obligato*. A wild track (sound without picture) exists of Laughton coaching little Sally through several attempts at the song. Her child's voice is quavery, but it sounds eerily like the adult-dubbed version we're now familiar with in the movie, and it would be fascinating to see and hear the effect of the scene as Laughton originally and more naturalistically conceived it. (Just possibly, it might have taken the kibosh off a moment which is lyrically beautiful but which some self-conscious modern audiences, long weaned away from accepting anything that smacks of musical drama in the cinema, sometimes are uncomfortable with and greet with nervous laughter.) "Sally, I want you to sing me your song," begins Laughton quietly, "very slowly and very sweetly." She sings it very simply and effectively, though she sometimes sings "petty" for "pretty," and she has a tendency to speed up on the phrase, "Flew away, flew away." Laughton attempts to correct her on this, then asks his sound recorder, "Can you understand those words?" "Yes," comes the reply, "She makes a little noise with her lips when she's starting." "Oh, that doesn't matter." Apparently they were trying to match the timing of what they had already filmed, but when someone points at the stopwatch, Laughton chooses to ignore it: "I can't be timed." Then, to Sally: "Sing to me, just sing to me, never mind that thing." And then, when they're reloading for another take, "Some of the words weren't quite clear, sweetheart. Try and sing the *story*."

Listening to little Sally Jane's rendition, one can appreciate how close an imitation of her child's sound was achieved by the adult who eventually dubbed the song for her.

For the moment, on screen, all is peace and safety. No longer captive to their stepfather's madness and greed, John and Pearl are welcomed by the river and its denizens like children in a fairy story fleeing a wicked stepparent, who are taken in by creatures of the woodland. A spider spins her dew-dropped web in the foreground as we see the children's skiff drift dreamily in the background. A frog rests on a foreground lily pad while the children's boat floats by in the background. (A shot was planned of "the drifting boat through fireflies," and its background, without fireflies, was photographed—high angle of the skiff crossing a bar of light on the water—but for whatever reason it wasn't used. Aside from that one shot, every dreamlike, nocturnal effect called for in Laughton's script made it into the film.) A soft breeze blows the moonlit filaments of a river weed, scattering them into the night . . .

Terry Sanders
There's some shots that were impossible to get on the second unit, like the spider web. I remember shooting a spider web, and photographically it was over-exposed, so we didn't use that. I mean, there were a lot of things that

John and Pearl, two pretty flies caught in a web of Hilyard Brown's devising.

one hoped for, you know, Laughton had a wish list, he didn't actually get everything. But, it was fun and exciting.

Hilyard Brown

For the shot of the kids drifting past a spider's web, I made a web out of nylon thread. I couldn't work at spider web size, so I made it greatly oversized, about three feet in diameter. Stanley just backed up and photographed it so that it looked like what it was supposed to be, while I was up there holding a little stick and dripping honey on the web so that the "dew" was dripping on it.

Brown's recollection of the spider web is substantially correct, but slightly incomplete. The white web was photographed against a plain black background, so that it could be combined optically with the shot of the boat in the background. (And, in point of fact, Brown dripped the honey not from a stick but from the more-controllable vehicle of a syringe.)

Hilyard Brown
But I didn't have to create everything from scratch like that. For one shot
of cattails spreading seeds in the wind, I picked up some real cattails out at
Rowland V. Lee's farm where we'd been shooting.

The film dissolves from the cattails to Spoon's ice cream parlor, where
Icey is listening to Walt reading aloud a postcard from Preacher:

> Dear Walt and Icey: I bet you been worried and gave us up for lost.
> Took the kids down here with me for a visit to my sister Elsie's
> farm. Thought a little change of scenery would do us all a world
> of good after so much trouble and heartache. At least the kids will
> get a plenty of good home cooking. Your devoted Harry Powell.

Don Beddoe
When I did my first scene with Charles Laughton, there was something to
do with a postcard. It was my opening shot of working—it wasn't the
opening shot that I had in the picture, but it was the opening shot of
working—and I was nervous about doing it, *very* nervous, because I had
tremendous admiration for Laughton as an actor. I had been a great ad-
mirer of his ever since he appeared first in New York with the play, *Payment Deferred.* I saw him in that on Broadway, and he was just wonderful
in it. And I'd always admired him since then, and particularly in *The Beach-
comber.* I thought he was just first-rate. So, working for him was a very
warm reunion. Of course, he didn't know *me* before, but as far as I was
concerned, it was a real idol that I was working for. I didn't know him as
a person at all, but just the professional stature of the man . . . I was wor-
rying about doing the postcard scene because I wanted to do it well, you
know, to feel that he would approve of me as an actor. But, I stumbled a
few times in the reading of the thing, and said, "Oh, damn!" you know.
And he looked at me and he said, "What's the matter? Are you nervous?"
And I said, "Well . . . (*Pause*) I might as well tell you, yes, I'm nervous,
working for you." He put his arm around me and he said, "You silly son
of a bitch! You're great, don't worry about it, come on now!" And of
course, that was the whole thing. It was a significant part of Laughton's
character, I think, and it meant a great deal to me, and I thought it was a
very generous thing to do, to put me at ease like that.

Icey + Walt (behind the confectionary counter)   bears/girls
read the postcard.

Laughton in this brief scene is putting the audience at ease—but only so that he can literally plunge them back into Preacher's relentless quest. Walt and Icey chat calmly about the "news" in Preacher's postcard:

ICEY: Now ain't you relieved, Walt?

WALT: Sure, but you was worried too, Mother; takin' off with never a word of goodbye. You know, I got to figurin' maybe them gypsies busted in and done off with all three of 'em.

ICEY: You and your gypsies! They been gone a week!

WALT: Sure. But not before one of 'em knifed a farmer and stole his horse. Never caught the gypsy—nor the horse.

Although the script now calls for a LAP DISSOLVE, the film much more powerfully CUTS to:

DESCENDING HELICOPTER SHOT — THE RIVER — DAY

A man is going along a river lane on horseback. It is PREACHER . . ."

The postcard
scene between
Walt and Icey
Spoon—
the eye of a
cinematic
hurricane . . .

Emphasizing the power of this transition is Schumann's score: swiftly descending strings over the helicopter shot of Mitchum's double, thunderous reprise of Preacher's motif when we cut to Mitchum himself.

Terry Sanders
Well, it's the music that makes that shot dramatic. But yes, it was another second unit shot. In those days, they didn't have zoom lenses, so you had to actually move in with the helicopter as close as you safely could.

At one point during the script writing stage, James Agee, in his notes, had imagined the need for "possibly: a helicopter shot linking Preacher, riding down a riverside road, and the children in their boat, a bend or two further downstream, beyond his seeing." Laughton's final draft, however, called for no such shot.

Terry Sanders
There are some more of my location shots coming up, but most of the rest of the river montage was shot in the studio. They did pretty well, considering they didn't have a river at all, just this little lake.

. . . which jump-cuts to a helicopter shot provided by Terry Sanders.

Davis Grubb

Laughton matched the movie I'd had in my head in this one way: He seized upon the real hero of the story, which is the river itself. And he did it in a way which grabbed that whole river in his film.

Perhaps I should say "heroine," not "hero." Once in 1958, on a St. Louis waterfront, I happened to bump into Richard Armfeld, the editor of the *Waterways Journal*. He said the Ohio River was different from other rivers. It's a river of pools, it's not a rushing, headlong river like the Mississippi which, even in the song, is "old man river." The Ohio is definitely feminine. I always knew that as a child; I didn't have it confirmed by literary sources until I grew up. I hadn't read Mark Twain, but I knew the river as well as I knew my front yard. It always had a way of reminding river people that it was there, particularly in the spring.

Again, from Grubb's letter to Laughton: "And yet I think we must keep the quick, bright edge of danger sharply at the corners of this sequence. The quick water running. The preacher on the shore. The snags and sawyers and sandbars. But *some* of this river sequence must flow gently and lead sweetly to Rachel on the bluff in the green, gentle morning under the willows. I will provide sketches for this." Grubb provided sketches, Laughton provided the scenes—and Walter Schumann provided a tone poem. As the composer explained, "Two themes in the form of songs had to be written before shooting was begun. The first, 'Pretty Fly,' was to be sung by the little girl. It developed into the main theme of the picture. The second was 'Lullaby,' which was to be used as a lonely setting for two tired children wandering down the river while escaping the preacher." It would actually be hard to cite any one melody as the film's "main theme," but Schumann's assessment is justified if we realize that the "Pretty Fly" tune becomes the theme associated, from the very first reel, with the River, and as we have seen the River is as much the leading character of our story as is the children's savior, Lillian Gish's Rachel.

Hilyard Brown

When Laughton filmed the sequences of the children drifting down the river, he put in a lot of things that were not in the book. He wanted the little kids to be associated with nature: rabbits, spiders, a little frog and all those things.

Laughton subsequently explained to Hollis Alpert at *Saturday Review* that he had wanted to surround the children with the creatures

"A little Disneyesque . . ." Trick question: How many rabbits are in this shot?

they might have encountered on their journey down river. "It was, in a way, a dream for them." (The optical effects team often created two slightly varied versions of a shot from which Laughton could choose. The shot of the children's boat in the background with two rabbits in the foreground is actually not a double but a *triple* exposure—they only had one rabbit, so the magic of cinema allowed this versatile mammal to portray both creatures.)

Paul Gregory
Charles discussed with me beforehand doing the trip down river from the point of view of the animals and cobwebs and things. He wanted to know if I thought that it would seem too artsy-fartsy to suddenly have the big rabbits and the big frog and what-have-you. I said, "Look, if you feel that language is necessary to tell your story, by all means do it." Which I do feel: one has to take that chance. Whether it was going to come off or not, I didn't know. I'd be the last one in the world to say, "No, it won't work."

What did I think of the idea? A little Disneyesque. But after all, Disney had used it to good advantage, and there was no license on it.

Davis Grubb

Laughton was criticized by some reviewers for using the animals. I thought it was beautiful. Why is it wrong to show a little frog? A rabbit? A turtle? After all, it worked pretty well in the great Steinbeck book, *The Grapes of Wrath*. He had the turtle as a metaphor in the novel.

Terry Sanders

This is my copy of the script of *Night of the Hunter* with all my notes for the second unit. So, basically every note here is something which came out of my discussions with Charles. We just went over it page by page, and I made little notes, as you see. Here's: "Animal picture book. Not John's point of view. A turtle waddling, moving in muddy water." I never got that shot. I think they hired a turtle in Los Angeles. "Nursery shot with turtle. Clean turtle up," it says.

Mrs. Sonya Goodman

My husband went to listen to Kitty White playing guitar and singing in a little nightclub. He felt that she was absolutely right for the lullaby, and he brought her to Mr. Laughton's attention.

Davis Grubb

I had a friend, a marvelous singer on the West Coast named Kitty White. But I had no connection with her being used on the picture. That was one of those coincidences peculiar to our business. I never even met Walter Schumann, I just talked to him on the phone. It was during the preproduction stage of the film. He called and said he needed a lyric for a lullaby. I don't remember why they were in such a hurry, but he needed it right away, so I said, "Call me back in twenty minutes."

I can't answer the immemorial question, which came first, the lyric or the tune. I think he may have played a phrase of it on the piano and just said, "I want it to be kind of a lullaby . . ." I just took it from there. I could have done a lot better, but they needed it in such a hurry. He called back, and I read it to him, and he said, "How does this sound?" He played something, I said, "It sounds great," and we made it up together. But I didn't spend an awful lot of time on that lyric. As a matter of fact, I didn't spend that much time on the book.

I think we worked on the little girl's song the same day.

Mrs. Sonya Goodman

My husband wrote the score in a very short time, less than a month, I think. He wrote very quickly, and rarely changed a theme that he'd developed. He was very, very careful in everything that he did, and I think the experience of having to write a weekly TV show like *Dragnet* helped him learn to write so quickly. A lot of *The Night of the Hunter* was written in his studio at home, and I recall him playing the lullaby for me right after it was written, saying, "How does this sound?" The things that he wanted to test before he tried them out on more people were the things that he himself liked very much. Sometimes he'd play something for the children, not asking their opinion but just to see their reaction. The lullaby was a favorite.

Davis Grubb

Laughton I don't think could have visualized—or, idealized—that music in his own mind.

Mrs. Sonya Goodman

My husband was a quiet man, not given to great verbal expression, but in his quiet way he was always very happy whenever he could put forth in music exactly what Laughton wanted, or even embellish Mr. Laughton's ideas. He wrote some beautiful music for that scene when finally the children escape down the river. I don't think Mr. Laughton had envisioned it quite that way, but he was just delighted with it. I remember my husband telling me that the music he was writing for certain areas was not necessarily for areas where Laughton thought music would be used. But all his new additions were kept, because they helped the picture.

Paul Gregory

Walter Schumann was with us for about three years prior to our making that picture, on the other projects, so when he came in exactly, I can't tell you. He read the book immediately, and loved it. Walter wasn't a man to volunteer. Once, he might come and say, "I've had an idea," and he would present it very well. But he wasn't at all one of those that today it was this idea and tomorrow it was another idea. There are some people who will rush in and say, "Oh, I've got a great idea for such-and-such!" Walter wasn't like that. Walter was a real businessman about his work. He would discuss it, and know how you felt musically this scene should develop, and then he'd bring it in and say, "Do you think this is it?" Oh, he was wonderful. Half of my heart was gone when Walter died.★ We had such plans to do so many things, the theatre, shows and things. He was a genius, a *real* genius, Walter.

Although Terry Sanders shot more second unit footage than he now remembers, he also shot more footage than was actually used in the film, but this is to be expected.

Terry Sanders

I don't remember any more how much we shot per day—it's probably in my production book, you know, how it shows the schedule—but it seems to me it took about three weeks. And, I was happy with some things, I wasn't so happy with other things, and we got back and ran the dailies with Charles. I sat and ran all of them with him. We'd sent them on ahead from back east, but he probably didn't look at them because a lot of them were background plates, which can be pretty boring to look at, you know. So he probably waited for me to come back. Although, somebody must have checked them as we were sending them back to ensure that they were there.

And he was pleased with them. I was mildly depressed. Because, first of all, that kind of stuff is not that rewarding. I mean, you do the best you can, you get what you can, but what is it? It's really just support for the film. Also, you always try to get a hundred percent, and you never do, so . . . But, Charles was very pleased, and I was happy with my work.

Stanley Cortez

Milt Carter, who has since passed on, was a tremendous help. He had a great sense of humor, and kind of a hoarse voice which gave him more

---

★The composer passed away following heart surgery in 1958.

character. He was always in on all the discussions, he was a very strong influence on Charles in terms of the logistics, and don't underestimate Milt's ability as an assistant director. Milt, Ruby Rosenberg, and I had worked with Charles on *The Man on the Eiffel Tower*.

Terry Sanders

The scandal was, with Ruby Rosenberg, when I *heard* . . . I don't know first-hand, but Paul Gregory was very upset . . . because for some reason there was a two-day or three-day shut-down in the production, (AUTHOR'S NOTE: *This possibly refers to Billy Chapin's appendicitis attack*), and apparently Rosenberg was taking the crew to build his swimming pool! You can ask Paul about that.

Stanley Cortez

Ruby was a fine fellow, and he was not the typical production manager, where all they think about is saving money. Sure, he had to stick by the budget, which was part of his function, but he knew values, and if Charles or somebody had a thought and if Ruby saw that this would add value to the film, or give it an extra bit of power, there was no problem. He would go right ahead and sort of juggle things around to make possible that which we thought was a good idea.

For instance, Terry went back east to secure footage of quite a few things: the children around the basement who discover the body in the beginning of the film, the exterior of the prison, the river countryside, Mitchum's double on a horse when he's stalking the children. They tried very hard, what they did was very good; the only one big moment that they tried to get but couldn't is the shot of Mitchum's double on a horse we originally planned to use for rear projection in the hayloft scene.

Terry Sanders

I'd have to check the production book; if it's in my notes, in my list of shots, then I'm sure I shot it, but I don't remember. I do remember that the actual shot was a studio shot. But that's always the way. You often try things two different ways, and then you use the best way. And what they did in this case was a great shot.

"Don't he never sleep?" The evolution of John's rude awakening in the hayloft by the sound and sight of Preacher on horseback is traced from the sketch that Grubb did for Laughton. . .

Terry Sanders' production book, laced with notes taken during Laughton's conversations with him and filled with Hilyard Brown sketches, designates: "Sc. 388-394 – PROCESS PLATE—NIGHT (Day for night/moonlight. Trees block view occasionally. INT. HAY LOFT. Preacher appears, astride walking horse, singing. He crosses the frame and passes out of frame. Try horse at varying distances. 384 – TWILIGHT - scene darkens. 388 – Back Lit. Fairy tale quality. Moon progression! Dog!" That dog, in the final film, ends up being heard but not seen, as effective a touch for Laughton as it had been for James Whale in the opening grave-

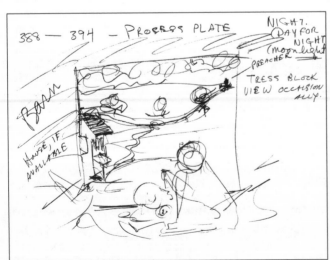

. . . to the sketches for a rear-projection plate which second unit director Terry Sanders photographed in West Virginia . . .
(*left & opposite*)

| PROC. |

BREAKDOWN SHEET

PRODUCTION NO_____ TITLE_____ PAGE _20_

NAME OF SET _BARN_ _DAY FOR NIGHT_ EXT INT NO. OF SCENES ___1___

CAST:	CAST AND WARD-ROBE CHANGE	SCENE NUMBERS AND SHORT RESUME OF ACTION
Preacher double horse dog	Preacher	(384 — . Twilight → night → moon Sc. 388 - 394 PROCESS PLATE INT. HAY LOFT. Preacher appears, astride walking horse, singing. He crosses the frame and passes out of frame. — MOON LIGHT
EFFECTS:		
MUSIC AND MISCELLANEOUS		
CONSTRUCTION ESSENTIALS:		Try horse at varying distances. 384 — TWILIGHT — SCENE DARKENS 388 ——→ BACK LIT. FAIRY TALE QUALITY
ESSENTIAL PROPS: (HOUSE IF EASY.)		Back lit? TWO ANGLES? OR CUTAWAYS? Moon progression! Dog!

yard scene of *Frankenstein*. But Sanders did shoot a double for Mitchum riding his horse, behind a log-fence, across a country landscape. It's a nicely composed shot, with three distant hills converging in the distance, and not without a certain mood provided by a cloud-darkened sky. Perhaps it might have been even more effective if the camera had been angled to position Preacher and his horse against that sky.

. . . to the final, forced-perspective solution executed on a soundstage by Brown and Cortez.

Stanley Cortez

I don't mean to speak derogatorily of Terry, but for some reason what he brought back for that one shot did not quite get over the thinking that Charles originally had and, had we used it, it would never have been as effective in terms of imagery as what we did. We concocted the idea of the hayloft, we took the idea to Ruby, who immediately saw the potentials of this thing, even though it was going to cost quite a bit more, and that's how we were able to go ahead and do it.

Hilyard Brown

Now, all that stuff, supposedly in late evening, where the kids stop at a house and hear the lullaby and see the canary in the window, and they go to the barn with the cows and climb up to the hay mow to sleep . . . At lunch one day, we were trying to figure out how to do that. I said, "Well, why don't we do it on the same set where we had the river chase?" So, those buildings were just cut-outs on a stage. They were like sheets of paper, just flat, painted cut-outs. If they didn't look quite real, that's the way we wanted them, that's exactly what we were trying to create.

Terry Sanders

One thing that's kind of interesting: If you ever get to see a 35mm print that isn't shown in the correct aspect ratio . . . *Night of the Hunter* is a *little* wide screen. Well, I remember seeing it projected at the time, where the wide screen matte wasn't put in, and you can see the set, and you can see *above* the set in the lullaby scene. That's supposed to be cut off. So, if it's projected wrong, if they have it framed wrong, you say, "What is this!?" You know, the top of the sky-scrim—that's a mistake.

After the children pause briefly to look at the farmhouse window, Kitty White's warm singing of Schumann's superbly tender lullaby continues while John and Pearl go into the barn to bed down for the night. Before they climb up into the hayloft, a tracking shot follows them across the barn floor, shooting through the legs and udders of several cows. Just before the shot ends, a drop of milk falls from one of the cow's udders.

Terry Sanders

Charles talked about shooting past the cow's udder. That was an important image to him. But I think that it was not lit right. I mean, they blasted the light on the udder so you can see all the bumps. They should have had it more in silhouette, I think, for my taste. I understand what he was going for, the concept of nurturing nature, symbolized by the milk . . . (*Smiles*) But for me, those udders are kind of a little bit frightening.

John and Pearl climb a ladder up into the hay loft, where they fall asleep beneath a wide-open window. The lullaby ends, and a brief passage of nighttime is indicated by a series of dissolves showing the crescent moon rising ever higher in the sky, another Rabin-DeWitt special effect. The wisps of clouds are apparently part of the on-stage cyclorama, but the moon and the stars were added in postproduction. That this was always the plan is indicated by the evidence of the out-takes in which the upper portion of the window is purposely blacked out by a board of some sort, thus to allow for the subsequent matting-in of optical work.

Hilyard Brown

Remember the business where Mitchum's riding across the horizon and the kids in the hay mow wake up and watch him back there riding by?

I had an idea that in order to make Preacher look like he's way out there, he should be much smaller, his travel should be much longer. We'd built the set in forced perspective, but, for the first time, I came up with the idea of having forced perspective people. So we went to one of those pony ride places and rented a white Shetland pony, and we used the little boy's double, who was a very small man, almost a midget, and had an outfit made for him just like Mitchum's. He rode on the pony in the background, Stanley backlit him in silhouette, and of course he was only about a third Mitchum's size, so he could travel three times as slowly. The set looked as though it were much bigger and he was really way over there. You hear Mitchum singing "Leaning on the Everlasting Arms," but what you see riding across in the background is not Mitchum at all. And it's not a process plate, which a lot of people think it is. It was shot real for real.

Stanley Cortez
The kind of things we did there illustrate, I feel, a phase of this business which is being lost. Unfortunately, many people today who are responsible for making films, for some reason and I don't know what it is, fail to realize that many things can be done on the camera or on the optical bench to give them the visual impression they want, a hundred times stronger, by doing it in a filmic way. Going to miniature sets, going to a miniature horse and rider, I don't want to use the word "tricks," I think it's a bad word, but these are the things that we don't use much today, unfortunately. And as a result, the so-called "realism" is a kind of disguise for the lack of know-how.

Now, I'm not criticizing my colleagues, or producers or directors, I'm only saying this in a constructive way. All that I am saying is that, if they were made aware that certain ideas and techniques exist to make what they visualize possible, they could then use them to the advantage of their pictures. And unfortunately, they are surrounded by people who don't have the years of experience to give them these imaginative concepts. Whereas, you take some of the directors who have been around and are aware of these things . . . Take a fellow like Freddie Zinneman for instance, or a person like Willie Wyler, or George Stevens, bless his soul, when he was alive, or any of these old pros, they knew the potentials—that's a key word—of how to achieve a certain result without going through all kinds of unnecessary expense under the guise of "naturalism."

And yet, ironically, naturalism is precisely what the film's star would have preferred to Laughton's more expressionistic approach, no matter how closely it may have been the cinematic approximation of Davis Grubb's lyrical and warmhearted prose.

Robert Mitchum

Yes, the book had its tenderness, but it was also . . . You had to stop every ten pages or so and say, "Holy Jesus!" It never quit. Relentless. Charles said he had to have some sort of a guideline, which was that he couldn't have women dragging their children off the streets every time I went to the market, or something like that. But I said, no, we should go for the ultimate, from the book, the inevitability, really, of Preacher, his ultimate evil.

"No, no, no," he said, he didn't want to portray that. He said it would really terrify people if you did it that way. It still came out that way, so he added all those things, you know, with the children, with the frogs, and the owls, he added all of that stuff to sweeten it.

No, I don't think he was just following the mood of the story. He *made* it the mood of the story. What would someone else have done? Run through a goat and make a couple of jokes? That's *Pounded to Death by Gorillas*. I'd *done* that. Still do it.

Agree with Mitchum or not on the aptness of Laughton's approach, the film reveals that the actor was completely correct on one point: Laughton made the mood of the story. And he made it with careful, conscious craftsmanship—God and the devil were both in the details. When the children's skiff approaches the farmhouse on the night of the lullaby, for instance, the river's water is smooth and calm. But after John hears Preacher's distant hymn and sees him on horseback traversing the horizon in silhouette—"Don't he never sleep?"—and the children rush back to the shore, the water is turbulent. (So is the music.)

Stanley Cortez

We thought that would tie in to the psychology of the scene, what Charles always called the "dramaturgy."

I've gotten many letters from people wanting to know how we did so-and-so. In fact, George Folsey, a very dear friend of mine, a very fine cinematographer, he called me and said, "How did you do that sequence down the river? Where did you go to get that?" I said, "Stage Fifteen at Culver City." A couple of years ago, the audience at the Filmex festival showing of the picture asked me the same thing, and they were amazed, they just couldn't believe it.

Hilyard Brown

Another idea that was all Charles Laughton's was that big close shot of the moon, craters and all, with wisps of clouds drifting in front of it. We took an already-existing shot of the moon and sent it to a lab for some special effects processing to put those clouds in.

Mitchum is not the only one who expresses reservations about Laughton's famously poetic imagery in this part of the film.

Paul Gregory

I thought the passage down the river was too dark, and it made it unbelievable. And I thought the things that were obvious cutouts for the barn and the house were unnecessary. It should have been real countryside, and we had it, we had it all there. We'd built sets on the Lee ranch that we didn't use. We didn't have to make these big cutouts. I don't think it's important, totally, to the standpoint of whether the picture can stand on its own or not, and I'm not saying that what I propose would have been any better, but I'm saying, had the children's flight down the river been more realistic, there would have been more drama, for me.

Because, I'm a realist, you see, I'm a very "real" individual. To me (*points to microphone*), this is a microphone—you see what I mean? And we had the river, we had the whole Ohio River, we sent the second unit back there. We could have had those children whirled out, we could have had them and their boat out in those rapids, and the stark horror of it, *being* more real . . . You see, the audiences went *mad* over the real thing of ol' Mitchum leaping after the children with his knife through the muck and mire. But then the picture demanded immediately that it not be real and be something else, only because they did it that way. That wasn't a dream, those kids weren't asleep in all that. They went to sleep once they were safely past Preacher, but they weren't dreaming that they were drifting down the river, they were drifting down the river. Why didn't we use the real river? Don't ask me. I think someone was afraid of drowning, or something. I don't know, because it was right there, it was absolutely right there, beautiful scenic values. I don't think this was Charles' deliberate decision, I think this had to do with too much icing on the cake. I think it had to do with a couple of departments that were more concerned with how a given thing was going to be that represented them than they were about the whole. And believe me, if we'd had the money, I would have reshot some stuff, and some of it would have involved that trip down the river. But we didn't have the money, so I just had to let it go.

Stanley Cortez
I think Charles was quite content with the picture. And if he hadn't been satisfied with any of the rushes as we went along, we would have reshot them, but we never did.

Robert Mitchum
In the beginning, when I said to Charles, "Let's make it for real," he was afraid of that. "No," he said, "We'll make a fairy story of it, as if it never really happened, as if it is a child's dream. Otherwise, we're adding to the spoilage." He was a moral ecologist.

Stanley Cortez
Charles would be so marvelous, he would say to me, "Stan, this is where we need fantasy, this is where we need so-and-so and so-and-so . . ." And then he'd walk away and leave me alone, and I would get these effects. He made a remark to me once when we were on the sequence of going down the river, he used the expression, "Fairy tale." And when he saw the rushes, he said, "My God, how did you do that?" I said, "Because you used the word 'fairy tale.'"

Robert Golden

Of course, that whole sequence of the kids' journey down the river was
the one that Stanley Cortez really did a magnificent job on. And
Laughton was very appreciative of it. He said it was beautiful, and he
said, "There is a true artist."

During the shooting of the picture, Gregory and Laughton gave each
of the key people—Brown, Cortez, Carter and myself—one percent of
the picture. All we were giving was help, but that was their way of ap-
preciating the help we were giving.

Hilyard Brown

I tell you, that was the most marvelous thing they could ever have done.
Here were four guys who normally just get a salary, and one morning, out
on location, somebody came and gave each of us a letter. We looked at
each other, opening them up, "What'd *you* get?" sort of thing. I thought,
"What's going on? Is the place folding up?" Inside was a letter, I think it
was notarized, saying something like, "We hereby give you thus-and-such
portion of the picture, due to your extraordinary help . . ." I tell you, it
really gives you a shot of adrenalin, a fantastic thing like that. I don't think
it amounted to much financially, but that wasn't the important thing. I
think Gregory and Laughton dreamed it up all by themselves. Some of the
people not involved in getting the percentage, their noses were out of joint
a little bit. But actually, this was an appreciation for the guys that would
meet and cooperate every night, the guys that made the picture.

Paul Gregory

Well, I've always given percentages of my productions to people that I
felt were worthy of it. Perhaps I shouldn't have been the one that decided their worthiness, but, since in most of the cases it was my money
anyway, I gave it as I chose. And it was a thing I'd planned to do if I felt
we had a unit at all. Not as an incentive, just as gratitude. Because, when
I got into the finances with United Artists, I didn't think we'd ever see
the time of day when we'd get a check from the picture. But I still
wanted these four to have the percentage, so they wouldn't feel that we
were selfish. And United Artists were very much against my doing it.
They felt the men were well-enough paid and they shouldn't partici-

Rachel

Davis Grubb

pate. But if you look into any of my shows, on almost all of them, people that have done themselves nobly I've hopefully rewarded.

Terry Sanders
I'm sure that Charles shot all of the children's river journey after the principal players were finished, because that's what one tends to do when you have actors you are paying a lot of money; you try to shoot them in a contained amount of time and . . . get rid of them.

Robert Mitchum
You see, after we finished the principal photography, then Charles went on for weeks doing the little boy and girl going down the river. They did effects, like the midget on the pony, they set up the owls and all that. And all the sets were stylized. That was how he planned to counterbalance the terror. And also, he wanted to bring some light into it from the old lady's character. "Mother Hubbard," he said. That's why he

chose Lillian Gish. I should have thought a much more *physically* capable image was needed from the old woman's character. But it works in the picture. With Lillian, *anything* works.

Terry Sanders
Charles discussed Lillian Gish as being kind of the most important element in the film. He always gave her great credit. He treated her like she was magical, you know.

The stage is set for Miss Gish's entrance when the children's skiff gently runs aground and the camera pans up to fill the screen with a starry night sky. (This nocturnal sky is courtesy of a vertically rotating drum, added to the scene by Rabin and DeWitt.) The film now dissolves from the starry night sky to a brilliant morning sky with sunbeams piercing the clouds. The last note of the Walter Schumann nocturne has died away, to be replaced by the sound of a rooster.

Terry Sanders

Oh, that's my shot of the clouds. I remember that shot. The script called for a sky at dawn, so I just kept a lookout for rays of sunlight poking through clouds, and when I saw them one day we grabbed the shot.

Contrary to the staging indicated in the script, we hear Miss Gish— "You two youngsters get up here to me this instant!"—before we actually see her. Davis Grubb's pre-production letter to Laughton had reflected on Rachel's entrance into the story: "I suddenly hear her crying down to the children from the bluff. Some willowy toughness . . . Rachel's whole life is crisis—toughness always. Toughness to cover the love and softness that if she kept it out in the open would spill out and spoil." Schumann's underscore immediately resumes, this time in a pastoral vein, sort of a wordless nursery rhyme. No sooner does Miss Gish make her appearance as Rachel (in long shot) than she grabs a willow switch and scoots John and Pearl along the riverbank and up to her farmhouse, where her three current charges—Ruby, Clary and Mary—are helping with the chores.

Rachel Cooper — a strong tree
with branches for many birds.

Terry Sanders

Laughton's image for Lillian Gish was Mother Goose, going along the
riverbank. There's all the geese on her front yard when she gets to her
house.

The presence of actual geese, perfectly natural in a barnyard, for all
their symbolic import, was apparently an inspiration of the production.
The script makes no mention of them, though it does hint at the symbolism Laughton intended for Miss Gish's character:

> She surrounds (John and Pearl) and drives them like geese up the
> bank . . . They move across the meadow like a nursery frieze.

Don Beddoe

I'd already met her, because I had played years ago with her sister Dorothy,
and as a matter of fact we did the play *Holiday*—remember the old Philip
Barry play?—together in stock. Oh, Dorothy was a love, oh, a complete

love, just a beautiful, beautiful person, and Lillian was the same thing she is always, gracious and lovely. Beautiful. Real lady.

Lillian Gish

It wasn't difficult to prepare to play Rachel Cooper. I am not a mother, but I had the most beautiful mother in the world, so I didn't have to go any further than home for that.

If I said some lines quietly that the script asked for "laughing loudly," or "sort of roughly," that's because I'd worked that out in rehearsal. You show to a director what you feel is right. Usually, when you're up there doing it, you're in this character, and if you're any good at all you're nearer the truth of it than someone who has so much to think about: story, sets, costumes. And Laughton, being an actor, would instinctively grasp a true, as opposed to an imposed, idea.

Of course, working with children, you had to be careful and do what was best for them. But there were no problems at all working with Billy Chapin. Wasn't he lovely in the picture? He was such a dear boy. He listened so carefully, and did so beautifully what he was told. It was a pleasure to work with him.

Only when they arrive at the house (filmed at the Lee ranch) do we— and John—get our first good look at Rachel, with a p.o.v. shot from her feet up to her face. Schumann's barnyard/nursery tune for Rachel now gives way to the same beautiful lullaby melody that underscored her appearance in the film's first scene and, more recently, provided vocal accompaniment for the children's night in the hayloft. A reverse angle gives us John's reaction, as coached by Laughton, standing in for Rachel and taking advantage of the chirping audible in the trees: "You look at me as if I was that funny bird or a giraffe or something you don't understand. You're trying to figure what the heck I'm about. Now, just cast your eyes down a second, down to my feet. Now, slowly look up . . . I'm going to look after you and care for you for the rest of my life. What I want you to do is, when I say that, it's a sort of look of, uh, you don't believe, you wonder. It's almost like somebody gave you an enormous big gift like Mitch did the other day, it's that kind of a look . . . No, it's more pleasant than that, Billy. It's almost crying. That's it."

Creative Play Period—Laughton and Miss Gish share some quality time with Rachel's orphans (*above & below*).

Don Beddoe

I thought the two children were good. I thought they were very well behaved, and they were good in the picture. I didn't see them give Laughton any trouble. I'm sure he handled them beautifully, because they seemed to be very compatible. I mean, he was not like the actor, he was just more like a father figure. Which was interesting, too, in its

way. Well, you don't think of Laughton as a family man, to begin with, you know, and he stepped into it just perfectly. I happened to notice a couple of little things where he'd give 'em a pat on the bottom, it was real cute, and they'd go off and they'd do what he wanted.

Stanley Cortez

I remember Charles working with the children, not just the little boy and girl, but also the other orphans that Lillian Gish's character was taking care of. He had a way with these children. They were never frightened of him. He became part of their group, so to speak, which was what he was trying to do. And Miss Gish was so marvelous with them. You know, Charles had a great love for kids, and they loved him. Unfortunately, he never had any of his own.

Childless indeed, Laughton once remarked to Grubb, "The only important thing for an artist is to communicate with another human being. It is not necessary for an actor to procreate." And another time, he said to the author, "Art is a kind of deviation from having children."

William Phipps

I've never told anybody this before. I remember Laughton used to say about himself and Elsa, the first ten years of their marriage was great—sex, and everything else. The first ten years. And, he said, he wanted children. And she refused him. She loved to go on record at the drop of a coin to say how much she disliked children. Did *not* like children. And, he never really forgave her. He never forgave her for that, he really wanted children. Oh, he *loved* children. He loved 'em. Kids loved Laughton, 'cause he was so *funny*. He would just charm the pants off the kids, and they were delighted. Because, you know, little kids like Santa Claus, and ogres, and stuff. And—where did I read it? He never described himself as "the back end of an elephant," the way somebody misquoted him, he used to say, "I look like the south end of an elephant going north."

Stanley Cortez

I think one of the great attributes that Charles had with kids was the instinctive reaction that children would have for Charles as a "foxy grandpa" type of a guy, you know, a great big wonderful, lovable red face like they saw in comic books and storybooks. He would call the children aside and give them certain things to think about without them knowing it. He would tell them certain stories, and they would think about them. He would inject an idea or a thought or a word, and they would keep thinking about that word, and that thinking would give Charles a certain expression when the camera was rolling. Mind you, he wouldn't say, "Think about it." He would never tell a child directly what to do. If you command a child, that's one approach, but if you approach a child indirectly it becomes a part of what *he* is thinking, as against part of your command and your thinking. So that was the whole idea, to get it out of the *child*.

Laughton's directorial technique with children was fondly remembered by Bill Chapin and his mother, according to the report filed by Elsa Lanchester's researchers. This description not only corroborates Cortez's perception of Laughton's methods but also casts doubt on Mitchum's assertion that Laughton gave up on working with the children:

> Billy, aware that children are really not actors, appreciates the personal way that Charles helped mold him the way he wanted the character to be. The picture was a memorable experience for Billy and he remembers even as a child how impressed he was that Charles would take so much time helping him interpret the role. Every character was important and special to him as a director, and he was willing to take the time and patience necessary to get exactly the interpretation he desired.
>
> Billy adored Laughton, felt he was a marvelous director because he spent so much time with him and because he established such an immediate direct and warm working relationship. Whenever Charles wanted Billy to do something in a scene, he took him off to the side, talked quietly with him. He never raised his voice, he discussed what he wanted in detail, listened to Billy's ideas and helped create the right mood for the scene.
>
> Once, in the middle of the shooting of the film, Billy had to go to the hospital for an appendectomy. He was there for a week, and during that time Charles came to visit him. He brought a very

personal gift—carefully chosen, expensive and personal—which thrilled the child actor. They sat and chatted in a relaxed manner for at least an hour.

There is a picture . . . taken by Don Ornitz, with Laughton and Billy standing together, thinking. Laughton had just whispered into Billy's ear about something that he wanted him to do, and the photographer caught that moment on film. The picture is signed, "To Billy who is a swell actor and a wonderful guy, Charles."

Shelley Winters' publicist at this time was Arthur P. Jacobs, who would become the producer of, among other films, the hit *Planet of the Apes* epics. In the midst of the *Hunter* shoot, his office prepared a press release which of course mentioned his client's starring role, but was mainly concerned with the child actors and Laughton's careful handling thereof. "One of the big mistakes in working with kids," we are told, "is to allow everyone on the set to talk to them, as this tends to confuse the children. Laughton and the principals in each scene are the only ones to have any contact with the children. The idea is to establish a close relationship between the kids and their acting elders. Laughton's iron-clad rule has been no contact; and the rule includes mothers, assistant directors and other crew personnel. When too many people are in touch with the children, they seem to lose all powers of concentration. Also, it is important that you treat the kids like everyone else—in a dignified adult way. This tends to make them feel that they are part of a team. Due to Laughton's brilliant skill as an actor, he is excellent as a teacher when he interprets the scenes for the children. Also, he is always ready to answer and explain any questions that the kids might have." The piece goes on to mention "Laughton's idea that the children should go out to play when they aren't working. Laughton also shies away from excessive rehearsals as they tend to make the children's performances too stilted and wooden." Of course, thanks to Laughton's unique method of keeping his camera rolling between takes, he was virtually filming his rehearsals anyway, thus assuring that no spontaneous moment of truth or inspiration would go unpreserved.

Paul Gregory
At the time, I thought the whole business of Rachel Cooper and the

Rachel Cooper's Kitchen—pre-production watercolor by Allan Abbott.

homeless children worked very well. I think if it were to be done today it would have to be done much more realistically in some aspects. It was easier to read that aspect of the story in the book than it was to film. Because, the very transfer of it from the book to film took on a Pollyanna, holier-than-thou kind of thing. Today, you'd almost need a Marjorie Main/Ma Kettle type of woman not to have it be so. Someone really grotesque, that's been scrubbin' the clothes and feedin' the hogs, who'd find the two children in their skiff on the shore and say, really crabby, "What are you two doin' over there, you little brats? You get out of there! What's the matter with you?" And have her suddenly be sweet, you know, "Ah, you poor little thing." And have her like that instead of the way Lillian was. Lillian played it straight, it wasn't caricatured at all. I don't think there was any other way to play it at that time. No other way to play it. But I don't think you could get away with that at all today, I think you'd have to caricature.

According to Davis Grubb, Laughton told him that Lillian Gish was "using some techniques from the old silent film days, but it was absolutely right for the film, and so he let her use them." If Grubb himself had had any doubts about the rightness of Miss Gish's interpretation of Rachel or the conviction in her performance, they were dispelled when the "real" Rachel saw the film. Being illiterate, she had never read Grubb's novel, but when she saw the movie she told Grubb that she recognized herself in Miss Gish and thanked him for the compliment he had paid her.

Stanley Cortez

I never saw anything but the most wonderful relationship between Miss Gish and Charles. Funny thing, Charles apologized to her for me one day. He was talking to her, and I was telling the boys to put certain lights in a certain place, and I used the expression, "Take this one, and give it to Gish." You see? "Gish." I meant no harm, but it's my way of working. This was at the beginning of the picture, and she didn't know quite how to take it. That's when Charles said to her, "Now, Lillian, Stan uses the word 'Gish,' not to be impolite, but rather out of respect for you, as he would use the word 'Caruso' or 'Michelangelo'—the great artists."

Before the two new children can join Rachel's family, they need a merciless scrubbing-down. After this clean-up, we see the children's baskets lined up on a shelf, which then dissolves to a tracking shot of the baskets as the kids carry them through town, trailing after Rachel on her errands. Apparently this was another instance where Laughton found in post-production that he didn't have the footage he needed— in this case, a tracking shot of the baskets. Here, once again, Rabin and DeWitt saved the day by optically enlarging the baskets from a tracking shot of the kids. Note the grainy texture of that one shot on the baskets as they're being carried through town.

Davis Grubb

That street scene was set up in such a funny way, it was like a stage set. But, when Rachel is walking through town with her children, I loved that.

Stanley Cortez

And that was not an easy set to light, incidentally. I gave Hilly Brown hell one day when he built that street on a very small stage. There is a law that every wall of a set must be four feet from the actual stage wall, in case of fire, but we didn't have the four feet. We had to follow Miss Gish and the kids along that street, into a store, out again. That was a difficult set to photograph, because the stage was so damn small, you could not get light where you wanted it. I gave Hilly hell, so to speak— but in a nice way. He took it in a nice way, too.

As a cattle dealer passes by Rachel and her children, he says, "Howdy, Miz Cooper, what happened to our milk supply?" This one-line bit is performed by veteran actor John Hamilton, at the time one of the co-stars of TV's *The Adventures of Superman,* portraying the cantankerous editor of the *Daily Planet,* Perry White. Those familiar with it recognize his voice in this street scene, but the camera angle conceals most of his face. Is it possible that Laughton knew of the infamous preview of *From Here to Eternity,* where audience members buzzed with distraction at their recognition of George "Superman" Reeves, and wished to avoid a similar moment in his own film? At a recent screening of *Hunter,* Jack Larson, who had portrayed cub reporter Jimmy Olsen on the *Superman* series, was delighted to recognize his old colleague in his walk-on bit: "'Well terrific!' I thought, 'John got a day off of Charles Laughton!'" This sighting prompted Larson to recall in turn that his script supervisor on a feature called *Johnny Trouble* had also worked on *The Night of the Hunter,* and had shared with him a memory from that production. Initially Laughton addressed his stars as "Mr. Mitchum" and "Miss Winters," all the while his former student and friend Miss Winters kept calling him "Charlie." Finally, Shelley said to her director, "Charlie, we've been shooting a couple of weeks now. Don't you think it's time you started calling us Shelley and Mitch?" "Very well," said the director, "and you can call me Mr. Laughton.")

With Miz Cooper and her other young charges, John and Pearl share days and nights of peace, but they are the eye of the hurricane. Inevitably, we know, Preacher will make his reappearance. In the meantime, however, we are presented with the quiet episode of Rachel reading a Bible story to the children. The mere sight of the Good Book, not surprisingly, is enough to freeze John's blood and send him into voluntary exile out on the front porch. Rachel gains his full attention by deciding to tell a tale with which he'll identify, the story of the Egyptian princess who found, in the bullrushes, "Moses—a king of men." Back in mid-July, when Laughton was still sweating over the script with Agee, he had sent him a memo concerning this scene:

A group shot, apparently taken while shooting the town scenes with Rachel Cooper, Ruby and the "Loafers." Stanley Cortez crouches in the front row, Hilyard Brown holds aloft Sally Jane Bruce on the left. Fourth from the left, of course, is Laughton, flanked by Billy Chapin and the other children, Lillian Gish and Robert Mitchum. The partially obscured gentleman in the black hat is probably Mitchum's stand-in. To his right is Gloria Castilo, and prop man Joe La Bella, his arm around Billy Chapin's brother Michael.

Dear Jim:

Re: Pg. #112 CLOSE SHOT — RACHEL — CHILDREN IN B-G-:

At the beginning of the Pharaoh story, I feel we haven't got it clear enough that John reacts badly when he sees the Bible. I am writing you about this because a copy of the script will be going into the Breen office; and if we make it very clear that we are for religion, and not against it in this passage, we shall have an easier time with them.

I suggest that the first shot is of the group, with John standing to one side; close-up of John; a close-up of the Bible as she opens it; back to the group with him leaving the shot and going outside the screen door; and back to her and the Bible, where she changes her mind about the story.

When it comes time to shoot the story-telling scene, Laughton prepares Miss Gish with the quiet words, "Eyes wise, wise, wise, wise and young and old and everything personal. Go ahead." Such language offers a glimpse of what Terry Sanders remembers about how Laughton saw Lillian Gish—or at least, the character she was portraying—as someone magical. After playing the off-camera children listening to her Bible story, Laughton becomes Rachel when the reverse angle photographs the children's reaction-and-response shot. Laughton, ever the master storyteller, begins not with the Bible tale, which by then the kids had heard several times, but with Hans Christian Andersen's "The Emperor's Nightingale." Only when he's sure that they're giving him the look of raptly attentive children does Laughton instantly segue into the Bible story.

After the other children go up to bed, Rachel asks John to bring her an apple—"And fetch one for yourself, too"—and then gently questions him about his history. Tentatively, he starts to open up to her. It is a scene executed with great delicacy—in one uninterrupted take—by both Miss Gish and young Chapin. Although Laughton, doubtless on the good advice of Bob Golden, protected himself in this scene by shooting closer angles on Gish and Chapin, in the end he decided he didn't need them.

Most of Rachel's orphans are grammar-school age, all save Ruby, a budding, yearning, early adolescent. On Thursday night, as usual, she leaves Rachel's farm and heads into town, ostensibly to take sewing lessons but actually to spend flirtatious time in the company of young men. Two local boys are lounging in an alleyway, vying for Ruby's attention, when who should enter the picture but Preacher Powell? Quickly charmed by Preacher, Ruby tells him, over a dish of ice cream, what he's hoping to hear: There are two new kids up at Miz Cooper's place, Pearl and John, and there's a doll with them—"Only they don't never let me play with it."

The source music for this city *noir*-scape is a big-band ballad arrangement of none other than Willa's waltz theme. Thus Mr. Schumann emphasizes the parallel between Willa and Ruby, each so desperate for love that she proves perfect prey for Preacher. (One of the two local youths is played, without credit, by Billy Chapin's older brother, Michael. The other anonymous actor is future director Corey Allen, who later that year would portray James Dean's nemesis Buzz in *Rebel Without a Cause*.)

Terry Sanders
I'd totally forgotten he was in this. Well, he was in *Time Out of War*. He played the young northerner. I'm sure that's why he's in *The Night of the Hunter*, because of our short film.

Davis Grubb
That whole scene where the guys were standing on the corner whistling at Ruby bothered me. The guys there were both city types, you see. Country boys wouldn't approach a girl like that. They'd do it, maybe, in a more crude way, or maybe a little more subtle. But it shouldn't have been done that way.

In directing the beginner, Gloria Castilo, Laughton's chief challenge seems to have been in calming her first-big-job butterflies in the stomach. Feeding her Preacher's lines for her close-up in the drugstore scene, Laughton senses the need to stop the action and remind her that all of this should be "*won*derful fun." Then, when they begin again, he catches her backsliding: "Ah! Don't get nervous, start again! Relax! Nothing's happening to you. No knives or anything . . ."

In addition to the dish of ice cream, Preacher has bought Ruby a pulp movie magazine. When next we see the periodical, it is in the hands of Miss Gish's Rachel. (A luridly romantic couple embraces on the front cover. The back cover is blank white. Perhaps prop master Joe La Bella was following Hilyard Brown's lead and including only those aspects of the magazine that a little boy might notice and pay attention to. More likely, here is an instance where the threadbare budget shows through. There was neither time nor money available to research and obtain authentic magazines of the period—one can glimpse a contemporary 1950s magazine cover of Ingrid Bergman at the newsstand—and they had to jury-rig something quickly for Ruby and Rachel's prop movie magazine.)

A tearful Ruby breaks down and confesses her nocturnal mating activities to old Rachel, who is instantly forgiving, (one of the few in-

One-take wonder: Lillian Gish and Gloria Castilo as Rachel and Ruby.

stances where the script contributes important lines and character in-sights not already present in the novel): "You were lookin' for *love*, Ruby, in the only foolish way you knew how. We all need love, Ruby. I lost the love of my son—I've found it with you-all . . . You're gonna grow up to be a strong, fine woman"—the script had said, "fine, full woman"—"and I'm gonna see to it you do." This sensitive scene, in which both women are moved to tears, is played out—like the earlier scene between Miss Gish and Billy Chapin—entirely in one take. While an old pro such as Miss Gish might have been expected readily to be able to carry an emotional, one-take scene, it is a measure of Laughton's courage and sensitivity as a director that he managed to entrust such scenes not only to the Iron Butterfly but also to a child actor and a first-time ingenue, and to ensure that they were as effective as they are.

Robert Mitchum

That was her first and, I believe, only picture. Castilo, Gloria Castilo. She worked in a flower shop, I used to see her there. Pretty girl. I don't know what happened to her.

Although Mitchum was wrong that *Hunter* was the late Miss Castillo's only picture, it was indeed her first picture and, unfortunately, destined to be her only film of real stature. The remainder of her filmography consists of sorority sister and juvenile delinquent roles in a roster of B-movies, of which the most frequently viewed on television—such is the popularity of even the most modest horror film—is *Invasion of the Saucer Men* (1957). But under Laughton's direction in *Hunter,* she gives a sensitive rendering of a difficult role. Gloria Castilo was the daughter of a Spanish family, which traced its presence in the Southwest back to the days of the conquistadores. A graduate of the University of New Mexico, where she had majored in music education, Miss Castilo joined the cast of the play *Late Love,* which a troupe called the Little Theatre of Albuquerque took on the road to Los Angeles.

Paul Gregory's casting director Mildred Gussey and the Pasadena Playhouse's Gilmore Brown recommended her to Gregory when he was still looking to cast the role of Ruby. After watching her in a Playhouse performance of *Late Love,* the producer went backstage, introduced himself to the startled and thrilled young actress, and arranged for her to meet Laughton. "It was an amazing interview," she recalled for the UA publicists. "I had read the book and knew the character, of course, and expected that Mr. Laughton would have me read the part." (Billy Chapin, Don Beddoe and the rest could have disabused her of that notion.) "But, instead, we simply sat around and discussed the role—the kind of girl Ruby was, her place in the scheme of the book. That's all. No reading, no screen test. Finally, Mr. Laughton smiled and said that I had the part."

Davis Grubb

Ruby was wrong. She was a good little actress, but I don't think the character was developed. I think she did as much as she could with the character as it was presented in the script and the direction. I guess if she'd tried to do any more they would have canned her, and said, "Look, this is not a picture about Ruby . . ." I'd like to have seen what an actress like Tammy Grimes would have done with it. She might seem too sophisticated, but she's a marvelous actress.

Shelley Winters shared no scenes with Lillian Gish, but here both actresses share a lunch with Laughton at the Rowland V. Lee ranch.

Meanwhile, "back at the (Roland V. Lee) ranch . . ."

Preacher shows up the next morning at Miz Cooper's farm, claiming to be John and Pearl's father. The hunter has finally run his two young quarries to ground—but he hasn't reckoned on Rachel's resourcefulness. Or her twelve-gauge shotgun.

Getting this important scene in the can taxed the resourcefulness of many of the filmmakers, from editor to producer. Lillian Gish, according to the Lanchester research, always felt that Paul Gregory "had a kind of reverence for Laughton's talent, and . . . tried to protect it." She even recalled that Gregory had spoken to her and the other cast members and explained to them that they had to shield Laughton from "as many problems as possible, even business concerns." Miss Gish's own experienced perspective was that "an artist is like a six-month-old kitten in business matters usually, and he needs someone he can trust, someone to manage the business for him. I often thought how nice it would have been if Griffith had had a Paul Gregory, as Charles had."

Paul Gregory

The thing that's of enormous interest to me, in the theater and in films, is that none of these things that are really worthwhile are born easily. They come a-borning through great ache and disappointment and shattering emotions and all that sort of thing. You don't just crack the shell open and you have the egg. For some reason, it's a Christ-awful carry-on with people that come and go and you wonder how you ever had them in there in the first place, and people at each other's throats . . .

You know, Laughton had been in business with Erich Pommer, and they'd done *Rembrandt* and two or three pictures, so there is no question that Laughton had had experience in the making of a motion picture. And yet, Laughton could never take a rough ship. If things got the slightest bit unsettling, Charles would flee. And yet, he wouldn't think about any of that when he would have meetings and meetings and meetings with an actor, and with a director, and then decide he didn't want them, and then they'd file suit against me, saying they'd given information to Laughton and they wanted to be paid for it, or that Laughton had said yes, this actor could be in it when maybe he'd gotten enthusiastic . . . You see, he never allowed for the fact that somebody had to keep all the strings pulled together and the thing sailing. Never allowed for that. And that was just his way, poor man, he couldn't help it, I don't hold it against him at all. But he was always vulnerable. And so he was vulnerable to the next person that came along and flattered him or something, and I was always having to rescue him from some venture.

Charles loved films but he didn't want to know anything about the business of the films, how much anything cost—anything. And the minute you'd say, "Charles, you can't do it," he'd snarl, "Why can't I do it?!" He'd go into a rage whenever there was no budget for something. Such an outrage as you've never heard, and slamming of doors, and I was the worst son of a bitch he'd ever known, and blah-blah-blah.

The money was being used up, and I had to give up my points in order to finish the picture. I gave up points from my side, I didn't discuss it with him at all. It wasn't a great crease, it was just that Laughton got behind schedule.

United Artists keep putting the interest on you, they compound the interest that they charge you for the money, so that you can *never* catch up. You can never catch up, it's impossible. You should look at their financial statement, it's an absolute farce; it's almost funny enough for Charlie Chaplin to make a movie out of it.

Call it Monday morning quarterbacking, but one person who came to feel that Gregory had only himself to blame was his star, Robert Mitchum. The actor subsequently told Lanchester's researchers that whatever the deal was with United Artists it was Gregory, after all, who had negotiated it and ultimately agreed to it. "He went in," said Mitchum, "and he was so arbitrary, and they didn't care if he made any money at all as long as they made money." Hence, Mitchum did agree with Gregory on his main point: "They simply buried the film." (Mitchum tended to be hard on Gregory in more ways than one, as we shall see. He even blamed Gregory for overworking Laughton, inasmuch as the actor/director had had to learn filmphotography and editing as preparation for directing *Hunter,* all while he was working on the script. An ironic opinion, in view of Gregory's stated position that the whole idea of Laughton directing films was proposed as a solution to his being overworked in the first place.)

Paul Gregory

And then, you know what United Artists did? They had Bob Mitchum booked for *Not As a Stranger* to start the week of our last week of shooting. We had to shoot around him, and hope to get him, and chase him all over the place and everything else.

But there were no battles on *The Night of the Hunter,* there positively were none. When Laughton once committed himself to something and started going, you didn't have battles. There was a good feeling, I'll tell you that, there was a good feeling on the set. The people all loved what was going on, the people who were doing it all loved it.

But I saw the key, in that picture, go down. For me, they lost the child's point-of-view the minute they went on all these horizons and showed all this stuff in the distance and what have you. To me, it went away. By horizon, I don't mean Mitchum's horse going by the barn window, no, that was all right. But I mean when they opened out, particularly that down-the-river stuff. That's where this picture got carried down in a path that it shouldn't have gone. And then, when we didn't have Mr. Mitchum, we had to come back to reality very quickly! To get him and to get the stuff that we had to have, we couldn't *wait* until the sun was almost gone, we couldn't *wait* until the clouds were this or that, they had to shoot it, because we had him on a Sunday morning and we had to have it. If you've noticed, those last scenes with Mitchum, it was a big, bright Sunday morning.

You see, it's an incredible business, show business, because for all of the brutality that is inflicted on it by itself, it still rolls on—and is fantastic. If you've got the hide to take it.

Robert Golden
The sequence that I was most disturbed about was one we shot on a Sunday, because Mitchum had started on a Stanley Kramer picture, *Not As a Stranger,* so his time had run out. And it was a sudden thing, we didn't have the usual preparation, the sketches and so forth. It was the scene outside Lillian Gish's house when Mitchum arrives for the first time. Mitchum dismounts and comes to the stairway, Lillian Gish and all the kids are all gathered there, and he's got his eyes on the doll. There wasn't time to shoot everything, and there was some maneuvering and scattering, and I was just afraid we couldn't put it together, because we couldn't go back, Mitchum was gone. That was, I would say, the most ad-libbed sequence in the picture.

Actually, in terms of time and place, the creation of this crucial sequence is not exactly the way it was recalled by the producer or his editor. The company began shooting the scene at the Lee ranch on Monday, September 13, and continued the next day. Some of the material shot included the beginning of the scene, where Mitchum rides up, and the climax where, under the watchful shotgun of Miss Gish, he rides off again. But the handling of the intermediate material, found among the out-takes, seems indeed slapdash, comprising mostly long shots, and the need for further coverage must have been apparent to Golden and Laughton the moment they viewed the rushes. With Mitchum's departure for *Not As a Stranger* imminent, the decision must have been made to squeeze in some further shooting on Sunday, the 26th—but not at the Lee ranch. Whether it was for the convenience of their star, or because the available rental time at the Lee ranch was running out, Hilyard Brown

mis Cooper: you say them kids is yours?

Grubb's sketch for Preacher's first visit to Rachel's farm.

was instructed to recreate the Cooper farmhouse on a sound stage. Taking no chances, on Saturday, the day before the special shoot, producer Gregory sent a Western Union wire to Robert Mitchum at his home:

> DEAR BOB: CONFIRMING CALL FOR SUNDAY SEPTEMBER 26TH, 1954 NINE A.M. READY STAGE FOURTEEN. WE GO ON STANDARD TIME TONIGHT SO BE CERTAIN YOU TURN YOUR CLOCK BACK. LOVE AND KISSES. PAUL GREGORY.

So the scene as it appears in the final film is a construct combining location footage at the ranch and sound stage footage on an interior-for-exterior recreation of the set, shot a week and a half later. (Ironically, *Not As a Stranger,* like *Hunter,* was a first-time project for *its* director, Stanley Kramer, who until this point had confined himself to producing. And, unlike Laughton, Kramer was in for a challenging experience dealing with "bad boy" Mitchum, as well as his equally bibulous co-stars, Frank Sinatra and Broderick Crawford—but that is another story.)

The actual scene was filmed on two locations: the Lee ranch and, here, on a soundstage.

Robert Mitchum

They asked me if I'd mind doing that last scene on Sunday. I said, "Yeah, I'll do it on Sunday, if you have breakfast on the set for everybody, and they serve *absynthe Suissesse* and brandy milk punch." We had a great prop man, Joe La Bella, he was great with the kids, and he was a great bartender.

One time, Paul and I were talking, and Max Youngstein and all these guys from United Artists were standing nearby. Ruby Rosenberg came over with a budget sheet, and one line said a hundred-and-sixty-six bucks or something, and it said, "Whiskey." Ruby said, "What's that?" and Paul said, "Well, I guess that's what it is." But Ruby said, "Can't we move it over to transportation or something like that?" Paul said, "Well, it's not transportation, is it? That's what it is, is whiskey." Ruby said, "I can't put a hundred-and-sixty-six dollars on the budget for whiskey!" The guys from United Artists turned around, and one of them said, "Why not, for Christ's sake?"

The amount of drinking and cursing which generally took place on the set—although, as we have seen, Laughton was careful to restrain himself around his younger actors—was apparently a source of concern for a woman from the Welfare Department whom Mitchum remembered frequenting the set and locations—ostensibly to protect the children. She wore a white hat to shade her face from the sun, "and she looked like a great lady who had somehow lost her way in Hollywood." According to the film's star, this lady was threatening to complain to the Welfare Department about the prevalent profanity and consumption of liquor. Mitchum prevented this by suggesting to the crew's still photographer, one day at the Lee location, that he catch a shot of the white-hatted lady at lunchtime drinking from a can of beer. The photo was duly snapped, and the woman made no further mention of negative reports to the home office.

Mitchum, on horseback off camera at the Lee ranch, hears his cue on the assistant director's bullhorn—"Come in, Bob. (*Pause*) Okay, Bob! Come on!" to which Mitchum shouts, "Don't hold your breath!" The horse, after all, cannot be hurried. Gloria Castilo's Rachel is emerging from the barn, eggs in hand, and is so startled to see Preacher that she drops the eggs and runs to Miz Cooper. "All right, sweetheart, relax, come on," Laughton tells her after her first take, "And don't twist your face up—you're too pretty." (When it's time for the eggs to shine in their big close-up as they splat on the ground at Gloria's feet, it is prop man La Bella who's dropping them off-camera. Laughton pronounces La Bella's work "Beautiful.") Then, it's on to Mitchum dismounting and approaching the house. Laughton's primary mandate to his star: "Action! Sex and hypocrisy, come on."

While Ruby fetches John and Pearl, Preacher sheds crocodile tears—which he wipes away with the heel of his hand, (a fine detail retained from the novel)—about his lost children, all for the benefit of Rachel. She remains unimpressed, even when Preacher starts to launch into his "Left Hand-Right Hand" sermon. "Don't forget that yours is a routine, Mitch—sex . . ." Laughton reminds Mitchum. "Like a medicine man."

Robert Golden

Of course, you've heard the expression of "cutters making pictures." Well, it's absurd. Because if you don't have the film, you're not going to make anything. I bow to Laughton and give him all the credit. But whatever values came out of this one scene—like when Mitchum says, "The Lord will provide," and we cut to the doll—were cutting values. Because shooting that scene was really winging it, and some guys can wing it, but that's one thing Laughton couldn't do, he couldn't wing it. He just didn't have the knowledge to. So, through no fault of his, he was not prepared for that scene, and we didn't have time to do it.

It is the location footage shot at the ranch that appears to be improvised. The studio-shot version is more careful, with much closer coverage of the principals. Significantly, it was at the studio that the team made sure to shoot that tight insert-shot of the fallen doll. No doubt, the most challenging aspect from Robert Golden's perspective was to combine the location work with the studio footage so that they would seamlessly blend into one effective scene, one whose dual origins would not be obvious to the audience.

Ruby brings Pearl and John into the scene. Pearl, arms outstretched to Preacher, lets her doll drop at the foot of the steps. (This beat of the scene, also shot in-studio, was filmed on Thursday, September 30. In the out-takes, one sees expert prop man La Bella adjusting Miss Jenny in Pearl's hand. When Sally Jane lets go of the doll, it lands perfectly in an upright position near the steps.) Rachel stays atop the steps, and John climbs to the railing on the side opposite her. Preacher keeps spreading his lies thickly in response to Rachel's skeptical questions, but the scene builds to the moment when the bond is finally solidified between the old woman and the boy. Rachel asks, "John, when your dad says come, you should mind him?" And John answers, "He—ain't—my—dad." Laughton directs Billy to say this last "as if you're telling the absolute, clear truth. So, keep your head quite, quite steady." (In the final film, Laughton and Golden created this moment by combining the visual of one shot with the audio of Billy's line-reading from a different shot.) That's all Rachel needs to hear—"No, and he ain't no preacher, neither!"—and she rushes back inside the house. John jumps off the porch. (This feat was executed by a boy stunt double, but the shot was not used.) John grabs the doll and dives under the steps, followed by Preacher, who opens his switchblade. Suddenly, we see why Rachel had to go back inside her house.

Robert Mitchum

Charles added a touch of slapstick here, too, when the Preacher dives after the boy under the steps and the old woman comes back out and taps the Preacher's ass with the barrel of her shotgun. Charles and I, we both said, "Well, the punch of the scene ends when (*slaps fist*) boom!— the Preacher looks up at the barrel." Because then, things started to look up in the picture. It's the first time you ever saw a double-barreled shotgun pointed right at somebody's nose. That thing can tear your head off. Literally tear your head off. It punctuated the scene, and it provided a comic relief, because the biggest laugh comes with that ultimatum. I think Charles was right to take that risk.

Davis Grubb

I didn't write the book for comedy. I wish I had written more comedy into it, because it certainly would have added another dimension to it. There was no comedy in the book. Laughton never mentioned to me his intentions about any of this, he kept that to himself. But his idea of poking Mitchum in the ass with Rachel's gun was brilliant. These are all things that added to my original conception.

Stanley Cortez

If you'll remember, Mitchum rides away from Gish and the children, screaming at them that he'll be back when it's dark, calling them "whores of Babylon." The word "whore" was not heard in movies in those days.

Paul Gregory

I just told them to *shoot* it. We could always dub it if we had to. The production code people read the script and called up and said, "You can't do this," and I said, "Well, I'm sorry, we're doing it."

Stanley Cortez

The Motion Picture Producers' Association didn't want to give the picture their seal of approval because of the word "whore." Charles got very angry about this, he showed them where the Bible says it, so why couldn't his character in the picture say it? He made his point, and they kept it in the picture.

The Rowland V. Lee ranch was the setting for perhaps the most infamous incident behind-the-scenes on *The Night of the Hunter*. For all that Mitchum loved Laughton and had been on his best behavior throughout the production, a day came when the "bad boy" star showed up at the Lee ranch more than slightly tipsy and, in Laughton's estimation, in no condition to act. Producer Gregory concurred with this assessment—but Mitchum did not. On many previous pictures, Mitchum had amazed his colleagues by carousing to all hours and yet arriving on set the next morning, letter-perfect in his lines, and highly professional in his performance. Doubtless, Mitchum thought he could pull off a similar feat this day, but Gregory insisted to his star that he was much too puffy-eyed to go before a camera. The argument which ensued was abruptly terminated when Mitchum unzipped his fly and performed a baptism on Paul Gregory's car, as he had once bestowed on David O. Selznick's carpet. "I stood there," Gregory recalled for Mitchum biographer Lee Server, "I couldn't believe it, that's all." When the ceremony was concluded, and the fly rezipped, Mitchum "turned around with a look on his face like that was just the *dearest* thing he had ever done in his life!"

Don Beddoe

Gregory told me about that. He was laughing about it, then. It probably wasn't funny at the time, I thought.

In his last years, Mr. Mitchum denied the episode had ever taken place, but when interviewed earlier by Miss Lanchester's researchers, he was not only still admitting to his misdeed, he was apparently unrepentant. "Gregory had to buy a new Cadillac," Mitchum said, "because you see, I peed on the radiator, and every time it heated up it smelled, and so he had to sell it." According to Davis Grubb, Laughton admonished his star, "Mitchum, you really mustn't do things like pissing on people's cars, even if you are angry!"

Robert Mitchum

Charles used to call me up. Once he said, "Hello, Bob, this is Charles here," and I said, "Yes," and he said, "I've been thinking about your attitude. You

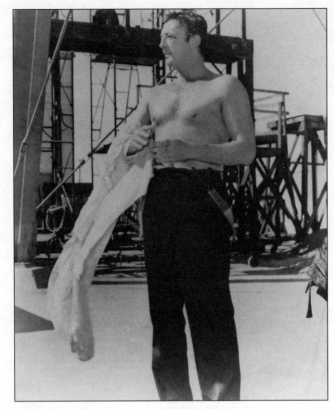

Robert Mitchum: actor, writer, singer, poet—and brandisher of skeletons.

know, all of us have skeletons in our closets, and we keep them in the closet and when people come by we look off in the other direction, pointing our toes at the rug, and whistling. I'm sure you get the picture." And I said, "Yes, Charles." So he said, "But you, not only do you open the door to your closet, but you snatch your skeleton out, and you *brandish* it. You've simply got to stop brandishing your skeleton." Then he hung up.

Preacher follows up on his threat and returns after dark. His siege of Rachel and her home is a study in the use of sight and sound to create suspense, and also in terms of Laughton's directorial choices, which depart from the original text, some for the better, some not. The sequence commences in a mood of eerie stillness—no musical underscore, just crickets—as Preacher sits on a stump outside Rachel's house, while Rachel sits inside the porch, shotgun in hand. Once more, Preacher starts to sing his favorite hymn:

Preacher's vigil in Rachel's garden

Leaning, leaning,
Safe and secure from all alarms . . .

But this time, Rachel sings in accompaniment:

Leaning on Jesus, leaning on Jesus,
Safe and secure from all alarms . . .

Neither the Grubb novel nor the film script specifies anything other than the fact that Rachel joins with Preacher in duet. But on screen, the moment is all the more telling because the old farm woman is not simply joining in on the song, she's joining in on counterpoint. And from her utterance of the Name we have never heard from Powell's lips we infer that she is closer in her heart to the tenets of the faith that Preacher has twisted and corrupted for his own ends. Preacher in the Grubb novel had no such compunction about invoking Jesus, and Laughton's choice to change this was probably extremely helpful in making his script acceptable to the Breen office. (As with earlier vocal moments in the film, this one was shot to a playback. The recording was on a disc, so that the sound man could quickly move the needle back to the beginning for repeated takes.)

Robert Mitchum
Apparently, that's the way they sang it in country churches or something. I don't remember, really, I guess Charles found that out from Walter; he was overjoyed to learn it, he said, "Let's do that." I remember, at the time somebody thought it was a little precocious.

Paul Gregory
I brought that counterpoint in the song to Laughton's attention. I'm the one that knew all about "Leaning on the Everlasting Arms"; I used to sing it at the old Baptist church where I went as a child in the country in Iowa. When he read the book, Laughton wanted to know if there was a song called "Leaning," and I said, "Yes." (*Sings*): "Leaning, leaning, leaning on the everlasting arms . . ." We men would sing it that way, and the women would all sing, "Leaning on Jesus, leaning on Jesus . . ." and so on, that's how we used to do it. And that's how it came to be used in that scene, Walter did whatever he did to arrange the duet. Well, it was lovely. I thought it showed the absolute devil and the absolute angel in perfect light.

Davis Grubb
It kind of bothered me at the time; it seemed a self-conscious thing. I guess it was supposed to mean that Rachel was putting Jesus back into the religion that Preacher had taken Him out of, but I never thought that device worked. I don't know, though, I'd like to see it again. It may start to work for me after a while.

After the singing, we—and Rachel—can still see Preacher outside on the stump. In the novel, Rachel nods off for just a moment and when she snaps back into alertness she quickly sees that Preacher has vanished from the stump. The screenplay improves on this moment with a classic bit of visual business. Ruby, carrying a candle, wanders into the scene and momentarily distracts Rachel; at the same time, her candle's light reflects off

Rachel guarding her brood—because it's a hard world for little things.

the porch screen, obscuring Preacher's stump. Almost immediately, Rachel gasps and blows out the candle, but it is too late—the stump is empty.

Knowing that Preacher will soon make his move to strike, Rachel sends for her brood of orphans to stand watch with her. Before they arrive, she witnesses an owl on a tree limb eyeing a rabbit and then taking off after its prey. (A wire attached to the owl's talon is used to make him fly off the branch. The rabbit attack is heard but not seen.)

Robert Golden

Laughton had such a great respect for Lillian Gish. And she's such a beautiful, wonderful lady, everybody on the set loved her. She was just so warm and kind and thoughtful—just delightful. To this day, I use an expression about three or four times a year: When she's sitting there on guard in the rocking chair, with the shotgun in her lap, and an owl gets this rabbit, she says, "It's a hard world for little things." I've used it as recently as a week ago. It's such a telling line, it's a whole book. And she says it so beautifully.

And, she says it incorrectly—in almost all of the out-takes. Repeatedly Miss Gish says, "It's a hard world *on* little things." Only after he's satisfied with the emotional resonance of Miss Gish's line-reading does Laughton notice the wrong word and correct her: "*For* little things."

Once the children come down to join Rachel, there is a brief exchange in the script which was filmed but not used. The old woman claims to be lonesome and invites the children to join her in some "games." One child offers to fetch the lamp, but Rachel says, "No, it's more fun playing games in the dark." (In the screenplay, it was "more fun hearin' stories in the dark.") In the film, we pick up the scene with Rachel, shotgun in hand, pacing back and forth in her darkened kitchen, telling the Bible story of King Herod and the slaughter of the innocents. "Well now," she begins, "there was this sneakin', no-'count, ornery King Herod! And he heard tell of this little King Jesus growin' up and old Herod figured: Well shoot! There sure won't be no room for the both of us! I'll just nip this in the bud . . ." (Laughton to the kids: "Watch her, children. Absolutely still, watching her. Very solemn, big eyed, children. Sally—are you looking at Lillian? Sally, the doll up higher, put your leg down, and look at Lillian, please, dear. And absolutely still, children. All right, Lillian.")

Typically, for a close reaction shot on the children, Laughton himself takes over the off-camera storyteller's duties. "Now, once upon a time, there was this mean, nasty, ornery old King Herod. And—he fell in a puddle." To their credit as young professionals, all the children keep a straight face at this improvised revision of the old Bible tale until Laughton says, "Okay, that'll do," and the camera crew cuts, then they break into laughter. "I know it's beastly standing there, horrible," Laughton sympathizes with his younger cast members before asking them to keep still for another take, and soon the shot is in the can.

At one point in Rachel's telling of the story, she puts to her kids the question, "And when little King Jesus' Ma and Pa heard about that plan, what do you reckon they went and done?" Of all her brood, each of whom pipes in with a far-fetched reply, it is John who answers Rachel correctly: "No; they went a-runnin'." "Billy, before you start again," Laughton tells him quietly, "don't forget that line is very warm and simple, and don't move your head much, just warm and friendly. It was a very nice memory, that apple business."

Played entirely without musical underscore, this final siege can't help falling a little short of the terror evoked by the river chase, but it's a chilling bit of business nevertheless, and it climaxes with one delicious little jolt. A distant shadow on the parlor mirror alerts Rachel that Preacher has gotten inside, so she raises her gun, ready to fire. Rachel talks to Preacher, and he responds. We hear him, but cannot see him. The camera remains focused on the far mirror, so we think of him as lurking somewhere across the room. "I'm givin' you to the count of three," she tells him, "then I'm comin' across this kitchen shootin'!" Here is how Davis Grubb tells his readers what happens next:

> Silence. And the prickle and gather quickened in her flesh and even as she shaped her mouth for the count she sensed a motion at her feet; though it seemed no more than the shadow of a leaf on the floor where the moon's square of light ended, a delicate shifting of air and space a yard and a half from her naked toes and she knew suddenly that he had stolen that close in that space of seconds. And now he rocketed suddenly upward before her very eyes, his twisted mask caught for one split second in the silver moonlight like the vision in a photograph negative and she saw the knife in his fist rise swiftly as the bobbin of a sewing machine just as she began pulling the trigger while the gun bucked and boomed in her hands. After the scream and the thunder, the room rang with echoing stillness and she saw him reel backward through the affrighted air onto the threshold, screaming again and cursing, then stumble into the broken shadow and light beneath the apple tree in the yard and up the rough ground toward the open barn.

Laughton captured the moment of Preacher's eruption and made it work on film by not letting us suspect how close Preacher has crept, until suddenly he rises into view, *very* close, and the focus swiftly shifts to clarify him for that almost subliminal shock image. (After Rachel shoots Preacher, we hear his cries and whelps of pain, as her terrorized face follows his off-screen exit. Preacher's howls were added to the soundtrack in post-production.) The children then gather around Rachel as she phones for the state troopers to retrieve the "something"

"I've got something trapped in my barn."

she's "(got) trapped in my barn." To young Mary Ellen Clemons, just before the take, Laughton reminds, "All right—soldier, Mary Ellen."

Lillian Gish

The company—Stanley Cortez, and the assistant, everyone—we all wanted to just have this be the finest thing ever done by Charles, because we all loved and admired this man. But he was so uncertain, and so frightened of the idea of directing his first picture that, if you made a suggestion, he would say, "Oh! Oh, what I'm doing is not right—it's wrong. You don't think it's right?" We found that the best way to help him was just to say, "Oh, that's fine, Charles." Because his ideas were good. We ended up putting support under him so that he could go ahead. He had no vanity, he had no security about what he was doing, and we had to try and supply that and not add, not tell him what to do or how to do it.

Paul Gregory

I wish you'd known him, because he was very coy and kittenish, you see, and he could act like he was very afraid and didn't know what he was doing, and give a facade of being absolutely the helpless little thing that's attacking something and "I don't know if I should be doing this or not . . ." and yet know every *minute* of what he's going to do.

Lillian Gish

Charles came to me at one time and he said, "This young man, Robert Mitchum, is worried about ruining his career, playing evil. And I don't want to do that to a young actor." That bothered me because, in all my acting days, if you could play evil you made as big a hit, almost bigger, than if you played the good side of it.

In the film, after I've shot Preacher, he runs through the kitchen, yelling. Charles put that in, that wasn't in the book. That was played for tragedy and fear in the book. Instead of standing your hair up with fear for the children, Charles was playing it for comedy. I remember I felt, "Oh, this should be played so that you're so frightened for everyone in this man's path," and it wasn't played that way. I could see what Charles was doing, and I knew his fear for this actor and knew why he was doing it. He softened it. He didn't want the man to be evil and feared. He didn't want the man to be so unsympathetic as he was in the book, and he should have been.

At least Miss Gish, true to her feelings, plays the moment as if *she* is frightened for everyone in this man's path, herself included. The look on her face when Preacher is screaming and running out is definitely not keyed to comedy. Actually, even Preacher's howls need not be construed as comedic. They are referred to in the novel (*see above*) and actually are perfectly in keeping with the animalistic nature of this madman and also with the pain he is now experiencing. Dig deeper into this scene, however, and you can discern where Laughton did weaken Preacher's evil and did back away from the fear we should be feeling. Preacher's uprising does provide a moment of shock, but contrast it with the shock in the book. In the film, Preacher is not rising into frame and raising his knife to strike. In the film, he is rising, startled—looking more scared than scary—because we hear the screech of a cat he has accidentally stepped on in the dark. A cat, I might add, whom we have never seen before in the film and will never see again, a *felinus ex machina* of pure, purring hokum straight out of any B-horror movie. Right there, if anywhere in the scene, is where Laughton has softened Preacher's evil by turning a moment of attack into a moment of clumsiness. The jolt is there, but how much more powerful if it had been the jolt from the book.

Terry Sanders
During this time, there was one worrisome thing that actually Lillian Gish picked up on, too. You saw my PBS film on Lillian Gish? Well, when I was filming her, we got to talking about *Hunter,* and it turns out that she, also, felt that Laughton's sense of Mitchum's role was a little bit off. Laughton felt two things: One, that there was a lot of humor there and that the audience would laugh, like when he was shot and he ran up into the barn, you know—and I didn't feel the audience would laugh. There was something a little off there. Laughton was somehow intending humor at the same time that it was heavy drama and melodrama. And he thought there would be a lot of humor all the way through, which I didn't think there would be. And Lillian picked up on his second thought . . . He had some conflict in Mitchum's role, because, he said to Lillian, "You know, I really shouldn't ask an actor to play this role, because it's going to hurt him," you know, "It's such an evil man." That's where I guess the humor came from, people should not really see him evil, "It'll hurt his career." And Lillian would say, "That's not right. Because, in *my* day, playing a villain was what you *loved* to do—you *wanted* that."

I remember at Laughton's dinner table one night, he was talking about how funny such and such a scene would be, and how the audiences would love it. And don't forget, Laughton came from huge success on the stage with *Caine Mutiny Court Martial* and some other things, so he really felt he knew audiences.

Paul Gregory
I don't recall ever having any conversation with Laughton about softening Preacher's evil. As I remember talking with him about my own feelings, the Preacher was a song that was heard in the land. He was just one of many singers at that time that went around our country taking people's money in the name of Jesus. I don't think we had any that became famous in the national sense, but there were many regional ones.

This is the way I was talking to Laughton, so for me, Preacher's song, his character and his presentation, couldn't have been too harsh. I thought he was a despicable character, so I wouldn't have thought that Charles could be too hard with him.

The policemen are pretty hard on Preacher when they come to arrest him the next morning. This is the payoff for the "ballet" of the beating and arrest of Peter Graves' Ben Harper early in the film. Laughton staged the arrest of Preacher with the same choreographed violence as the arrest of Harper—starting with the shot inside the police car, shooting from behind the trooper's heads as they approach—and it hits the boy John in the same way. "Do a yawning stretch as you come out of the barn," Laughton tells Mitchum. He does, and the troopers trounce him. Laughton calls out each step in the choreography numerically: "One!" The cops come up behind Preacher. "Two!" They club the back of his head. "Three!" They grab him, pull his hands back. "Four!" They throw him face-forward to the ground, guns drawn at his back. Thus, the movements precisely mirror the same beats utilized in the Peter Graves arrest scene. To young John, the wounded Preacher somehow becomes his wounded father as he watches the cops take him down. As before, young Chapin grabs his stomach. "Billy, it's too much," says Laughton. "Let's rehearse it." Billy repeats the gesture. "No, Billy, it's too much. You did it for me in rehearsal. It's just that." Laughton snaps his fingers. Billy gestures. "You lean forward too much. What do you lean for?" Billy tries again. "That's it." By now, it is late September, pressures are mounting, and Laughton is no longer above giving Billy a line-reading, feeding him the two different emphases of the repeated word: "Don't . . . *Don't!*" and the cry of "Dad!" "Listen. It's a recognition, somebody come back from the dead, like a ghost: 'Da-aa-ad!'" (Laughton gets the effect he is after, but will later delete the one-word line in the final cut.)

Robert Mitchum
Charles said he wanted it to be as theatrical as possible, without a lot of exaggeration, so it had to be sort of illusionary. That's the way he saw it, all these people surging up to tear him down.

It is the last brick on the load for the boy, who snaps and cries. "Billy, imitate me!" says Laughton to get the tearful reaction from Billy he wants for the film. Billy starts flailing Preacher/Dad with the doll full of money. "Don't! Don't! Take it back, Dad! Here! Here! Take it back! I don't want it, Dad! It's too much! Here! Here!" As with the earlier farmyard scene with Preacher, shots filmed at the Lee ranch are intercut with studio footage. For a key shot of Preacher lying face down while John pummels him with the doll, the subdued madman (presumably Mitchum's double) is actually on a raised platform, and the barn in the background is either rear-projection or a cyclorama. For the tight shot on Preacher's back with the money flying out of the doll, other hands— probably Joe La Bella's—are dropping extra bills on Preacher's back from just above camera range. (Surprisingly, the burst doll and the spilled bills are a seemingly inevitable image which apparently never occurred to novelist Grubb and are only to be found in Laughton's film.)

After John's crying jag, Rachel cradles the collapsed boy in her arms and carries him away from Preacher for the last time, the camera following along. But Grubb and Laughton still have more dramaturgy up their sleeves. The film dissolves to Preacher's trial. "Lynch him! Lynch him! Bluebeard!" cries the betrayed Icey Spoon, sitting in the gallery with husband Walt. Laughton wants the crowd to "grumble, grumble." "Let's try it again," says Laughton. "Start grumbling again. (*To Varden*) It's the word, the ugliness of the word, '*Lyynnnch!*' I want the staring eyes, and the *drunken* face. (*To the crowd of extras*) Start bubbling." The crowd murmurs, Evelyn says her lines. Laughton: "Do it again with staring eyes. Your eyes were half closed. All right, start grumbling. (*Assuming Preacher's position off-camera*) I'm the biggest so-and-so in the world. *Come on!*"

On the witness stand, young John has been so traumatized by his adventure that he cannot bring himself to look at Preacher and identify him for the district attorney. Laughton emphasizes the child's isolation by keeping the camera firmly on him. There are no cutaways to Preacher, and even the D.A. is seen only by his hands—first, pointing: "Please, little lad. Won't you look yonder and tell the Court if that is the man that killed your mother?" and then, patting John reassuringly on his shoulder, "It's all right, Mrs. Cooper. You can take the little fellow away." (The faceless attorney was played by James Griffith, a gangling character actor who

Always eloquent with or without dialog, silent screen legend Miss Gish here mimes the winding, and listening to the ticking of a watch, in answer to the offscreen Attorney's question about what Santa has in store for young John.

in those days kept busy on TV and film. Fans of *Hunter* curious to know what he looks like might check out Warner Bros.' 1954 big-screen version of Jack Webb's long-running radio/TV hit, *Dragnet*, in which Griffith plays reluctant crime witness Quinn, and watch for the tell-tale ring on his right hand. By doing this, they can also hear a Walter Schumann musical score which, although it doesn't scale the lyrical heights of his work on *Hunter*, does foreshadow the blending of music and sound as heard in Preacher's scream when, at *Dragnet*'s climax, a clap of thunder blends into the drum roll leading into the famous "dum-da-dum-dum" motif . . .)

Once more, Laughton the visual storyteller takes full advantage of silent film star Gish's eloquence of expression and gesture. In answer to the offscreen attorney's question about what Santa has in store for John, she pantomimes winding and listening to the ticking of a wristwatch. ("Cut," says Laughton. "Did you get the pantomime of the watch?" In fact, Miss Gish

(scene)

Lynch him! Lynch him!

tries it at least two slightly different ways.) God is still in the details, and the director is recalling seeds he planted in the film's first reel that are about to blossom in its final scenes. One important seed was the ticking watch in Miz Cunningham's window at which John gazed so yearningly. Another was Bart the reluctant hangman. We are about to meet him again, but not before a turbulent and dramatic sequence in which the vengeful—and tipsy—Spoons, obviously unmindful of Rachel's curtain-raising quotation "Judge not, lest ye be judged," instigate the formation of a lynch mob.

Don Beddoe

That mob scene went very smoothly. It was done outdoors on some back lot or other, shot Night for Night. I remember, we did it, I think, in one or two takes at the outside. There were a lot of people, it was a mixed-up rabble, and I think that Laughton just inspired the people, both by his reputation and by himself, to really become members of a mob and not just: "Screen Extras Guild call: for Mob Scene," in other words, where they all run on and go, "Yeah!" and go home. They were all individual people, and I think he brought that out in them. And that's the reason that it was so effective, I think. Because, it was effective, it was really effective.

Schumann's score fans the flames as the torch-bearing citizens break into a furniture store and loot it for improvised clubs and weapons. "Come on, you murderous bastards!" commands Laughton. The day before, on October 5, Laughton had finished shooting the climactic Christmas scene. The mob-scene shoot is on October 6 and 7, the last two days of the "official" production schedule, and the director manages to squeeze in a lot of coverage—more, in fact, than he will end up using. (The shots of Mitchum and the police officers already have been in the can since September 21.) As the mob rampages toward us in a backward-trucking shot, the crowd responds to the incitements of Walt and Icey. (In typical movie technique, the mob pantomimes its shouts so that the sound technician can record the Spoons' lines. Later, the crowd sounds will be mixed into the soundtrack.) Having been spotted eating in a diner by the Spoons and their fellow vigilantes, Rachel quickly leads her brood out the back way—all save Ruby, who, still nursing a crush for Preacher, is found mooning outside the police station. Rachel pulls Ruby away—there were more shots of this, including more of Ruby's protestations, than Laughton kept in the film—and leads her children around the rear of the station house where we see Preacher being snuck out the back way by some policemen and into a patrol car. Just as a cop is ready to say his line, Mitchum tosses his cigarette out the window. "Christmas atmosphere!" says Laughton. The officer catches sight of Bart at his door and calls out, "Hey *Bart!* . . . We're savin' this bird up fer you!" With a tip of his hat, Bart calls back at the cops, "This time it'll be a privilege." Thus does the film, unlike the novel, provide Bart with some form of redemption. "Do it and smile, you son of a bitch, at the end, come on," says Laughton. Done, and done. "Good. Cut."

Now Laughton cuts to a tracking shot of Rachel leading her brood in a straight line along the sidewalk. ("Mother Goose triumphant, Lillian. All right.") We will see no more of Preacher, and in Schumann's underscore the heavily clashing chords of Preacher's theme now give way to the light tinkling of sleigh-bells. Once again, the musical sound is a preview of our next scene, which will be an exterior shot of Rachel's farmhouse on a snowy Christmas day. (This is the re-constructed farmhouse on a sound-stage, and sharp-eyed viewers might notice that it is different from the farmhouse that was used on the Lee ranch exteriors. For one thing, the ranch chimney was in the middle of the roof and, here, it is on the roof's far right corner. Actually, the entire frontage is different. Part of the problem is the approach—from the river first, from the road second; one is never sure which is the main entrance. Neither the mailbox nor the road is on the river side.) The scene's action calls for Rachel to come out and check her mailbox, then return to her kitchen, grousing all the while about her own, grown children not having sent her anything for Christmas. On the stage, the snow machine is making so much noise it sounds like D-Day, but Miss Gish gamely speaks her lines, all of which of course will have to be dubbed in later. Except for the racket, it is a perfectly realized image of a Christmas card.

Stanley Cortez

Of course, Charles was the great devotee of David Wark Griffith, and the pictorial concept of Griffith's films influenced Charles in the structure—"structure," underline that three times—of the film. Charles had his own way of doing it, but I felt he was learning from Griffith. If you'll notice in *The Night of the Hunter,* there were many times where Charles would go back to the exact same shot or the exact same angle to serve as a sort of psychological reminder for the audience, which is what Griffith did. Griffith would start off on a long shot of a set of a scene, and he would cut back to that master shot several times. It's rudimentary today, but it was not in Griffith's time. It was Griffith's thought to cut back to the same shot to remind the audience of what the whole thing was about. In the last scene of our picture, Charles started with the exterior of Lillian Gish's house, and then went back to it for the last shot of the picture. In my opinion, it became a symphonic concept, because, in great pieces of music, you start with the main theme and you invariably end with that theme. In this case, the theme was her home, with the snow falling down; that, by the way, was an exterior shot inside on a stage. That's one of the charming things about that film.

Inside the house, where Miss Gish is with the children, Walter's music is very fast, kind of a scherzo quality, it sort of lilts, like sparkling dia-

monds. It was lit in that vein, because Charles explained that in his mind, "This is like wrapping up a Christmas package, with a fancy ribbon, and that's it, ladies and gentlemen, boom." That was the end of the picture and they'd all walk away. While I was lighting it, I had in my head the Mendelssohn scherzo, *Midsummer Night's Dream*. These were the things that were marvelous.

Laughton calls for "bright eyes" from the children as they poke their faces around the kitchen staircase wall. This image was apparently inspired by a Davis Grubb sketch in which the kids' smiling faces peer from behind a Christmas tree. "Now, all Christmas, and very bright, everybody. All right, go!" And for another (twelfth) take: "Christmas, children, presents! All right, go!" For Rachel, each of the children has made, with Rachel's own assistance, the same gift: a pot-holder. Rachel sends the kids—all save Ruby—into the next room to discover and unwrap their own presents. But for Ruby, Rachel has a more grown-up sort of gift: a beautiful brooch. It is like a benediction from the old lady to the budding child-woman, and Ruby, verging on tears, hugs Rachel and then runs to show off her brooch

Rachel thinking how it is for children in the world —
their running feet — Lord save little children!
They abide! The wind blows and
the rain is cold. Yet they abide!!

for the other kids. As with Laughton's healing reprise of Bart the Hangman, this redemption comes for Ruby only in the film, not in the original novel. Together with the earlier extension of the Rachel/Ruby movie-
magazine sequence, this scene illustrates Laughton's sensitivity to Grubb's
themes and his ability to enlarge upon them in his dramatization. Walter
Schumann tenderly underlines this intimate moment between Rachel and
Ruby by referring one last time to "Willa's Waltz," but this time without
anything sinister around the edges, just pure, heartfelt lyricism.

John's Christmas gift from Rachel, sure enough, is a pocketwatch.
Rachel chats with him a bit about the watch—"a fine, loud ticker"—as
John heads up to his room. Laughton again keeps the spoken word to a
minimum, deleting John's mini-soliloquy as he ascends the stairs: "I ain't
afraid no more! I got a watch that ticks! I got a watch that shines in the
dark!" In production, Laughton decided that what he had already visualized and dramatized was sufficient and these words from the novel were

unnecessary. Lillian Gish has already articulated her own beatific soliloquy while stirring a pot on the stove:

> RACHEL: Lord save little children! You'd think the world'd be ashamed to name such a day as Christmas for one of them and then go on in the same old way. My soul is humble when I see the way little ones accept their lot. Lord save little children! The wind blows and the rains are cold. Yet, they abide.

Laughton shot, but did not use, some more of Rachel's soliloquy, originally intended to be delivered while John discovers his new watch: "For every young'n, rich or poor, there's a time of running through a dark place; and there's no word for a young'n's fear. A young'n sees a shadow on the wall, and sees a Tiger. And the old ones say, 'Go to sleep, there's no tiger.' But when that young'n sleeps, it's a Tiger's sleep, and a Tiger's night, and a Tiger's breath on the windowpane. Lord save little children!" It's another slice of pure Grubb, delivered by Miss Gish just as beautifully as the part Laughton kept, but the director was wise not to push the envelope of philosophical sentiment one bit more than he had already dared.

. . . and they endure.

Whatever is in the pot, it is cooking for real. In the out-takes, (minus Schumann's underscore,) one can hear it bubbling, and, between takes, a crew member fans the steam or blows on it to get it to rise. As so often in earlier crucial scenes, the camera holds on Rachel and doesn't cut away while John passes through the kitchen with his new watch, whereas using John's scripted lines would have required a separate close shot of the boy on the stairway. Laughton cues his young star: "Billy . . . shining . . . And these are two people that don't want to show they love each other." After the brief dialogue about the watch, and then John's exit, the camera moves in closer on the old farm woman:

RACHEL: (*telling us*) They abide and they endure.

James Agee had prepared, during the early pre-production period, four single-space typed pages outlining "INTERIORS AND EXTERIORS FOR 'THE NIGHT OF THE HUNTER'." One of the more detailed entries describes his poetic vision for the film's climax, one which presumably for budgetary reasons never made it into the script's final draft: "A Model, centering Rachel's home, from which we pull up and away to embrace the whole world of River Country and deep starlight. The landscape in this night shot is snowed under; all glows white in the darkness except the blackness of homes & outbuildings and of woodland and of towns. There are lights in the homes, and light sheds upward from villages like shallow thistles into the darkness; the starlight is brilliant. Model could be based on a helicopter shot or, for greater scope, on aerial map photography." Absent this spectacular imagery, the film nonetheless manages to achieve the same poignant poetry, thanks simply to Miss Gish's line-reading and the support Cortez's snowy vision receives from Schumann's exultant score. The melody of the lullaby surges heavenward like a prayer, and, in a final feat of musical magic, the piece concludes with the four notes of Preacher's theme—two rising, two falling—but harmonically transformed, the nightmare at last transcended into nocturne. In his Christmas novel, *A Tree Full of Stars,* Davis Grubb would write, "For what is Hate but Love that has lost its way home in the dark?" Mr. Schumann's music, in these four final chords, shows Love how to find its way back home.

At the conclusion of filming, the cast and crew gave Laughton this affectionate souvenir, sketched by Hilyard Brown, full of in-jokes. Note the reference to editor Golden's anecdote, "What the hell do I do now?" and Golden's recollection of Laughton's constant confusion over the technique of "complete reverse" (*above & overleaf*).

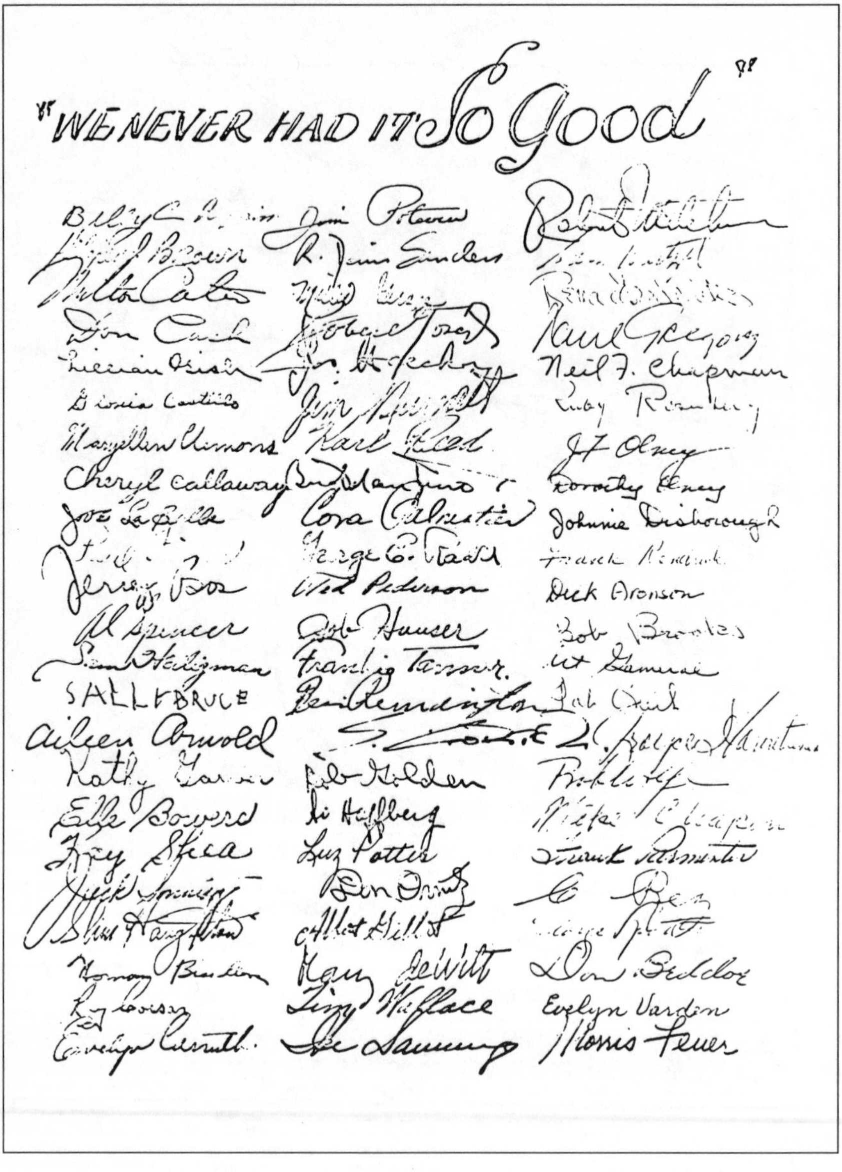
"WE NEVER HAD IT SO Good"
Neil F. Chapman
Paul Gregory
Cheryl Callaway
Dick Aronson
Al Spencer
SALLY BRUCE
Aileen Arnold
Evelyn Varden
Morris Feuer

III

POSTPRODUCTION

"This whole picture had been done by Laughton with the thought, 'This is right. And I am going to rise or fall on this opinion.'"

—Robert Golden

Even before the *Hunter* shoot was completed, Paul Gregory had acquired another literary property for his next movie project with Laughton, and it would be hard to imagine a more challenging novel to film: Norman Mailer's World War II epic, *The Naked and the Dead*. Nor was Laughton ready to stop there: the actor-turned-director told Davis Grubb that Thomas Wolfe was the greatest American novelist of all time, and Laughton very much wanted to make a movie of *You Can't Go Home Again*. But, first things first. Opus One was in the can, and people would now need to be made aware of its existence. Rather than rely on United Artists to promote his picture—for fear, wisely as it turned out, that *Hunter* would merely get lost in the shuffle of the company's proliferation of product—Paul Gregory took the initiative of commissioning the services of Saul Bass, a graphic designer of prodigious skill and imagination. Bass had recently been making a name for himself by executing main title sequences, which were often hailed as more visually arresting than the motion pictures to which they served as prelude. He had a long-term association with the films of Otto Preminger, highlighted by striking title sequences—customarily echoed in the art for the print ads—for such films as *Carmen Jones* and *Anatomy of a Murder*. Non-Preminger projects such as Hitchcock's *Psycho* and Kubrick's *Spartacus* also benefitted from Bass's modernistic design and cinematic savvy. His main title sequences were more like short films unto themselves: for example, the stalking cat-fight synchronized to Elmer Bernstein's jazzy score which begins *Walk on the Wild Side*. The first fruit of Bass's Gregory commission was an ad for the trade papers, featuring the stark image of Preacher's HATE hand clutching Pearl's Raggedy Ann doll, and the headline: "Finished!" (Never mind that the ad shows Preacher's right hand, not his left, spelling HATE.) The text is terse and to the point. It also ignores the fact that a lot of very important filming was executed on *The Night of the Hunter* for weeks after its official completion date: "On Thursday, October 7, filming was completed on the initial Paul Gregory Production, NIGHT OF THE HUNTER, based on the Davis Grubb novel. Robert Mitchum, Shelley Winters and Lillian Gish co-star/ James Agee wrote the screenplay Walter Schumann, the music/ Charles Laughton directed. A United Artists release."

Paul Gregory

There are always little things that are shot but not used, but I don't think
we shot any whole sequences of any kind that weren't used. That's one
thing I'll say, we had a tight, tight screenplay. Tight. I think it took five
weeks to shoot.

Stanley Cortez

We finished *The Night of the Hunter* in wonderful shape. The picture was
made, I believe, in thirty-six days. Would you believe that? Thirty-six
days. Through it all, there were two men at Charles' side every minute,
Milt Carter and myself. But after shooting, I left, and Bob Golden became the key figure with Laughton. They spent weeks editing the picture, with Walter Schumann and a piano on hand all the time.

Robert Golden

Laughton supervised the entire editing of the picture. It took a lot
longer this way, the fact that we didn't sit down to edit until the shooting was finished. The first time we went to the cutting room together,
he said, "My God, what a barren, terrible looking place!" The next
time, he brought Japanese prints to hang in the cutting room. And he
brought a couple of director's chairs to put outside the cutting room,
where we'd go sit and talk.

And sometimes we had to talk. I told you about that scene we weren't
fully prepared for, where Mitchum first shows up at Lillian Gish's farm.
That scared me more than any other sequence we worked on in the cutting room. I didn't think we could do it. Remember how Hugo Fregonese
warned me about Laughton's charm when I began the picture? Well,
Laughton and I kept working and working on that sequence, and I was
getting annoyed—as I've said, it could be very trying. Finally, I threw the
scissors up in the air, and I said, "Charles, I can't satisfy you!" I was T'd off.

He said, "Bob—come outside."

We went out and sat in the chairs.

He said, "I want you to realize . . . I'm here . . . as your guest."

That was when I finally caught on to what Fregonese had warned me
about. But, we went back in and we finished the sequence.

When I saw the picture again a couple of years ago, I realized there was one sequence that practically defeats the whole picture from a commercial and artistic standpoint. I didn't realize it in 1955, we had all become so close to this picture. Of course, you wouldn't even think of it, this was the most expensive scene in the picture, we had to shoot it at night, with lots of extras. I'm talking about when the lynch mob forms and is going to get Mitchum. Just think of how much we could have saved in the making of the picture, and I'm sure the picture would have been a hundred percent better, if, from the scene where Mitchum is arrested, we'd dissolved to the beautiful Christmas scene. I think that the lynch mob scene is just so anticlimactic, it accomplishes nothing; Evelyn Varden is back again as Icey Spoon and you don't know whether she's drunk or what.

Don Beddoe

I thought that the scene was valuable in that it took it out of the more machine-like murder or maniac thing, you know, and brought it home to the *people*. And that's why it was effective. You know how you read in the paper about these guys who kill six or seven people on the freeway, or do this and that, and you think, "Aw, there's some bad fellows," or, "They must be nuts," you know, and then you drop it. But this was somebody they *knew*. They *all* knew him. And it was a case of . . . Well, the nearest parallel I could think of would be a western in which the town folk found out that the sheriff had been crooked. All the different people would have different reactions in different ways, but they'd all want to kill him. They trusted him and he'd betrayed them. Which is exactly what the scene is about. This was a personal relationship between the people and a lunatic, which is not always brought out in a lunatic picture. It's usually just a lunatic against the law, or against the people who are trying to psychoanalyze him.

Robert Golden

I have a theory that if the audience is distracted, either by, "What did he mean by that line?" or by, "Why are they doing that?" you have lost them for a certain amount of the next footage and Lord knows when you're going to get them back.

I just know that that last scene is absolutely exquisite, even more beautiful than the opening scene. To bring this work to its final, lovely completion, it's just a beautiful, beautiful frame. But before you can get to it, the mob scene interrupts the continuity and flow—which I think, from a cutter's standpoint, is the most important thing—with a very sharp, jagged, violent piece of business that has no meaning. Although it's important to get your audience with you from the very first reel, a reviewer, for example, doesn't write his review until he's seen the whole picture. And the reviews help to pull in the audience, as does word of mouth. I've often thought that Laughton was way ahead of his time in making the picture. I think, during this time of so-called art pictures and so forth, that this could have taken its place right with them. But even at that time, I think, if it hadn't had this lynch scene it would have been a more perfect work. It's awfully hard to say that this would have made that difference at the box office, but I'd just love to see the picture that way and be willing to bet that it made that difference.

Davis Grubb

That lynch scene was never done right, never done right. It wasn't done right in the book. I couldn't tell you in what way, because I had a picture in my mind and I couldn't describe it. I tried my best to get it on paper. I make my work *from* movie images in my mind. I'm always cutting, and splicing, and everything else.

I think a film critic said that I had condoned lynching, or something. But you see, I don't think that's fair, because I tried not to be a judge. I'd already been a judge of Preacher by letting him be what he was. I don't think I should have had him insane at the end, or killed defensively by Rachel. I don't think that would have worked, somehow. He had to be burned up, as an effigy is burned up.

Whereas in Grubb's novel the implication of lines like "Preacher's last, terrible night on earth" is that the lynch mob succeeded in prying Preacher loose from the blue men, the film handles this problem by having Preacher rescued by the police only so that they can "save this bird up fer" Bart, the same hangman who had dispatched John and Pearl's father.

Davis Grubb

That was entirely somebody else's idea, but I think it's an excellent one, I admire it. I think it was Laughton's idea, very definitely.

Davis Grubb

Paul Gregory

We didn't change that mob scene or anything else. Well, when the thing was over it was over. I think that the whole thing of the girl, Ruby, breaking away and going back to the prison again where they were holding Preacher after all of this was a little garnishing. Poor old, dear old Grandma Goose still had her hands full, you see, when you look at it that way. For some reason or other, Laughton seemed to think he had to cross that *t* again and dot that *i*, and maybe for him, he did. I didn't think they had to be, but Lord knows, I forgive him for that. And, I'm a great one for when a thing is over, let it go, it's over.

Robert Golden

Laughton was a bugger for work, and even though working on Saturdays was *verboten* at that time, we were running film on Saturday after the picture was finished shooting. Our new associate was the projectionist, Charlie McCleod, whom I'd known for years and who happened to be quite a guy. I remember one Saturday, Laughton, McCleod, Walter Schumann and myself went to the Devonshire Inn for lunch. Laughton was quite a gourmet, and a most charming, delightful individual.

Actor Charles Laughton
Directs His First Movie

(*Charles Laughton Biography*)

Charles Laughton is at once one of Hollywood's most colorful and talented creative artists, a fact which has now been acknowledged by the public and leading figures in the entertainment field alike.

Following a long and highly successful career as an actor—Charles Laughton has never been in a bad or indifferent picture—he took the one step which has been characterized as hazardous, and joined the roster of Hollywood directors.

His first film directing venture, which follows spectacular success in stage direction including "Don Juan in Hell," "John Brown's Body," "Caine Mutiny Court Martial" and "That Fabulous Redhead," is the Paul Gregory Production, "The Night of the Hunter," co-starring Robert Mitchum, Shelley Winters and Lillian Gish, for United Artists release. The picture opens ...... at the .... Theatre.

Laughton is what one might call "The Compleat Director," for there is no phase of the creative side of film making or stage show production in which he is not interested.

Laughton was groomed for the hotel business (which had been the business of his parents), but his heart was really in the theatre. He attended some London stage plays as many as thirteen times. It was during World War I, while in the Army, that he joined a company of theatrical players. After that, he let his brother take care of the hotel business, while Charles joined the Royal Academy of Dramatic Art.

Laughton established himself as a first-rate actor on the London stage. Shortly after his marriage to Elsa Lanchester, he made his bid on the New York stage where he was acclaimed with the same enthusiasm that London showed.

It wasn't long before Hollywood beckoned, and American audiences associated Laughton with important roles and fine performances. With the release of "The Night of the Hunter," audiences will associate his name with fine directorial efforts too.

Laughton biography from the *Night of the Hunter* press kit.

You couldn't be with Laughton for this length of time without certain things taking place that are worth repeating. We were talking about things that had taken place during the shooting, and I said to Laughton, "Charles, for Charlie McCleod, give your imitation of Stanley Cortez." I forget what the imitation was, but it was very hilarious. Well, Charles wasn't in the mood to do it, and he said, "You should see the one I do of *you!*"

I said, "Oh, would you do that one? *Please?*"

He said, "NO!"

With editor Golden, years after the fact, repeatedly offering the lion's share of the credit for the editing to Laughton, it is worth noting that in 1955 James Agee felt the same way about the writing credit. In a January 14 letter to Paul Gregory, he was insistent on that point:

Dear Paul:

The script-authorship forms are enclosed, signed. While I'm about it, I'd like to bring up once more, a matter which I discussed at length, but inconclusively, with Charles, last summer: the whole question of proper script credit, and the verbalization of it. My feeling was, and is, that Charles had such an immense amount to do with the script, that it seems to me absurd to take solo credit, much as I'd like it. Charles' own feeling, as he can fill in (so I'll only outline it here), fell into 2 parts: 1) he doesn't like the idea of being talked of as a "genius" or a credit-hog, as he felt might happen if we split credit; 2) realizing how intricate the collaboration is, in actual practice, in crystallizing any kind of show, he felt, strongly, that the front, the thing presented to the world, should remain ultra-simple and clear. There is such virtue in both points that I can't pretend or try to argue them out of existence. Nevertheless I'm sure you know as well as I do, or better, how embarrassed a writer should rightly feel in being given full credit, who has done a piece of work for and with Charles. It's on this basis that I feel very strongly that credit on the script should be double. At times I've even felt that it should be given him entirely; I can withdraw from that position only in realizing that I *was* useful, as a sort of combination sounding-board and counterirritant. I'll be grateful if you'll discuss this whole business with him, taking my point of view as strongly as you may happen to feel it: strongly, I hope. On another point I fully concur with Charles' suggestion; that in all reference to the initial novel we give maximal credit to Davis Grubb—who after all furnished much more of a movie story than is ordinarily done by a novelist. I.e., that the credit NOT read, "Screenplay by whosis, based on a novel by Grubb," or words to that effect, but rather: "Adapted to the screen by Whosis and

Whosis, from the novel by Grubb," or words to *that* effect. Need-less to say, I am deeply eager to see the picture, at whatever stage it's see-able. (If you send a rough print East, I'd be grateful if you'd let me know and let me see it.) I'm fascinated, and about 95 per-cent confident, in many things which Charles learned, and showed me, out of the Griffith films we saw. If they do work, and I think they will, they're going to make movie story-telling faster, and more genuinely movie, than they've been in many years.

My warm regards to you and, if it isn't too late, my best wishes for the slightly shopworn but still new year.

Sincerely,
Jim
Jim Agee

The producer's reply was dated February 10:

Dear Jim:

Your letter of January 14th has been received, and of course I have read it, considered it and discussed it in great detail with Charles.

We do not feel, in any sense, that a change in the credit should be made where you are concerned. We feel that you made a great contribution to "THE NIGHT OF THE HUNTER."

I tell you very honestly if we thought the picture were bad, in order to protect you we would be more than happy to remove your name, but since we think it is great we feel that you will be happy and proud that you had something to do with it—and nei-ther Charles nor I feel that under any circumstances should you be embarrassed over the credit, etc.

Best personal regards to you.

Sincerely,
GREGORY ASSOCIATES, INC.
Paul Gregory

Terry Sanders

To the best of my recollection, there was no Writers Guild arbitration. Charles did not *want* credit. He just didn't care about the credit at all.

The film was scheduled to open that summer. James Agee never saw *The Night of the Hunter.* He died in a Manhattan taxicab of a coronary occlusion the afternoon of Monday, May 16. Agee biographer Laurence Bergreen, whose research had included interviews with Paul Gregory and Terry Sanders, wrote: "Not everyone in California reacted with sorrow to Agee's death. Laughton and Gregory, whose *Night of the Hunter* was about to open, felt an enormous sense of relief that they would not have to put up with him anymore." A Western Union telefax from Charles Laughton to Agee's widow, Mia, dated May 19, reads in its entirety:

JUST HEARD SAD NEWS OF JAMES PASSING. I LOVED HIM.

Terry Sanders

Well, Charles was very sheepish about the relationship with Agee, and would kind of mutter, "We killed him." Meaning the stress. It was half a joke, and half feeling badly. There was a certain glee and guilt, about Agee.

In the early sixties, they published a book of Agee's screenplays. I had to loan my copy of Charles' shooting script to James Agee's widow, because she had no copy of the script at all. So, this was the actual script that the publisher used for the book. So, Agee, even though he gets full credit, did not write it, Charles did.

True to the preproduction discussions between Agee and Laughton, the on-screen script credit gives pride of place, not to the scenarist, but to the novelist:

From the Novel by
DAVIS GRUBB
Screen Play by
JAMES AGEE

Naturally, the film had a book tie-in, with Dell publishing the first paperback edition of Grubb's novel. Oddly, although book stores were
provided with plenty of displays featuring Mitchum and scenes from the
film to promote the paperback, the book itself carried no image, nor
even any reference to the film. The cover art was even more abstract
than that of the Harper hardback which had been illustrated with a watercolor of a tree and the moon; the paperback had merely the moon.
Did somebody at Dell fear that it wouldn't be classy to put Mitchum's
picture on the cover? Not until late in the 1990's did bright and enterprising Prion finally publish such an edition of *The Night of the Hunter.*

Book tie-in promotion from the *Night of the Hunter* press kit.

Although the headline in Saul Bass's trade ad for *Hunter* had read: "Finished!", it turned out that what was finished were Saul Bass's services for *The Night of the Hunter*. The designer did not go on to create the film's title sequence, nor was his HATE-hand-on-the-doll image used as the motif in any of the subsequent ad art. (A slightly similar Bass image for *The Man with the Golden Arm*, however, was very much in evidence that year.) This last is probably for the best, as the image for *Hunter* might otherwise have tipped off brighter audience members too soon as to the blood money's hiding place. It may be that Gregory had hoped to utilize Bass' services throughout the campaign, but reluctantly had to scale down his promotional budget after getting his first look at the rough cut of his film. That fateful viewing by producer and director took place, according to Mitchum biographer Lee Server, in a small screening room at the Beverly Hills Hotel.

Paul Gregory

There were areas in the picture where, on a couple of occasions, clearer statements could have been made, but twenty years later it's hard for me to remember all of them. But I do remember Laughton and I discussed it at great length when we saw the rough cut of the whole picture for the first time together, and he was not happy that it had slipped into that little-too-dark a look.

As Gregory recollected the experience for Server, he was duly impressed by the actors' performances and the production unit's artistry and creativity, but—had they been perhaps a little *too* artistic, a tad *too* creative, a little too far off the beaten path? When the lights came up, and the two partners sat there, said Gregory, "You had to be careful what you said to Charles. He didn't believe you if you said it was wonderful, and he would have killed you if you said you thought it was awful. But . . . I was not one to bullshit him. I looked him right in the eye and I said, 'Charlie, they're not going to know how to sell this picture.' And he said, 'Oh, my God, why, old boy?' I said, 'It's . . . they're going to call it an art film, a picture for the art houses. And I think we're going to be in trouble. It has nothing to do with the fact that you did a fantastic job, but I think it's going to be a tough sale.' Well, he hadn't dreamed of such a possibility."

This concern was reflected in a conversation between Laughton and

Denis Sanders, though it's not known whether it took place before or after the screening of *Hunter* with Gregory. In one of many discussions the director and his protege had regarding aesthetics, both men agreed that "the final problem in making a film is the reception. A sensational movie with rotten material can very often be highly successful. To achieve an extremely beautiful film that will also be successful is dangerous. Because *Night of the Hunter* was a non-sensational film, the danger was greater than it would have been had they settled for making a kind of horror movie." It is interesting to note in this regard that, as part of the film's publicity campaign, pre-release quotes were obtained from the two rival queens of Tinseltown columny, Hedda Hopper and Louella Parsons. From Hedda: "A winner! Paul Gregory and Charles Laughton's first picture is a wow!" And from Louella: "Terrifying and brooding! *Night of the Hunter* is the most completely different horror movie I have ever seen!" And yet, when this latter quote is emblazoned on the front of *Hunter*'s press book, the word "horror" is deleted.

In any event, with the footage assembled into its nearly-final form, Walter Schumann was free to complete the writing and recording of his score.

Paul Gregory

This was one of the areas where I thought Laughton was absolutely super. He sat with the rough-cut film, and Charles listened . . . He and Walter Schumann didn't run that film just once, they ran it two or three times, and discussed it, and I stayed out of it completely. Completely. Because I felt that there might be sounds and tones and tunes and words that Laughton would have heard in his mind's ear when he directed a given scene that I wouldn't be in tune with, and it was better to just allow it. He and Walter did it all.

As an unofficial member of Laughton's production unit, Davis Grubb had been contributing what he could from his Philadelphia stronghold by communicating with the director via correspondence and phone calls—as well as those sketches Laughton had requested. For a man who loved words, Charles Laughton was not a voluminous correspondent. But then he was a master of the *spoken* word, and no doubt felt most at home getting his ideas across to Grubb via the telephone. A rare letter scribbled in Laughton's often undecipherable hand survives from the preproduction period, in which at one point he queries the author about music to accompany his melodramatic tale:

> The kind of river music will be most gratefully received. This same river music will have to cover our whole opening sequence. I'm going to write you further about that when it has jelled in my mind. I'm seeing Walter Schumann . . .

Davis Grubb wrote back to Laughton on April 19, 1954, and his six-page, single-spaced epistle covers many topics they had been discussing, including the composer's contribution:

> Now for the answer to Mr. Schumann's queries about folk music, etc . . .. Riverboat minstrel tunes of a much earlier day than the time of this novel . . . would not suggest the river mood in the film as dramatically as something completely original would do . . . Please, PLEASE no folksy mouth-harp concerti with full Hollywood Bowl orchestra behind them. There are folk in this story. We need no folksyness (sic). But you know this and it is perhaps impertinent of me to remind you of it . . . I think the Everlasting Arms hymn needs to be part of the music.

Walter Schumann, however, had a very definite opinion about the advisability of utilizing "Everlasting Arms" in his underscore. As the composer related the process of scoring *The Night of the Hunter,* "In the novel, the Preacher continually sang the religious hymn, 'Everlasting Arms.' In the picture he does so on four separate occasions. However, I could not use this hymn as underscoring for the Preacher since it would dignify and create sympathy for his psychopathic religious beliefs. Therefore, for Preacher's theme, I wrote what I considered a pagan motif, consisting of clashing fifths in the lower register."

The score was orchestrated for Schumann by a veteran Hollywood composer, the late Arthur Morton. He had been the orchestrator of many distinguished soundtracks, including George Antheil's music for *The Juggler,* and would eventually become Jerry Goldsmith's constant

collaborator, orchestrating dozens of the maestro's Hollywood master-
works. Morton occasionally got a chance to shine on his own, as when
scoring episodes of the classic Americana TV series, *The Waltons*. Contacted by phone, orchestrator Morton could be cordially gruff, and he
was very shy about discussing any of his past work, including *The Night
of the Hunter*. "All I can tell you," he claimed, "is that when I saw
Preacher's theme, I told Walter, 'We're going to need four trombones.'
Aside from that, if the music's any good, blame it on the composer."

As that blamed composer recalled in his *Film Music Notes* article, "My
first meetings with Mr. Laughton on the *Night of the Hunter* project were
concerned with the philosophical approach of developing the novel and
the musical pre-scored themes necessary for a shooting script . . . In our
preliminary discussions Mr. Laughton and I agreed that since melodrama
was ever-present in the plot, that photography and music would be used
to capture the lyric quality of Davis Grubb's writing . . . We decided
upon the scenes where music would be of primary importance. As Mr.
Laughton put it, 'In these scenes you are the right hand and I am the
left.' So in the shooting of these scenes he purposely went far over
footage. This, of course, is a composer's dream; to have flexibility and not
be tied to exact timings. In actuality, to edit the film to the music.

"During the shooting of the picture, I was present at all of the scenes
where music was to be used. At its conclusion I attended all of the editing sessions with Mr. Laughton and our editor, Bob Golden. A rough
cut was completed with all of the 'music' sequences left overlength until
the score was finished."

Robert Golden

Walter Schumann was a very brilliant man. I can't remember leaving
scenes overlength as a general thing, but if there was any particular
problem, if there was any consideration, it was certainly done to accommodate him in any way possible. And it was a pleasure to do it, because whatever he would ask for was so meaningful.

Schumann's association with Laughton and Gregory was a special one.
He was on this picture long before any of the rest of us were. I would say
Walter Schumann was absolutely, next to Laughton, the most important
contributor to the picture. He was a beautiful man, and also the man

Laughton had the most respect for. By that I mean, they had worked together before, there was a mutual respect, and this was a superb talent. I
can't say enough about him. I remember the recording sessions of the
music, and one of the musicians saying that Schumann's music was so easily understood—it had simplicity—and yet, outstanding.

Those two recording sessions occurred in early July, at Radio
Records in Hollywood, with technician Henri Rene supervising as
Walter Schumann conducted an orchestra of fifty-one pieces—including, as Arthur Morton had prescribed, four trombones. Meanwhile,
plans were hatching at Gregory's office and United Artists for various
ways in which the film could be promoted. Even though Laughton did
not appear in his film, he was still a star, and surely there must be some
way the film could capitalize on that fact? The answer, it turned out,
came from an unexpected quarter, not the producer or the releasing
company, but the story's original author.

Davis Grubb

As for Walter Schumann's score, the more I hear it, the better it wears.
You know, you listen to *The Man with the Golden Arm* right now, and I
don't think it holds up as well. I don't know what it was, Schumann just
wasn't into that kind of querulous atonalism which Elmer Bernstein and
Alex North were into at that time. Although, I always thought a lot of
the score for *Rebel Without a Cause* by a guy I used to know on the
coast, Leonard Rosenman. Schumann was in a straight Brahms tradition, I would say, maybe as late as some of the better Richard Strauss.
Well, the waltz was lovely. And funny, the first four notes are almost
identical to the first four notes of Johnny Carson's TV theme.

The revolution in film marketing which had been spurred by the phe-
nomenal success of Dmitri Tiomkin's song for *High Noon,* "Do Not For-
sake Me Oh My Darlin'," was still in full-swing in 1955. Consequently, it
was felt that *Hunter,* like every other major motion picture, should not be
released without an accompanying title song. Of course, *Hunter* had songs
such as the "Lullaby" already woven into the fabric of the score, but none
of them, for all their inherent beauty, were deemed to have the proper

commercial potential, so yeoman Tinseltown lyricist Paul Francis Webster was hired to add lyrics to "Willa's Waltz." Waltzes, after all, can always be performed in a "jazz-pop" rendition, as Schumann's score had in fact treated Willa's theme to underscore the sequence of Ruby sashaying into town. (Actually, Ruby merely walks; it is the music that sashays.)

Sheet-music does survive of "Willa's Waltz, The Theme from 'The Night of the Hunter,'" but it isn't known whether any attempt was ever made to produce a commercial recording of the song.

Davis Grubb

I really flipped over the score when I first heard it. United Artists had a big reception at a hotel in Philadelphia, and I met Mr. Crown and Mr. (Robert) Benjamin. They were just lovely guys. Just as tough and as smart as the Harry Cohn/Warner Brothers kind of people were, but with a real gentility and sweetness about them. I'm not certain, but I'm pretty sure I was on the phone with one of them and it was he who sent me these acetate discs with the music on them.

I think my agent may have sold the idea of a soundtrack album, with Laughton narrating, to the executives. Laughton had already recorded, you see, *Don Juan in Hell* and the Bible stories, so it seemed a natural progression. My agent said, "If we don't do the record, it'll be all right. But it would be a nice thing; it'll mean _____"—I've forgotten how much they paid.

He said Laughton needed the narration fast. I just took the book, got out of my apartment and holed up in a room at the Drake Hotel with a tiny Olivetti typewriter, and I knocked that out in a couple of days. I had worked enough with advertising on radio to know how to synchronize solo narration and "b.g. music." So that's all I did. It really turned out surprisingly well.

I didn't realize at the time it was going to be a very small edition. I recently talked to a friend of mine named Jay down at Dayton Records, where they specialize in collectors' items, and he said that he'd only seen two copies in the last twenty years. When I listen to it now, I hear certain phrases that grate on my ear sometimes. I wish I'd paid a little more time with it.

But I was really a very dumb person in those days. I was drunk with success, really a pain in the ass. Although, I worked very hard on *Dream of*

Kings, my second novel; I worked harder on *Dream of Kings,* as a matter of fact, than I did on *Night of the Hunter,* because I was much more self-conscious—you know, a first-time success's second attempt. Scott Fitzgerald said a funny thing once, he said, "There are no second acts in American life." So I'm looking forward to my third act. Somewhere up ahead.

In addition to the narration, Grubb also wrote the liner notes for the LP, and they are a valentine to his director and the time-honored tradition he had revived in his cross-country tours. Grubb here also harks back to the evocative moment in his novel, lovingly recreated by Laughton, when little Pearl asks her big brother to tell her a story:

> I can somehow imagine a quiet autumn evening several million years ago—some aeons before television or radio or the film. A congenial coterie of Neanderthal men and women have settled back to digest their meals around the crackling flames of the supper fire. One of them turns to another of their number and commands: 'Tell us a story.' Something of the same sort of thing, I rather believe, has been happening among human beings ever since. Everyone loves to be told a story—and the chillier and scarier the better. Around the time that books were invented the storyteller fell by the wayside and the human voice as an instrument of narration succumbed to the drama and the printed page. And yet children—being true primitives, true aborigines in a sense—know this wondrously personal thrill of being told a tale. It's better than theater—better than movies in its curious, ancient way. Perhaps it's because we can provide our own actors, our own scenery, within the magic proscenium of Imagination. Charles Dickens' narration of his own works held audiences spellbound in a strangely different way than a dramatization of them could ever have done. A Greek storyteller named Homer made himself a reputation of considerable duration by the same device. Perhaps our original Neanderthal storyteller had a friend who supplied background music on a reed flute. Charles Laughton, who has restored the art of storytelling to its former place of majesty and great art, fares much better with background music in this narration of The

Night of the Hunter, which Laughton, in his first role as film director, has recently brought to the screen in a harrowing, moving
film starring Robert Mitchum, Shelley Winters and Lillian Gish.
Walter Schumann, whom I have long admired for his brilliant
background music for the Charles Laughton-Paul Gregory Production of John Brown's Body, has written what seems to me to
be one of the most haunting and original film scores of the past
decade for the Laughton-Gregory filming of the story. Schumann
knew instinctively from the outset that the essential fabric of The
Night of the Hunter was wound in and out with two principal
themes: The River and Little Children.

Sometimes during the writing of the book it seemed to me that
I could remember from my Ohio Valley childhood, almost as a
dimly recollected symphonic theme, the majesty and motion and
wonder of the great river. Schumann more than sensed this great
rhythm—he heard it in his creative imagination and put it down.
And he has captured the sorrow, the plight and the beauty of children in two charming songs—Once Upon a Time There Was a
Pretty Fly and the Lullaby, beautifully sung by Kitty White. Incidentally, I had to write the lyric for the latter in a frantic twenty
minutes one spring day last year, and ten minutes later Schumann
and I worked it out between us on the phone between Philadelphia and Redondo Beach, California.

When RCA Victor decided that the entire film score was so
beautiful and strong as to merit an album all its own, Charles
Laughton consented to weave the score together by telling the
story he had so brilliantly brought to the screen as director. And I
must confess that when I first heard his reading I found myself as
spellbound and anxious as if I had no notion as to how the story
would turn out. The two small children, John and Pearl, orphaned
and cast upon the saving waters of the great river, make their terrified and then idyllic exodus from the clutches of the villainous
Preacher. (The authority and authenticity of Mitchum's solo of
Leaning on the Everlasting Arms took me back to West Virginia
campground days when Billy Sunday and Sam Jones roared Salvation against the hills.) And once more the tale builds in suspense

as Laughton casts the ancient storyteller's spell, and Schumann's surging music conjures up the piteous children's terror, the beauty and mercy and majesty of the great river that carries them onward, and finally the great warmth and human dignity of the staunch farm woman Rachel Cooper who saves them from the hunter's knife. As I listened on I found myself closing my eyes and hearing the tale of The Night of the Hunter told to me as if I had never written it at all, as if it were something new, as if I had no idea what would happen next. But then hearing a story told is different—it is magic. Close your eyes and—listen.

For admirers of the film and its score, that RCA album has been a mixed blessing. Featured on the cover is a photo of Mitchum as Preacher, switchblade in hand, superimposed against misty clouds and a blue evening sky. Although the bold lettering proclaims, "PAUL GREGORY presents CHARLES LAUGHTON in a reading of THE NIGHT OF THE HUNTER by DAVIS GRUBB, Music by WALTER SCHUMANN," the storyteller's text was derived not from Grubb's novel but from the author's specially prepared narration for the LP. Notwithstanding the distinct pleasure to be derived from hearing Laughton's masterful delivery of prose written by the man whose novel had so moved him, and that Schumann's music superbly establishes the same mood and excitement on the disc as it does in the film, it would have been far better had there been two albums. In a literate LP such as Caedmon produces, Laughton could have read actual highlights from Grubb's novel, playing all the parts as he had off-camera during the film's shooting. And, the beautiful Schumann score could have had to itself the album it deserved: unabridged, and unencumbered by unnecessary narration.

A limited edition it may have been, but the RCA album was heavily promoted or, more properly speaking, it was heavily used to promote the movie. Several complete radio broadcasts were scheduled, and duly ballyhooed in the press—a very odd promotional gimmick, given that this narrative-with-music gave away the film's entire story. (Nowadays, movie trailers have been much criticized for divulging almost the whole picture, but in the fifties this wasn't the norm, and movies and their audiences were both the better for it.)

William Phipps

I saw *The Night of the Hunter* at a screening, and Bob Mitchum hadn't seen it yet. I told him how good it was, and how great he was. He said—"But, is it commercial?"

Turned out, it wasn't too commercial at the time, was it?

Robert Golden

We had a preview of the picture, and it was not successful. It's a gut instinct, sensing the audience's reaction. I had talked Laughton and Gregory into previewing a composite print. Now, that's a gamble. A composite print—the "marriage print"—that's when you've cut the negative, you've dubbed the picture, and the film and the soundtrack are on one piece of film. You can go back and do some cutting, and maybe some spot dubbing, and make a new print, but it's expensive. In a major studio, the cost isn't quite so important, but this was an independent production. I'd seen so many cases of supposedly knowledgeable people going into a projection room and looking at a rough cut without the music, without certain effects, and they just didn't get a proper or valuable response. So, since we were going into a little theater down in Manhattan Beach or wherever, and showing an audience this picture which we knew was unusual, my opinion was that it should be presented in its best possible form, technically. Also, production had gone on for a long time and I felt a responsibility to the people in the distribution company who wanted the picture. And I did say, "We can still make changes," but I didn't think anything would be changed.

No one said, "We should take out the mob scene," for example. And I don't know, outside of that, what we could have done to improve the picture. What would have been done if we hadn't had it on a composite print, I don't know. This was for Gregory's benefit, too, because it wouldn't have helped for the thing to go on and on and on, unless there was something to be done. If someone had had a suggestion that looked like it would have made a marked difference in the picture, we could have gone ahead and made these changes. Milt Carter, I remember, thought the whole opening should be changed. Now, I don't remember the details, but it was very possible that the audience didn't understand what the hell was happening. This was discussed, there was a pro

Caricature of Charles
Laughton supplied for
publicity use in the *Night
of the Hunter* press kit.

and con, and Laughton didn't agree. This is just my philosophical opinion, but I think that he gave the picture everything that he had—this
was *his,* you see—and unless someone had a startling idea that he agreed
with, nothing was going to be done. And no one did have that startling
idea.

There was disappointment, but no one knew the answer, and we were
all too close to it. You get to a point in a picture where you do it because,
"Well, maybe that's right." But this whole picture had been done with the
thought, "This is right. And I am going to rise or fall on this opinion."

Laughton fell. Oh, the film received many excellent reviews when it
opened that summer, and even wound up on several year-end "Best of
1955" lists. But by then, the film had already played itself out to a disappointing box-office.

Don Beddoe

Oh, I loved it. I thought it was a great picture. I thought it was going
to be sensational. I guess it wasn't, particularly, was it?

Robert Golden

Previews can tear your guts out, but they aren't as important as when the picture is released and is not a success—that *really* just tears your guts out. When you give yourself for the better part of a year—and I mean give, give, give—a flop is horrible. But I don't think Laughton had lost faith, and I wouldn't ever think that Laughton felt the picture fell way short of his personal vision, because Lord knows he was there during shooting and nothing got away from him.

Paul Gregory

The picture premiered on "Paul Gregory Day" in Des Moines, Iowa. I don't think it helped the picture, I don't think it helped me. All that stuff, the visiting movie stars and the big premiere, was for the people that put it on, it wasn't for me, they just used me to hang it on. We were going to sneak-preview the picture in Des Moines, and they heard about it and suddenly called up and said, "My goodness, can we make this a Paul Gregory day?"

I said, "Well, what have I done to deserve it?"

"Well, you're from Des Moines," and blah, blah, blah, "and we can raise fifty thousand for the new YMCA building . . ."

So I said, "Well, if it'll help the picture, fine."

July 25 was designated Paul Gregory Day by Mayor Joe Van Dreser, initiating plans for a twenty-four-hour celebration of Des Moines' native son, to culminate in a star-studded premiere of *The Night of the Hunter*. Lillian Gish, when invited to attend, cabled Gregory from Rome: "WILL FLY AUSTRIA DES MOINES AND BACK VERY EXPENSIVE AM I WORTH IT LETTER FOLLOWS MUCH LOVE= LILLIAN=." Gregory wrote a letter, replying in part: "You are worth every cent it would cost to fly you to Des Moines from Austria and back; however, I wouldn't put you through such an ordeal if you were my worst enemy. All I would like to have you do is wire Mr. Stanley Friedman, president of the Des Moines Chamber of Commerce, your sentiments (if you have any) towards the fat boy and me and your regrets for not being able to attend . . ."

Actor Don Taylor was himself from Pennsylvania, but being "a shining young light" at the time—he was groom to Elizabeth Taylor in the

Spencer Tracy comedy *Father of the Bride*—Paul Gregory invited him to add his luster to the guest list. On the flight to Iowa, Don Taylor's *Blue Veil* co-star Laughton—perhaps instinctively sensing in Taylor the future director-to-be—befriended him, and they sat together at the rear of the plane. Laughton shared with the young man his adventures working on *Hunter*, but unfortunately the flight was interrupted by a storm and was forced to land in Denver. Laughton and the other luminaries—including Elsa Lanchester, Don DeFore, Agnes Moorehead and Cesar Romero—sought shelter in the Denver Skychief restaurant. As it happened, several patrons that night seemed to be having birthdays, which the management was duly honoring with complimentary birthday cakes and singing waiters. Some time, probably around the third rousing rendition of "Happy Birthday," it was decided that if all these Denver denizens were having birthdays then, by God, Charles Laughton ought to be having one, too. Taylor told the waiter that it was Charles' birthday, and, sure enough, the great man got his cake and his song.

A special green-tinted insert in the *Hunter* press kit immortalizes the

events of Paul Gregory Day with several pictures and the banner headline, "'SALUTE TO PAUL GREGORY' WORLD PREMIERE IN DES MOINES EX-
PLODES BALLY BOMBSHELL HEARD 'ROUND THE NATION! BIZ TERRIFIC!"
In addition to the visiting celebrities, all of whom submitted to radio
interviews, the governor and other local dignitaries were in attendance
for the gala day. The main events were the Chamber of Commerce Tes-
timonial Luncheon honoring Paul Gregory—"Luncheon set in motion
the biggest movie event in Des Moines history!"—and of course, that
evening, the big premiere. Laughton, not surprisingly, was the highlight
among the speakers paying tribute to Gregory at his luncheon: "He has
pinned to the ground that scabby lie that the intelligence of the American audience is average age Twelve . . . We have a word in the theater
that you use in Iowa, only we don't use it in quite the same way. To you
the word is sacred. It is corn . . . If Mr. Gregory and I ever allow corn
to creep into our productions, we hope it will be the quality of Iowa
corn. I also hope it will bear a billion-dollar crop." According to *Des
Moines Register* reporter Robert Barewald, Gregory was stunned by all
the testimonials, "almost overcome with emotion," and spoke his thanks
with long pauses between his words: "I can only tell you one thing. This
day—this occasion—would never exist if it were not for my association
with Charles Laughton. To be able to come back to Des Moines and
have him with me for this occasion is almost more than I can talk about.
Thank you."

   The big noise in Des Moines was broadcast live via a remote hook-
up on NBC-TV's *The Tonight Show*, hosted by Steve Allen. "HOLLY-
WOOD STARS IN PERSON" promised the marquee of the Paramount Theater (right next to the bus depot), and *The Night of the Hunter* opened
to an impressive crowd of thousands, whose reactions to the screening
Laughton found most gratifying: "I set out to make audiences scream,"
he said, "and, by Jove, I did it!" Such ballyhoo was, according to the
press kit insert, "the prelude for a 2-state saturation send-off across Iowa
and Nebraska . . . Coverage of the event by newspapers, magazines,
radio and TV makes *The Night of the Hunter* one of the top pre-sold pictures of the year!" Which, of course, it unfortunately would not prove
to be.

Paul Gregory

We did well in Des Moines, though. We did very well in Iowa, and all through that part of the country.

But the marketing of the picture was dreadful. Dreadful.

Ideally, a film's promoters should seek for a single image which will convey the movie's story and mood to the prospective ticket-buyer. The ad art which came closest to achieving this goal for *Hunter*—or, at least, as close as possible given the film's highly unusual plot—depicted a full moon framing Willa and Preacher, locked in an embrace, their faces looking in different directions, his LOVE hand holding her, his HATE hand holding his knife. But this image lacked any reference to John, or the

child's-eye view of terror. Sadly more typical of the overall campaign was
the largish newspaper ad which hit all over the target and completely
missed the bull's-eye. Beneath the full moon a collage of no less than ten
separate stills from the film is anchored in the center by a giant book
bearing the film's title, and because the cover says, "PAUL GREGORY presents," it conveys the impression that he, not Davis Grubb, wrote the
novel. "Towering above all others . . ." is the headline, followed by, "
. . .the warmth and passion and suspense of the gripping best seller!
. . .the powerful performances of a superb, distinguished cast! . . .the creative genius of Paul Gregory and Charles Laughton, the famed
producing-directing team that brought 'The Caine Mutiny Court Martial' to the stage! . . .these are the exciting raw materials of screen greatness . . . but greater than them all—is the impact of the motion picture
itself!" This rather typical fifties everything-but-the-kitchen-sink movie
advertising features generalized verbiage which says nothing except "It's
great, folks!" and presents a mulligan stew of images (including an
anachronistically contemporary, and inappropriately glamorized, portrait
of Miss Winters, pearls and all). Thus did United Artists' promotion department attempt in vain to fit the round peg of Laughton's quirky masterpiece into the square hole of Hollywood blockbuster potboilers.

With such puffery pushing the picture into theaters nationwide, *Hunter* couldn't compete with the Cinemascoped and Technicolored extravaganzas that were themselves competing with the riveting little black-and-white screens which were keeping more and more Americans home in their living rooms. Critic Pauline Kael recalled going to see *The Night of the Hunter* its opening week and finding herself among a few hundred people in a theater built to hold a thousand.

One indication of U-A's approach to *Hunter*'s distribution and marketing can be found in an October 16 column by film-writer Eleanor Keen in the *Chicago Sun-Times*. Miss Keen reports that Paul Gregory "enjoyed the experience (of producing *Hunter*) tremendously. He was startled, he says, to discover what a sense of relief, as well as a sense of accomplishment, there is in finishing a film. 'There it all is, finally, wrapped up, finished, on film. In the theater nothing is ever that complete. There are always new problems, new audiences, new stages. Every night is an opening.'" But, after extolling the pedigree of *Hunter*'s cast and creators, the columnist announces, "The picture starts Wednesday at the Roosevelt Theater. It is being presented on the same program with *Robbers' Roost*. The latter is Zane Grey's story. It stars George Montgomery and Richard Boone." Clearly it is a gauge of United Artists' faith in *The Night of the Hunter* that they would introduce it to a major city like Chicago by throwing it away on a double-bill with a B-western.

Paul Gregory

It should never have been mass-booked at all. I tried to get them not to, but I just ran into a stone wall. You see, a releasing company like United Artists, they have so much money out and they want to get it back right away and start investing in more pictures, and so on. They didn't give a damn at all; they had decided how much they'd be happy to have from our picture, and so they didn't go out and do a campaign on it at all. If it could have started in Des Moines and then built like a prairie fire, it would have built its own. It should *never* have gone into New York until it had played around the country and we'd begun to get the reaction, the word-of-mouth and all that kind of thing.

But, they didn't have time to do that, they had to print hundreds of copies and get all their money at once, or some damn thing. They had

no sense of salesmanship at all, and the reason was very simple, they were after the big money in *Not As a Stranger,* that's what they put all their campaign money into. And so you had Frank Sinatra and Bob Mitchum in *Not As a Stranger,* you had Bob Mitchum in something else, and you had Bob Mitchum in *The Night of the Hunter.* You see? There was no dis-

tinction. They put you out of business before you have a chance to be in business. You might say, "Who's 'they'?" Well, Arthur Krim, and all these *nice* people that you never see and that are just like voices in a tunnel. Charles was disappointed. He was very disappointed because he didn't feel that they gave it the importance that they had promised us. And I agree with him completely. You see, I think this is a picture that we could have taken to England first, and not released it first in the United States at all, and then released it in some choice bookings. Because, it was well-received in England, we got wonderful reviews.

Now, I must say, in all fairness to United Artists, they did not interfere at all with the way we filmed it when once we started shooting. They didn't come and look at dailies. I must say they didn't, because I remember the first time they saw it was when I took the film into New York, and they didn't want any changes made after that first cut.

But we never made a nickel on *The Night of the Hunter,* and they made a lot of money. Oh, yes, you always hear about the film being a financial flop, but they've made a lot of money, they've done very well with all of their hidden interest charges and all of their compounding . . . I ran into one of their top executives not long ago, and he said, "Why don't you go to United Artists with your new project? They'll finance you. You know, we did very well on your picture."

I said, "Well, I'm glad you did. But we never made a dime."

They had no sense of sale, no sense of showmanship with it at all. When I produce a show, before I just say "Oh, I'm going to open up here," instead, I try to "cast" where I am, look at what other shows are around me, so that I have the best chance for the audience I'm after. Which is exactly what United Artists didn't do. You see, that picture didn't cost anything to make. $425,000 is all, and it's grossed over two and a half million, but the costs on it are . . . We still have, like, $300,000 to get back, we've made no dent in our possible profits. I think that if United Artists had promoted the picture properly, it could have made them a lot more money than it did, so in a sense they lost money. How much would I say they lost? Well, whether they consider it a loss or not, I would never work for them again, period. And perhaps that's not a loss. (*Laughs*) I might have lost them a lot of money.

Stanley Cortez

This is only my opinion, but I think the picture was badly released. It was a very distinctive type of picture, it should have been released in, perhaps, an art house to begin with. It should never have been released in what is known as saturation booking. I know it hurt Charles terribly to think that the picture in America was not the success that it could have been. Little did he know that what he did would be acclaimed in later years.

Also, one of the sad things about *The Night of the Hunter* is the fact that in Europe it had a limited success because many European countries don't have what we unfortunately have here in America, which is, by buying a collar, you become a phony priest. The concept in Europe is, a priest is a priest, this is a very holy thing, there are no phony priests. And so, since the film was based on a phony priest, it was banned in many countries in Europe.

And not only in Europe, as it turns out. *The Night of the Hunter* was banned from at least one Bible Belt city, Memphis, Tennessee. Mr. Lloyd T. Binford, 88, Chairman of the Memphis board of censors, wrote to the United Artists branch manager and asserted that *Hunter* was "the rawest film (he) had ever seen." (Binford subsequently admitted that, due to trouble with his car and chauffeur, he had not actually made it to the screening, and had therefore never seen the film.)

Paul Gregory

It was too bad the picture was made at that time. For one thing, today you could make it and not have all that "Christian" nonsense. We were just bombarded by all the church associations of censors, or whatever they called themselves. Protestant censor committees and all the church groups just bombarded us with silly things, threats of boycotting the picture and so forth. Yes, even though Preacher was clearly a phony. It didn't make any difference to them, he was peddling God. I said to a meeting of three hundred of these people, "If you can see one ounce of recognition of yourselves in this man, then you're tragedies." Which is so. But they put up many, many barriers, so that we didn't get certain bookings that we needed to get it started off right. They just made it generally difficult.

(Here Gregory seems to be referring to the episode Laughton had reported to Davis Grubb, but casting himself in the role of Laughton. Or, had Laughton cast himself in the role of Gregory, as Gregory says he did when discussing *Caine Mutiny* with that Boston journalist . . .?)

Paul Gregory

What about Laughton's own spirituality? All I can tell you is, he said to me one day, "The Bible is the biggest crock of bullshit I ever read in my life, but if I can be paid to read it, I'll read the son of a bitch." That's what he said. I don't have it in writing, but that's what he said.

Robert Mitchum

Charles was one of the very few people who was qualified to be a director. He was a very tolerant man, he had great humor, and he was . . . He would scream for what he wanted, but he was very humble. He realized that this film was a great opportunity, which it was, of course. The fact that he had actually come through it and done all these things was a source of great wonder to him. And it's unfortunate that he hadn't done that from the very beginning. He should have been doing that all the time. I told him he was too timid. He used to have a thing, if he had a film to do, that the first two day's work didn't count.

He liked doing what he was doing. He liked to be involved. He was a teacher, you know. He used to have people come and have classes in his house. He used to try to teach them that, in order to read Shakespeare, they didn't have to speak with a broad English accent as long as they spoke clear and intelligible English and knew what they were talking about. It was very difficult, because a lot of them had been schooled before, orators or declamation contest winners from Long Beach or whatever.

He was always at me to do Shakespeare. He gave me a long speech one time, he wanted me to do *Richard the Third* in England. He said he'd direct it. I said no, I said, "So? What? Then I come back and do the same lousy picture I would have done had I not done that." For me to do Shakespeare in England, I'd just be breathing someone else's air; to someone else, it might be valuable. I finally said to Charles, "For what? For what reason?"

And he said, "For *us*, you cunt!"

As it happens, Robert Mitchum actually did execute one job of live stage-acting for Charles Laughton: He performed as Preacher in excerpts from *The Night of the Hunter* on CBS-TV's *The Ed Sullivan Show.* In today's television marketplace, the commonplace practice for film-plugging is simply for an actor to put in an appearance on the couch of some talk-show host, accompanied by a short clip from his or her movie. But in the golden age of live TV, there were few "talk shows" as we know them today, and a great proliferation of variety shows. King of them all was newspaper columnist Ed Sullivan's *The Toast of the Town,* later rechristened *The Ed Sullivan Show.* (Few people remember that the famous night that Elvis Presley made his debut on the Sullivan show, Ed wasn't there. The guest host? Charles Laughton.) Ed used to regale his audiences with genuine movie stars, "live, on our stage," recreating scenes from their current motion pictures: Gary Cooper endured the withering cross-examination of prosecutor Rod Steiger in a tense moment from the script of *The Court Martial of Billy Mitchell;* Henry Fonda, who had played *Mister Roberts* hundreds of times on Broadway, repeated the role once more to promote the Warner Brothers film version, with James Cagney and a young Jack Lemmon recreating a hilarious shipboard encounter between the Captain and Ensign Pulver. And, even though so much of *The Night of the Hunter* depended on its unique sets and lighting and music for its effectiveness, stars Mitchum and Winters were assigned to bring Preacher and Willa back to life one more time. Considering the Sullivan Show's enormous popularity, more people probably saw the "Left Hand-Right Hand" sermon enacted that Sunday on their TV screens than ever paid to see it in a movie theater.

Robert Mitchum

I don't even remember doing it. I had just fallen off a plane from Europe, and came in, and the next thing I knew, I was dodging stagehands. That set looks enormous, I suppose, on the tube, but the stage was really only half that deep. They were moving sets and flats around, and Jesus Christ, you'd be impaled if you didn't jump out of the way. One of the guys says, "This is nothing. You ought to be here when we do the Gleason show. *Nothin'* makes sense on that."

I said, "How the hell do you handle this?"

He reaches off behind a flat and he pulls out a big quart bottle of Jack Daniels, and says, "This helps."

"Sunday was a disappointing night," wrote Ken Murphy, noted TV critic and columnist, and heading his roster of let-downs was the following commentary: "Now 'Night of the Hunter' may be an excellent movie, just as it undoubtedly was an excellent book, but I still can't believe that even Ed Sullivan fans want to look at a half-hour trailer of any film, however excellent." This "too much of a good thing" approach curiously clung to the *Hunter* promotion, from the broadcasts of the Laughton soundtrack-narration to the newspaper serialization of the story—"It will come to (name of newspaper) readers, starting Monday, with all its brilliant storytelling and its gripping characters intact from the pages of the novel." Why bother to see the movie?

Stanley Cortez

Who am I to criticize United Artists? But I think our little picture kind of got lost in that big corporation. It was an unusual picture, it was ahead of its time, its appeal was a very unique one, and I just don't think it should have been given that big saturation booking. I remember Charles was upset about this, too. If Charles were alive today, I know that he would be delighted to know that at last his and our efforts are being acclaimed. We've always known that the picture was a classic, but it's become more evident the past few years, I would imagine because of exposure on television. Those who hadn't seen it, or were too young when it first came out, are seeing it for the first time. They realize the greatness of this thing, that the term "classic" is the proper definition. And the proof of that is that the picture is being shown over and over and over again, not only here but in Europe as well. People stop me in Paris and ask me all kinds of questions about it.

Mrs. Sonya Goodman

I think Mr. Laughton recognized that there were some actors and actresses whose ability had never really been used to its fullest, and the actors he used in his productions surprised a lot of Hollywood people. Tyrone Power had been used in pretty-boy roles and swashbucklers, but somehow Mr. Laughton had always understood that there was a lot more acting depth and range of emotion to Tyrone Power, and he waited a long time to get the chance to use him. When the reviews came out on *John Brown's Body,* they said that Tyrone Power was a revelation, a discovery. In the same way, Mr. Laughton understood that Robert Mitchum had a tremendous depth that had never really been explored before. Putting him in the part of this mad murderer was really an offbeat bit of casting, but a lot of people say that that was Mitchum's most interesting role, and I think he will say so himself.

Robert Mitchum

My best performance? Probably. There are things I didn't like about my work in it, but I haven't seen it in a long time. I'd have to point to it, frame by frame. I'd have to qualify it. I always do, because I don't spend too much time honing it up with makeup and eyebrows and a lot of study. I don't like to detract from the general scene. I learned that early on: stay out of the shot. "Hey, wait a minute, we didn't get Mitchum."

"Of course we did, he was—" "No, he wasn't, he was over here." "Right. Okay, later."

Do I wish more people had seen this picture? Not particularly. That's up to them, you know. I'm not in the picture-selling business, and I'm not too concerned with posterity. No, I don't think I got a raw deal by not getting an Oscar nomination. It depends upon what you mean by getting nominated for an Oscar. I worked one year with a lady who had received the Academy Award the year before for a really dumb performance. I was doing a picture with her and we were well into it before I realized that she didn't know it was a comedy. The writer knew, I knew. Nobody else knew. She had convinced them that she wanted to do it because (*Hushed, reverent tone*) "It's the Bible," you know. So, I don't know. Charles would be the first one to say . . . You'd have to calm him down, really, because his personal instinct would be to denounce the whole Academy business.

The people who say the picture was "too arty"? I don't know, I guess they're just tone-deaf, that's all. *Jaws* isn't excessive for *Jaws,* is it? Is it? I don't know. No, I shouldn't think so.

Stanley Cortez

To me, the word "arty" is a disgraceful, horrible, insulting word to use, it has connotations of being phony, or pretentious, of bad taste, of kitsch—all the things that Charles Laughton was not. I despise that word. You'll hear it coming from some uninformed person on the set or some man who sits back in his chair in some office and always plays it safe, who doesn't have the guts or the courage to at least *try* to do something different, something truly worthwhile.

Paul Gregory

"Too arty"? I don't know what they mean. It's only too many potatoes on your plate if you don't like potatoes, but it's not too many if you happen to like potatoes, you know what I mean? I never thought about it being arty or not being arty, I thought about it being truthful. That's all I ever thought about. I think it's awfully easy to say something's too arty or too this or too that, if you weren't there when it was being done. And it's such a difficult job, the *easiest* aspect of it is so difficult, to get a thing on, that by the time it's on and it's over, I never give a damn what they say. I never read a review on *The Night of the Hunter.* I never read a review on anything that I do. Ever. If someone comes to me and tells me, "Jesus, isn't it marvelous, you've had a hit" (*Laughs*) I say, "Yes, it's marvelous," and let it go at that. Because I can't be bothered. I think that the reviewers and the critiques and all that stuff are the unnecessary aspect of our business anyway.

When Lillian Gish had likened most artists to six-month-old kittens in matters of business, she must have had the skittish Laughton in mind. "Once, admiring the Gregory-Laughton relationship," she recalled, "I said to Charles, 'I hope nothing ever happens to you and Paul and your friendship.'" Laughton surprised her with the intensity of his reaction: "What? What could happen? What do you mean?" She explained that something could happen, time can change everything. She hoped it never would and, in truth, didn't think they would ever split up. "I was shocked by their parting," she admitted, "and have always wondered what came between them, or what happened."

Lillian Gish

Oh, they were a beautiful combination, Paul and Charles, it was a pity they ever broke up. They did such lovely things, *Don Juan in Hell* and all the others. I don't know whatever happened to them. I see Paul Gregory sometimes now with Janet.★ Oh, that combination never should have broken up.

Paul Gregory

I'd say the separation came out of *The Night of the Hunter.* Laughton and my relationship was a very special and very close one, but very few relationships, if you look at others, can survive the separation that being in production demands, you know, being around other people. You see, I had the responsibility of maintaining a company, of paying Laughton a big salary, so I had to do things. I couldn't not do something while the

---

★the late Janet Gaynor, Mrs. Paul Gregory.

picture was going on, I had to have something else going, because we weren't getting any money from the picture at all, and I didn't feel that we would be getting anything. And so, there were elements, people who got next to Laughton and said, "What's Gregory trying to do without you? He's gone on to something else . . ." And Laughton never, ever, ever, *ever* could see reason. Ever. It wasn't in his vocabulary. About anything. He'd get a bug in his ear that someone had planted, then he'd be suspicious, and I just couldn't work that way.

And he had a lawyer that was in our company that was my lawyer, too, but he was an irascible old son of a bitch, Lloyd Wright, and he's dead, and I would say it if he were alive, he was the main reason for Laughton and my not going on. He was a lawyer who took ten percent, too, and he suddenly saw an opportunity after Laughton had become prominent again of setting up a company with he and Charles, but it never happened.

So, I don't fight any of those kinds of things. If someone comes along and thinks they can do better and they want to try it, fine, they have my blessing, "Wonderful, go and try it." But it was over, and I went on to other things, and had equal successes. After all, the biggest success I had was *Marriage-Go-Round,* the play with Charles Boyer and Claudette Col-

bert. It wasn't the artistic satisfaction of some of the others, but nevertheless it was very successful. And my days at CBS were enormously successful, and so I was satisfied with what I did. But I'd much rather work
with someone. I missed working with Laughton, because we worked well
together. And that's one of the reasons I haven't done very much, is because I like to work with another individual. I'm not a lone wolf.

Robert Mitchum

I stayed in touch with Charles. You know, he was not too prudent in his
keep. He paid $36,000 for a Rubens bathing picture; he had bought a num-
ber of paintings . . . Suddenly he owed the government $86,000 in taxes—
there they were, in the paintings. He said he'd rather worry about that than
give up the paintings. So, his husbandry was probably a little slack.

When we lived in Maryland, he was working on *Advise and Consent*.
He came over to ask me to read his speeches with him, to coach him
through his speeches. We had a great mutual admiration society. He
used to call me up. He talked to me once about *The Night of the Hunter*
after it was all over. He told me, "There are desperate areas of embarrassment." He thought I was great, and the same for everybody else.

Paul Gregory

Laughton never spoke about how close he felt the film came to what he
had wanted to achieve. He never spoke in those terms, on any of our
productions. You see, Laughton wasn't the man on fire, you never felt
from Charles that he *had* to do something because it was something he
had to do. You never felt that. Charles was very surgical. Even though
there's fire in what you see on the screen, in the result.

All I understood from Davis Grubb was that he liked the picture. He
should have liked it, it was true to his story, and an author can't ask any
more than that. (*Laughs*) He might ask you to make it better than his
story. But, I think it was true to the book.

Davis Grubb

I just loved Evelyn Varden. I sat with her up in the United Artists' viewing room the day I saw the answer print. Laughton was on the coast and
couldn't make it. She sat there in the viewing room just squeezing my

"I just loved Evelyn Varden . . ." The actress and Davis Grubb saw *The Night of the Hunter* together for the first time in a United Artists screening room.

hand as hard as she could, hoping I'd be pleased, and I was hoping that she was pleased . . .

What was my reaction? Well, George Grizzard, a very fine actor, [and co-star with Laughton on *Advise and Consent*], said to me once at P.J. Clarke's, "Charles Laughton really ruined your book." I said, "Laughton *couldn't* ruin the book. He might have ruined his *film* . . ." Grizzard said, "Well, I apologize, you're right." But, I did at first think Laughton had ruined *The Night of the Hunter*. His film was faithful to my book, but it wasn't faithful to the film I'd had in my head while I was writing it. How could it have been? I would have felt that Griffith had ruined the book.

Since then, I've seen the film many times, and I've come to appreciate it for the fine work it is. I'm always surprised to see that it's lasted as long as it has. And I'm proud of that, because I did contribute something to it. I think it's a wonderful picture, and I wouldn't want to change a single thing about it.

But, I would kind of like to do it over again.

Now, I know the people who admire the film might say that sounds like sacrilege, but I don't think so. Laughton's film was a fine one, but there's more than one way to tell a good story. If I had a hand in making a new version of *Night of the Hunter,* I might try to put in some of the things that Laughton left out, things I wished I'd seen more of when I first saw the film. There were lots of things. For example, the woman who ran the secondhand furniture store, Miz Cunningham. There wasn't enough of her. And I'd like to have seen something more of Uncle Birdie. I'd have liked to have seen that character developed more. If we ever do a remake, I'd like to see it really built up, and I'd like to see Ruby built up.

Anyway, I think Laughton made a marvelous movie. I also think he was disappointed with it. Because, I think he was a good artist, a great artist in many ways, and I think every great artist is disappointed in what he has not been able to personally control. In other words, if I write a book, I can be pleased with it. But if I write a movie, I have to subdivide this into all the different other egos and talents and gifts and hates and loves that went into it. I'm sure Laughton wasn't pleased. I can't imagine anybody ever being totally pleased with a movie.

He talked to me about the picture after it finished, but he was very shy about it. I'd been living the Civil War writing my second novel, I was like breathing it night and day. That was in '55; I had a meeting with Laughton in 1956. I talked to him about *A Dream of Kings,* and I don't think it grabbed him. We parted in the lobby of the St. Moritz. He said, "I've been thinking about if we make a movie again together—"

I said, "When, not if."

He said, "We'll have a success next time."

We shook on it, then he turned and walked out through the revolving doors and I never saw him again.

It was like a pledge had been made, that we would make a movie again. And I've often wondered if it might have been *The Watchman,* which was written in '59, not long before he died, because so many actors and actresses have expressed such interest in playing the main roles. Of course, over time and after the fact, *Hunter* has turned out to be a kind of success. Several years ago, here in New York, I noticed that, at the same time, *Night of the Hunter* was being shown at the Museum of Modern Art, a cheap theater on 42nd Street, and on *The Late, Late Show* on TV.

Robert Mitchum

I wonder if Charles never felt, before that, that he was ready to direct a film, or that he wanted to. I suppose nobody would have taken him seriously, although a lot of people that knew him might have, especially actors.

William Phipps

He didn't plan on having a movie-directing career. Not at that time, when he was in his mid-fifties. Later than that, I guess when he was about sixty, I remember his saying—shortly before he got cancer—that he didn't care about acting any more. He didn't want to learn the lines: he said, "I only want to direct." But, he didn't have any burning ambition, even at the time of *The Night of the Hunter,* to go on and direct. Of course, he could pick and choose, you know. I mean, this *excited* him— he would never have touched *Night of the Hunter* if he didn't see the potential there, if he didn't love the story.

Paul Gregory

Well, I don't think he will go down as having been unique as a director. That's right, even though his picture was unique itself. I think there's no way Charles Laughton could have gone down in history as a director. This one picture was not enough to decide that he was a great director. He had an enormous amount of help on this picture, an *enormous* amount, and many of the decisions were not his. He directed the actors, and he worked with Stanley Cortez deciding where to place the camera, but until that moment of decision, in that sense, was made, all the other stuff was done for Charles, by the unit: Golden, Cortez, Brown, Carter. And myself. It was quiet, because I never walked on the stage or in that unit, but Laughton felt very responsible to that film and we talked about it all. Laughton conveyed to that group what he and I had discussed way into the night every night. And yet, I'm not saying for a minute that I could have made the picture. I could not have. But I think this was a unique marriage of Laughton and material—and the unit.

Now, in a theater, here again, if Laughton would have, he could have been probably the most exciting director in the theatre in America. He directed *Don Juan in Hell*, he directed *John Brown's Body*, he directed *Caine Mutiny.* But—you couldn't pin it down. You see, it was mercury. He couldn't hold it, like this. Suddenly it would go *psssst!* and it'd pop out of there. Then you'd get that pushed down, and you'd go like this again, "I got it, I got the genie in my hand," and suddenly up your arm it would go. He couldn't hang on to it.

Stanley Cortez

Charles and I spent nine months preparing a film of *The Naked and the Dead,* and just what actually happened I really don't know, but what I do know is that when I see the final picture, it made my . . . It was not what it should have been. Someday I'll show you the script, I have it at home, it's that thick. That's Charles Laughton's script, marvelous, really great, he had dramatic devices he called "time machines" in it. You see, he was going to go for a really big cast, a big production. I think he had in mind Jimmy Stewart, Burt Lancaster, Richard Widmark, many top, top names. Milt Carter and I spent weeks in Hawaii scouting locations. Laughton couldn't go because he had to get the script finished. We made about five hundred stills of potential locations. One of the high points was the mountain Norman Mailer speaks of in his powerful book. When I saw that film and compared it to what Charles Laughton had in mind, it was like day and night. I don't mean to speak disrespectfully of Raoul Walsh, but they were two different concepts. One was made for X amount of dollars, and this is what you get. But Charles' thought was a very big picture.

Terry Sanders

Well, it *had* to be a big picture, because it was a lot of soldiers and guns and shooting . . . Laughton was talking about big names. At one point, Laughton thought he would lose weight and maybe play the General himself. But who he really wanted to play the General was Robert Montgomery. He would have been a great General.

Terry Sanders has good reason to remember this second "epic that never was," because the involvement in it of him and his brother was much more central than had been their participation on *Hunter*. As with *Hunter*, however, Laughton felt that his first obligation was to collaborate as closely and intensely as possible with the book's author. *The Naked and the Dead*, like *The Night of the Hunter*, was its author's first published novel, but whereas Laughton had welcomed young Davis Grubb to "the aristocracy of the arts," by the time Laughton became involved with Mr. Mailer, the author had been in that aristocracy for some years and had grown accustomed to his position in its hierarchy. Laughton still kept in touch with Grubb, and ruefully reported that his newest author-director collaboration was not going as smoothly as his first had done. Grubb had put his faith in what he termed "Laughton's artist's trustworthiness," but Mr. Mailer, according to Laughton, was not so disposed. Nor was the truculent Young Turk of American letters inclined to conceal what would nowadays be called his attitude problem. "Throughout all of Laughton's painstaking work," according to Grubb, "and I am absolutely certain that Laughton approached that task with as much reverence for a splendid novel as he had with my own modest tour de force—constantly, persistently, naggingly Mailer kept implying that Laughton was going to make it all Hollywood shit." Things came to a head one day when Laughton had to patiently endure Mailer's use of the word "verisimilitude" about forty-nine times. Imagine Laughton's infinite patience snapping when he hears Mailer uttering the word for the fiftieth time. Picture Laughton now turning slowly on young Mailer and asking, with the quiet unctuousness of Sir Wilfred addressing a *Witness for the Prosecution*: "Mister Mailer—will you be kind enough to tell me where in the Pacific Ocean is located the island of solid rock upon which the action of your fine story takes place?" Mailer hems. Mailer haws. He bobs, he weaves—then he admits, "Well, as a matter of fact—there isn't any such island. I made it up." Now imagine Laughton rising before an unsuspecting Mailer, and roaring with all the Captain Bligh that's in him: "Yes. Yes, Mr. Mailer! I know fucking bloody well you made it up! And it cost me three-thousand fucking bloody dollars of research to ascertain that fiction! Now—let us have no more of your fucking bloody palaver about verisimilitude!"

Terry Sanders

It was during the marketing of *Night of the Hunter,* Paul Gregory had bought *The Naked and the Dead,* and Laughton was already starting on his second picture. At that point, he got along so well with Denis and me and really respected us, and so he wanted us to be his collaborators in writing the screenplay, which turned out to be a long-term project. So we spent a lot of time every day, writing, but also talking. The writing plan was such that we would write for two hours in the morning, and then have this incredible lunch that this lovely cook, German lady, would make for us, and the rest of the afternoon we would read Shakespeare aloud, or Dickens, or whatever. We would take turns reading. I'm not an actor, although I did a little acting at UCLA, and Charles wanted me to play Goldstein, one of the soldiers in *The Naked and the Dead.*

As Denis recalled the project, the brothers were each hired at $250 a week, and the work proceeded not only at the Laughton home—at the pool and in the "school room"—but also *chez* Sanders, because Charles loved the boys' mother, Tina, and always enjoyed visiting. It didn't feel like work writing a script with the master, enjoying those meals, talking around the pool, listening to Laughton read Shaw and the Bible when the mood struck him, or hearing him hold forth on art—"It was almost an unbelievable experience to two young men who had just recently graduated from the university."

Terry Sanders

What an incredible career Charles Laughton had. I mean, he did so many wonderful films. *Mutiny on the Bounty,* which I loved. We used to drive along, go to a restaurant, and people would lean out of their cars and say, "Captain Bligh!"

"On one occasion, Charles stood nude in the pool looking very much like Captain Bligh," Denis remembered, "shouting out ideas with the two of us poised at the side of the pool with pads and pencils, taking down every word." Apparently, it took a little while before Laughton had gotten himself up to that speed. "At first," said Denis, "Charles had great doubts about doing the script. First of all, he felt he was too old a man to give an honest treatment to Mailer's book, because Mailer was a young man. He also had a great aversion to the subject matter. Hated war. He recognized that both of us Sanders brothers were very enthusiastic and excited about the book, and that's one reason he wanted us to work with him. He also knew that for Terry and me, the men's emotions were real. Charles could understand them, but he didn't like them. He was repelled by some of the things in the book. But he was able to see that our main purpose was to abstract the material—to find poetic lines beyond the obvious story line. To give, for instance, in a scene in which a soldier was being carried on a stretcher a number of universal discomforts—all the discomforts that could happen. Therefore, as we worked on the script, Charles became completely enthusiastic. We would talk for hours about particular aspects of the film that we wished to achieve.

"At times, however, Charles would 'pull rank.' If I had written a scene which I was particularly proud of and Charles didn't like it, he'd say, 'But my dear Denis, it's not theatrical.' At first, this intimidated me because there was no answer, you couldn't argue with that kind of statement. But, after a while, I learned to say, 'You son of a bitch, you're wrong.' And tell him the scene was right. To which, Charles would mutter, and then later we'd talk about it. It was an experience of sharing and a rich one.

"We worked together for weeks on the script and finally, one day, Charles took me aside and confessed, 'You know, originally I didn't think you had any talent, I thought your brother had it all. And I simply hired you because I didn't want to break up a pleasant sibling relationship. But now I recognize, my boy, that you have equal talents, and I'm glad to be working with you.' Of course, I had recognized the reason for having been hired originally, but it pleased me that Charles had changed his mind. I told him, 'I knew that, Charles. I was simply waiting for you to recognize the truth.'"

"Charles had a number of innovations in mind for the film. He wished to show a sort of circular motion so that the person on the screen would be on the borders and his thoughts would be revealed in the center of the screen. It was an effect that he could never completely work out, but we were talking a great deal about these flashbacks, going backwards, rather than flashing back to a scene and then going forward chronologically. The idea was not used, but it was an intriguing one."

Terry Sanders

Well, *The Naked and the Dead,* if you've read the book, has cameos—vignettes—that are called "time machine." That's where Charles got the phrase that Stanley Cortez remembered, it comes right out of the book. There are, like, twelve or fifteen people in the platoon that are followed, and there's also the officers. The book has a very strong storyline, but every so often Mailer stops and does a little portrait called "time machine," of Martinez, or of Reb, or of Hearn, or of the General. And the time machine is just a little three-page sketch of their history, like, just what was important in the history to bring them to that point, and it's done starting when they're tiny and bringing them forward in age. And Laughton, we were talking this out in writing the script, you know, Laughton turned to me one time and said, "That's a great idea."

I said, "What do you mean?"

He said, "Instead of you doing these time machines forward, we'll do them backwards, as you just suggested."

And I don't remember suggesting that. So I always felt, "Maybe I did suggest it, but the other thing that might have happened was that Laughton thought this was such an outlandish idea that he didn't want to just say, "I have an idea, let's do it backwards." He said, "Your idea to do it backwards is so great!"

Backwards—in other words, you start when the soldier is twenty-five and you work back to when he was one year old. It's just like, if you were cutting a scene, you just put it in reverse order, you get younger and younger and younger in the flashback, instead of starting with them young and coming forward again. The time machine might be two, three minutes at most, and the first thirty seconds you might see them in civilian life, just the year before they got into the army, and then the next thirty seconds you'd see them in high school, and the next thirty seconds you'd see how the mother beat them, or something. Mailer had the idea of these little portraits of the characters, and Laughton decided they'd be good if you could just run them in reverse order.

William Phipps

I remember working with Laughton on that, down at their house at Palos Verdes, many, many times. And, I remember being there many times, reading the scenes aloud, and Charles making notes and stuff. He'd act them with me, he needed to hear how they played. I remember, he was almost in despair over that, because he couldn't whip it into shape. Laughton and Terry Sanders, they couldn't get from that brilliant book to the screen, like *Night of the Hunter*. And I remember, he was very frustrated about that. And it went on for a long time, but they never could get it just right. He couldn't get it to where he could say, "This'll be a movie, I can shoot this." He never could get it.

As fate would have it, another Paul Gregory project intervened and took the Sanders brothers back further in history, like characters in a reverse-order time machine, to the Civil War once more. According to Denis Sanders, "During the time we were working on *Naked and the Dead,* we were interrupted. Paul called us one day to say that the woman who had written the script for the TV show, *The Day Lincoln Was Shot,* had not done a satisfactory job." (Shades of *Night of the Hunter!*) "It was three weeks before broadcast and Paul needed a script in one week, and he asked us to do it. We went to Paul's offices with our sleeping bags, worked night and day, and came up with a script in one week."

(The late Raymond Massey played the title role of the President—for the umpteenth time in his career—and he once confided to me that, during the *Lincoln* broadcast, the actor portraying the Vice-President whispered into Massey/Lincoln's ear on his deathbed, "After you're gone, Abe—I'm gonna be top banana.")

"With this interruption," as Denis Sanders went on to recollect, "Charles and we never really got back to working on the script together. We finally finished it by ourselves. The final script was quite magnificent, and Mailer loved it. As a matter of fact, it was the only script that he did like."

Terry Sanders

When I first met Charles Laughton, just when he was about to start filming *The Night of the Hunter,* he was very successful. He was riding high, you know, really, really feeling good about his powers, and his knowledge of audiences. So, the tragic thing that happened to Laughton with *Night of the Hunter* was the audiences not only didn't laugh at the spots where he thought they would, they didn't really go see the film, at that time. And it crushed Laughton's spirit. And that is so sad, because, you know, the movie business is all about surviving success, and surviving failure. You have to go forward, you cannot be crushed by whatever happens. But he . . . I guess his ego was just crushed. And then he lost *The Naked and the Dead*. So, Laughton declined, really, after that.

William Phipps

Did it break his heart? He had a way of feeling—"That happened, it's over with—what's next?" I don't think he was grieving, not at all. Not at all. And after that, he did that *wonderful* performance in *Advise and Consent*. And *Witness for the Prosecution*.

"When the picture was not a success," Davis Grubb told Miss Lanchester's researcher, "Charles was terribly disappointed. He liked to pretend that he did not care what critics thought, but their reaction to *Night of the Hunter* undoubtedly gave him great sadness, was a bitter disappointment, and prevented him from doing more experimental work in the future."

Terry Sanders

This was the terrible thing about the movie business. Movies cost so much money that ultimately money people, for better or worse, they can pull the plug. And basically the plug was pulled on Laughton directing *The Naked and the Dead,* which is also a great tragedy, because it could have been a great film. I think that what happened was that the financing wouldn't support Laughton directing it. Simply because *Night of the Hunter* had not been a success. Had *Night of the Hunter* been a success, there would have been no problem. But . . . I think that was the reason that the Gregory/Laughton partnership split.

Work on *The Naked and the Dead* was shifted to RKO, and then, finally, the film was produced at Warner Brothers. The end result? "As it was," says Terry, "it was a parody of itself."

Terry Sanders

I always felt if *Bridge on the River Kwai* had come out first, then some-body—even Jack Warner—might have had the guts to let *The Naked and the Dead* be made the way it should have been made. But actually, Jack Warner *hated* Norman Mailer. Hated him, thought he was a Commie fink, hated the story, *loved* the title—*The Naked and the Dead,* you know?—and decided to make it like *Battle Cry,* just a patriotic kind of film, as much as possible. In fact, Jack Warner said to Denis and me, one time we actually met, he said, "Now, don't have them slipping around in shit." That was his guidance. Well, I mean, it was colorful.

But the film at Warner Brothers was just the biggest mess I ever saw. And the really troublesome thing for Denis and me is: We had our choice of taking our names off of it, or leaving them on and getting full credit for a terrible film. I mean, we had the sole screenplay credit, and in fact it was screwed up after we left. Marion Hargrove and probably two or three other people just tore it up and did whatever Jack Warner told them to do. It was a mess.

I saw Norman Mailer just last year. He came out because "American Masters" did a portrait film of him, and he came out to a PBS press event, and I saw him there: "Norman!" And we talked about the script. He loved the script that Denis and I did. I still would love to do it, be-cause it's never been done. *The Naked and the Dead* has never been made. So he said, "Why don't you *do* it?"

Paul Gregory

Laughton didn't do *The Naked and the Dead* because we split up, and that property was mine. And so I took it to RKO, and then to Warner Brothers. It's a funny thing: *That* property just grossed millions and mil-lions and millions, and it was a lousy picture. Disheartening. But Laughton would have been brilliant with that, because he hated war, and that's why I wanted him to direct it. Because it was an antiwar pic-ture. He had been in the First World War, he hated war, and he would have been a superb director of that picture, because it had poetry, it had great poetry in it. That's what I think Mr. Walsh missed. Raoul Walsh wouldn't know a piece of prose from a piece of horse-shit. He's a com-

petent, competent director, but he has no flight in him at all, and
Laughton had. Laughton had flight.

Laughton told Grubb that the Second World War, in his opinion, was
"a war which we didn't really win. Nor, what's more, ever shall." Having
served in the First World War, "Laughton . . . looked with somewhat jaun-
diced eye upon the 30,000,000 dead of his big show's re-run. He didn't
think we won either war. He didn't think anybody ever wins any war."

Terry Sanders
You know, I think *Hunter* only cost $800,000, that's the figure I heard.
And, that's very little, even at that time, considering Robert Mitchum
was a star. When I look at *Night of the Hunter* today, it's so incredible to
me that $800,000 could buy all of this production. It's amazing. I re-
member, when Norman Mailer saw *The Night of the Hunter,* he said to
Charles, "You're not a good editor." Which Charles got sort of indig-
nant and upset about. "Can you imagine," he said, "that's what he said!"
And I think that Mailer meant that there's a kind of choppiness, often,
to the editing. But that's what he said, in any case.

My impression was that Laughton was totally pleased with what he did,
that he accomplished what he'd wanted to do, that it was completely successful from his point of view. That's why it was such a shock when audiences didn't respond, or it wasn't sold well, or whatever happened. I liked
the film. I felt shivery. It grabs you, this film. I thought Mitchum was
amazing, and I loved Lillian Gish, and Shelley Winters was . . . pathetic.
She was wonderful in this. I thought the children were very awkward, particularly the little girl. I didn't feel comfortable watching her. I thought it
was a very, very good film; I didn't think it was a great film. Whatever that
means, "great film." It was not a perfect film, the way maybe *Citizen Kane*
is a perfect film. And, certain things, like where Mitchum is shot and runs
off into the barn . . . It's a little bit short-handed, you know?

Look, God bless Charles Laughton. It was a *wonderful* first film. It was
an incredible first film. It was fabulous, and he should have gone on and
made a second, and the third. What a pity he didn't go on to make more
movies. If it wasn't *Naked and the Dead,* he could have done something
else. You know, why should he have made a perfect film for his first

film? I think he certainly could have learned from it, and done a really fabulous second film. But, it was daring, it was exciting, because it was innovative, and it was doing things that hadn't been done before, and taking a lot of risks, and it was an exciting film from that standpoint, the whole creative aspect. And I think there are some little mistakes he made, but . . . I think his main problem was a certain lack of awareness, or miscalculation of the impact of certain scenes. Not only those bits of humor, I think that audiences didn't have the deep love for Lillian Gish that he had, the sweetness that he wanted to project. Somehow, it didn't work, I don't know. No, it was mainly the humor thing, in fact, maybe that's the only place that I really felt he was off. There was some conflict, there, about not really playing the evil fully, and pulling back a little, and making it lighthearted, slightly, at the end . . .

Maybe the budget did hurt a little, because there are a lot of things, really, a little crimped at the end, like the lynch mob, and that kind of thing. It could have been bigger, you know? But I think the choice was good, to put the money into getting Mitchum and doing the important scenes well and maybe skimping on some of the lesser scenes. There's a certain awkwardness sometimes in the blocking and staging, like when they arrest Peter Graves and Shelley Winters walks on. But there are a lot of great moments, too, like the honeymoon scene, or when the kids are playing with the doll and the money and Preacher walks out onto the porch.

I feel that films that you see at a certain age, particularly when you're sixteen to eighteen, or maybe a little younger—they last your whole life. They just hit you when you're open to them, vulnerable to them . . . We all have those particular films. This is a pretty extraordinary movie. For me, as I say, the extraordinary thing is that Laughton never made any others.

And he was bitter. When I saw him afterwards, I felt the joy had gone out. The enthusiasm when I first met him, the excitement, and the enthusiasm, and the discovery . . . Being on top of the world, and being the master director of stage plays and great success with *Caine Mutiny* . . . When I first knew him, he was doing everything, including going off to play *King Lear* on the stage. He was at the height of his powers. That was all gone when I saw him a few years later. To see someone at the height of his powers, and then sort of crumple . . . I remember he was working on *Spartacus*. He hated Stanley Kubrick. Called him "That little shit." I guess Stanley was mean and nasty to him, or something. Charles was just acting, doing his work, and he just didn't have the joy. I doubt he had any inkling that *Night of the Hunter* was eventually going to be so highly regarded, because I don't think it was at that time. When did he die, 1962? I guess he didn't really have all that much time after *Hunter,* if you think about it.

Terry's brother Denis also kept in touch with Laughton. He prized his work on *Hunter* as "one of the rare experiences of my life," and felt that he'd learned a great deal from working with Laughton. "Charles was ahead of his time. Perhaps because *Night of the Hunter* was a first film, we are, at times, almost too conscious of the wheels turning. But there is no doubt that, had Charles had more experience with making films, and had he been given more opportunities, he would have been one of the truly great filmmakers. Despite the reception of the critics, which was mixed, with most of them missing the real beauty of the film, the people involved with it liked what they had done. Time has proved that they were right."

Davis Grubb and
Rowdy Charlie.

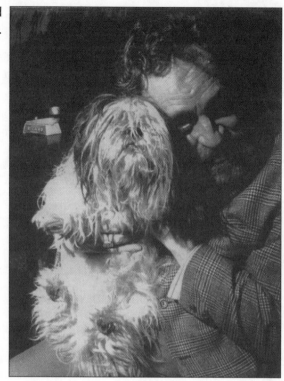

Davis Grubb

Laughton and I didn't go on binges or anything together, but I remember
drinking with him three times. And then I went up to the St. Moritz drunk
one time, and poor Miss Lanchester was there, and I was in bad shape, and
she was never quite the same again. I must have been awful. And I love her.
I don't remember being rowdy, I just think I'd intervened at a bad time.

I doubt very much if she's had any thoughts of me at all in the past
decade. If she has, then I hope they have not been unpleasant feelings,
because I don't want to pass through life with any of that kind of thing.
It's like a check you've written without money in the bank for, or something; you have to make good.

I know that years later she called me, because I was of use to her, I think,
and that's understandable. It was up at the St. Moritz with Burgess Meredith, and the three of us sat there: they were drinking, and I was with my
Lhasa Apso, Rowdy Charlie, my roommate. And *he* was having a good
time, 'cause he was diggin' Burgess. And I don't know him well enough to

refer to him as Buzz, but he's a charming man and an enormously talented actor, and very funny. He and Elsa were sitting there sipping; she wanted to pick our minds about Charles during the different periods of our relationships. Burgess' memory, of course, was much longer than mine. I was coming out with things that I hoped would help her in some small way.

Laughton and I were sitting there drinking at the St. Moritz one time, and I said, "Could I have an old shirt of yours?" He gave me a flannel shirt, from Ziedler and Ziedler in Hollywood, I think. Beautiful shirt, and it was a little ragged, but it was his shirt and I kept it for a long time. It was huge, it was big enough for a bedspread. He was a very tall man. I never realized that so much from his movies, but he was several inches taller than I was.

He was really a Dickens character. You see, he was a very large man in many senses besides the physical. He told me, "I've been studying *Lear* now for forty years, and I think I'm almost ready to do it." And he did it the next year in England. I'd have loved to have seen him.

Laughton died at around the same time my mother died, so I was hardly aware of it, my mind was in such a blur. I miss him. I missed him particularly in the years after I'd begun to find my feet again and I wanted to talk to him about them. And there have been so many questions through the years I've wanted to ask him about people in Hollywood, like Jean Renoir, and Clifford Odets.

Stanley Cortez

Charles never said in so many words what he wanted *The Night of the Hunter* to say. But instinctively, we knew what he was trying to say with the phony priest and the love-and-hate concept, that it existed among the peoples of the world. He was very much aware of what was happening in the world. When the children drift down the river, hungry, until Lillian Gish finds them in the bulrushes—well, that would signify in Charles' mind not only an era in our country, the 1930's, it still existed even when the film was made, as it does today in certain parts of the world. He was very much aware of the hunger of children, the poverty, the pathos, how children without knowing it are persecuted by people. He had contempt for the phonies, for the people who take advantage of other people. Sometimes, you can't delineate and be definitive, but you feel it, you sense it.

Certainly I did, I felt this was what Charles was thinking. I knew this was behind the whole thing . . . And sort of a fairy-like, fairyland concept.

Who was it? Somebody stopped me one day and said, "Gee, that's the way I was when I was a kid." I said, "That's what was behind Charles' thinking." This picture has a very special effect on the young people and the children who see it.

Paul Gregory

You know why? Because they see the truth in it. Just like the boy in the story sees the truth in Preacher when none of the grown-ups see it. That's what I wanted, that's the only thing I wanted. I didn't want a message at all. I wasn't interested in that, per se, I couldn't say, "This is the message of it." But I wanted an imprint on the mind of any child that saw it. So that he would have had that mental experience, in his childish way, of discerning responsibility and what it means. And I think it succeeded there. As I've said, these are the reasons why I chose the book for our film, the resonances it shared with my own childhood . . .

I was born Jason Lenhart, and when the Depression really got rough, my father just couldn't take it, he left my mother and the five children to fend for themselves. My mother carried on. I didn't see my father again until Paul Gregory Day in Des Moines. There was a knock on my hotel room door; I opened it and he didn't recognize me, but I knew him.

He asked for Jason Lenhart.

I said, "He's not here," and closed the door.

Then I went into the bathroom and threw up. I never saw him again.

Mrs. Sonya Goodman

It was an extraordinary movie, there was nothing like it. I guess a lot of people didn't know what to make of it. It was scary, maybe too scary. And they were so used to seeing Robert Mitchum as just a cowboy. And yet, it's funny, in a strange way he was probably sexier playing that awful villain than he's ever been in anything else.

Robert Mitchum

I haven't seen it for a long time. I've seen parts of it on television. I liked it. It's one of my favorite pictures. That, and *Cape Fear.*

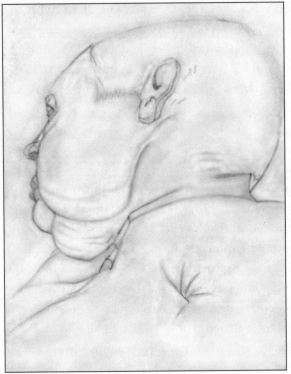

Sketch of Laughton by
Mrs. Sonya Goodman.

Paul Gregory

Well, I think some of what Charles and I set out to do was lost, but not
all of it. On the whole, I agree with Phillip Scheuer. You know, he was
the critic for the *Los Angeles Times.* He listed it as number three of the
ten best pictures of the year. I think it was a fabulous picture. I think it's
unfortunate it had to come out when it did. If it had been made today,
it would be colossal.

Robert Golden

This kind of opportunity doesn't come to too many people, and I was
fortunate in that respect. There are a lot of *A*'s for effort, everybody
works hard in this business. But the kind of thing that Laughton undertook to do was unusual, and I can understand how young people today
would appreciate what he did, because that's what they try to do, control every phase of a production.

I think it's a wonderful picture. "They don't make 'em like that."

They didn't make 'em that way then, either. And that's why you can imagine the disappointment. But it's like a tooth-ache. When it's hurting, it hurts like hell, and after it's over you've forgotten about it. It doesn't hurt anymore. And when I go on the golf course, and something happens and I say, "It's a hard world for little things," I remember that. I remember the good things.

Hilyard Brown

I think *The Night of the Hunter* worked probably as well as any movie I've ever worked on. Whether the general public appreciates what it did is another matter, but I must say we did ninety-nine percent of what we hoped to do. I'd like to do more and more of the same thing with various directors. But there aren't many pictures where you have that satisfaction. Every day was fun, and you always looked forward to getting to the rushes. You'd take a look at what you had discussed two nights before and done the next day. And the big satisfaction was hoping you'd get to see what you wanted on the screen and, sure enough, there it was.

Lillian Gish

I think Laughton was pleased, but I think it took so much out of him that he never directed a film again. I'd hoped he'd go on and make films. His work was beautiful, he had sensitivity and taste, and I thought the film had great feeling and understanding of the basics of the human equation. We've lost that now, we depend upon automobiles and explosions in our pictures. We need good and sensitive directors.

"Charles put his heart and blood into the film," said Lillian Gish, "and, though it was not a commercial success, he should have felt satisfied because it was such a moving and beautiful film . . . He was a wonderful man, and he gave a great gift to the world." In September of 1975, when Davis Grubb sent Miss Gish a copy of his newest novel, she wrote a thank-you note:

Dear Davis Grubb,

The treasure of treasures arrived in my morning mail. Books are truly my only possessions and to receive your beautifully inscribed copy is a rare gift for which I am most grateful.

"Night of the Hunter" holds such fond and good memories for me and I must tell you that it now has become a true classic. For the past five years I have traveled to thirty-six of our states in over three hundred and sixty colleges with my Art of Film program and the young people have been most responsive . . . So many of the questions they ask pertain to "Night of the Hunter" and my mail weekly contains numerous questions, information, etc., about the film . . . It truly has become a deserved classic. I know whatever cloud Charles Laughton is looking down on us from he is enormously pleased and our dear Evelyn Varden as well.

Whatever the cloud and wherever its location, there came a night when Grubb felt that Laughton's spirit had left that perch and descended to Philadelphia. It was a night when Grubb was completely broken up upon learning of the death of the original Rachel, the Rachel he had christened Cooper in his first novel and accurately described as "a strong tree with branches for many birds." Luckily for him, Grubb was not alone that evening, he was in the company of three friends, one of whom happened to be Miles Davis. "Miles had a gig to do with his combo that night at a squalid but tasty jazz joint called the Blue Note at 15th and Ridge Avenue in Philadelphia's ugliest tenderloin . . . Miles is one of the most restrained, unsentimental, cynical and toughest (in the good way) friends I ever had. He quietly mounted the bandstand, blew into his microphone to test its liveness and then, in his well-known husky voice, announced his first number—'Blues For Rachel.' It lasted thirty-five minutes. And it wasn't the Jack Daniels anymore—for I was stone sober now—that made me aware of a huge, hulking Yorkshireman who, save for the three Sitwells, might still be a fat hotel bellboy in Scarborough by the sea—standing, towering somewhere back in the shadows beyond the farthest, checkered table cloth: actor, writer, genius, Christ knows what all—I don't know all of him even now, what he was . . . Rachel Cooper—Charles Laughton—Miles Davis: all on my side that night . . . Amid the azure haze of Miles' never-more-moving horn—as hallowed to me as any Trinity of Holy Writ."

Stanley Cortez

When I went to Charles' funeral it was one of the saddest experiences of my life. His death was the industry's loss. As far as I'm concerned, the name of Charles Laughton will always be indelible in my thinking.

One of the most touching experiences in my life happened a few years ago at the Filmex festival here in L.A. The year before, they had honored writers, and this year, they were honoring cinematographers. They asked me what film of mine I would like to have shown, and when I suggested *The Night of the Hunter,* they readily accepted the idea.

That night, there were maybe a thousand people there, (AUTHOR'S NOTE: Including MC William Friedkin, director of *The Exorcist* and a big fan of *Hunter*), and I got up after the showing to have a question-and-answer session. But before I took the questions, I said, "Ladies and Gentlemen, I thank you very much for your kind applause. Tonight, you are honoring me, but this film, *The Night of the Hunter,* could never have been made without the genius of Charles Laughton. I would like to ask you, please, to rise for a minute of silence in his memory." And immediately, they all stood up. I suddenly felt very priestly, everybody rising at my words, and then motioning with my hands and everybody sitting down. I laugh about that part of it now, while I'm telling you this, but at the time it was a wonderful moment, the tribute these people were paying to this great man.

Paul Gregory

I've told you what Laughton had to say about the Bible and what a crock he thought it was. I never saw Charles Laughton exude one ounce of spiritual quality that would be recognized as such in the terms that we know. But yet, he was kind. At times, very kind, when you would least expect it. He would be kind after he had been terrible to someone, and then his overabundance of kindness would be sort of to repay himself for what he had done to someone else. Yes, I know, he didn't just read the Bible, he told audiences the story of how that old man showed him the Chartres Cathedral when he was young, and all of that, but . . .

I think he had an enormous sense of appreciation, you see. And they had to be damn good words. The man knew words like no one I've ever

known, and they had to be damn good words or he wouldn't have repeated them. And there had to be showmanship in the showing him of
the Chartres Cathedral. I was there with him one time, I saw it the first
time with him, and he repeated to me the same things that the man had
said to him. He was a great showman on hanging on to something that
would have an impact, or a shock, he was very, very good at all of this.
But I don't think he cared at all. I think he cared about the writing. I
think he was impressed by the fact that they don't know how many hundreds of years ago and who the people actually were that built it. I think
all that impressed him, and I think he was in awe of what it meant to
them, and respected that. But I don't think it moved his blood pressure
one degree up or down so far as *his* spiritual self was concerned, at all.

William Phipps
Oh, my God, he was *deeply* spiritual. I mean, look at his renditions of
poetry, and his writing in the books about poetry . . . Oh, Christ, yes,
he was spiritual. He was acknowledged to have one of the best eyes in
the world for paintings. I mean, he had a deep reverence for beautiful,
beautiful things. How could that not be spiritual?

Paul Gregory
I don't think he loved a thing. I don't think he loved a thing, except
words and literature. If you'd ever see his bed, it was always strewn with
Phaedo, and Plato, *The Republic,* and Socrates and this and that. He read
all of those old things. He'd say, "Listen to this passage, old boy," then
he'd go into a thing that'd put you to sleep. He loved all of that, you see,
the words, and the way Socrates would go into these dissertations on
this and that. He could keep you occupied for the whole night reading
to you. Loved to read. But I don't think Charles Laughton had any deep
humanity in him at all. At least, I didn't recognize it. Maybe he had
great gallons of it.

   Laughton was a renegade. He left England, and he felt all the English
hated him. He hated everything. Everything and everybody. There was
no *ground*. No ground, no one plateau that you could reach with Charles
Laughton and say, "Now, here, sweetie, is where we'll have our next battle." You could never reach that. You could never get from here to there.

William Phipps in more
recent years.

You'd get to a point, and then you'd wake up the next morning, you'd be clear back to here. You'd spend the whole day pulling him back to there again, and then maybe you could keep him there for two days, and then he'd be way back here again. Such depression as you'd never believe.

Hated everything. No, he didn't love the theatre. He didn't want to be in the theatre, he would do something that would have a short run, but he didn't want to be in the theatre. Then why did he do it? You go upstairs and ask him, is all I can tell you. He did it for money, he did it for a living. And I'll tell you that Charles Laughton never did anything for nothing that I ever had anything to do with.

But let the last words on Laughton come from the man whose words were transformed by Laughton into this one-of-a-kind film. "Charles Laughton knew movies inside and out," Davis Grubb once said. "And, as things turned out, he knew more about *The Night of the Hunter* than I did."

Davis Grubb

I've told you what Laughton felt about Lear, that he was primitive man reaching for God, and I would say that in his way Laughton was reach-

ing, too. He had been a Catholic, and he told me about the time when
he was facing one of the bloodiest engagements of World War I.
Laughton was in the trenches, prepared to go over the top. It was some
bridge, I think. It was a word like "Armageddon," only it wasn't Armageddon, so it must have been Armentieres. The chaplain came
through to give the Catholic soldiers absolution, and when he came to
Laughton, Laughton said, "No thanks, father, I think I can take it from
here alone." "And," Laughton told me, "I never went back to church."

Laughton was absorbed in the intellectual activity of the time that he
was growing up, as I was. He was probably a better student of the Bible
than most—certainly than some of the ministers I've known in West
Virginia. I think he found his own religion and didn't need the priest.
When he said what he did to the chaplain, I don't think he meant, "I
don't need God." I think he was saying, "I don't need the priest."

Because, Laughton was a man of great devotion. In the first place, he
was devoted to the word. And, "In the beginning was the Word."

IV

THE MORNING AFTER

"And the Spirit'll go on from there."

—Charles Laughton, *The Storyteller,*
an LP record album of one of his reading concerts

Billy Wilder, while directing Laughton in the film version of Agatha Christie's *Witness for the Prosecution* (1957), chanced to pick up the actor's script one day, and was impressed to find every page completely packed with Laughton's multi-nuanced notes. Wilder had come to regard Laughton as the Compleat Actor, a conviction that was reinforced on a day when Laughton was not even supposed to be at the set. Wilder had scheduled the time to film the reactions of the extras in the jury box. The reading of lines to which extras would respond was normally a script supervisor's task, but when Laughton heard what Wilder had planned he begged to be allowed to read his lines himself. What's more, after Wilder relented and let Laughton read his role as master barrister Sir Wilfred for the "jury," the actor went on to read the parts of his co-stars, Tyrone Power and Marlene Dietrich, plus all of the supporting players' lines as attorneys, policemen and witnesses. For Wilder, it was a memorable day and for Laughton, an exhausting pleasure—his first off-camera opportunity to play every role in a movie since directing his actors in *The Night of the Hunter.*

Billy Wilder (L) directs Laughton—out of costume, and presumably off-camera—and Marlene Dietrich in *Witness for the Prosecution.*

Laughton's portrayal of Sir Wilfred was the first role in a long time for which he would be nominated for an Academy Award, (and the last). I've always felt that, of all his screen roles, Laughton's turn in *Witness* was the closest to a representation of the actual artist, a somewhat sweetened portrait of the curmudgeonly and consummate craftsman who told Bible stories to enraptured audiences and who directed *The Night of the Hunter.* Thanks to screenings of the restored print of *Spartacus* (1960) in recent years, contemporary film goers have had an opportunity to discover Laughton in his colorful role as Senator Gracchus. His final acting on film was as a more contemporary politico, the Southern Senator Seab Cooley in Otto Preminger's film of *Advise and Consent* (1962) from Alan Drury's novel.

Directors were not the only ones who could be impressed by Laughton's dedication to his craft. The production secretary on *Advise,* Florence Nerlinger, once told me that Preminger and his stellar cast (including Laughton's old nemesis from *Caine Mutiny,* Henry Fonda, and his old buddy from *Eiffel Tower,* Burgess Meredith) had all been invited one evening to visit the Kennedy White House. The director and all the stars gladly accepted this rare privilege—except one. "Charles Laughton came to me," Ms. Nerlinger remembered, "and said, 'Can you please call the White House people and get me out of this somehow? My long monologue is coming up tomorrow, and I've got to be working on it tonight, I'll need to be sensitive to all its details, and how can I prepare to do that if I'm socializing this evening?'" In truth, Laughton was probably concerned not only with the next day's work but also with the fact that he needed to conserve his energy in general: He was already suffering intimations of the illness which would claim his life within a year.

During Laughton's final months, his friend Billy Wilder helped to sustain his spirits by promising him the role of Moustache in his upcoming production of *Irma La Douce* with Jack Lemmon and Shirley MacLaine. Wilder knew that the actor would probably never live to shoot a day on his movie, but it was a fantasy Laughton embraced, even to growing a luxuriant white mustache so that he would look the part. Poignant testimony of Laughton's last year can be found in the memoirs of Ruth Gordon and Elsa Lanchester: the pain, the pills, the cobalt treatments, the nightmares, the delusions . . . A friend of Laughton's, Bruce Zortman, was delegated

Laughton in *Spartacus.*

by Laughton to take down the autobiography he was "dictating," but Laughton would usually end up falling asleep before he could offer a single word for his friend to jot down. Once, however, Laughton managed to dictate one sentence before succumbing to slumber. In his morphine dreams that day, he convinced himself that he had written something profound and important, and said so upon awakening. But what had he actually said? Duly recorded on Zortman's pad was the solitary statement:

"I was in love with Lillian Gish."

Even though Laughton's movie-directing career seemed to have gone kaput after *Hunter*, had he lived longer, one still can wonder if he might have kept his implicit pact with Davis Grubb to film another of his stories. Although by its very nature the young author's sophomore effort, the Civil War coming-of-age saga *A Dream of Kings,* was not likely to be as compelling as *The Night of the Hunter,* during the almost two decades Grubb survived Laughton's passing he managed to produce many fine novels.

Some of Grubb's early, macabre short stories proved helpful to the producers of such television anthology series as *Alfred Hitchcock Presents* and *Rod Serling's Night Gallery.*

"The Horsehair Trunk," a tale of a would-be out-of-body murderer, was televised once, faithfully, with Vincent Price, and once, abominably, with Jack Cassidy. Peter Fonda portrayed the vengeful title character in "The Return of Verge Likens" on the Hitchcock-produced TV version of the psychological drama. "Where the Woodbine Twineth," also on *Hitchcock,* told a haunting tale of transformation in which, as in *Hunter,* a little girl and her doll figure prominently. The author recreated his boyhood home, address and all, in a story about menacing miniature soldiers called "The Siege of 318," which was dramatized on a short-lived ABC series called *Dark Room.*

One Grubb novel, *Fools' Parade,* provided James Stewart with his last big-screen leading role. There were no supernatural elements in the book, but it was Davis Grubb at his scary-funny best, full of lyric descriptions of Depression-era West Virginia, dark, outrageous humor, and a hunt-to-the-death in which the villains are as quirky as their quarry. The 1971 feature film version had James Stewart as one-eyed ex-convict Mattie Appleyard, and George Kennedy as ex-prison guard and professional assassin "Doc" Counsel (with welcome support from character actor Strother Martin and a still-boyish Kurt Russell as Mattie's pals). Although this film's director, the reliable action-movie maestro Andrew McLaglen, was never mistaken for a genius of Laughton's caliber, he did manage to film *Fools' Parade* on location in Davis Grubb country, and, with help from a fine script by James Lee Barrett and atmospheric production design, he captured on-screen some of the author's uniquely nightmarish vision. One thing McLaglen's film had in common with Laughton's, unfortunately, was a fast and sloppy release, which virtually guaranteed its quick disappearance from theaters. And although not a masterpiece like *Hunter, Fools' Parade* was similarly under-appreciated by the critics. Even today it has never really had its due. Typically dismissive is the usually astute Leonard Maltin in his annual survey of films on TV, whose critique claims that Stewart's fine performance is wasted in a film which is unintentionally funny too many times to be taken seriously. I would submit, however, that *Fools' Parade* is intentionally funny too many times not to be taken seriously. (The late

A suspenseful scene on the Ohio river—but this time in the skiff, instead of Billy and Sally Jane, it's James Stewart and Strother Martin in the film of Davis Grubb's *Fool's Parade.*

Anne Baxter, who had yearned to play Willa in *Hunter,* here steals the show as an outrageous riverboat madam who is deeply hurt because she has been denied membership in the D.A.R.)

Over the years, other Davis Grubb books have been considered for various film projects, but they have never materialized. Various leading men in the sixties expressed an interest in playing the title character in *The Watchman,* a sheriff in a small prison town whose teen daughter becomes involved in an unsolved murder. There was even talk of Sophia Loren playing Grubb's *Talley Vengeance,* the title character in one of the chapters from his epic panorama of a turn-of-the-century small town, *The Voices of Glory.* Talley is a down-on-her-luck widow who ultimately sees that her well-to-do and hypocritical tormenters get their come-uppance, and a film of her story might have become a seriocomic Capraesque movie with Preston Sturges overtones. Grubb was always rooting for the societal underdog, whether he was examining race relations in *Shadow of My Brother* or writing about violent coal-mine labor disputes in *The*

Barefoot Man. A lighthearted Christmas fantasy, *A Tree Full of Stars,* about a yuletide tree which takes root and refuses to come down after the holiday, embraces some serious spiritual issues.

Remember how Grubb told me that he had it in mind to write a fairy story? He finally began such a tale in the late seventies, while he was living once more in the Deep South. But fairies were only one component of what he planned would be a crazy-quilt tale of the near future, examining issues of spirituality and sexuality in a uniquely Grubbian mixture of comedy and terror. As Davis' brother Lou explained it to me, this latest novel—*Ancient Lights*—was designed to be "a combination of the Bible, the Kama Sutra and Lenny Bruce." Davis was deep into working on this magnum opus when he suddenly became sick and was diagnosed with a disease branching off the same family tree that had killed Charles Laughton. His doctors strongly urged him to travel to New York so that he could get the best possible medical care for his cancer, but the writer was reluctant to interrupt working on a book in which he so deeply believed, and made the firm decision to stay put and devote his energies to *Ancient Lights*—whereupon his illness went into remission. And it stayed in remission until he had finished this most unorthodox book of his career. But then the cancer returned quickly, forcing him into his final hospitalization. He died in 1980. *Ancient Lights* was published in 1982, with its publisher's fervent hopes that it might attain the successful cult status of a *V,* a *One Flew Over the Cuckoo's Nest,* or an *Even Cowgirls Get the Blues.* To date, Grubb's last book has never earned that hoped-for wide readership, but for such a one-of-a-kind novel, there is always the chance of rediscovery and appreciation, just as there has proved to be for Laughton's one-of-a-kind film, *The Night of the Hunter.*

As noted previously, in 1955 there were some critics who could appreciate Laughton's ground-breaking effort, among them Francois Truffaut, who praised *Hunter* for exemplifying "an experimental cinema which truly experiments." But many critics were blind to the film's originality. One scribe claimed that Laughton, lacking any fresh ideas for his own film, had merely remade everybody else's. Filmmakers, unlike some critics, recognize that even the most innovative art always fuses elements from its predecessors; these writers and directors recognized the accomplishment of Laughton's fusion, and in turn have incorporated elements from *Hunter* in their own subsequent films. Sometimes the reflection of Laughton's opus takes the form of a clear homage, as in Spike Lee's *Do the Right Thing,* and sometimes it is more a matter of general inspiration, as in the dreamlike nostalgia of the films of Terence Davies (*The Long Day Closes*). Steven Spielberg screened *The Night of the Hunter* for his crew to show them the child's viewpoint he hoped to emulate in *E.T.* References to *Hunter* abide in our current culture, from the lyrics of Bruce Springsteen's "Cautious Man" to the *Simpsons* episode "Cape Feare" (in which a character named Sideshow Bob, having only three fingers on each hand, has tattooed them with "LUV" and "HAT"). Stephen King dedicated his graphic-art novel, *Cycle of the Werewolf,* to Lou Grubb and his family. In this tale, which was filmed in 1985 under the title *Silver Bullet,* the lycanthrope turns out to be the town preacher.

Various producers and directors over the years have toyed with the idea of remaking *The Night of the Hunter.* A made-for-TV version a few years ago was, according to author/critic Jessica Amanda Salmonson, "so bad somebody better go to hell for it." Richard Chamberlain, an actor who has striven mightily to overcome his matinee idol image, was actually an interesting casting choice for Preacher, and director David (*Godspell*) Greene has demonstrated that he can do imaginative things with a camera, but this version of Grubb's story was completely botched. Laughton's old pal Burgess Meredith was on hand as Uncle Birdie, but unlike James Gleason he was given virtually nothing to do. This version should have been called *The Day of the Hunter* because the big chase down to the river takes place at high noon. As if that weren't bad enough, the film ends right there at the river, completely eliminating "Rachel Cooper" and the second half of the story.

A strange but suitably dreamlike arrangement of Pearl's "Pretty Fly" song by Walter Schumann and Grubb has been recorded by the contemporary music group, Mono Puff, on their album titled *It's Fun to Steal* (Bar None records A-HAON 101). And for the Varese Sarabande label, Bruce Kimmel has produced an entire album devoted to a new musical version of *The Night of the Hunter* (VSD-5876) by composer Claibe Richardson and lyricist Stephen Cole. Although the work has yet to receive its first stage presentation, based on the evidence of the CD it is very faithful both to the letter of Grubb's novel and the spirit of Laughton's film.

The original RCA *Night of the Hunter* soundtrack album, with
Laughton narrating Schumann's score, is currently available on two different CD's, both of them imports. A Spanish BMG version replicates the
packaging of the old LP and includes Grubb's original liner notes. The
edition from Germany's The Bear Family, however, is packaged with many
evocative frame blow-ups from the film and, unlike the BMG disc, sequences the material into a dozen or so individual tracks. Incredibly, this
job of narration is Charles Laughton's only appearance on a CD to date.
None of his radio or record dramatizations have been released on CD, not
even *Don Juan in Hell,* and none of his marvelous story-telling performances are available. Perhaps this gap in our contemporary culture may some
day be rectified. One can only hope.

At this writing, tentative plans are being formulated which may finally
lead to a recording of Walter Schumann's complete musical score to *The
Night of the Hunter.* One can only pray.

In the meantime, Grubb's first novel is once again in print, and a beautiful UCLA restoration of Laughton's first-and-last film is being screened
at theaters and major film festivals.

"They abide, and they endure."

The Night of the Hunter
CAST & CREDITS

Rev. Harry Powell . . . . Robert Mitchum
Willa Harper . . . . Shelley Winters
Rachel Cooper . . . . Lillian Gish
Uncle Birdie . . . . James Gleason
Icey Spoon . . . . Evelyn Varden
Ben Harper . . . . Peter Graves
Walt Spoon . . . . Don Beddoe
John Harper . . . . Billy Chapin
Pearl Harper . . . . Sally Jane Bruce
Ruby . . . . Gloria Castilo
Mary . . . . Cheryl Callaway
Clary . . . . Mary Ellen Clemons
Young Man in Town . . . . Corey Allen (uncredited)
Second Young Man . . . . Michael Chapin (uncredited)
Bart the Hangman . . . . Paul Bryar (uncredited)
Burlesque Dancer . . . . Gloria Pall (uncredited)
Cattle Rancher . . . . John Hamilton (uncredited)
District Attorney . . . . James Griffith (uncredited)
Miz Cunningham . . . . (unknown)
Old Farm Woman . . . . (unknown)
Prison Guard . . . . (unknown)
Bart's Wife . . . . (unknown)
Judge . . . . (unknown)

Released by United Artists
Directed by Charles Laughton
Produced by Paul Gregory
From the Novel by Davis Grubb
Screenplay by James Agee (credited), Charles Laughton (uncredited)
Cinematography by Stanley Cortez
Camera Operator: Bud Martino (uncredited)
Assistant Cameraman: Sy Hoffberg (uncredited)
Music composed and conducted by Walter Schumann
Orchestrated by Arthur Morton (uncredited)
Vocals (uncredited) by Kitty White, Betty Benson
Art Direction by Hilyard Brown
Set Decorator: Alfred E. Spencer
Edited by Robert Golden
Assistant Director: Milton Carter
Production Manager: Ruby Rosenberg
Second Unit Director: Terry Sanders (uncredited)
Wardrobe by Jerry Bos; Evelyn Carruth, assistant
Props by Joseph LaBella
Hair Stylist: Kay Shea
Sound by Stanford Naughton
Special Photographic Effects by Jack Rabin & Louis DeWitt
Makeup by Don L. Cash
Special Make-up by Maurice Seiderman (uncredited)
Production Assistant: Denis Sanders (uncredited)
Running Time: 93 Minutes

ABOUT THE AUTHOR

According to **Preston Neal Jones,** he was one of those fans of *The Night of the Hunter* who first encountered the film when he was young and impressionable. He adds: "Now that I'm middle-aged and impressionable, I still love the movie; hence, this book." Jones's other writings have appeared in periodicals as disparate as *Cinefantastique* and *American Art Review*; he has contributed entries to *Groves' New Dictionary of Music and Musicians* and *The St. James Encyclopedia of Popular Culture.* At UCLA, Jones has lectured on the subject of film music, and at Roanoke College in Virginia (where he was Writer in Residence) he taught on the topics of *Star Trek* and *The Night of the Hunter.* He lives in Los Angeles.